MEN ARE FROM MARS,

Women Are from Venus

AND

MARS AND VENUS IN THE BEDROOM

JOHN GRAY, Ph.D.

 HarperCollins*Publishers*

MEN ARE FROM MARS
WOMEN ARE FROM VENUS

A Practical Guide for
Improving Communication
and Getting What You Want
in Your Relationships

John Gray, Ph.D.

HarperCollins*Publishers*

Library of Congress Cataloging-in-Publication Data is available
upon request.

ISBN: 978-0-06-190800-2

09 10 11 12 13   /RRD   10 9 8 7 6 5 4 3 2 1

This book is dedicated with
deepest love and affection
to my wife, Bonnie Gray.
Her love, vulnerability, wisdom, and strength
have inspired me to be the best I can be
and to share what we have learned together.

Contents

Acknowledgments

I thank my wife, Bonnie, for sharing the journey of developing this book with me. I thank her for allowing me to share our stories and especially for expanding my understanding and ability to honor the female point of view.

I thank our three daughters, Shannon, Julie, and Lauren, for their continued love and appreciation. The challenge of being a parent has allowed me to understand the struggles my parents had and love them even more. Being a father has especially assisted me in understanding and loving my father.

I thank my father and mother for their loving efforts to raise a family of seven children. I thank my oldest brother, David, for understanding my feelings and admiring my words. I thank my brother William for motivating me to higher achievements. I thank my brother Robert for all the long and interesting conversations we had until dawn and for his brilliant ideas, from which I always benefit. I thank my brother Tom for his encouragement and positive spirit. I thank my sister Virginia for believing in me and appreciating my seminars. I thank my deceased younger brother Jimmy for his love and admiration, which continue to support me through my difficult times.

I thank my agent Patti Breitman, whose help, brilliant creativity, and enthusiasm have guided this book from its conception to its completion. I thank Carole Bidnick for her inspired support at the beginning of this project. I thank Susan Moldow and Nancy Peske for their expert feedback and advice. I thank the staff at HarperCollins for their continued responsiveness to my needs.

I thank all the thousands who participated in my relationship seminars, shared their stories, and encouraged me to write this book. Their positive and loving feedback has supported me in developing this simple presentation of such a complex subject.

I thank my clients who have shared their struggles so intimately and trusted my assistance in their journey.

I thank Steve Martineau for his skillful wisdom and influence, which can be found sprinkled through this book.

I thank my different promoters, who have put their hearts and souls into producing the John Gray Relationship Seminars where this material was tried, tested, and developed: Elley and Ian Coren in Santa Cruz; Debra Mudd, Gary and Helen Francell in Honolulu; Bill and Judy Elbring in San Francisco; David Obstfeld and Fred Kliner in Washington, D.C.; Elizabeth Kling in Baltimore; Clark and Dottie Bartell in Seattle; Michael Najarian in Phoenix; Gloria Manchester in L.A.; Sandee Mac in Houston; Earlene Carrillo in Las Vegas; David Farlow in San Diego; Bart and Merril Jacobs in Dallas; and Ove Johhansson and Ewa Martensson in Stockholm.

I thank Richard Cohen and Cindy Black at Beyond Words Publishing for their loving and genuine support of my last book, *Men, Women, and Relationships,* which gave birth to the ideas in this book.

I thank John Vestman at Trianon Studios for his expert audio recordings of my whole seminar and Dave Morton and the staff of Cassette Express for their continued appreciation of this material and their quality service.

I thank the members of my men's group for sharing their stories, and I especially thank Lenney Eiger, Charles Wood, Jacques Early, David Placek, and Chris Johns, who gave me such valuable feedback for editing the manuscript.

I thank my secretary, Ariana, for efficiently and responsibly taking over the office during this project.

I thank my lawyer (and adopted grandfather of my children), Jerry Riefold, for always being there.

I thank Clifford McGuire for his continued friendship of twenty years. I could not ask for a better sounding board and friend.

MEN ARE FROM MARS
WOMEN ARE FROM VENUS

Introduction

A week after our daughter Lauren was born, my wife Bonnie and I were completely exhausted. Each night Lauren kept waking us. Bonnie had been torn in the delivery and was taking painkillers. She could barely walk. After five days of staying home to help, I went back to work. She seemed to be getting better.

While I was away she ran out of pain pills. Instead of calling me at the office, she asked one of my brothers, who was visiting, to purchase more. My brother, however, did not return with the pills. Consequently, she spent the whole day in pain, taking care of a newborn.

I had no idea that her day had been so awful. When I returned home she was very upset. I misinterpreted the cause of her distress and thought she was blaming me.

She said, "I've been in pain all day.... I ran out of pills. I've been stranded in bed and nobody cares!"

I said defensively, "Why didn't you call me?"

She said, "I asked your brother, but he forgot! I've been waiting for him to return all day. What am I supposed to do? I can barely walk. I feel so deserted!"

At this point I exploded. My fuse was also very short that day. I was angry that she hadn't called me. I was furious that she was blaming me when I didn't even know she was in pain. After exchanging a few harsh words, I headed for the door. I was tired, irritable, and had heard enough. We had both reached our limits.

Then something started to happen that would change my life.

Bonnie said, "Stop, please don't leave. This is when I need you the most. I'm in pain. I haven't slept in days. Please listen to me."

I stopped for a moment to listen.

She said, "John Gray, you're a fair-weather friend! As long as I'm sweet, loving Bonnie you are here for me, but as soon as I'm not, you walk right out that door."

Then she paused, and her eyes filled up with tears. As her tone shifted she said, "Right now I'm in pain. I have nothing to give, this is when I need you the most. Please, come over here and hold me. You don't have to say anything. I just need to feel your arms around me. Please don't go."

I walked over and silently held her. She wept in my arms. After a few minutes, she thanked me for not leaving. She told me that she just needed to feel me holding her.

At that moment I started to realize the real meaning of love–unconditional love. I had always thought of myself as a loving person. But she was right. I had been a fair-weather friend. As long as she was happy and nice, I loved back. But if she was unhappy or upset, I would feel blamed and then argue or distance myself.

That day, for the first time, I didn't leave her. I stayed, and it felt great. I succeeded in giving to her when she really needed me. This felt like real love. Caring for another person. Trusting in our love. Being there at her hour of need. I marveled at how easy it was for me to support her when I was shown the way.

How had I missed this? She just needed me to go over and hold her. Another woman would have instinctively known what Bonnie needed. But as a man, I didn't know that touching, holding, and listening were so important to her. By recognizing these differences I began to learn a new way of relating to my wife. I would have never believed we could resolve conflict so easily.

In my previous relationships, I had become indifferent and unloving at difficult times, simply because I didn't know what else to do. As a result, my first marriage had been very painful and difficult.

This incident with Bonnie revealed to me how I could change this pattern.

It inspired my seven years of research to help develop and refine the insights about men and women in this book. By learning in very practical and specific terms about how men and women are different, I suddenly began to realize that my marriage did not need to be such a struggle. With this new awareness of our differences Bonnie and I were able to improve dramatically our communication and enjoy each other more.

By continuing to recognize and explore our differences we have discovered new ways to improve all our relationships. We have learned about relationships in ways that our parents never knew and therefore could not have taught us. As I began sharing these insights with my counseling clients, their relationships were also enriched. Literally thousands of those who attended my weekend seminars saw their relationships dramatically transform overnight.

Seven years later individuals and couples still report successful benefits. I receive pictures of happy couples and their children, with letters thanking me for saving their marriage. Although their love saved their marriage, they would have divorced if they hadn't gained a deeper understanding of the opposite sex.

Susan and Jim had been married nine years. Like most couples they started out loving each other, but after years of increasing frustration and disappointment they lost their passion and decided to give up. Before getting a divorce, however, they attended my weekend relationship seminar. Susan said, "We have tried everything to make this relationship work. We are just too different."

During the seminar they were amazed to learn that their differences were not only normal but were to be expected. They were comforted that other couples had experienced the same patterns of relating. In just two days, Susan and Jim gained a totally new understanding of men and women.

They fell in love again. Their relationship miraculously changed. No longer heading toward a divorce, they looked forward to sharing the rest of their lives together. Jim said, "This information about our differences has given me back my wife. This is the greatest gift I could ever receive. We are loving each other again."

Six years later, when they invited me to visit their new home and family, they were still loving each other. They were still thanking me for helping them to understand each other and stay married.

Although almost everyone would agree that men and women are different, *how* different is still undefined for most people. Many books in the last ten years have forged ahead, attempting to define these differences. Though important advances have been made, many books are one-sided and unfortunately reinforce mistrust and resentment toward the opposite sex. One sex is generally viewed as being victimized by the other. A definitive guide was needed for understanding how *healthy* men and women are different.

To improve relations between the sexes it is necessary to create an understanding of our differences that raises self-esteem and personal dignity while inspiring mutual trust, personal responsibility, increased cooperation, and greater love. As a result of questioning more than 25,000 participants in my relationship seminars I have been able to define in positive terms how men and women are different. As you explore these differences you will feel walls of resentment and mistrust melting down.

Opening the heart results in greater forgiveness and increased motivation to give and receive love and support. With this new awareness, you will, I hope, go beyond the suggestions in this book and continue to develop ways in which you can relate lovingly to the opposite sex.

All of the principles in this book have been tested and tried. At least 90 percent of the more than 25,000 individuals questioned have enthusiastically recognized themselves in these descriptions. If you find yourself nodding your head while reading this book, saying "Yes, yes this is me you're talking about," then you are definitely not alone. And just as others have benefited from applying the insights in this book, you can as well.

Men Are from Mars, Women Are from Venus reveals new strategies for reducing tension in relationships and creating more love by first recognizing in great detail how men and women are different. It then offers practical suggestions about how to reduce frustration and disappointment and to create increasing happiness and intimacy. Relationships do not have to be such a struggle. Only when we do not understand one another is there tension, resentment, or conflict.

So many people are frustrated in their relationships. They love their partners, but when there is tension they do not know what to do to make things better. Through understanding how completely different men and women are, you will learn new ways for successfully relating with, listening to, and supporting the opposite sex. You will learn how to create the love you deserve. As you read this book you may wonder how anybody succeeds in having a successful relationship without it.

Men Are from Mars, Women Are from Venus is a manual for loving relationships in the 1990s. It reveals how men and women differ in all areas of their lives. Not only do men and women communicate differently but they think, feel, perceive, react, respond, love, need, and appreciate differently. They almost seem to be from different planets, speaking different languages and needing different nourishment.

This expanded understanding of our differences helps resolve much of the frustration in dealing with and trying to understand the opposite sex. Misunderstandings can then be quickly dissipated or avoided. Incorrect expectations are easily corrected. When you remember that your partner is as different from you as someone from another planet, you can relax and cooperate with the differences instead of resisting or trying to change them.

Most important, throughout this book you will learn practical techniques for solving the problems that arise from our differences. This book is not just a theoretical analysis of psychological differences but also a practical manual for how to succeed in creating loving relationships.

The truth of these principles is self-evident and can be validated by your own experience as well as by common sense. Many examples will simply and concisely express what you have always intuitively known. This validation will assist you in being you and in not losing yourself in your relationships.

In response to these insights, men often say "This is exactly how I am. Have you been following me around? I no longer feel like something is wrong with me."

Women often say "Finally my husband listens to me. I don't have to fight to be validated. When you explain our differences, my husband understands. Thank you!"

These are but a few of the thousands of inspirational comments that people have shared after learning that men are from Mars and women are from Venus. The results of this new program for understanding the opposite sex are not only dramatic and immediate but also long lasting.

Certainly the journey of creating a loving relationship can be rocky at times. Problems are inevitable. But these problems either can be sources of resentment and rejection or can be opportunities for deepening intimacy and increasing love, caring, and trust. The insights of this book are not a "quick fix" to eliminate all problems. Instead they provide a new approach whereby your relationships can successfully support you in solving life's problems as they arise. With this new awareness you will have the tools you need to get the love you deserve and to give your partner the love and support he or she deserves.

I make many generalizations about men and women in this book. Probably you will find some comments truer than others...after all, we are unique individuals with unique experiences. Sometimes in my seminar couples and individuals will share that they relate to the examples of men and women but in an opposite way. The man relates to my descriptions of women and the woman relates to my descriptions of men. I call this role reversal.

If you discover you are experiencing role reversal, I want to assure you that everything is all right. I suggest that when you do not relate to something in this book, either ignore it (moving on to something you do relate to) or look deeper inside yourself. Many men have denied some of their masculine attributes in order to become more loving and nurturing. Likewise many women have denied some of their feminine attributes in order to earn a living in a work force that rewards masculine attributes. If this is the case, then by applying the suggestions, strategies, and techniques in this book you not only will create more passion in your relationships but also will increasingly balance your masculine and feminine characteristics.

In this book I do not directly address the question of *why* men and women are different. This is a complex question to which there are many answers, ranging from biological differences, parental influence, education, and birth order to cultural conditioning by society, the media, and history. (These issues are explored in great depth in my book *Men, Women, and Relationships: Making Peace with the Opposite Sex.*)

Although the benefits of applying the insights in this book are immediate, this book does not replace the need for therapy and counseling for troubled relationships or survivors of a dysfunctional family. Even healthy individuals may need therapy or counseling at challenging times. I believe strongly in the powerful and gradual transformation that occurs in therapy, marriage counseling, and twelve-step recovery groups.

Yet repeatedly I have heard people say that they have benefited more from this new understanding of relationships than from years of therapy. I however believe that their years of therapy or recovery work provided the groundwork that allowed them to apply these insights so successfully to their life and relationships.

If our past was dysfunctional, then even after years of therapy or attending recovery groups we still need a positive picture of healthy relationships. This book provides that vision. On the other hand, even if our past has been very loving and nurturing, times have changed, and a new approach to relationships between the sexes is still required. It is essential to learn new and healthy ways of relating and communicating.

I believe everyone can benefit from the insights in this book. The only negative response I hear from participants in my seminars and in the letters I receive is "I wish someone had told me this before."

It is never too late to increase the love in your life. You only need to learn a new way. Whether you are in therapy or not, if you want to have more fulfilling relationships with the opposite sex, this book is for you.

It is a pleasure to share with you *Men Are from Mars, Women Are from Venus.* May you always grow in wisdom and in love. May the frequency of divorce decrease and the number of happy marriages increase. Our children deserve a better world.

John Gray
November 15, 1991
Mill Valley, California

CHAPTER

1

MEN ARE FROM MARS
WOMEN ARE FROM VENUS

Imagine that men are from Mars and women are from Venus. One day long ago the Martians, looking through their telescopes, discovered the Venusians. Just glimpsing the Venusians awakened feelings they had never known. They fell in love and quickly invented space travel and flew to Venus.

The Venusians welcomed the Martians with open arms. They had intuitively known that this day would come. Their hearts opened wide to a love they had never felt before.

The love between the Venusians and Martians was magical. They delighted in being together, doing things together, and sharing together. Though from different worlds, they reveled in their differences. They spent months learning about each other, exploring and appreciating their different needs, preferences, and behavior patterns. For years they lived together in love and harmony.

Then they decided to fly to Earth. In the beginning everything was wonderful and beautiful. But the effects of Earth's atmosphere took hold, and one morning everyone woke up with a peculiar kind of amnesia—*selective amnesia!*

Both the Martians and Venusians forgot that they were from different planets and were supposed to be different. In one morning everything they had learned about their differences was erased from their memory. And since that day men and women have been in conflict.

REMEMBERING OUR DIFFERENCES

Without the awareness that we are supposed to be different, men and women are at odds with each other. We usually become angry or frustrated with the opposite sex because we have forgotten this important truth. We expect the opposite sex to be more like ourselves. We desire them to "want what we want" and "feel the way we feel."

We mistakenly assume that if our partners love us they will react and behave in certain ways–the ways we react and behave when we love someone. This attitude sets us up to be disappointed again and again and prevents us from taking the necessary time to communicate lovingly about our differences.

> We mistakenly assume that if our partners love us they
> will react and behave in certain ways–the ways
> we react and behave when we love someone.

Men mistakenly expect women to think, communicate, and react the way men do; women mistakenly expect men to feel, communicate, and respond the way women do. We have forgotten that men and women are supposed to be different. As a result our relationships are filled with unnecessary friction and conflict.

Clearly recognizing and respecting these differences dramatically reduce confusion when dealing with the opposite sex. When you remember that men are from Mars and women are from Venus, everything can be explained.

AN OVERVIEW OF OUR DIFFERENCES

Throughout this book I will discuss in great detail our differences. Each chapter will bring you new and crucial insights. Here are the major differences that we will explore:

In chapter 2 we will explore how men's and women's values are inherently different and try to understand the two biggest mistakes we make in relating to the opposite sex: men mistakenly offer solutions and invalidate feelings while women offer unsolicited advice and direction. Through understanding our Martian/Venusian background it becomes obvious why men and women *unknowingly* make these mistakes. By remembering these differences we can correct our mistakes and immediately respond to each other in more productive ways.

In chapter 3 we'll discover the different ways men and women cope with stress. While Martians tend to pull away and silently think about what's bothering them, Venusians feel an instinctive need to talk about what's bothering them. You will learn new strategies for getting what you want at these conflicting times.

We will explore how to motivate the opposite sex in chapter 4. Men are motivated when they feel needed while women are motivated when they feel cherished. We will discuss the three steps for improving relationships and explore how to overcome our greatest challenges: men need to overcome their resistance to giving love while women must overcome their resistance to receiving it.

In chapter 5 you'll learn how men and women commonly misunderstand each other because they speak different languages. A *Martian/Venusian Phrase Dictionary* is provided to translate commonly misunderstood expressions. You will learn how men and women speak and even stop speaking for entirely different reasons. Women will learn what to do when a man stops talking, and men will learn how to listen better without becoming frustrated.

In chapter 6 you will discover how men and women have different needs for intimacy. A man gets close but then inevitably needs to pull away. Women will learn how to support this pulling-away process so he will spring back to her like a rubber band. Women also will learn the best times for having intimate conversations with a man.

We will explore in chapter 7 how a woman's loving attitudes rise and fall rhythmically in a wave motion. Men will learn how correctly to interpret these sometimes sudden shifts of feeling. Men also will learn to recognize when they are needed the most and how to be skillfully supportive at those times without having to make sacrifices.

In chapter 8 you'll discover how men and women give the kind of love they need and not what the opposite sex needs. Men primarily need a kind of love that is trusting, accepting, and appreciative. Women primarily need a kind of love that is caring, understanding, and respectful. You will discover the six most common ways you may unknowingly be turning off your partner.

In chapter 9 we will explore how to avoid painful arguments. Men will learn that by acting as if they are always right they may invalidate a woman's feelings. Women will learn how they unknowingly send messages of disapproval instead of disagreement, thus igniting a man's defenses. The anatomy of an argument will be explored along with many practical suggestions for establishing supportive communication.

Chapter 10 will show how men and women keep score differently. Men will learn that for Venusians every gift of love scores equally with every other gift, regardless of size. Instead of focusing on one big gift men are reminded that the little expressions of love are just as important; 101 ways to score points with women are listed. Women, however, will learn to redirect their energies into ways that score big with men by giving men what they want.

In chapter 11 you'll learn ways to communicate with each other during difficult times. The different ways men and women hide feelings are discussed along with the importance of sharing feelings. The Love Letter Technique is recommended for expressing negative feelings to your partner, as a way of finding greater love and forgiveness.

You will understand why Venusians have a more difficult time asking for support in chapter 12, as well as why Martians commonly resist requests. You will learn how the phrases "could you" and "can you" turn off men and what to say instead. You will learn the secrets for encouraging a man to give more and discover in various ways the power of being brief, direct, and using the correct wording.

In chapter 13 you'll discover the four seasons of love. This realistic perspective of how love changes and grows will assist you in overcoming the inevitable obstacles that emerge in any relationship. You will learn how your past or your partner's past can affect your relationship in the present and discover other important insights for keeping the magic of love alive.

In each chapter of *Men Are from Mars, Women Are from Venus* you will discover new secrets for creating loving and lasting relationships. Each new discovery will increase your ability to have fulfilling relationships.

GOOD INTENTIONS ARE NOT ENOUGH

Falling in love is always magical. It feels eternal, as if love will last forever. We naïvely believe that somehow we are exempt from the problems our parents had, free from the odds that love will die, assured that it is meant to be and that we are destined to live happily ever after.

But as the magic recedes and daily life takes over, it emerges that men continue to expect women to think and react like men, and women expect men to feel and behave like women. Without a clear awareness of our differences, we do not take the time to understand and respect each other. We become demanding, resentful, judgmental, and intolerant.

With the best and most loving intentions love continues to die. Somehow the problems creep in. The resentments build. Communication breaks down. Mistrust increases. Rejection and repression result. The magic of love is lost.

We ask ourselves:

How does it happen?

Why does it happen?

Why does it happen to us?

To answer these questions our greatest minds have developed brilliant and complex philosophical and psychological models. Yet still the old patterns return. Love dies. It happens to almost everyone.

Each day millions of individuals are searching for a partner to experience that special loving feeling. Each year, millions of couples join together in love and then painfully separate because they have lost that loving feeling. From those who are able to sustain love long enough to get married, only 50 percent stay married. Out of those who stay together, possibly another 50 percent are not fulfilled. They stay together out of loyalty and obligation or from the fear of starting over.

Very few people, indeed, are able to grow in love. Yet, it does happen. When men and women are able to respect and accept their differences then love has a chance to blossom.

> **When men and women are able
> to respect and accept their differences
> then love has a chance to blossom.**

Through understanding the hidden differences of the opposite sex we can more successfully give and receive the love that is in our hearts. By validating and accepting our differences, creative solutions can be discovered whereby we can succeed in getting what we want. And, more important, we can learn how to best love and support the people we care about.

Love is magical, and it can last, if we remember our differences.

CHAPTER 2

MR. FIX-IT AND THE HOME-
IMPROVEMENT COMMITTEE

The most frequently expressed complaint women have about men is that men don't listen. Either a man completely ignores her when she speaks to him, or he listens for a few beats, assesses what is bothering her, and then proudly puts on his Mr. Fix-It cap and offers her a solution to make her feel better. He is confused when she doesn't appreciate this gesture of love. No matter how many times she tells him that he's not listening, he doesn't get it and keeps doing the same thing. She wants empathy, but he thinks she wants solutions.

The most frequently expressed complaint men have about women is that women are always trying to change them. When a woman loves a man she feels responsible to assist him in growing and tries to help him improve the way he does things. She forms a home-improvement committee, and he becomes her primary focus. No matter how much he resists her help, she persists–waiting for any opportunity to help him or tell him what to do. She thinks she's nurturing him, while he feels he's being controlled. Instead, he wants her acceptance.

These two problems can finally be solved by first understanding why men offer solutions and why women seek to improve. Let's pretend to go back in time, where by observing life on Mars and Venus —before the planets discovered one another or came to Earth—we can gain some insights into men and women.

LIFE ON MARS

Martians value power, competency, efficiency, and achievement. They are always doing things to prove themselves and develop their power and skills. Their sense of self is defined through their ability to achieve results. They experience fulfillment primarily through success and accomplishment.

> **A man's sense of self is defined through his ability to achieve results.**

Everything on Mars is a reflection of these values. Even their dress is designed to reflect their skills and competence. Police officers, soldiers, businessmen, scientists, cab drivers, technicians, and chefs all wear uniforms or at least hats to reflect their competence and power.

They don't read magazines like *Psychology Today, Self,* or *People.* They are more concerned with outdoor activities, like hunting, fishing, and racing cars. They are interested in the news, weather, and sports and couldn't care less about romance novels and self-help books.

They are more interested in "objects" and "things" rather than people and feelings. Even today on Earth, while women fantasize about romance, men fantasize about powerful cars, faster computers, gadgets, gizmos, and new more powerful technology. Men are preoccupied with the "things" that can help them express power by creating results and achieving their goals.

Achieving goals is very important to a Martian because it is a way for him to prove his competence and thus feel good about himself. And for him to feel good about himself he must achieve these goals by himself. Someone else can't achieve them for him. Martians pride themselves in doing things all by themselves. Autonomy is a symbol of efficiency, power, and competence.

Understanding this Martian characteristic can help women understand why men resist so much being corrected or being told what to do. To offer a man unsolicited advice is to presume that he doesn't know what to do or that he can't do it on his own. Men are very touchy about this, because the issue of competence is so very important to them.

> **To offer a man unsolicited advice**
> **is to presume that he doesn't know what to do**
> **or that he can't do it on his own.**

Because he is handling his problems on his own, a Martian rarely talks about his problems unless he needs expert advice. He reasons: "Why involve someone else when I can do it by myself?" He keeps his problems to himself unless he requires help from another to find a solution. Asking for help when you can do it yourself is perceived as a sign of weakness.

However, if he truly does need help, then it is a sign of wisdom to get it. In this case, he will find someone he respects and then talk about his problem. Talking about a problem on Mars is an invitation for advice. Another Martian feels honored by the opportunity. Automatically he puts on his Mr. Fix-It hat, listens for a while, and then offers some jewels of advice.

This Martian custom is one of the reasons men instinctively offer solutions when women talk about problems. When a woman innocently shares upset feelings or explores out loud the problems of her day, a man mistakenly assumes she is looking for some expert advice. He puts on his Mr. Fix-It hat and begins giving advice; this is his way of showing love and of trying to help.

He wants to help her feel better by solving her problems. He wants to be useful to her. He feels he can be valued and thus worthy of her love when his abilities are used to solve her problems.

Once he has offered a solution, however, and she continues to be upset it becomes increasingly difficult for him to listen because his solution is being rejected and he feels increasingly useless.

He has no idea that by just listening with empathy and interest he can be supportive. He does not know that on Venus talking about problems is not an invitation to offer a solution.

LIFE ON VENUS

Venusians have different values. They value love, communication, beauty, and relationships. They spend a lot of time supporting, helping, and nurturing one another. Their sense of self is defined through their feelings and the quality of their relationships. They experience fulfillment through sharing and relating.

> **A woman's sense of self
> is defined through her feelings
> and the quality of her relationships.**

Everything on Venus reflects these values. Rather than building highways and tall buildings, the Venusians are more concerned with living together in harmony, community, and loving cooperation. Relationships are more important than work and technology. In most ways their world is the opposite of Mars.

They do not wear uniforms like the Martians (to reveal their competence). On the contrary, they enjoy wearing a different outfit every day, according to how they are feeling. Personal expression, especially of their feelings, is very important. They may even change outfits several times a day as their mood changes.

Communication is of primary importance. To share their personal feelings is much more important than achieving goals and success. Talking and relating to one another is a source of tremendous fulfillment.

This is hard for a man to comprehend. He can come close to understanding a woman's experience of sharing and relating by comparing it to the satisfaction he feels when he wins a race, achieves a goal, or solves a problem.

Instead of being goal oriented, women are relationship oriented; they are more concerned with expressing their goodness, love, and caring. Two Martians go to lunch to discuss a project or business goal; they have a problem to solve. In addition, Martians view going to a restaurant as an efficient way to approach food: no shopping, no cooking, and no washing dishes. For Venusians, going to lunch is an opportunity to nurture a relationship, for both giving support to and receiving support from a friend. Women's restaurant talk can be very open and intimate, almost like the dialogue that occurs between therapist and patient.

On Venus, everyone studies psychology and has at least a master's degree in counseling. They are very involved in personal growth, spirituality, and everything that can nurture life, healing, and growth. Venus is covered with parks, organic gardens, shopping centers, and restaurants.

Venusians are very intuitive. They have developed this ability through centuries of anticipating the needs of others. They pride themselves in being considerate of the needs and feelings of others. A sign of great love is to offer help and assistance to another Venusian without being asked.

Because proving one's competence is not as important to a Venusian, offering help is not offensive, and needing help is not a sign of weakness. A man, however, may feel offended because when a woman offers advice he doesn't feel she trusts his ability to do it himself.

A woman has no conception of this male sensitivity because for her it is another feather in her hat if someone offers to help her. It makes her feel loved and cherished. But offering help to a man can make him feel incompetent, weak, and even unloved.

On Venus it is a sign of caring to give advice and suggestions. Venusians firmly believe that when something is working it can always work better. Their nature is to want to improve things. When they care about someone, they freely point out what can be improved and suggest how to do it. Offering advice and constructive criticism is an act of love.

Mars is very different. Martians are more solution oriented. If something is working, their motto is don't change it. Their instinct is to leave it alone if it is working. "Don't fix it unless it is broken" is a common expression.

When a woman tries to improve a man, he feels she is trying to fix him. He receives the message that he is broken. She doesn't realize her caring attempts to help him may humiliate him. She mistakenly thinks she is just helping him to grow.

GIVE UP GIVING ADVICE

Without this insight into the nature of men, it's very easy for a woman unknowingly and unintentionally to hurt and offend the man she loves most.

For example, Tom and Mary were going to a party. Tom was driving. After about twenty minutes and going around the same block a few times, it was clear to Mary that Tom was lost. She finally suggested that he call for help. Tom became very silent. They eventually arrived at the party, but the tension from that moment persisted the whole evening. Mary had no idea of why he was so upset.

From her side she was saying "I love and care about you, so I am offering you this help."

From his side, he was offended. What he heard was "I don't trust you to get us there. You are incompetent!"

Without knowing about life on Mars, Mary could not appreciate how important it was for Tom to accomplish his goal without help. Offering advice was the ultimate insult. As we have explored, Martians never offer advice unless asked. A way of honoring another Martian is *always* to assume he can solve his problem unless he is asking for help.

Mary had no idea that when Tom became lost and started circling the same block, it was a very special opportunity to love and support him. At that time he was particularly vulnerable and needed some extra love. To honor him by not offering advice would have been a gift equivalent to his buying her a beautiful bouquet of flowers or writing her a love note.

After learning about Martians and Venusians, Mary learned how to support Tom at such difficult times. The next time he was lost, instead of offering "help" she restrained herself from offering any advice, took a deep relaxing breath, and appreciated in her heart what Tom was trying to do for her. Tom greatly appreciated her warm acceptance and trust.

Generally speaking, when a woman offers unsolicited advice or tries to "help" a man, she has no idea of how critical and unloving she may sound to him. Even though her intent is loving, her suggestions do offend and hurt. His reaction may be strong, especially if he felt criticized as a child or he experienced his father being criticized by his mother.

> Generally speaking, when a woman offers unsolicited advice or tries to "help" a man, she has no idea of how critical and unloving she may sound to him.

For many men, it is very important to prove that they can get to their goal, even if it is a small thing like driving to a restaurant or party. Ironically he may be more sensitive about the little things than the big. His feelings are like this: "If I can't be trusted to do a small thing like get us to a party, how can she trust me to do the bigger things?" Like their Martian ancestors, men pride themselves on being experts, especially when it comes to fixing mechanical things, getting places, or solving problems. These are the times when he needs her loving acceptance the most and not her advice or criticism.

LEARNING TO LISTEN

Likewise, if a man does not understand how a woman is different, he can make things worse when he is trying to help. Men need to remember that women talk about problems to get close and not necessarily to get solutions.

So many times a woman just wants to share her feelings about her day, and her husband, thinking he is helping, interrupts her by offering a steady flow of solutions to her problems. He has no idea why she isn't pleased.

> Many times a woman just wants to share her feelings about her day, and her husband, thinking he is helping, interrupts her by offering a steady flow of solutions to her problems.

For example, Mary comes home from an exhausting day. She wants and needs to share her feelings about the day.

She says, "There is so much to do; I don't have any time for myself."

Tom says, "You should quit that job. You don't have to work so hard. Find something you like to do."

Mary says, "But I like my job. They just expect me to change everything at a moment's notice."

Tom says, "Don't listen to them. Just do what you can do."

Mary says, "I *am!* I can't believe I completely forgot to call my aunt today."

Tom says, "Don't worry about it, she'll understand."

Mary says, "Do you know what she is going through? She needs me."

Tom says, "You worry too much, that's why you're so unhappy."

Mary angrily says, "I am not always unhappy. Can't you just listen to me?"

Tom says, "I *am* listening."

Mary says, "Why do I even bother?"

After this conversation, Mary was more frustrated than when she arrived home seeking intimacy and companionship. Tom was also frustrated and had no idea what went wrong. He wanted to help, but his problem-solving tactics didn't work.

Without knowing about life on Venus, Tom didn't understand how important it was just to listen without offering solutions. His solutions only made things worse. You see, Venusians never offer solutions when someone is talking. A way of honoring another

Venusian is to listen patiently with empathy, seeking truly to under-stand the other's feelings.

Tom had no idea that just listening with empathy to Mary express her feelings would bring her tremendous relief and fulfill-ment. When Tom heard about the Venusians and how much they needed to talk, he gradually learned how to listen.

When Mary now comes home tired and exhausted their conver-sations are quite different. They sound like this:

Mary says, "There is so much to do. I have no time for me."

Tom takes a deep breath, relaxes on the exhale, and says, "Humph, sounds like you had a hard day."

Mary says, "They expect me to change everything at a mo-ment's notice. I don't know what to do."

Tom pauses and then says, "Hmmm."

Mary says, "I even forgot to call my aunt."

Tom says with a slightly wrinkled brow, "Oh, no."

Mary says, "She needs me so much right now. I feel so bad."

Tom says, "You are such a loving person. Come here, let me give you a hug."

Tom gives Mary a hug and she relaxes in his arms with a big sigh of relief. She then says, "I love talking with you. You make me really happy. Thanks for listening. I feel much better."

Not only Mary but also Tom felt better. He was amazed at how much happier his wife was when he finally learned to listen. With this new awareness of their differences, Tom learned the wisdom of listening without offering solutions while Mary learned the wisdom of letting go and accepting without offering unsolicited advice or criticism.

To summarize the two most common mistakes we make in relationships:

1. A man tries to change a woman's feelings when she is upset by becoming Mr. Fix-It and offering solu-tions to her problems that invalidate her feelings.

2. A woman tries to change a man's behavior when he makes mistakes by becoming the home-improvement committee and offering unsolicited advice or criticism.

IN DEFENSE OF MR. FIX-IT AND THE HOME-IMPROVEMENT COMMITTEE

In pointing out these two major mistakes I do not mean that everything is wrong with Mr. Fix-It or the home-improvement committee. These are very positive Martian and Venusian attributes. The mistakes are only in timing and approach.

A woman greatly appreciates Mr. Fix-It, as long as he doesn't come out when she is upset. Men need to remember that when women seem upset and talk about problems is not the time to offer solutions; instead she needs to be heard, and gradually she will feel better on her own. She does not need to be fixed.

A man greatly appreciates the home-improvement committee, as long as it is requested. Women need to remember that unsolicited advice or criticism–especially if he has made a mistake–make him feel unloved and controlled. He needs her acceptance more than her advice, in order to learn from his mistakes. When a man feels that a woman is not trying to improve him, he is much more likely to ask for her feedback and advice.

> When our partner resists us
> it is probably because we have made a mistake
> in our timing or approach.

Understanding these differences makes it easier to respect our partner's sensitivities and be more supportive. In addition we recognize that when our partner resists us it is probably because we have made a mistake in our timing or approach. Let's explore this in greater detail.

WHEN A WOMAN RESISTS A MAN'S SOLUTIONS

When a woman resists a man's solutions he feels his competence is being questioned. As a result he feels mistrusted, unappreciated, and stops caring. His willingness to listen understandably lessens.

By remembering that women are from Venus, a man at such times can instead understand why she is resisting him. He can reflect and discover how he was probably offering solutions at a time when she was needing empathy and nurturing.

Here are some brief examples of ways a man might mistakenly invalidate feelings and perceptions or offer unwanted solutions. See if you can recognize why she would resist:

1. "You shouldn't worry so much."
2. "But that is not what I said."
3. "It's not such a big deal."
4. "OK, I'm sorry. Now can we just forget it."
5. "Why don't you just do it?"
6. "But we do talk."
7. "You shouldn't feel hurt, that's not what I meant."
8. "So what are you trying to say?"
9. "But you shouldn't feel that way."
10. "How can you say that? Last week I spent the whole day with you. We had a great time."
11. "OK, then just forget it."
12. "All right, I'll clean up the backyard. Does that make you happy?"
13. "I got it. This is what you should do."
14. "Look, there's nothing we can do about it."
15. "If you are going to complain about doing it, then don't do it."
16. "Why do you let people treat you that way? Forget them."
17. "If you're not happy then we should just get a divorce."
18. "All right, then you can do it from now on."
19. "From now on, I will handle it."

20. "Of course I care about you. That's ridiculous."
21. "Would you get to the point?"
22. "All we have to do is…"
23. "That's not at all what happened."

Each of these statements either invalidates or attempts to explain upset feelings or offers a solution designed suddenly to change her negative feelings to positive feelings. The first step a man can take to change this pattern is simply to stop making the above comments (we explore this topic more fully in chapter 5). To practice listening without offering any invalidating comments or solutions is, however, a big step.

By clearly understanding that his timing and delivery are being rejected and not his solutions, a man can handle a woman's resistance much better. He doesn't take it so personally. By learning to listen, gradually he will experience that she will appreciate him more even when at first she is upset with him.

WHEN A MAN RESISTS
THE HOME-IMPROVEMENT COMMITTEE

When a man resists a woman's suggestions she feels as though he doesn't care; she feels her needs are not being respected. As a result she understandably feels unsupported and stops trusting him.

At such times, by remembering that men are from Mars, she can instead correctly understand why he is resisting her. She can reflect and discover how she was probably giving him unsolicited advice or criticism rather than simply sharing her needs, providing information, or making a request.

Here are some brief examples of ways a woman might unknowingly annoy a man by offering advice or seemingly harmless criticism. As you explore this list, remember that these little things can add up to create big walls of resistance and resentment. In some of the statements the advice or criticism is hidden. See if you can recognize why he might feel controlled.

1. "How can you think of buying that? You already have one."
2. "Those dishes are still wet. They'll dry with spots"
3. "Your hair is getting kind of long, isn't it?"
4. "There's a parking spot over there, turn [the car] around."
5. "You want to spend time with your friends, what about me?"
6. "You shouldn't work so hard. Take a day off."
7. "Don't put that there. It will get lost."
8. "You should call a plumber. He'll know what to do."
9. "Why are we waiting for a table? Didn't you make reservations?"
10. "You should spend more time with the kids. They miss you."
11. "Your office is still a mess. How can you think in here? When are you going to clean it up?"
12. "You forgot to bring it home again. Maybe you could put it in a special place where you can remember it."
13. "You're driving too fast. Slow down or you'll get a ticket."
14. "Next time we should read the movie reviews."
15. "I didn't know where you were." (You should have called.)
16. "Somebody drank from the juice bottle."
17. "Don't eat with your fingers. You're setting a bad example."
18. "Those potato chips are too greasy. They're not good for your heart."
19. "You are not leaving yourself enough time."
20. "You should give me more [advance] notice. I can't just drop everything and go to lunch with you."
21. "Your shirt doesn't match your pants."
22. "Bill called for the third time. When are you going to call him back?"

23. "Your toolbox is such a mess. I can't find anything. You should organize it."

When a woman does not know how to directly ask a man for support (chapter 12) or constructively share a difference of opinion (chapter 9), she may feel powerless to get what she needs without giving unsolicited advice or criticism (again, we explore this topic more fully later on). To practice giving acceptance and not giving advice and criticism is, however, a big step.

By clearly understanding he is rejecting not her needs but the way she is approaching him, she can take his rejection less personally and explore more supportive ways of communicating her needs. Gradually she will realize that a man wants to make improvements when he feels he is being approached as the solution to a problem rather than as the problem itself.

> **A man wants to make improvements when he feels he is being approached as the solution to a problem rather than as the problem itself.**

If you are a woman, I suggest that for the next week practice restraining from giving *any* unsolicited advice or criticism. The men in your life not only will appreciate it but also will be more attentive and responsive to you.

If you are a man, I suggest that for the next week you practice listening *whenever* a woman speaks, with the sole intention of respectfully understanding what she is going through. Practice biting your tongue whenever you get the urge to offer a solution or change how she is feeling. You will be surprised when you experience how much she appreciates you.

CHAPTER 3

MEN GO TO THEIR CAVES
AND WOMEN TALK

One of the biggest differences between men and women is how they cope with stress. Men become increasingly focused and withdrawn while women become increasingly overwhelmed and emotionally involved. At these times, a man's needs for feeling good are different from a woman's. He feels better by solving problems while she feels better by talking about problems. Not understanding and accepting these differences creates unnecessary friction in our relationships. Let's look at a common example.

> When Tom comes home, he wants to relax and unwind by quietly reading the news. He is stressed by the unsolved problems of his day and finds relief through forgetting them.
>
> His wife, Mary, also wants to relax from her stressful day. She, however, wants to find relief by talking about the problems of her day. The tension slowly building between them gradually becomes resentment.
>
> Tom secretly thinks Mary talks too much, while

Mary feels ignored. Without understanding their
differences they will grow further apart.

You probably can recognize this situation because it is just one
of many examples where men and women are at odds. This problem is not just Tom and Mary's but is present in almost every relationship.

Solving this problem for Tom and Mary depends not on how
much they loved each other but on how much they understood the
opposite sex.

Without knowing that women really do need to talk about
problems to feel better, Tom would continue to think Mary talked
too much and resist listening to her. Without knowing that Tom was
reading the news to feel better, Mary would feel ignored and
neglected. She would persist in trying to get him to talk when he
didn't want to.

These two differences can be resolved by first understanding in
greater detail how men and women cope with stress. Let's again
observe life on Mars and Venus and glean some insights about men
and women.

COPING WITH STRESS ON MARS AND VENUS

When a Martian gets upset he never talks about what is bothering
him. He would never burden another Martian with his problem
unless his friend's assistance was necessary to solve the problem.
Instead he becomes very quiet and goes to his private cave to think
about his problem, mulling it over to find a solution. When he has
found a solution, he feels much better and comes out of his cave.

If he can't find a solution then he does something to forget his
problems, like reading the news or playing a game. By disengaging
his mind from the problems of his day, gradually he can relax. If his
stress is really great it takes getting involved with something even
more challenging, like racing his car, competing in a contest, or
climbing a mountain.

> **To feel better Martians go to their caves**
> **to solve problems alone.**

When a Venusian becomes upset or is stressed by her day, to find relief, she seeks out someone she trusts and then talks in great detail about the problems of her day. When Venusians share feelings of being overwhelmed, they suddenly feel better. This is the Venusian way.

> **To feel better Venusians get together**
> **and openly talk about their problems.**

On Venus sharing your problems with another actually is considered a sign of love and trust and not a burden. Venusians are not ashamed of having problems. Their egos are dependent not on looking "competent" but rather on being in loving relationships. They openly share feelings of being overwhelmed, confused, hopeless, and exhausted.

A Venusian feels good about herself when she has loving friends with whom to share her feelings and problems. A Martian feels good when he can solve his problems on his own in his cave. These secrets of feeling good are still applicable today.

FINDING RELIEF IN THE CAVE

When a man is stressed he will withdraw into the cave of his mind and focus on solving a problem. He generally picks the most urgent problem or the most difficult. He becomes so focused on solving this one problem that he temporarily loses awareness of everything else. Other problems and responsibilities fade into the background.

At such times, he becomes increasingly distant, forgetful, unresponsive, and preoccupied in his relationships. For example, when having a conversation with him at home, it seems as if only 5 percent of his mind is available for the relationship while the other 95 percent is still at work.

His full awareness is not present because he is mulling over his problem, hoping to find a solution. The more stressed he is the more gripped by the problem he will be. At such times he is incapable of giving a woman the attention and feeling that she normally receives and certainly deserves. His mind is preoccupied, and he is powerless to release it. If, however, he can find a solution, instantly he will feel much better and come out of his cave; suddenly he is available for being in a relationship again.

However, if he cannot find a solution to his problem, then he remains stuck in the cave. To get unstuck he is drawn to solving little problems, like reading the news, watching TV, driving his car, doing physical exercise, watching a football game, playing basketball, and so forth. Any challenging activity that initially requires only 5 percent of his mind can assist him in forgetting his problems and becoming unstuck. Then the next day he can redirect his focus to his problem with greater success.

Let's explore in greater detail a few examples. Jim commonly uses reading the newspaper to forget his problems. When he reads the paper he is no longer being confronted with the problems of his day. With the 5 percent of his mind that is not focused on his work problems, he begins forming opinions and finding solutions for the world's problems. Gradually his mind becomes increasingly involved with the problems in the news and he forgets his own. In this way he makes the transition from being focused on his problems at work to focusing on the many problems of the world (for which he is not directly responsible). This process releases his mind from the gripping problems of work so he can focus on his wife and family again.

Tom watches a football game to release his stress and unwind. He releases his mind from trying to solve his own problems by solving the problems of his favorite team. Through watching sports he can vicariously feel he has solved a problem with each play. When his team scores points or wins, he enjoys the feeling of success. If his team loses, he suffers their loss as his own. In either case, however, his mind is released from the grip of his real problems.

For Tom and many men the inevitable release of tension that

occurs at the completion of any sporting event, news event, or movie provides a release from the tension he feels in his life.

How Women React to the Cave

When a man is stuck in his cave, he is powerless to give his partner the quality attention she deserves. It is hard for her to be accepting of him at these times because she doesn't know how stressed he is. If he were to come home and talk about all his problems, then she could be more compassionate. Instead he doesn't talk about his problems, and she feels he is ignoring her. She can tell he is upset but mistakenly assumes he doesn't care about her because he isn't talking to her.

Women generally do not understand how Martians cope with stress. They expect men to open up and talk about all their problems the way Venusians do. When a man is stuck in his cave, a woman resents his not being more open. She feels hurt when he turns on the news or goes outside to play some basketball and ignores her.

To expect a man who is in his cave instantly to become open, responsive, and loving is as unrealistic as expecting a woman who is upset immediately to calm down and make complete sense. It is a mistake to expect a man to always be in touch with his loving feelings just as it is a mistake to expect a woman's feelings to always be rational and logical.

When Martians go to their caves they tend to forget that their friends may be having problems too. An instinct takes over that says before you can take care of anybody else, you must first take care of yourself. When a woman sees a man react in this way, she generally resists it and resents the man.

She may ask for his support in a demanding tone, as if she has to fight for her rights with this uncaring man. By remembering that men are from Mars, a woman can correctly interpret his reaction to stress as his coping mechanism rather than as an expression of how he feels about her. She can begin to cooperate with him to get what she needs instead of resisting him.

On the other side, men generally have little awareness of how distant they become when they are in the cave. As a man recognizes how withdrawing into his cave may affect women, he can be compassionate when she feels neglected and unimportant. Remembering that women are from Venus helps him to be more understanding and respectful of her reactions and feelings. Without understanding the validity of her reactions, a man commonly defends himself, and they argue. These are five common misunderstandings:

1. When she says "You don't listen," he says "What do you mean I don't listen. I can tell you everything you said."

When a man is in the cave he can record what she is saying with the 5 percent of mind that is listening. A man reasons that if he is listening with 5 percent, then he is listening. However, what she is asking for is his full undivided attention.

2. When she says "I feel like you are not even here," he says "What do you mean I'm not here? Of course I am here. Don't you see my body?"

He reasons that if his body is present then she shouldn't say he is not there. However, though his body is present, she doesn't feel his full presence, and that is what she means.

3. When she says "You don't care about me," he says "Of course I care about you. Why do you think I am trying to solve this problem?"

He reasons that because he is preoccupied with solving a problem that will in some way benefit her, she should know he cares for her. However, she needs to feel his direct attention and caring, and that is what she is really asking for.

4. When she says "I feel like I am not important to you," he says "That's ridiculous. Of course you are important."

He reasons that her feelings are invalid because he is solving problems to benefit her. He doesn't realize that when he focuses on one problem and ignores the problems she is bothered by that almost any woman would have the same reaction and take it personally and feel unimportant.

5. When she says "You have no feelings. You are in your head," he says "What's wrong with that? How else do you expect me to solve this problem?"

He reasons that she is being too critical and demanding because he is doing something that is essential for him to solve problems. He feels unappreciated. In addition he doesn't recognize the validity of her feelings. Men generally don't realize how extremely and quickly they may shift from being warm and feeling to being unresponsive and distant. In his cave a man is preoccupied with solving his problem and is unaware of how his indifferent attitude might feel to others.

To increase cooperation both men and women need to understand each other better. When a man begins to ignore his wife, she often takes it personally. Knowing that he is coping with stress in his own way is extremely helpful but does not always help her alleviate the pain.

At such times she may feel the need to talk about these feelings. This is when it is important for the man to validate her feelings. He needs to understand that she has a right to talk about her feelings of being ignored and unsupported just as he has a right to withdraw into his cave and not talk. If she does not feel understood then it is difficult for her to release her hurt.

FINDING RELIEF THROUGH TALKING

When a woman is stressed she instinctively feels a need to talk about her feelings and all the possible problems that are associated with her feelings. When she begins talking she does not prioritize the significance of any problem. If she is upset, then she is upset about it all, big and small. She is not immediately concerned with finding solutions to her problems but rather seeks relief by expressing herself and being understood. By randomly talking about her problems, she becomes less upset.

> A woman under stress is not immediately concerned with
> finding solutions to her problems
> but rather seeks relief
> by expressing herself and being understood.

As a man under stress tends to focus on one problem and forget others, a woman under stress tends to expand and become overwhelmed by all problems. By talking about all possible problems without focusing on problem solving she feels better. Through exploring her feelings in this process she gains a greater awareness of what is really bothering her, and then suddenly she is no longer so overwhelmed.

To feel better, women talk about past problems, future problems, potential problems, even problems that have no solutions. The more talk and exploration, the better they feel. This is the way women operate. To expect otherwise is to deny a woman her sense of self.

When a woman is overwhelmed she finds relief through talking in great detail about her various problems. Gradually, if she feels she is being heard, her stress disappears. After talking about one topic she will pause and then move on to the next. In this way she continues to expand talking about problems, worries, disappointments, and frustrations. These topics need not be in any order and tend to be logically unrelated. If she feels she is not being understood, her awareness may expand even further, and she may become upset about more problems.

Just as a man who is stuck in the cave needs little problems to distract him, a woman who doesn't feel heard will need to talk about other problems that are less immediate to feel relief. To forget her own painful feelings she may become emotionally involved in the problems of others. In addition she may find relief through discussing the problems of her friends, relatives, and associates. Whether she is talking about her problems or others' problems, talking is a natural and healthy Venusian reaction to stress.

> **To forget her own painful feelings**
> **a woman may become emotionally involved**
> **in the problems of others.**

How Men React When Women Need to Talk

When women talk about problems, men usually resist. A man assumes she is talking with him about her problems because she is holding him responsible. The more problems, the more he feels blamed. He does not realize that she is talking to feel better. A man doesn't know that she will appreciate it if he just listens.

Martians talk about problems for only two reasons: they are blaming someone or they are seeking advice. If a woman is really upset a man assumes she is blaming him. If she seems less upset, then he assumes she is asking for advice.

If he assumes she is asking for advice, then he puts on his Mr. Fix-It hat to solve her problems. If he assumes she is blaming him, then he draws his sword to protect himself from attack. In both cases, he soon finds it difficult to listen.

If he offers solutions to her problems, she just continues talking about more problems. After offering two or three solutions, he expects her to feel better. This is because Martians themselves feel better with solutions, as long as they have asked for a solution to be offered. When she doesn't feel better, he feels his solutions have been rejected, and he feels unappreciated.

On the other hand, if he feels attacked, then he begins to defend himself. He thinks if he explains himself that she will stop blaming him. The more he defends himself, however, the more upset she becomes. He doesn't realize that explanations are not what she needs. She needs him to understand her feelings and let her move on to talk about more problems. If he is wise and just listens, then a few moments after she is complaining about him, she will change the subject and talk about other problems as well.

Men also become particularly frustrated when a woman talks about problems that he can do nothing about. For example, when a woman is stressed she could complain:

- "I'm not getting paid enough at work."
- "My Aunt Louise is getting sicker and sicker, each year she gets sicker."
- "Our house just isn't big enough."
- "This is such a dry season. When is it going to rain?"
- "We are almost overdrawn in our bank account."

A woman might make any of the above comments as a way of expressing her worries, disappointments, and frustrations. She may know that nothing more can be done to solve these problems, but to find relief she still needs to talk about them. She feels supported if the listener relates to her frustration and disappointment. She may, however, frustrate her male partner—unless he understands that she just needs to talk about it and then she will feel better.

Men also become impatient when women talk about problems in great detail. A man mistakenly assumes that when a woman talks in great detail that all the details are necessary for him to find a solution to her problem. He struggles to find their relevance and becomes impatient. Again he doesn't realize that she is looking not for a solution from him but for his caring and understanding.

In addition, listening is difficult for a man because he mistakenly assumes there is a logical order when she randomly changes from one problem to another. After she has shared three or four problems he becomes extremely frustrated and confused trying logically to relate these problems.

Another reason a man may resist listening is that he is looking for the bottom line. He cannot begin formulating his solution until he knows the outcome. The more details she gives the more he is frustrated while listening. His frustration is lessened if he can remember that she is greatly benefiting by talking about the details. If he can remember that talking in detail is helping her to feel good, then he can relax. Just as a man is fulfilled through working out the intricate details of solving a problem, a woman is fulfilled through talking about the details of her problems.

> Just as a man is fulfilled through working out the intricate details of solving a problem, a woman is fulfilled through talking about the details of her problems.

Something a woman can do to make it a little easier for a man is to let him know in advance the outcome of the story and then go back and give the details. Avoid keeping him in suspense. Women commonly enjoy letting the suspense build because it brings more feeling into the story. Another woman appreciates this buildup, but a man can be easily frustrated.

The degree to which a man does not understand a woman is the degree to which he will resist her when she is talking about problems. As a man learns more how to fulfill a woman and provide her emotional support he discovers that listening is not so difficult. More important, if a woman can remind a man that she just wants to talk about her problems and that he doesn't have to solve any of them, it can help him to relax and listen.

HOW THE MARTIANS AND VENUSIANS FOUND PEACE

The Martians and Venusians lived together in peace because they were able to respect their differences. The Martians learned to respect that Venusians needed to talk to feel better. Even if he didn't have much to say, he learned that by listening he could be very supportive. The Venusians learned to respect that Martians needed to withdraw to cope with stress. The cave was no longer a great mystery or cause for alarm.

What the Martians Learned

The Martians realized that even when they felt they were being attacked, blamed, or criticized by the Venusians it was only temporary; soon the Venusians would suddenly feel better and be very appreciative and accepting. By learning to listen, the Martians discovered how much the Venusians really thrived on talking about problems.

Each Martian found peace of mind when he finally understood that a Venusian's need to talk about her problems was not because he was failing her in some way. In addition he learned that once a Venusian feels heard she stops dwelling on her problems and becomes very positive. With this awareness, a Martian was able to listen without feeling responsible for solving all her problems.

Many men and even women are very judgmental of the need to talk about problems because they have never experienced how healing it can be. They have not seen how a woman who feels heard suddenly can change, feel better, and sustain a positive attitude. Generally they have seen how a woman (probably their mother) who did not feel heard continued to dwell on her problems. This happens to women when they do not feel loved or heard over an extended period of time. The real problem, however, is that she feels unloved, not that she is talking about problems.

After the Martians learned how to listen they made a most amazing discovery. They began to realize that listening to a Venusian talk about problems could actually help them come out of their caves in the same way as watching the news on TV or reading a newspaper.

Similarly, as men learn to listen without feeling blamed or responsible, listening becomes much easier. As a man gets good at listening, he realizes that listening can be an excellent way to forget the problems of his day as well as bring a lot of fulfillment to his partner. But on days when he is really stressed he may need to be in his cave and slowly come out by some other distraction, like the news or a competitive sport.

What the Venusians Learned

The Venusians also found peace of mind when they finally understood that a Martian going into his cave was not a sign that he didn't love her as much. They learned to be more accepting of him at these times because he was experiencing a lot of stress.

The Venusians were not offended when Martians were easily distracted. When a Venusian talked and a Martian became distracted, she would very politely stop talking, stand there, and wait for him to notice. Then she would begin talking again. She understood that sometimes it was hard for him to give his full attention. The Venusians discovered that by asking for the Martians' attention in a relaxed and accepting manner the Martians were happy to redirect their attention.

When the Martians were completely preoccupied and in their caves, the Venusians also did not take it personally. They learned that this was not the time to have intimate conversations but a time to talk about problems with their friends or have fun and go shopping. When the Martians thereby felt loved and accepted, the Venusians discovered that the Martians would more quickly come out of their caves.

CHAPTER 4

HOW TO MOTIVATE
THE OPPOSITE SEX

Centuries before the Martians and Venusians got together they had been quite happy living in their separate worlds. Then one day everything changed. The Martians and Venusians on their respective planets suddenly became depressed. It was this depression, however, that motivated them eventually to come together.

Understanding the secrets of their transformation helps us today to recognize how men and women are motivated in different ways. With this new awareness you will be better equipped to support your partner as well as get the support you need at difficult and stressful times. Let's go back in time and pretend to witness what happened.

When the Martians became depressed, everyone on the planet left the cities and went to their caves for a long time. They were stuck and couldn't come out, until one day when a Martian happened to glimpse the beautiful Venusians through his telescope. As he quickly shared his telescope, the sight of these beautiful beings inspired the Martians, and their depression miraculously lifted. *Suddenly they felt needed.* They came out of their caves and began building a fleet of spaceships to fly to Venus.

When the Venusians became depressed, to feel better they formed circles and began talking with one another about their problems. But this didn't seem to relieve the depression. They stayed depressed for a long time until through their intuition they experienced a vision. Strong and wondrous beings (the Martians) would be coming across the universe to love, serve, and support them. *Suddenly they felt cherished.* As they shared their vision their depression lifted, and they happily began preparing for the arrival of the Martians.

Men are motivated and empowered
when they feel needed....
Women are motivated and empowered
when they feel cherished.

These secrets of motivation are still applicable. Men are motivated and empowered *when they feel needed.* When a man does not feel needed in a relationship, he gradually becomes passive and less energized; with each passing day he has less to give the relationship. On the other hand, when he feels trusted to do his best to fulfill her needs and appreciated for his efforts, he is empowered and has more to give.

Like the Venusians, women are motivated and empowered *when they feel cherished.* When a woman does not feel cherished in a relationship she gradually becomes compulsively responsible and exhausted from giving too much. On the other hand when she feels cared for and respected, she is fulfilled and has more to give as well.

WHEN A MAN LOVES A WOMAN

A man falling in love with a woman is similar to what took place when the first Martian discovered the Venusians. Stuck in his cave and unable to find the source of his depression, he was searching the sky with his telescope. As if he had been struck by lightning, in one glorious moment his life was permanently changed. He had glimpsed through his telescope a vision he described as awesome beauty and grace.

He had discovered the Venusians. His body lit on fire. As he watched the Venusians, for the first time in his life he began to care about someone other than himself. From just one glimpse his life had new meaning. His depression lifted.

Martians have a win/lose philosophy–I want to win, and I don't care if you lose. As long as each Martian took care of himself this formula worked fine. It worked for centuries, but now it needed to be changed. Giving primarily to themselves was no longer as satisfying. Being in love, they wanted the Venusians to win as much as themselves.

In most sports today we can see an extension of this Martian competitive code. For example, in tennis I not only want to win but also try to make my friend lose by making it difficult for him to return my shots. I enjoy winning even though my friend loses.

Most of these Martian attitudes have a place in life, but this win/lose attitude becomes harmful in our adult relationships. If I seek to fulfill my own needs at the expense of my partner, we are sure to experience unhappiness, resentment, and conflict. The secret of forming a successful relationship is for both partners to win.

Differences Attract

After the first Martian fell in love, he began manufacturing telescopes for all his brother Martians. Very quickly they all came out of their depressions. They too began to feel love for the Venusians. They started to care about the Venusians as much as themselves.

The strange and beautiful Venusians were a mysterious attraction to the Martians. Their differences especially attracted the Martians. Where the Martians were hard, the Venusians were soft. Where the Martians were angular, the Venusians were round. Where the Martians were cool, the Venusians were warm. In a magical and perfect way their differences seemed to complement each other.

In an unspoken language the Venusians communicated loud and

clear: "We need you. Your power and strength can bring us great fulfill-ment, filling a void deep within our being. Together we could live in great happiness." This invitation motivated and empowered the Martians.

Many women instinctively understand how to give this message. In the beginning of a relationship, a woman gives a man a brief look that says you could be the one to make me happy. In this subtle way she actually initiates their relationship. This look encourages him to come closer. It empowers him to overcome his fears of having a rela-tionship. Unfortunately, once they are in a relationship and as the problems begin to emerge, she doesn't know how important that message still is to him and neglects to send it.

The Martians were very motivated by the possibility of making a difference on Venus. The Martian race was moving to a new level of evolution. They were no longer satisfied by just proving them-selves and developing their power. They wanted to use their power and skills in the service of others, especially in the service of the Venusians. They were beginning to develop a new philosophy, a win/win philosophy. They wanted a world where everyone cared for themselves as well as for others.

Love Motivates Martians

The Martians began building a fleet of spaceships that would carry them across the heavens to Venus. They had never felt so alive. Through glimpsing the Venusians, they were beginning to have unselfish feelings for the first time in their history.

Similarly, when a man is in love he is motivated to be the best he can be in order to serve others. When his heart is open, he feels so confident in himself that he is capable of making major changes. Given the opportunity to prove his potential, he expresses his best self. Only when he feels he cannot succeed does he regress back to his old selfish ways.

When a man is in love, he begins to care about another as much as himself. He is suddenly released from the binding chains of being

> Given the opportunity to prove his potential,
> a man expresses his best self.
> Only when he feels he cannot succeed does he
> regress back to his old selfish ways.

motivated for himself alone and becomes free to give to another, not for personal gain, but out of caring. He experiences his partner's fulfillment as if it were his own. He can easily endure any hardship to make her happy because her happiness makes him happy. His struggles become easier. He is energized with a higher purpose.

In his youth he can be satisfied by serving himself alone, but as he matures self-gratification is no longer as satisfying. To experience fulfillment he must begin to live his life motivated by love. Being inspired to give in such a free and selfless way liberates him from the inertia of self-gratification devoid of caring for others. Although he still needs to receive love, his greatest need is to give love.

Most men are not only hungry to give love but are starving for it. Their biggest problem is that they do not know what they are missing. They rarely saw their fathers succeed in fulfilling their mothers through giving. As a result they do not know that a major source of fulfillment for a man can come through giving. When his relationships fail he finds himself depressed and stuck in his cave. He stops caring and doesn't know why he is so depressed.

At such times he withdraws from relationships or intimacy and remains stuck in his cave. He asks himself what it is all for, and why he should bother. He doesn't know that he has stopped caring because he doesn't feel needed. He does not realize that by finding someone who needs him, he can shake off his depression and be motivated again.

> Not to be needed is a slow death for a man.

When a man doesn't feel he is making a positive difference in someone else's life, it is hard for him to continue caring about his life and relationships. It is difficult to be motivated when he is not needed. To become motivated again he needs to feel appreciated, trusted, and accepted. Not to be needed is a slow death for a man.

WHEN A WOMAN LOVES A MAN

A woman falling in love with a man is similar to what took place when the first Venusian believed that the Martians were coming. She dreamed that a fleet of spaceships from the heavens would land and a race of strong and caring Martians would emerge. These beings would not need nurturing but instead wanted to provide for and take care of the Venusians.

These Martians were very devoted and were inspired by the Venusian beauty and culture. The Martians recognized that their power and competence were meaningless without someone to serve. These wondrous and admirable beings had found relief and inspiration in the promise of serving, pleasing, and fulfilling the Venusians. What a miracle!

Other Venusians had similar dreams and instantly came out of their depressions. The realization that transformed the Venusians was the belief that help was on the way because the Martians were coming. The Venusians had been depressed because they felt isolated and alone. To come out of depression they needed to feel that loving help was on the way.

Most men have little awareness of how important it is to a woman to feel supported by someone who cares. Women are happy when they believe their needs will be met. When a woman is upset, overwhelmed, confused, exhausted, or hopeless what she needs most is simple companionship. She needs to feel she is not alone. She needs to feel loved and cherished.

Empathy, understanding, validation, and compassion go a long way to assist her in becoming more receptive and appreciative of his support. Men don't realize this because their Martian instincts tell them it's best to be alone when they are upset. When she is upset, out of respect he will leave her alone, or if he stays he makes matters worse by trying to solve her problems. He does not instinctively realize how very important closeness, intimacy, and sharing are to her. What she needs most is just someone to listen.

Through sharing her feelings she begins to remember that she is worthy of love and that her needs will be fulfilled. Doubt and mistrust melt away. Her tendency to be compulsive relaxes as she remembers that she is worthy of love–she doesn't have to earn it; she can relax, give less, and receive more. She deserves it.

> **A woman's tendency to be compulsive relaxes as she
> remembers that she is worthy of love–
> she doesn't have to earn it;
> she can relax, give less, and receive more. She deserves it.**

Too Much Giving Is Tiring

To deal with their depression the Venusians were busy sharing their feelings and talking about their problems. As they talked they discovered the cause of their depression. They were tired of giving so much all the time. They resented always feeling responsible for one another. They wanted to relax and just be taken care of for a while. They were tired of sharing everything with others. They wanted to be special and possess things that were their own. No longer were they satisfied being martyrs and living for others.

On Venus, they lived by lose/win philosophy–"I lose so that you can win." As long as everyone made sacrifices for others, then everyone was taken care of. But after doing this for centuries the Venusians were tired of always caring about one another and sharing everything. They also were ready for a win/win philosophy.

Similarly, many women today are also tired of giving. They want time off. Time to explore being themselves. Time to care about themselves first. They want someone to provide emotional support, someone they don't have to take care of. The Martians fit the bill perfectly.

At this point the Martians were learning to give while the Venusians were now ready to learn how to receive. After centuries the Venusians and Martians had reached an important stage in their evolution. The Venusians needed to learn how to receive while the Martians needed to learn how to give.

This same change commonly takes place in men and women as they mature. In her younger years, a woman is much more willing to sacrifice and mold herself to fulfill her partner's needs. In a man's younger years, he is much more self-absorbed and unaware of the needs of others. As a woman matures she realizes how she may have been giving up herself in order to please her partner. As a man matures he realizes how he can better serve and respect others.

As a man matures he also learns that he may be giving up himself, but his major change is becoming more aware of how he can succeed in giving. Likewise, as a woman matures she also learns new strategies for giving, but her major change tends to be learning to set limits in order to receive what she wants.

Giving Up Blame

When a woman realizes she has been giving too much, she tends to blame her partner for their unhappiness. She feels the injustice of giving more than she has received.

Although she has not received what she deserved, to improve her relationships she needs to recognize how she contributed to the problem. When a woman gives too much she should not blame her partner. Similarly, a man who gives less should not blame his partner for being negative or unreceptive to him. In both cases, blaming does not work.

Understanding, trust, compassion, acceptance, and support are the solution, not blaming our partners. When this situation occurs, instead of blaming his female partner for being resentful, a man can be compassionate and offer his support even if she doesn't ask for it, listen to her even if at first it sounds like blame, and help her to trust and open up to him by doing little things for her to show that he cares.

Instead of blaming a man for giving less, a woman can accept and forgive her partner's imperfections, especially when he disappoints her, trust that he wants to give more when he doesn't offer his support, and encourage him to give more by appreciating what he does give and continuing to ask for his support.

SETTING AND RESPECTING LIMITS

Most important, however, a woman needs to recognize her boundaries of what she can give without resenting her partner. Instead of expecting her partner to even the score, she needs to keep it even by regulating how much she gives.

Let's look at an example. Jim was thirty-nine and his wife, Susan, was forty-one when they came for counseling. Susan wanted a divorce. She complained that she had been giving more than he had for twelve years and could not take it any more. She blamed Jim for being lethargic, selfish, controlling, and unromantic. She said she had nothing left to give and was ready to leave. He convinced her to come to therapy, but she was doubtful. In a six-month period they were able to move through the three steps for healing a relationship. Today they are happily married with three children.

Step 1: Motivation

I explained to Jim that his wife was experiencing twelve years of accumulated resentment. If he wanted to save this marriage, he would have to do a lot of listening for her to be motivated to work on their marriage. For the first six sessions together, I encouraged Susan to share her feelings and helped Jim patiently to understand her negative feelings. This was the hardest part of their healing process. As he began to really hear her pain and unfulfilled needs, he became increasingly motivated and confident that he could make the changes necessary to have a loving relationship.

Before Susan could be motivated to work on their relationship, she needed to be heard and feel that Jim validated her feelings: this was the first step. After Susan felt understood, they were able to proceed to the next step.

Step 2: Responsibility

The second step was taking responsibility. Jim needed to take responsibility for not supporting his wife, while Susan needed to take responsibility for not setting boundaries. Jim apologized for the ways he had hurt her. Susan realized that just as he had stepped over her boundaries by treating her in disrespectful ways (such as yelling, grumbling, resisting requests, and invalidating feelings), she had not set her boundaries. Although she did not need to apologize, she did acknowledge some responsibility for their problems.

As she gradually accepted that her inability to set limits and her tendency to give more had contributed to their problems, she was able to be more forgiving. Taking responsibility for her problem was essential to releasing her resentment. In this way they both were motivated to learn new ways of supporting each other through respecting limits.

Step 3: Practice

Jim particularly needed to learn how to respect her boundaries, while Susan needed to learn how to set them. Both of them needed to learn how to express honest feelings in a respectful way. They agreed in this third step to practice setting and respecting limits, knowing that at times they would make mistakes. Being able to make mistakes gave them a safety net while they both practiced. These are some examples of what they learned and practiced:

- Susan practiced saying "I don't like the way you are talking. Please stop yelling or I will leave the room." After leaving the room a few times, she didn't need to do it anymore.
- When Jim would make requests that she would later resent doing, she practiced saying "No, I need to relax" or "No, I'm too busy today." She discovered that he was more attentive to her because he

understood how busy or tired she was.
• Susan told Jim that she wanted to go on a vacation, and when he said he was too busy she said that she would go alone. Suddenly he shifted his schedule and wanted to go.
• When they talked and Jim interrupted, she practiced saying "I'm not finished, please hear me out." Suddenly he started listening more and interrupting less.
• Susan's most difficult task was to practice asking for what she wanted. She said to me, "Why should I have to ask, after all I have done for him?" I explained that making him responsible for knowing her wants was not only unrealistic but a big part of her problem. She needed to be responsible for getting her needs fulfilled.
• Jim's most difficult challenge was to be respectful of her changes and not expect her to be the same accommodating partner he originally married. He recognized that it was as difficult for her to set limits as it was for him to adjust to them. He understood that they would become graceful as they had more practice.

As a man experiences limits, he is motivated to give more. Through respecting limits, he automatically is motivated to question the effectiveness of his behavior patterns and to start making changes. When a woman realizes that in order to receive she needs to sets limits, then automatically she begins to forgive her partner and explore new ways of asking for and receiving support. When a woman set limits, she gradually learns to relax and receive more.

LEARNING TO RECEIVE

Setting limits and receiving are very scary for a woman. She is commonly afraid of needing too much and then being rejected, judged, or abandoned. Rejection, judgment, and abandonment are most painful because deep inside her unconscious she holds the incorrect belief that she is unworthy of receiving more. This belief was formed and reinforced in childhood every time she had to suppress her feelings, needs, or wishes.

A woman is particularly vulnerable to the negative and incorrect belief that she doesn't deserve to be loved. If as a child she witnessed abuse or was directly abused, then she is even more vulnerable to feeling unworthy of love; it is harder for her to determine her worth. Hidden in the unconscious, this feeling of unworthiness generates the fear of needing others. A part of her imagines that she will not be supported.

Because she is afraid of not being supported, she unknowingly pushes away the support she needs. When a man receives the message that she doesn't trust him to fulfill her needs, then he feels immediately rejected and is turned off. Her hopelessness and mistrust transform her valid needs into desperate expressions of neediness and communicate to him the message that she doesn't trust him to support her. Ironically, men are primarily motivated by being needed, but are turned off by neediness.

At such times, a woman mistakenly assumes that having needs has turned him off when in truth it is her hopelessness, desperation, and mistrust that has done so. Without recognizing that men need to be trusted, it is difficult and confusing for women to understand the difference between needing and neediness.

"Needing" is openly reaching out and asking for support from a man in a trusting manner, one that assumes that he will do his best. This empowers him. "Neediness," however, is desperately needing support because you don't trust you will get it. It pushes men away and makes them feel rejected and unappreciated.

For women, not only is needing others confusing but being disappointed or abandoned is especially painful, even in the smallest ways. It is not easy for her to depend on others and then be ignored, forgotten, or dismissed. Needing others puts her in a vulnerable position. Being ignored or disappointed hurts more because it affirms the incorrect belief that she is unworthy.

How the Venusians Learned to Feel Worthy

For centuries the Venusians compensated for this fundamental fear of unworthiness by being attentive and responsive to the needs of others. They would give and give, but deep inside they did not feel worthy of receiving. They hoped that by giving they would become more worthy. After centuries of giving they finally realized that they were worthy of receiving love and support. Then they looked back and realized that they had always been worthy of support.

This process of giving to others prepared them for the wisdom of self-esteem. Through giving to others they came to see that others truly were worthy of receiving, and thus they began to see that everyone deserved to be loved. Then, finally, they saw that they too deserved to receive.

Here on Earth, when a little girl experiences her mother receiving love, then automatically she feels worthy. She is able easily to overcome the Venusian compulsion to give too much. She doesn't have to overcome a fear of receiving because she identifies so closely with her mother. If her mother has learned this wisdom then the child automatically learns it through observing and feeling her mother. If the mother is open to receive, then the child learns how to receive.

The Venusians, however, did not have role models, so it took them thousands of years to give up their compulsive giving. Through gradually seeing that others were worthy of receiving, they realized that they also were worthy of receiving. At that magical moment the Martians also went through a transformation and began building spaceships.

When the Venusian Is Ready the Martian Will Appear

When a woman realizes that she truly deserves to be loved, she is opening the door for a man to give to her. But when it takes her ten years of overgiving in a marriage to realize that she deserves more, ironically, she feels like closing the door and not giving him the chance. She may feel something like this: "I have given to you and you have ignored me. You had your chance. I deserve better. I can't trust you. I am too tired, I have nothing left to give. I will not let you hurt me again."

Repeatedly, when this is the case, I have assured women that they don't have to give more to have a better relationship. Their partner actually will give them more if they give less. When a man has been ignoring her needs, it is as though they have both been asleep. When she wakes up and remembers her needs, he also wakes up and wants to give her more.

> **When she wakes up and remembers her needs,**
> **he also wakes up and wants to give her more.**

Predictably, her partner will wake up from his passive state and truly make many of the changes she requires. When she is no longer giving too much, because she is feeling worthy inside herself, he comes out of his cave and starts building spaceships to come and make her happy. It may take him a while actually to learn to give her more, but the most important step is taken—he is aware that he has neglected her and he wants to change.

It also works the other way around. Usually when a man realizes that he is unhappy and wants more romance and love in his life, his wife will suddenly begin to open up and love him again. The walls of resentment begin to melt, and love comes back to life. If there has been a lot of neglect it may take a while truly to heal all the accumulated resentments, but it is possible. In chapter 11, I will discuss easy and practical techniques to heal these resentments.

Quite often, when one partner makes a positive change the other will also change. This predictable coincidence is one of those magical things about life. When the student is ready the teacher appears. When the question is asked then the answer is heard. When we are truly ready to receive then what we need will become available. When the Venusians were ready to receive, the Martians were ready to give.

LEARNING TO GIVE

A man's deepest fear is that he is not good enough or that he is incompetent. He compensates for this fear by focusing on increasing his power and competence. Success, achievement, and efficiency are foremost in his life. Before they discovered the Venusians, the Martians were so concerned with these qualities that they didn't care about anything or anybody else. A man appears most uncaring when he is afraid.

> **A man's deepest fear is that he is not good enough or that he is incompetent.**

Just as women are afraid of receiving, men are afraid of giving. To extend himself in giving to others means to risk failure, correction, and disapproval. These consequences are most painful because deep inside his unconscious he holds an incorrect belief that he is not good enough. This belief was formed and reinforced in childhood every time he thought he was expected to do better. When his accomplishments went unnoticed or were unappreciated, deep in his unconscious he began forming the incorrect belief that he was not good enough.

> **Just as women are afraid of receiving, men are afraid of giving.**

A man is particularly vulnerable to this incorrect belief. It generates within him the fear of failing. He wants to give but is afraid he will fail, so he doesn't try. If his biggest fear is inadequacy, he naturally is going to avoid any unnecessary risks.

Ironically, when a man really cares a lot his fear of failure increases, and he gives less. To avoid failure he stops giving to the people he wants to give to the most.

When a man is insecure he may compensate by not caring about anybody except himself. His most automatic defensive response is to say "I don't care." For this reason, the Martians did not let themselves feel or care too much for others. By becoming successful and powerful they finally realized that they were good enough and that they could succeed in giving. They then discovered the Venusians.

Although they had always been good enough, the process of proving their power prepared them for the wisdom of self-esteem. Through becoming successful and then looking back, they realized that their every failure was necessary to achieve their later successes. Every mistake had taught them a very important lesson necessary to achieve their goals. Thus they realized they had always been good enough.

It Is OK to Make Mistakes

The first step for a man in learning how to give more is to realize that it is OK to make mistakes and it is OK to fail and that he doesn't have to have all the answers.

I remember the story of a woman who complained that her partner would never make a commitment to marriage. To her it seemed that he did not care as much as she did. One day, however, she happened to say that she was so happy being with him. Even if they were poor, she would want to be with him. The next day he proposed. He needed the acceptance and encouragement that he was good enough for her, and then he could feel how much he cared.

Martians Need Love Too

Just as women are sensitive to feeling rejected when they don't get the attention they need, men are sensitive to feeling that they have failed when a woman talks about problems. This is why it is so hard for him to listen sometimes. He wants to be her hero. When *she* is disappointed or unhappy over anything, *he* feels like a failure. Her unhappiness confirms his deepest fear: he is just not good enough. Many women today don't realize how vulnerable men are and how much they need love too. Love helps him to know that he is enough to fulfill others.

It is difficult for a man to listen to a woman when she is unhappy or disappointed because he feels like a failure.

A young boy who is fortunate enough to see his father succeed in fulfilling his mother enters relationships as an adult with a rare confidence that he can succeed in fulfilling his partner. He is not terrified of commitment because he knows he can deliver. He also knows that when he doesn't deliver he is still adequate and still deserves love and appreciation for doing his best. He does not condemn himself because he knows he is not perfect and that he is always doing his best and his best is good enough. He is able to apologize for his mistakes because he expects forgiveness, love, and appreciation for doing his best.

He knows that everyone makes mistakes. He saw his father make mistakes and continue to love himself. He witnessed his mother loving and forgiving his father through all his mistakes. He felt her trust and encouragement, even though at times his father had disappointed her.

Many men did not have successful role models while they were growing up. For them staying in love, getting married, and having a family is as difficult as flying a jumbo jet without any training. He may be able to take off, but he is sure to crash. It is difficult to continue flying once you have crashed the plane a few times. Or if you witnessed your father crash. Without a good training manual for relationships, it is easy to understand why many men and women give up on relationships.

5

DIFFERENT LANGUAGES

When the Martians and Venusians first got together, they encountered many of the problems with relationships we have today. Because they recognized that they were different, they were able to solve these problems. One of the secrets of their success was good communication.

Ironically, they communicated well because they spoke different languages. When they had problems, they would just go to a translator for assistance. Everyone knew that people from Mars and people from Venus spoke different languages, so when there was a conflict they didn't start judging or fighting but instead pulled out their phrase dictionaries to understand each other more fully. If that didn't work they went to a translator for help.

> **The Martian and Venusian languages had the same words,**
> **but the way they were used gave different meanings.**

You see the Martian and Venusian languages had the same words, but the way they were used gave different meanings. Their expressions were similar, but they had different connotations or emotional emphasis. Misinterpreting each other was very easy. So when communication problems emerged, they assumed it was just one of those expected misunderstandings and that with a little assistance they would surely understand each other. They experienced a trust and acceptance that we rarely experience today.

EXPRESSING FEELINGS VERSUS EXPRESSING INFORMATION

Even today we still need translators. Men and women seldom mean the same things even when they use the same words. For example, when a woman says "I feel like you *never* listen," she does not expect the word *never* to be taken literally. Using the word *never* is just a way of expressing the frustration she is feeling at the moment. It is not to be taken as if it were factual information.

> To fully express their feelings, women
> assume poetic license to use various superlatives,
> metaphors, and generalizations.

To fully express their feelings, women assume poetic license and use various superlatives, metaphors, and generalizations. Men mistakenly take these expressions literally. Because they misunderstand the intended meaning, they commonly react in an unsupportive manner. In the following chart ten complaints easily misinterpreted are listed, as well as how a man might respond unsupportively.

TEN COMMON COMPLAINTS THAT ARE EASILY MISINTERPRETED

Women say things like this	Men respond like this
"We never go out."	"That's not true. We went out last week."
"Everyone ignores me."	"I'm sure some people notice you."

Women say things like this	**Men respond like this**
"I am so tired, I can't do anything."	"That's ridiculous. You are not helpless."
"I want to forget everything."	"If you don't like your job, then quit."
"The house is always a mess."	"It's not always a mess."
"No one listens to me anymore."	"But I am listening to you right now."
"Nothing is working."	"Are you saying it is my fault?"
"You don't love me anymore."	"Of course I do. That's why I'm here."
"We are always in a hurry."	"We are not. Friday we were relaxed."
"I want more romance."	"Are you saying I am not romantic?"

You can see how a "literal" translation of a woman's words could easily mislead a man who is used to using speech as a means of conveying only facts and information. We can also see how a man's responses might lead to an argument. Unclear and unloving communication is the biggest problem in relationships. The number one complaint women have in relationships is: "I don't feel heard." Even this complaint is misunderstood and misinterpreted!

> The number one complaint women have in relationships is:
> "I don't feel heard."
> Even this complaint is misunderstood by men!

A man's literal translation of "I don't feel heard" leads him to invalidate and argue with her feelings. He thinks he *has* heard her if he can repeat what she has said. A translation of a woman saying "I don't feel heard" so that a man could correctly interpret it is: "I feel as though you don't fully understand what I really mean to say or care about how I feel. Would you show me that you are interested in what I have to say?"

If a man really understood her complaint then he would argue less and be able to respond more positively. When men and women are on the verge of arguing, they are generally misunderstanding each other. At such times, it is important to rethink or translate what they have heard.

Because many men don't understand that women express feelings differently, they inappropriately judge or invalidate their partner's feelings. This leads to arguments. The ancient Martians learned to avoid many arguments through correct understanding. Whenever listening stirred up some resistance, they consulted their *Venusian/Martian Phrase Dictionary* for a correct interpretation.

WHEN VENUSIANS TALK

The following section contains various excerpts from the lost *Venusian/Martian Phrase Dictionary*. Each of the ten complaints listed above is translated so that a man can understand their real and intended meaning. Each translation also contains a hint of how she wants him to respond.

You see, when a Venusian is upset she not only uses generalities, and so forth, but also is asking for a particular kind of support. She doesn't directly ask for that support because on Venus everyone knew that dramatic language implied a particular request.

In each of the translations this hidden request for support is revealed. If a man listening to a woman can recognize the implied request and respond accordingly, she will feel truly heard and loved.

The Venusian/Martian Phrase Dictionary

"We never go out" translated into Martian means "I feel like going out and doing something together. We always have such a fun time, and I love being with you. What do you think? Would you take me out to dinner? It has been a few days since we went out."

Without this translation, when a woman says "We never go out" a man may hear "You are not doing your job. What a disappointment you have turned out to be. We never do anything together anymore because you are lazy, unromantic, and just boring."

> **"Everyone ignores me"** translated into Martian means "Today, I am feeling ignored and unacknowledged. I feel as though nobody sees me. Of course I'm sure some people see me, but they don't seem to care about me. I suppose I am also disappointed that you have been so busy lately. I really do appreciate how hard you are working and sometimes I start to feel like I am not important to you. I am afraid your work is more important than me. Would you give me a hug and tell me how special I am to you?"

Without this translation, when a woman says "Everyone ignores me" a man may hear "I am so unhappy. I just can't get the attention I need. Everything is completely hopeless. Even you don't notice me, and you are the person who is supposed to love me. You should be ashamed. You are so unloving. I would never ignore you this way."

> **"I am so tired, I can't do anything"** translated into Martian means "I have been doing so much today. I really need a rest before I can do anything more. I am so lucky to have your support. Would you give me a hug and reassure me that I am doing a good job and that I deserve a rest?"

Without this translation, when a woman says "I am so tired, I can't do anything" a man may hear "I do everything and you do nothing. You should do more. I can't do it all. I feel so hopeless. I want a 'real man' to live with. Picking you was a big mistake."

> **"I want to forget everything"** translated into Martian means "I want you to know that I love my work and my life but today I am so overwhelmed. I would love to do something really nurturing for myself before I have to be responsible again. Would you ask me 'What's the matter?' and then listen with empathy without offering any solutions? I just want to feel you understanding the pressures I feel. It would make me feel so much better. It helps me to relax. Tomorrow I will get back to being responsible and handling things."

Without this translation, when a woman says "I want to forget everything" a man may hear "I have to do so much that I don't want to do. I am so unhappy with you and our relationship. I want a better partner who can make my life more fulfilling. You are doing a terrible job."

> **"This house is always a mess"** translated into Martian means "Today I feel like relaxing, but the house is so messy. I am frustrated and I need a rest. I hope you don't expect me to clean it all up. Would you agree with me that it is a mess and then offer to help clean up part of it?"

Without this translation, when a woman says "This house is always a mess" a man may hear "This house is a mess because of you. I do everything possible to clean it up, and before I have finished, you have messed it up again. You are a lazy slob and I don't want to live with you unless you change. Clean up or clear out!"

> **"No one listens to me anymore"** translated into Martian means "I am afraid I am boring to you. I am

afraid you are no longer interested in me. I seem to be very sensitive today. Would you give me some special attention? I would love it. I've had a hard day and feel as though no one wants to hear what I have to say.

"Would you listen to me and continue to ask me supportive questions such as: 'What happened today? What else happened? How did you feel? What did you want? How else do you feel?' Also support me by saying caring, acknowledging, and reassuring state-ments such as: 'Tell me more' or 'That's right' or 'I know what you mean' or 'I understand.' Or just listen, and occasionally when I pause make one of these reassuring sounds: 'oh,' 'humph,' 'uh-huh,' and 'hmmm.'" *(Note:* Martians had never heard of these sounds before arriving on Venus.)

Without this translation, when a woman says "No one listens to me anymore" he may hear "I give you my attention but you don't listen to me. You used to. You have become a very boring person to be with. I want someone exciting and interesting and you are definitely not that person. You have disappointed me. You are selfish, uncaring, and bad."

"Nothing is working" translated into Martian means "Today I am so overwhelmed *and* I am so grateful that I can share my feelings with you. It helps me so much to feel better. Today it seems like nothing I do works. I know that this is not true, but I sure feel that way when I get so overwhelmed by all the things I still have to do. Would you give me a hug and tell me that I am doing a great job. It would sure feel good."

Without this translation, when a woman says "Nothing is working" a man may hear "You never do anything right. I can't trust you. If I hadn't listened to you I wouldn't be in this mess. Another man would have fixed things, but you made them worse."

"You don't love me anymore" translated into Martian means "Today I am feeling as though you don't love me. I am afraid I have pushed you away. I know you really do love me, you do so much for me. Today I am just feeling a little insecure. Would you reassure me of your love and tell me those three magic words, I love you. When you do that it feels so good."

Without this translation, when a woman says "You don't love me anymore" a man may hear "I have given you the best years of my life, and you have given me nothing. You used me. You are selfish and cold. You do what you want to do, for you and only you. You do not care about anybody. I was a fool for loving you. Now I have nothing."

"We are always in a hurry" translated into Martian means "I feel so rushed today. I don't like rushing. I wish our life was not so hurried. I know it is nobody's fault and I certainly don't blame you. I know you are doing your best to get us there on time and I really appreciate how much you care.

"Would you empathize with me and say something like, 'It *is* hard always rushing around. I don't always like rushing either.'"

Without this translation, when a woman says "We are always in a hurry" a man may hear "You are so irresponsible. You wait until the last minute to do everything. I can never be happy when I am with you. We are always rushing to avoid being late. You ruin things every time I am with you. I am so much happier when I am not around you."

"I want more romance" translated into Martian means "Sweetheart, you have been working so hard lately. Let's take some time out for ourselves. I love it

when we can relax and be alone without the kids
around and no work pressures. You are so romantic.
Would you surprise me with flowers sometime soon
and take me out on a date? I love being romanced."

Without this translation, when a woman says "I want more romance" a man may hear "You don't satisfy me anymore. I am not turned on to you. Your romantic skills are definitely inadequate. You have never really fulfilled me. I wish you were more like other men I have been with."

After using this dictionary for a few years, a man doesn't need to pick it up each time he feels blamed or criticized. He begins to understand the way women think and feel. He learns that these kinds of dramatic phrases are not to be taken literally. They are just the way women express feeling more fully. That's the way it was done on Venus and people from Mars need to remember that!

WHEN MARTIANS DON'T TALK

One of the big challenges for men is correctly to interpret and support a woman when she is talking about her feelings. The biggest challenge for women is correctly to interpret and support a man when he isn't talking. Silence is most easily misinterpreted by women.

> The biggest challenge for women
> is correctly to interpret and support a man
> when he *isn't* talking.

Quite often a man will suddenly stop communicating and become silent. This was unheard of on Venus. At first a woman thinks the man is deaf. She thinks that maybe he doesn't hear what's being said and that is why he is not responding.

You see men and women think and process information very differently. Women think out loud, sharing their process of inner discovery with an interested listener. Even today, a woman often discovers what she wants to say through the process of just talking. This process of just letting thoughts flow freely and expressing them out loud helps her to tap into her intuition. This process is perfectly normal and especially necessary sometimes.

But men process information very differently. Before they talk or respond, they first silently "mull over" or think about what they have heard or experienced. Internally and silently they figure out the most correct or useful response. They first formulate it inside and then express it. This process could take from minutes to hours. And to make matters even more confusing for women, if he does not have enough information to process an answer, a man may not respond at all.

Women need to understand that when he is silent, he is saying "I don't know what to say yet, but I am thinking about it." Instead what they hear is "I am not responding to you because I don't care about you and I am going to ignore you. What you have said to me is not important and therefore I am not responding."

How She Reacts to His Silence

Women misinterpret a man's silence. Depending on how she is feeling that day she may begin to imagine the very worst–"He hates me, he doesn't love me, he is leaving me forever." This may then trigger her deepest fear, which is "I am afraid that if he rejects me then I will never be loved. I don't deserve to be loved."

When a man is silent it is easy for a woman to imagine the worst because the only times a woman would be silent are when what she had to say would be hurtful or when she didn't want to talk to a person because she didn't trust him anymore and wanted to have nothing to do with him. No wonder women become insecure when a man suddenly becomes quiet!

> When a man is silent it is easy
> for a woman to imagine the worst.

When a woman listens to another woman, she will continue to reassure the speaker that she is listening and that she cares. Instinctively when the speaker pauses the female listener will reassure the speaker by making reassuring responses like "oh, uh-huh, hmmm, ah, ah-ha, or humph."

Without these reassuring responses, a man's silence can be very threatening. Through understanding a man's cave, women can learn to interpret a man's silence correctly, and to respond to it.

Understanding the Cave

Women have a lot to learn about men before their relationships can be really fulfilling. They need to learn that when a man is upset or stressed he will automatically stop talking and go to his "cave" to work things out. They need to learn that no one is allowed in that cave, not even the man's best friends. This was the way it was on Mars. Women should not become scared that they have done something terribly wrong. They need gradually to learn that if you just let men go into their caves, after a while they will come out and everything will be fine.

This lesson is difficult for women because on Venus one of the golden rules was never to abandon a friend when she was upset. It just doesn't seem loving to abandon her favorite Martian when he is upset. Because she cares for him, a woman wants to come into his cave and offer him help.

In addition, she often mistakenly assumes that if she could ask him lots of questions about how he is feeling and be a good listener, then he would feel better. This only upsets Martians more. She instinctively wants to support him in the way that she would want to be supported. Her intentions are good, but the outcome is counterproductive.

Both men and women need to stop offering the method of caring they would prefer and start to learn the different ways their partners think, feel, and react.

Why Men Go into Their Caves

Men go into their caves or become quiet for a variety of reasons.

1. He needs to think about a problem and find a practical solution to the problem.

2. He doesn't have an answer to a question or a problem. Men were never taught to say "Gee, I don't have an answer. I need to go into my cave and find one." Other men assume he is doing just that when he becomes quiet.

3. He has become upset or stressed. At such times he needs to be alone to cool off and find his control again. He doesn't want to do or say anything he might regret.

4. He needs to find himself. This fourth reason becomes very important when men are in love. At times they begin to lose and forget themselves. They can feel that too much intimacy robs them of their power. They need to regulate how close they get. Whenever they get too close so as to lose themselves, alarm bells go off and they are on their way into the cave. As a result they are rejuvenated and find their loving and powerful self again.

Why Women Talk

Women talk for a variety of reasons. Sometimes women talk for the same reasons that men stop talking. These are four common reasons that women talk:

1. To convey or gather information. (This is generally the only reason a man talks.)

2. To explore and discover what it is she wants to say. (He stops talking to figure out inside what he wants to say. She talks to think out loud.)

3. To feel better and more centered when she is upset. (He stops talking when he is upset. In his cave he has a chance to cool off.)

4. To create intimacy. Through sharing her inner feelings she is able to know her loving self. (A Martian stops talking to find himself again. Too much intimacy, he fears, will rob him of himself.)

Without this vital understanding of our differences and needs it is easy to see why couples struggle so much in relationships.

Getting Burned by the Dragon

It is important for women to understand not to try and get a man to talk before he is ready. While discussing this topic in one of my seminars, a Native American shared that in her tribe mothers would instruct young women getting married to remember that when a man was upset or stressed he would withdraw into his cave. She was not to take it personally because it would happen from time to time. It did not mean that he did not love her. They assured her that he would come back. But most important they warned the young woman never to follow him into his cave. If she did then she would get burned by the dragon who protected the cave.

> Never go into a man's cave
> or you will be burned by the dragon!

Much unnecessary conflict has resulted from a woman following a man into his cave. Women just haven't understood that men really do need to be alone or silent when they are upset. When a man withdraws into his cave a woman just doesn't understand what is happening. She naturally tries to get him to talk. If there is a problem she hopes to nurture him by drawing him out and getting him to talk about it.

She asks "Is there something wrong?" He says "No." But she can feel he is upset. She wonders why he is withholding his feelings. Instead of letting him work it out inside his cave she unknowingly interrupts his internal process. She asks again "I know something is bothering you, what is it?"

He says "It's nothing."

She asks "It's not nothing. Something's bothering you. What are you feeling?"

He says "Look, I'm fine. Now leave me alone!"

She says "How can you treat me like this? You never talk to me anymore. How am I supposed to know what you are feeling? You don't love me. I feel so rejected by you."

At this point he loses control and begins saying things that he will regret later. His dragon comes out and burns her.

WHEN MARTIANS DO TALK

Women get burned not only when they unknowingly invade a man's introspective time but also when they misinterpret his expressions, which are generally warnings that he is either in his cave or on his way to the cave. When asked "What's the matter?" a Martian will say something brief like "It's nothing" or "I am OK."

These brief signals are generally the only way a Venusian knows to give him space to work out his feelings alone. Instead of saying "I am upset and I need some time to be alone," men just become quiet.

In the following chart six commonly expressed abbreviated warning signals are listed as well as how a woman might unknowingly respond in an intrusive and unsupportive manner:

SIX COMMON ABBREVIATED WARNING SIGNALS

When a woman asks "What's the matter?"

A man says	A woman may respond
"I'm OK" or "It's OK."	"I know something's wrong. What is it?"
"I'm fine" or "It's fine."	"But you seem upset. Let's talk."
"It's nothing."	"I want to help. I know something is bothering you. What is it?"
"It's all right" or "I'm all right."	"Are you sure? I am happy to help you."
"It's no big deal."	"But something is upsetting you. I think we should talk."
"It's no problem."	"But it is a problem. I could help."

When a man makes one of the above abbreviated comments he generally wants silent acceptance or space. At times like this, to avoid misinterpretation and unnecessary panic, the Venusians consulted their *Martian/Venusian Phrase Dictionary*. Without this assistance, women misinterpret these abbreviated expressions.

Women need to know that when a man says "I am OK" it is an abbreviated version of what he really means, which is "I am OK because I can deal with this alone. I do not need any help. Please support me by not worrying about me. Trust that I can deal with it all by myself."

Without this translation, when he is upset and says "I am OK" it sounds to her as if he is denying his feelings or problems. She then attempts to help him by asking questions or talking about what she thinks the problem is. She does not know that he is speaking an abbreviated language. The following are excerpts from their phrase dictionary.

The Martian/Venusian Phrase Dictionary

"I'm OK" translated into Venusian means "I am OK, I can deal with my upset. I don't need any help, thank you."

Without this translation, when he says "I am OK" she may hear "I am not upset because I do not care" or she may hear "I am not willing to share with you my upset feelings. I do not trust you to be there for me."

"I'm fine" translated into Venusian means "I am fine because I am successfully dealing with my upset or problem. I don't need any help. If I do I will ask."

Without this translation, when he says "I am fine" she may hear "I don't care about what has happened. This problem is not important to me. Even if it upsets you, I don't care."

"It's nothing" translated into Venusian means "Nothing is bothering me that I cannot handle alone. Please don't ask any more questions about it."

Without this translation, when he says "Nothing is bothering me" she may hear "I don't know what is bothering me. I need you to ask me questions to assist me in discovering what is happening." At this point she proceeds to anger him by asking questions when he really wants to be left alone.

"It's all right" translated into Venusian means "This is a problem but you are not to blame. I can resolve this within myself if you don't interrupt my process by asking more questions or offering suggestions. Just act like it didn't happen and I can process it within myself more effectively."

Without this translation, when he says "It's all right" she may hear "This is the way it is supposed to be. Nothing needs to be changed. You can abuse me and I can abuse you" or she hears "It's all right this time, but remember it is your fault. You can do this once but don't do it again or else."

> **"It's no big deal"** translated into Venusian means "It is no big deal because I can make things work again. Please don't dwell on this problem or talk more about it. That makes me more upset. I accept responsibility for solving this problem. It makes me happy to solve it."

Without this translation, when he says "It's no big deal" she may hear "You are making a big deal out of nothing. What concerns you is not important. Don't overreact."

> **"It's no problem"** translated into Venusian means "I have no problem doing this or solving this problem. It is my pleasure to offer this gift to you."

Without this translation, when he says "It's no problem" she may hear "This is not a problem. Why are you making it a problem or asking for help?" She then mistakenly explains to him why it is a problem.

Using this *Martian/Venusian Phrase Dictionary* can assist women in understanding what men really mean when they abbreviate what they are saying. Sometimes what he is really saying is the opposite of what she hears.

WHAT TO DO WHEN HE GOES INTO HIS CAVE

In my seminars when I explain about caves and dragons, women want to know how they can shorten the time men spend in their caves. At this point I ask the men to answer, and they generally say that the more women try to get them to talk or come out, the longer it takes.

Another common comment by men is "It is hard to come out of the cave when ❢ feel my mate disapproves of the time I spend in the cave." To make a man feel wrong for going into his cave has the effect of pushing him back into the cave even when he wants to come out.

When a man goes into his cave he is generally wounded or stressed and is trying to solve his problem alone. To give him the support that a woman would want is counterproductive. There are basically six ways to support him when he goes into his cave. (Giving him this support will also shorten the time he needs to spend alone.)

How to Support a Man in His Cave

1. Don't disapprove of his need for withdrawing.
2. Don't try to help him solve his problem by offering solutions.
3. Don't try to nurture him by asking questions about his feelings.
4. Don't sit next to the door of the cave and wait for him to come out.
5. Don't worry about him or feel sorry for him.
6. Do something that makes you happy.

If you need to "talk," write him a letter to be read later when he is out, and if you need to be nurtured, talk to a friend. Don't make him the sole source of your fulfillment.

A man wants his favorite Venusian to trust that *he* can handle what is bothering him. To be trusted that he can handle his problems is very important to his honor, pride, and self-esteem.

Not worrying about him is difficult for her. Worrying for others is one way women express their love and caring. It is a way of showing love. For a woman, being happy when the person you love is upset just doesn't seem right. He certainly doesn't want her to be happy *because* he is upset, but he does want her to be happy. He wants her to be happy so that he has one less problem to worry about. In addition he wants her to be happy because it helps him to feel loved by her. When a woman is happy and free from worry, it is easier for him to come out.

Ironically men show their love by not worrying. A man questions "How can you worry about someone whom you admire and trust?" Men commonly support one another by saying phrases such as "Don't worry, you can handle it" or "That's their problem, not yours" or "I'm sure it will work out." Men support one another by not worrying or minimizing their troubles.

It took me years to understand that my wife actually wanted me to worry for her when she was upset. Without this awareness of our different needs, I would minimize the importance of her concerns. This only made her more upset.

When a man goes into his cave he is generally trying to solve a problem. If his mate is happy or *not* needy at this time, then he has one less problem to solve before coming out. Knowing that she is happy with him also gives him more strength to deal with his problem while in the cave.

Anything that distracts her or helps her to feel good will be helpful to him. These are some examples:

Read a book

Listen to music

Work in the garden

Exercise

Get a massage

Listen to self-
improvement tapes

Treat yourself to
something delicious

Call a girlfriend for a
good chat

Write in a journal

Go shopping

Pray or meditate

Go for a walk

Take a bubble bath

See a therapist

Watch TV or a video

The Martians also recommended that the Venusians do something enjoyable. It was hard to conceive of being happy when a friend was hurting, but the Venusians did find a way. Every time their favorite Martian went into his cave, they would go shopping or out on some other pleasing excursion. Venusians love to shop. My wife, Bonnie, sometimes uses this technique. When she sees I am in my cave, she goes shopping. I never feel like I have to apologize for my Martian side. When she can take care of herself I feel OK taking care of myself and going into my cave. She trusts that I will come back and be more loving.

She knows that when I go into my cave is not the right time to talk. When I begin showing signs of interest in her, she recognizes that I am coming out of the cave, and it is then a time to talk. Sometimes she will casually say, "When you feel like talking, I would like to spend some time together. Would you let me know when?" In this way she can test the waters without being pushy or demanding.

HOW TO COMMUNICATE SUPPORT TO A MARTIAN

Even when they are out of the cave men want to be trusted. They don't like unsolicited advice or empathy. They need to prove themselves. Being able to accomplish things without the help of others is a feather in their cap. (While for a woman, when someone assists her, having a supportive relationship is a feather in her cap.) A man feels supported when a woman communicates in a way that says "I trust you to handle things unless you directly ask for help."

Learning to support men in this way can be very difficult in the beginning. Many women feel that the only way they can get what they need in a relationship is to criticize a man when he makes mistakes and to offer unsolicited advice. Without a role model of a mother who knew how to receive support from a man, it does not occur to women that they can encourage a man to give more by directly asking for support–without being critical or offering advice. In addition, if he behaves in a manner that she does not like she can simply and directly tell him that she doesn't like his behavior, without casting judgment that he is wrong or bad.

How to Approach a Man with Criticism or Advice

Without an understanding of how they are turning men off with unsolicited advice and criticism, many women feel powerless to get what they need and want from a man. Nancy was frustrated in her relationships. She said, "I still don't know how to approach a man with criticism and advice. What if his table manners are atrocious or he dresses really, really badly? What if he's a nice guy but you see he's got a pattern of behaving with people in a way that makes him look like a jerk and that's causing him trouble in relationships with others? What should I do? No matter how I tell him, he gets angry or defensive or just ignores me."

The answer is that she should definitely not offer criticism or advice unless he asks. Instead, she should try giving him loving acceptance. This is what he needs, not lectures. As he begins to feel her acceptance, he will begin to ask what she thinks. If, however, he detects her demanding that he change, he will not ask for advice or suggestions. Especially in an intimate relationship, men need to feel very secure before they open up and ask for support.

In addition to patiently trusting her partner to grow and change, if a woman is not getting what she needs and wants, she can and should share her feelings and make requests (but again without giving advice or criticism). This is an art that requires caring and creativity. These are four possible approaches:

> 1. A woman can tell a man that she doesn't like the way he dresses without giving him a lecture on how to dress. She could say casually as he is getting dressed "I don't like that shirt on you. Would you wear another one tonight?" If he is annoyed by that comment, then she should respect his sensitivities and apologize. She could say "I'm sorry—I didn't mean to tell you how to dress."

2. If he is that sensitive–and some men are–then she could try talking about it at another time. She could say "Remember that blue shirt you wore with the green slacks? I didn't like that combination. Would you try wearing it with your gray slacks?"

3. She could directly ask "Would you let me take you shopping one day? I would love to pick out an outfit for you." If he says no, then she can be sure that he doesn't want any more mothering. If he says yes, be sure not to offer too much advice. Remember his sensitivities.

4. She could say "There is something I want to talk about but I don't know how to say it. [*Pause.*] I don't want to offend you, but I also really want to say it. Would you listen and then suggest to me a better way I could say it?" This helps him to prepare himself for the shock and then he happily discovers that it is not such a big deal.

Let's explore another example. If she doesn't like his table manners and they are alone, she could say (without a disapproving look) "Would you use your silverware?" or "Would you drink from your glass?" If, however, you are in front of others, it is wise to say nothing and not even notice. Another day you could say "Would you use your silverware when we eat in front of the kids?" or "When you eat with your fingers, I hate it. I get so picky about these little things. When you eat with me, would you use your silverware?"

If he behaves in a way that embarrasses you, wait for a time when no one else is around and then share your feelings. Don't tell him how he "should behave" or that he is wrong; instead share honest feelings in a loving and brief way. You could say "The other night at the party, I didn't like it when you were so loud. When I'm around, would you try to keep it down?" If he gets upset and doesn't like this comment, then simply apologize for being critical.

This art of giving negative feedback and asking for support is discussed thoroughly in chapters 9 and 12. In addition, the best times for having these conversations is explored in the next chapter.

When a Man Doesn't Need Help

A man may start to feel smothered when a woman tries to comfort him or help him solve a problem. He feels as though she doesn't trust him to handle his problems. He may feel controlled, as if she is treating him like a child, or he may feel she wants to change him.

This doesn't mean that a man does not need comforting love. Women need to understand that they are nurturing him when they abstain from offering unsolicited advice to solve his problems. He needs her loving support but in a different way than she thinks. To withhold correcting a man or trying to improve him are ways to nurture him. Giving advice can be nurturing only if he directly asks for it.

A man looks for advice or help only after he has done what he can do alone. If he receives too much assistance or receives it too soon, he will lose his sense of power and strength. He becomes either lazy or insecure. Instinctively men support one another by not offering advice or help unless specifically approached and asked.

In coping with problems, a man knows he has to first go a certain distance by himself, and then if he needs help he can ask for it without losing his strength, power, and dignity. To offer help to a man at the wrong time could easily be taken as an insult.

When a man is carving the turkey for Thanksgiving and his partner keeps offering advice on how and what to cut, he feels mistrusted. He resists her and is determined to do it his way on his own. On the other hand, if a man offers her assistance in cutting the turkey she feels loved and cared for.

When a woman suggests that her husband follow the advice of some expert, he may be offended. I remember one woman asking me why her husband got so angry at her. She explained to me that before sex she had asked him if he had reviewed his notes from a taped lecture by me on the secrets of great sex. She didn't realize this was the ultimate insult to him. Although he had appreciated the tapes, he didn't want her telling him what to do by reminding him to follow my advice. He wanted her to trust that he knew what to do!

While men want to be trusted, women want caring. When a man says to a woman "What's the matter, honey?" with a concerned look on his face, she feels comforted by his caring. When a woman in a similar caring and concerned way says to a man "What's the matter, honey?" he may feel insulted or repulsed. He feels as though she doesn't trust him to handle things.

It is very difficult for a man to differentiate between empathy and sympathy. He hates to be pitied. A woman may say "I am so sorry I hurt you." He will say "It was no big deal" and push away her support. She on the other hand loves to hear him say "I'm sorry I hurt you." She then feels he really cares. Men need to find ways to show they care while women need to find ways to show they trust.

> It is very difficult for a man to differentiate
> between empathy and sympathy.
> He hates to be pitied.

Too Much Caring Is Smothering

When I first married Bonnie, the night before I would leave town to teach a weekend seminar, she would ask me what time I was getting up. Then she would ask what time my plane left. Then she would do some mental figuring and warn me that I hadn't left enough time to catch my plane. Each time she thought she was supporting me, but I didn't feel it. I felt offended. I had been traveling around the world for fourteen years teaching courses, and I had never missed a plane.

Then in the morning, before I left, she asked me a string of questions such as, "Do you have your ticket? Do you have your wallet? Do you have enough money? Did you pack socks? Do you know where you are staying?" She thought she was loving me, but I felt mistrusted and was annoyed. Eventually I let her know that I appreciated her loving intention but that I didn't like being mothered in this way.

I shared with her that if she wanted to mother me, then the way I wanted to be mothered was to be unconditionally loved and trusted. I said, "If I miss a plane, don't tell me 'I told you so.' Trust that I will learn my lesson and adjust accordingly. If I forget my toothbrush or shaving kit, let me deal with it. Don't tell me about it when I call." With an awareness of what I wanted, instead of what she would have wanted, it was easier for her to succeed in supporting me.

A Success Story

Once, on a trip to Sweden to teach my relationship seminar, I called back to California from New York, informing Bonnie that I had left my passport at home. She reacted in such a beautiful and loving way. She didn't lecture me on being more responsible. Instead she laughed and said, "Oh my goodness, John, you have such adventures. What are you going to do?"

I asked her to fax my passport to the Swedish consulate, and the problem was solved. She was so cooperative. Never once did she succumb to lecturing me on being more prepared. She was even proud of me for finding a solution to my problem.

MAKING LITTLE CHANGES

One day I noticed that when my children asked me to do things I would always say "no problem." It was my way of saying I would be happy to do that. My stepdaughter Julie asked me one day, "Why do you always say 'no problem'?" I didn't actually know right away. After a while I realized that it was another of those deeply ingrained Martian habits. With this new awareness I started saying "I would be happy to do that." This phrase expressed my implied message and certainly felt more loving to my Venusian daughter.

This example symbolizes a very important secret for enriching relationships. Little changes can be made without sacrificing who we are. This was the secret of success for the Martians and Venusians. They were both careful not to sacrifice their true natures, but they were also willing to make small changes in the way they interacted. They learned how relationships could work better by creating or changing a few simple phrases.

The important point here is that to enrich our relationships we need to make little changes. Big changes generally require some suppression of who we truly are. This is not good.

Giving some reassurance when he goes into his cave is a small change that a man can make without changing his nature. To make this change he must realize that women really do need some reassurance, especially if they are to worry less. If a man doesn't understand the differences between men and women, then he cannot comprehend why his sudden silence is such a cause for worry. By giving some reassurance he can remedy the situation.

On the other hand if he does not know how he is different, then when she is upset by his tendency to go into his cave, he may give up going into his cave in an attempt to fulfill her. This is a big mistake. If he gives up the cave (and denies his true nature) he becomes irritable, overly sensitive, defensive, weak, passive, or mean. And to make matters worse, he doesn't know why he has become so unpleasant.

When a woman is upset by his going into the cave, instead of giving up the cave, a man can make a few small changes and the problem can be alleviated. He does not need to deny his true needs or reject his masculine nature.

HOW TO COMMUNICATE SUPPORT TO A VENUSIAN

As we have discussed, when a man goes into his cave or becomes quiet he is saying "I need some time to think about this, please stop talking to me. I will be back." He doesn't realize that a woman may hear "I don't love you, I can't stand to listen to you, I am leaving and I am never coming back!" To counteract this message and to give her the correct message he can learn to say the four magic words: "I will be back."

When a man pulls away, a woman appreciates him saying out loud "I need some time to think about this, I will be back" or "I need some time to be alone. I will be back." It is amazing how the simple words "I will be back" make such a profound difference.

Women greatly appreciate this reassurance. When a man understands how important this is to a woman, then he is able to remember to give this reassurance.

If a woman felt abandoned or rejected by her father or if her mother felt rejected by her husband, then she (the child) will be even more sensitive to feeling abandoned. For this reason, she should never be judged for needing this reassurance. Similarly, a man should not be judged for his need for the cave.

A woman should not be judged for needing this reassurance, just as a man should not be judged for needing to withdraw.

When a woman is less wounded by her past and if she understands a man's need to spend time in the cave, then her need for reassurance will be less.

I remember making this point in a seminar and a woman asking, "I am so sensitive to my husband's silence, but as a child I never felt abandoned or rejected. My mother never felt rejected by my father. Even when they got a divorce they did it in a loving way."

Then she laughed. She realized how she had been duped. Then she started to cry. Of course her mother had felt rejected. Of course she had felt rejected. Her parents were divorced! Like her parents, she also had denied their painful feelings.

In an age when divorce is so common, it is even more important that men be sensitive to giving reassurance. Just as men can support women by making little changes, women need to do the same.

HOW TO COMMUNICATE WITHOUT BLAME

A man commonly feels attacked and blamed by a woman's feelings, especially when she is upset and talks about problems. Because he doesn't understand how we are different, he doesn't readily relate to her need to talk about all of her feelings.

He mistakenly assumes she is telling him about her feelings because she thinks he is somehow responsible or to be blamed. Because she is upset and she is talking to him, he assumes she is upset with him. When she complains he hears blame. Many men don't understand the (Venusian) need to share upset feelings with the people they love.

With practice and an awareness of our differences, women can learn how to express their feelings without having them sound like blaming. To reassure a man that he is not being blamed, when a woman expresses her feelings she could pause after a few minutes of sharing and tell him how much she appreciates him for listening.

She could say some of the following comments:

- "I'm sure glad I can talk about it."
- "It sure feels good to talk about it."
- "I'm feeling so relieved that I can talk about this."
- "I'm sure glad I can complain about all this. It makes me feel so much better."
- "Well, now that I've talked about it, I feel much better. Thank you."

This simple change can make a world of difference.

In this same vein, as she describes her problems she can support him by appreciating the things he has done to make her life easier and more fulfilling. For example, if she is complaining about work, occasionally she could mention that it is so nice to have him in her life to come home to; if she is complaining about the house, then she could mention that she appreciates that he fixed the fence; or if she is complaining about finances, mention that she really appreciates how hard he works; or if she is complaining about the frustrations of being a parent, she could mention that she is glad she has his help.

Sharing Responsibility

Good communication requires participation on both sides. A man needs to work at remembering that complaining about problems does not mean blaming and that when a woman complains she is generally just letting go of her frustrations by talking about them. A woman can work at letting him know that though she is complaining she also appreciates him.

For example, my wife just came in and asked how I was doing on this chapter. I said, "I'm almost done. How was your day?"

She said, "Oh, there is so much to do. We hardly have any time together." The old me would have become defensive and then reminded her of all the time we have spent together, or I would have told her how important it was to meet my deadline. This would have just created tension.

The new me, aware of our differences, understood she was looking for reassurance and understanding and not justifications and explanations. I said, "You're right, we have been really busy. Sit down here on my lap, let me give you a hug. It's been a long day."

She then said, "You feel really good." This was the appreciation I needed in order to be more available to her. She then proceeded to complain more about her day and how exhausted she was. After a few minutes she paused. I then offered to drop off the babysitter so she could relax and meditate before dinner.

She said, "Really, you'll take the babysitter home? That would be great. Thank you!" Again she gave me the appreciation and acceptance I needed to feel like a successful partner, even when she was tired and exhausted.

Women don't think of giving appreciation because they assume a man knows how much she appreciates being heard. He doesn't know. When she is talking about problems, he

88   John Gray

needs to be reassured that he is still loved and appreciated.

Men feel frustrated by problems unless they are doing something to solve them. By appreciating him, a woman can help him realize that just by listening he is also helping.

A woman does not have to suppress her feelings or even change them to support her partner. She does, however, need to express them in a way that doesn't make him feel attacked, accused, or blamed. Making a few small changes can make a big difference.

Four Magic Words of Support

The four magic words to support a man are "It's not your fault." When a woman is expressing her upset feelings she can support a man by pausing occasionally to encourage him by saying "I really appreciate your listening, and if this sounds as if I'm saying it's your fault, that's not what I mean. It's not your fault."

A woman can learn to be sensitive to her listener when she understands his tendency to start feeling like a failure when he hears a lot of problems.

Just the other day my sister called me and talked about a difficult experience that she was going through. As I listened I kept remembering that to support my sister I didn't have to give her any solutions. She needed someone just to listen. After ten minutes of just listening and occasionally saying things like "uh-huh," "oh," and "really!" she then said, "Well, thank you, John. I feel so much better."

It was much easier to hear her because I knew she was not blaming me. She was blaming someone else. I find it more difficult when my wife is unhappy because it is easier for me to feel blamed. However, when my wife encourages me to listen by appreciating me, it becomes much easier to be a good listener.

What to Do When You Feel Like Blaming

Reassuring a man that it is not his fault or that he is not being blamed works only as long as she truly is not blaming him, disapproving of him, or criticizing him. If she is attacking him, then she should share her feelings with someone else. She should wait until she is more loving and centered to talk to him. She could share her resentful feelings with someone she is not upset with, who will be able to give her the support she needs. Then when she feels more loving and forgiving she can successfully approach him to share her feelings. In chapter 11 we will explore in greater detail how to communicate difficult feelings.

How to Listen Without Blaming

A man often blames a woman for being blaming when she is innocently talking about problems. This is very destructive to the relationship because it blocks communication.

Imagine a woman saying "All we ever do is work, work, work. We don't have any fun anymore. You are so serious." A man could very easily feel she is blaming him.

If he feels blamed, I suggest he not blame back and say "I feel like you are blaming me."

Instead I suggest saying "It is difficult to hear you say I am so serious. Are you saying it is all my fault that we don't have more fun?"

Or he could say "It hurts when I hear you say I am so serious and we don't have any fun. Are you saying that it is all my fault?"

In addition, to improve the communication he can give her a way out. He could say "It feels like you are saying it is all my fault that we work so much. Is that true?"

Or he could say "When you say we don't have any fun and that I am so serious, I feel like you are saying it is all my fault. Are you?"

All of these responses are respectful and give her a chance to take back any blame that he might have felt. When she says "Oh, no, I'm not saying it's all your fault" he will probably feel somewhat relieved.

Another approach that I find most helpful is to remember that she always has a right to be upset and that once she gets it out, she will feel much better. This awareness allows me to relax and remember that if I can listen without taking it personally, then when she needs to complain she will be so appreciative of me. Even if she was blaming me, she will not hold on to it.

The Art of Listening

As a man learns to listen and interpret a woman's feelings correctly, communication becomes easier. As with any art, listening requires practice. Each day when I get home, I will generally seek out Bonnie and ask her about her day, thus practicing this art of listening.

If she is upset or has had a stressful day, at first I will feel that she is saying I am somehow responsible and thus to blame. My greatest challenge is to not take it personally, to not misunderstand her. I do this by constantly reminding myself that we speak different languages. As I continue to ask "What else happened?" I find that there are many other things bothering her. Gradually I start to see that I am not solely responsible for her upset. After a while, when she begins to appreciate me for listening, then, even if I was *partially* responsible for her discomfort, she becomes very grateful, accepting, and loving.

Although listening is an important skill to practice, some days a man is too sensitive or stressed to translate the intended meaning of her phrases. At such times he should not even attempt to listen. Instead he could kindly say "This isn't a good time for me. Let's talk later."

Sometimes a man doesn't realize that he can't listen until she begins talking. If he becomes very frustrated, while listening he should not try to continue—he'll just become increasingly upset. That does not serve him or her. Instead, the respectful thing to say is "I really want to hear what you are saying, but right now it is very difficult for me to listen. I think I need some time to think about what you have just said."

As Bonnie and I have learned to communicate in a way that respects our differences and understand each other's needs, our marriage has become so much easier. I have witnessed this same transformation in thousands of individuals and couples. Relationships thrive when communication reflects a ready acceptance and respect of people's innate differences.

When misunderstandings arise, remember that we speak different languages; take the time necessary to translate what your partner really means or wants to say. This definitely takes practice, but it is well worth it.

CHAPTER 6

MEN ARE LIKE
RUBBER BANDS

Men are like rubber bands. When they pull away, they can stretch only so far before they come springing back. A rubber band is the perfect metaphor to understand the male intimacy cycle. This cycle involves getting close, pulling away, and then getting close again.

Most women are surprised to realize that even when a man loves a woman, periodically he needs to pull away before he can get closer. Men instinctively feel this urge to pull away. It is not a decision or choice. It just happens. It is neither his fault nor her fault. It is a natural cycle.

> **When a man loves a woman,**
> **periodically he needs to pull away**
> **before he can get closer.**

Women misinterpret a man's pulling away because generally a woman pulls away for different reasons. She pulls back when she doesn't trust him to understand her feelings, when she has been hurt and is afraid of being hurt again, or when he has done something wrong and disappointed her.

Certainly a man may pull away for the same reasons, but he will also pull away even if she has done nothing wrong. He may love and trust her, and then suddenly he begins to pull away. Like a stretched rubber band, he will distance himself and then come back all on his own.

A man pulls away to fulfill his need for independence or autonomy. When he has fully stretched away, then instantly he will come springing back. When he has fully separated, then suddenly he will feel his need for love and intimacy again. Automatically he will be more motivated to give his love and receive the love he needs. When a man springs back, he picks up the relationship at whatever degree of intimacy it was when he stretched away. He doesn't feel any need for a period of getting reacquainted again.

WHAT EVERY WOMAN SHOULD KNOW ABOUT MEN

If understood, this male intimacy cycle enriches a relationship, but because it is misunderstood it creates unnecessary problems. Let's explore an example.

> Maggie was distressed, anxious, and confused. She and her boyfriend, Jeff, had been dating for six months. Everything had been so romantic. Then without any apparent reason he began to distance himself emotionally. Maggie could not understand why he had suddenly pulled away. She told me, "One minute he was so attentive, and then the next he didn't even want to talk to me. I have tried everything to get him back but it only seems to make matters worse. He seems so distant. I don't know what I did wrong. Am I so awful?"

When Jeff pulled away, Maggie took it personally. This is a common reaction. She thought she had done something wrong and blamed herself. She wanted to make things "right again," but the more she tried to get close to Jeff the more he pulled away.

After taking my seminar Maggie was so relieved. Her anxiety and confusion immediately disappeared. Most important, she stopped blaming herself. She realized that when Jeff pulled away it was not her fault. In addition she learned why he was pulling away and how gracefully to deal with it. Months later at another seminar, Jeff thanked me for what Maggie had learned. He told me they were now engaged to be married. Maggie had discovered a secret that few women know about men.

Maggie realized that when she was trying to get close while Jeff was trying to pull away, she was actually preventing him from stretching his full distance and then springing back. By running after him, she was preventing him from ever feeling that he needed her and wanted to be with her. She realized that she had done this in every relationship. Unknowingly she had obstructed an important cycle. By trying to maintain intimacy she had prevented it.

How a Man Is Suddenly Transformed

If a man does not have the opportunity to pull away, he never gets a chance to feel his strong desire to be close. It is essential for women to understand that if they insist on continuous intimacy or "run after" their intimate male partner when he pulls away, then he will almost always be trying to escape and distance himself; he will never get a chance to feel his own passionate longing for love.

In my seminars I demonstrate this with a big rubber band. Imagine that you are holding a rubber band. Now begin stretching your rubber band by pulling it to your right. This particular rubber band can stretch twelve inches. When the rubber band is stretched twelve inches there is nowhere left to go but back. And when it returns it has a lot of power and spring.

Likewise, when a man has stretched away his full distance, he will return with a lot of power and spring. Once he pulls away to his limit, he begins to go through a transformation. His whole attitude begins to shift. This man who did not seem to care about or be interested in his partner (while he was pulling away) suddenly cannot live without her. He is now feeling again his need for intimacy. His power is back because his desire to love and be loved have been reawakened.

This is generally puzzling for a woman because in her experience if she has pulled away, becoming intimate again requires a period of reacquaintance. If she doesn't understand that men are different in this way, she may have a tendency to mistrust his sudden desire for intimacy and push him away.

Men also need to understand this difference. When a man springs back, before a woman can open up again to him she generally wants and needs time and conversation to reconnect. This transition can be more graceful if a man understands a woman may need more time to regain the same level of intimacy–especially if she felt hurt when he pulled away. Without this understanding of differences, a man may become impatient because he is suddenly available to pick up the intimacy at whatever level of intensity it was when he pulled away and she is not.

Why Men Pull Away

Men begin to feel their need for autonomy and independence after they have fulfilled their need for intimacy. Automatically when he begins to pull away, she begins to panic. What she doesn't realize is that when he pulls away and fulfills his need for autonomy then suddenly he will want to be intimate again. A man automatically alternates between needing intimacy and autonomy.

> **A man automatically alternates between needing intimacy and autonomy.**

For example, in the beginning of his relationship Jeff was strong and full of desire. His rubber band was fully stretched. He wanted to impress her, fulfill her, please her, and get close to her. As he succeeded she also wanted to get closer. As she opened her heart to him he got closer and closer. When they achieved intimacy he felt wonderful. But after a brief period a change took place.

Imagine what happens to the rubber band. The rubber band becomes limp. Its power and stretch are gone. There is no longer any movement. This is exactly what happens to a man's desire to get close after intimacy has been achieved.

Even though this closeness is fulfilling to a man, he will inevitably begin to go through an inner shift. He will begin to feel the urge to pull away. Having temporarily fulfilled his hunger for intimacy, he now feels his hunger to be independent, to be on his own. Enough of this needing another person. He may feel he has become too dependent or may not know why he feels a need to pull away.

Why Women Panic

As Jeff instinctively pulls away without any explanation to Maggie (or to himself), Maggie reacts with fear. She panics and runs after him. She thinks she has done something wrong and has turned him off. She imagines he is expecting her to reestablish intimacy. She is afraid he will never come back.

To make matters worse, she feels powerless to get him back because she doesn't know what she did to turn him off. She doesn't know that this is just a part of his intimacy cycle. When she asks him what's the matter, he doesn't have a clear answer, and so he resists talking about it. He just continues to distance her even more.

Why Men and Women Doubt Their Love

Without an understanding of this cycle it is easy to see how men and women begin to doubt their love. Without seeing how she was preventing Jeff from finding his passion, Maggie could easily assume that Jeff didn't love her. Without getting the chance to pull away, Jeff would lose touch with his desire and passion to be close. He could easily assume that he no longer loved Maggie.

After learning to let Jeff have his distance or "space," Maggie discovered that he did come back. She practiced not running after him when he would withdraw and trusted that everything was OK. Each time he did come back.

As her trust in this process grew, it became easier for her not to panic. When he pulled away she did not run after him or even think something was wrong. She accepted this part of Jeff. The more she just accepted him at those times the sooner he would return. As Jeff began to understand his changing feelings and needs, he became more confident in his love. He was able to make a commitment. The secret of Maggie and Jeff's success was that they understood and accepted that men are like rubber bands.

HOW WOMEN MISINTERPRET MEN

Without an understanding of how men are like rubber bands, it is very easy for women to misinterpret a man's reactions. A common confusion arises when she says "Let's talk" and immediately he emotionally distances himself. Right when she wants to open up and get closer, he wants to pull away. Commonly I hear the complaint "Every time I want to talk, he pulls away. I feel like he doesn't care about me." She mistakenly concludes that he doesn't *ever* want to talk to her.

This rubber band analogy explains how a man may care very much about his partner but suddenly pull away. When he pulls away it is not because he does not want to talk. Instead, he needs some time alone; time to be with himself when he is not responsible for anyone else. It is a time for him to take care of himself. When he returns then he is available to talk.

To a certain extent a man *loses* himself through connecting with his partner. By feeling her needs, problems, wants, and emotions he may lose touch with his own sense of self. Pulling away allows him to reestablish his personal boundaries and fulfill his need to feel autonomous.

> To a certain extent a man *loses* himself
> through connecting with his partner.

Some men, however, may describe this pulling away differently. To them it is just a feeling of "I need some space" or "I need to be alone." Regardless of how it is described, when a man pulls away, he is fulfilling a valid need to take care of himself for a while.

Just as we do not *decide* to be hungry, a man does not decide to pull away. It is an instinctual urge. He can only get so close, and then he begins to lose himself. At this point he begins to feel his need for autonomy and begins to pull away. By understanding this process, women can begin correctly to interpret this pulling away.

Why Men Pull Away When Women Get Close

For many women, a man tends to pull away precisely at the time when she wants to talk and be intimate. This occurs for two reasons.

> 1. A woman will unconsciously sense when a man is pulling away and precisely at those times she will attempt to reestablish their intimate connection and say "Let's talk." As he continues to pull away, she mistakenly concludes that he doesn't want to talk or that he doesn't care for her.

> 2. When a woman opens up and shares deeper and more intimate feelings it may actually trigger a man's need to pull away. A man can only handle so much intimacy before his alarm bells go off, saying it is time to find balance by pulling away. At the most intimate moments a man may suddenly automatically switch to feeling his need for autonomy and pull away.

It is very confusing for a woman when a man pulls away because something she says or does often triggers his departure. Generally when a woman starts to talk about things with *feeling* a man starts to feel this urge to pull away. This is because feelings draw men closer and create intimacy, and when a man gets too close he automatically pulls away.

It is not that he doesn't want to hear her feelings. At another time in his intimacy cycle, when he is needing to get close, the same *feelings* that could have triggered his departure will draw him closer. It is not *what* she says that triggers his departure but *when* she says it.

WHEN TO TALK WITH A MAN

When a man is pulling away is not the time to talk or try to get closer. Let him pull away. After some time, he will return. He will appear loving and supportive and will act as though nothing has happened. *This is the time to talk.*

At this golden time, when a man wants intimacy and is actually available to talk, women generally don't initiate conversations. This occurs for these three common reasons:

1. A woman is afraid to talk because the last time she wanted to talk he pulled away. She mistakenly assumes that he doesn't care and he doesn't want to listen.

2. A woman is afraid the man is upset with her and she waits for him to initiate a conversation about his feelings. She knows that if she were suddenly to pull away from him, before she could reconnect she would need to talk about what happened. She waits for him to initiate a conversation about what upset him. He, however, doesn't need to talk about his upset feelings because he is not upset.

3. A woman has so much to say that she doesn't want to be rude and just begin talking. To be polite, instead of talking about *her own* thoughts and feelings she makes the mistake of asking him questions about *his* feelings and thoughts. When he has nothing to say, she concludes he doesn't want to have a conversation with her.

With all of these incorrect beliefs about why a man is not talking, it is no wonder that women are frustrated with men.

HOW TO GET A MAN TO TALK

When a woman wants to talk or feels the need to get close, she should do the talking and not expect a man to initiate the conversation. To initiate a conversation she needs to be the first to begin sharing, even if her partner has little to say. As she appreciates him for listening, gradually he will have more to say.

A man can be very open to having a conversation with a woman but at first have nothing to say. What women don't know about Martians is that they need to have a reason to talk. They don't talk just for the sake of sharing. But when a woman talks for a while, a man will start to open up and share how he relates to what she has shared.

For example, if she talks about some of her difficulties during the day he may share some of the difficulties of his day so that they can understand each other. If she talks about her feelings about the kids, he may then talk about his feelings about the kids. As she opens up and he doesn't feel blamed or pressured, then he gradually begins to open up.

How Women Pressure Men to Talk

A woman sharing her thoughts naturally motivates a man to talk. But when he feels a demand is being made that he talk, his mind goes blank. He has nothing to say. Even if he has something to say he will resist because he feels her demand.

It is hard for a man when a woman demands that *he* talk. She unknowingly turns him off by interrogating him. Especially when he doesn't feel the need to talk. A woman mistakenly assumes that a man "needs to talk" and therefore "should." She forgets that he is from Mars and doesn't feel the need to talk as much.

She even feels that unless *he* talks, he doesn't love her. To reject a man for not talking is to ensure that he has nothing to say. A man needs to feel accepted just the way he is, and then he will gradually open up. He does not feel accepted when she wants him to talk more or resents him for pulling away.

A man who needs to pull away a lot before he can learn to share and open up will first need to listen a lot. He needs to be appreciated for listening, then gradually he will say more.

How to Initiate a Conversation with a Man

The more a woman tries to get a man to talk the more he will resist. Directly trying to get him to talk is not the best approach, especially if he is stretching away. Instead of wondering how she can get him to talk a better question might be "How can I achieve greater intimacy, conversation, and communication with my partner?"

If a woman feels the need for more talk in the relationship, and most women do, then she can initiate more conversation but with a mature awareness that not only accepts but also expects that sometimes he will be available and at other times he will instinctively pull away.

When he is available, instead of asking him twenty questions or demanding that he talk, she could let him know that she appreciates him even if he just listens. In the beginning she should even discourage him from talking.

For example, Maggie could say "Jeff, would you listen to me for a while? I've had a hard day and I want to talk about it. It will make me feel much better." After Maggie talked for a couple of minutes then she could pause and say "I really appreciate when you listen to my feelings, it means a lot to me." This appreciation encourages a man to listen more.

Without appreciation and encouragement, a man may lose interest because he feels as though his "listening" is "doing nothing." He doesn't realize how valuable his listening is to her. Most women, however, instinctively know how important listening is. To expect a man to know this without some training is to expect him to be like a woman. Fortunately, after being appreciated for listening to a woman, a man does learn to respect the value of talking.

WHEN A MAN WON'T TALK

> Sandra and Larry had been married for twenty years. Sandra wanted a divorce and Larry wanted to make things work.
>
> She said, "How can he say he wants to stay married? He doesn't love me. He doesn't feel anything. He walks away when I need him to talk. He is cold and heartless. For twenty years he has withheld his feelings. I am not willing to forgive him. I will not stay in this marriage. I am too tired of trying to get him to open up and share his feelings and be vulnerable."

Sandra didn't know how she had contributed to their problems. She thought it was all her husband's fault. She thought she had done everything to promote intimacy, conversation, and communication, and he had resisted her for twenty years.

After hearing about men and rubber bands in the seminar, she burst into tears of forgiveness for her husband. She realized that "his" problem was "their" problem. She recognized how she had contributed to their problem.

She said, "I remember in our first year of marriage I would open up, talk about my feelings, and he would just walk away. I thought he didn't love me. After that happened a few times, I gave up. I was not willing to be hurt again. I did not know that at another time he would be able to listen to my feelings. I didn't give him a chance. I stopped being vulnerable. I wanted him to open up before I would."

One-sided Conversations

Sandra's conversations were generally one-sided. She would try to get him to talk first by asking him a string of questions. Then, before she could share what she wanted to talk about, she would become upset with his short answers. When she finally did share her feelings, they were always the same. She was upset that he was not open, loving, and sharing.

A one-sided conversation might go like this:

SANDRA:	How was your day?
LARRY:	OK.
SANDRA:	What happened?
LARRY:	The usual.
SANDRA:	What do you feel like doing this weekend?
LARRY:	I don't care. What do you want to do?
SANDRA:	Do you want to invite our friends over?
LARRY:	I don't know... Do you know where the TV schedule is?
SANDRA:	(*upset*) Why don't you talk to me?
LARRY:	(*Stunned and silent.*)
SANDRA:	Do you love me?
LARRY:	Of course I love you. I married you.
SANDRA:	How could you love me? We never talk anymore. How can you just sit there and say nothing. Don't you care?

At this point, Larry would get up and go for a walk. When he came back he would act as though nothing had happened. Sandra would also act as though everything was fine, but inside she would withdraw her love and warmth. On the surface she would try to be loving, but on the inside her resentment increased. From time to time it would boil up and she would begin another one-sided interrogation of her husband's feelings. After twenty years of gathering evidence that he did not love her, she was no longer willing to be deprived of intimacy.

Learning to Support Each Other Without Having to Change

At the seminar Sandra said, "I have spent twenty years trying to get Larry to talk. I wanted him to open up and be vulnerable. I didn't realize that what I was missing was a man who would support *me* in being open and vulnerable. That is what I really needed. I have shared more intimate feelings with my husband this weekend than in twenty years. I feel so loved. This is what I have been missing. I thought he had to change. Now I know nothing is wrong with him or me. We just didn't know how to support each other."

Sandra had always complained that Larry didn't talk. She had convinced herself that his silence made intimacy impossible. At the seminar she learned to share her feelings without expecting or demanding Larry to reciprocate. Instead of rejecting his silence she learned to appreciate it. It made him a better listener.

Larry learned the art of listening. He practiced listening without trying to fix her. It is much more effective to teach a man to listen than to open up and be vulnerable. As he learns to listen to someone he cares for and is appreciated in response, he gradually will open up and share more automatically.

When a man feels appreciated for listening and he doesn't feel rejected for not sharing more, he will gradually begin to open up. When he feels as though he doesn't have to talk more, then naturally he will. But first he needs to feel accepted. If she is still frustrated by his silence she is forgetting that men are from Mars!

WHEN A MAN DOESN'T PULL AWAY

Lisa and Jim had been married for two years. They did everything together. They were never apart. After a while, Jim became increasingly irritable, passive, moody, and temperamental.

In a private counseling session, Lisa told me, "He is no longer any fun to be with. I have tried everything to cheer him up, but it doesn't work. I want to do fun things together, like going to restaurants, shopping, traveling, going to plays, parties, and dancing, but he doesn't. We never do anything anymore. We just watch TV, eat, sleep, and work. I try to love him, but I am angry. He used to be so charming and romantic. Living with him now is like living with a slug. I don't know what to do. He just won't budge!"

After learning about the male intimacy cycle–the rubber band theory–both Lisa and Jim realized what had happened. They were spending too much time together. Jim and Lisa needed to spend more time apart.

When a man gets too close and doesn't pull away, common symptoms are increased moodiness, irritability, passiveness, and defensiveness. Jim had not learned how to pull away. He felt guilty spending time alone. He thought he was supposed to share everything with his wife.

Lisa also thought they were supposed to do everything together. In counseling I asked Lisa why she had spent so much time with Jim.

She said, "I was afraid he would get upset if I did anything fun without him. One time I went shopping and he got really upset with me."

Jim said, "I remember that day. But I wasn't upset with you. I was upset about losing some money in a business deal. I actually remember that day because I remember noticing how good I felt having the whole house to myself. I didn't dare tell you that because I thought it would hurt your feelings."

Lisa said, "I thought you didn't want me to go out without you. You seemed so distant."

Becoming More Independent

With this new awareness, Lisa got the permission she needed not to worry so much about Jim. Jim pulling away actually helped her become more autonomous and independent. She started taking better care of herself. As she started doing the things she wanted to do and getting more support from her girlfriends she was much happier.

She released her resentment toward Jim. She realized that she had been expecting too much from him. Having heard about the rubber band she realized how she was contributing to their problem. She realized that he needed more time to be alone. Her loving sacrifices were not only preventing him from pulling away and then springing back but her dependent attitude was also smothering him.

Lisa started doing fun things without Jim. She did some of the things that she had been wanting to do. One night she went out to eat with some girlfriends. Another night she went to a play. Another night she went to a birthday bowling party.

Simple Miracles

What amazed her was how quickly their relationship changed. Jim became much more attentive and interested in her. Within a couple of weeks, Jim started to come back to his old self again. He was wanting to do fun things with her and started planning dates. He got his motivation back.

In counseling he said, "I feel so relieved. I feel loved...when Lisa comes home she is happy to see me. It feels so good to miss her when she is gone. It feels good to 'feel' again. I had almost forgotten what it was like. Before it seemed like nothing I did was good enough. Lisa was always trying to get me to do things, telling me what to do and asking me questions."

Lisa said, "I realized I was blaming him for my unhappiness. As I took responsibility for my happiness, I experienced that Jim was more energetic and alive. It's like a miracle."

OBSTRUCTING THE INTIMACY CYCLE

There are two ways a woman may unknowingly obstruct her male partner's natural intimacy cycle. They are: (1) chasing him when he pulls away; and (2) punishing him for pulling away.

The following is a list of the most common ways a woman "chases a man" and prevents him from pulling away:

CHASING BEHAVIORS

1. Physical
When he pulls away, she physically follows him. He may walk into another room and she follows. Or as in the example of Lisa and Jim, she does not do the things she wants to do so that she can be with her partner.

2. Emotional
When he pulls away, she emotionally follows him. She worries about him. She wants to help him feel better. She feels sorry for him. She smothers him with attention and praise.

Another way she may emotionally stop him from pulling away is to disapprove of his need to be alone. Through disapproving she is also emotionally pulling him back.

Another approach is to look longingly or hurt when he pulls away. In this way she pleads for his intimacy and he feels controlled.

3. Mental
She may try to pull him back mentally by asking him guilt-inducing questions such as "How could treat me this way?" or "What's wrong with you?" or "Don't you realize how much it hurts me when you pull away?"

Another way she may try to pull him back is to try to please him. She becomes overly accommodating. She tries to be perfect so he would never have any reason to pull away. She gives up her sense of self and tries to become what she thinks he wants.

She is afraid to rock the boat for fear that he might

pull away, and so she withholds her true feelings and avoids doing anything that may upset him.

The second major way a woman may unknowingly interrupt a man's intimacy cycle is to punish him for pulling away. The following is a list of the most common ways a woman "punishes a man" and prevents him from coming back and opening up to her:

PUNISHING BEHAVIORS

1. Physical

When he begins to desire her again she rejects him. She pushes away his physical affection. She may reject him sexually. She doesn't allow him to touch her or be close. She may hit him or break things in order to show her displeasure.

When a man is punished for pulling away, he can become afraid of ever doing it again. This fear may prevent him from pulling away in the future. His natural cycle is then broken. It may also create an anger that blocks him from feeling his desire for intimacy. He may not come back when he has pulled away.

2. Emotional

When he returns, she is unhappy and she blames him. She does not forgive him for neglecting her. There is nothing he can do to please her or make her happy. He feels incapable of fulfilling her and gives up.

When he returns, she expresses her disapproval through words, tone of voice, and by looking at her partner in a certain wounded way.

3. Mental

When he returns, she refuses to open up and share her feelings. She becomes cold and resents him for not opening up and talking.

She stops trusting that he really cares and punishes him by not giving him a chance to listen and be the "good" guy. When he happily returns to her, he is in the doghouse.

When a man feels punished for pulling away, he can become afraid of losing her love if he pulls away. He begins to feel unworthy of her love if he pulls away. He may become afraid to reach out for her love again because he feels unworthy; he assumes he will be rejected. This fear of rejection prevents him from coming back from his journey into the cave.

HOW A MAN'S PAST MAY AFFECT HIS INTIMACY CYCLE

This natural cycle in a man may already be obstructed from his childhood. He may be afraid to pull away because he witnessed his mother's disapproval of his father's emotional distancing. Such a man may not even know that he needs to pull away. He may unconsciously create arguments to justify pulling away.

This kind of man naturally develops more of his feminine side but at the expense of suppressing some of his masculine power. He is a sensitive man. He tries hard to please and be loving but loses part of his masculine self in the process. He feels guilty pulling away. Without knowing what has happened he loses his desire, power, and passion; he becomes passive or overly dependent.

He may be afraid to be alone or to go into his cave. He may think he doesn't like being alone because deep inside he is afraid of losing love. He has already experienced in childhood his mother rejecting his father or directly rejecting him.

While some men don't know how to pull away, others don't know how to get close. The macho man has no problem pulling away. He just can't come back and open up. Deep inside he may be afraid he is unworthy of love. He is afraid of being close and caring a lot. He does not have a picture of how welcomed he would be if he got closer. Both the sensitive male and the macho male are missing a positive picture or experience of their natural intimacy cycle.

Understanding this male intimacy cycle is just as important for men as it is for women. Some men feel guilty needing to spend time in their caves or they may get confused when they start to pull away and then later spring back. They may mistakenly think something is wrong with them. It is such a relief for both men and women to understand these secrets about men.

WISE MEN AND WOMEN

Men generally don't realize how their suddenly pulling away and then later returning affects women. With this new insight about how women are affected by his intimacy cycle, a man can recognize the importance of sincerely listening when a woman speaks. He understands and respects her need to be reassured that he is interested in her and he does care. Whenever he is not needing to pull away, the wise man takes the time to initiate conversation by asking his female partner how she is feeling.

He grows to understand his own cycles and reassures her when he pulls away that he will be back. He might say "I need some time to be alone and then we will have some special time together with no distractions." Or if he starts to pull away while she is talking he might say "I need some time to think about this and then we can talk again."

> The man grows to understand his own cycles and
> reassures her when he pulls away that he will be back.

When he returns to talk, she might probe him to understand why he left. If he's not sure, which is many times the case, he might say "I'm not sure. I just needed some time to myself. But let's continue our conversation."

He is more aware that she needs to be heard and he needs to listen more when he is not pulling away. In addition, he knows that listening helps him to become aware of what he wants to share in a conversation.

To initiate a conversation the wise woman learns not to demand that a man talk but asks that he truly listen to her. As her emphasis changes, the pressure on him is released. She learns to open up and share her feelings without demanding that he do the same.

She trusts that he will gradually open up more as he feels accepted and listens to her feelings. She does not punish him or chase after him. She understands that sometimes her intimate feelings trigger his need to pull away while at other times (when he is on his way back) he *is* quite capable of hearing her intimate feelings. This wise woman does not give up. She patiently and lovingly persists with a knowing that few women have.

CHAPTER 7

WOMEN
ARE LIKE WAVES

A woman is like a wave. When she feels loved her self-esteem rises and falls in a wave motion. When she is feeling really good, she will reach a peak, but then suddenly her mood may change and her wave crashes down. This crash is temporary. After she reaches bottom suddenly her mood will shift and she will again feel good about herself. Automatically her wave begins to rise back up.

When a woman's wave rises she feels she has an abundance of love to give, but when it falls she feels her inner emptiness and needs to be filled up with love. This time of bottoming out is a time for emotional housecleaning.

If she has suppressed any negative feelings or denied herself in order to be more loving on the upswing of her wave, then on the downswing she begins to experience these negative feelings and unfulfilled needs. During this down time she especially needs to talk about problems and be heard and understood.

My wife, Bonnie, says this experience of "going down" is like going down into a dark well. When a women goes into her "well" she is consciously sinking into her unconscious self, into darkness and diffused feeling. She may suddenly experience a host of unexplained emotions and vague feelings. She may feel hopeless, thinking she is all alone or unsupported. But soon after she reaches the bottom, if she feels loved and supported, she will automatically start to feel better. As suddenly as she may have crashed, she will automatically rise up and again radiate love in her relationships.

A woman's self-esteem rises and falls like a wave.
When she hits bottom
it is a time for emotional housecleaning.

A woman's ability to give and receive love in her relationships is generally a reflection of how she is feeling about herself. When she is not feeling *as* good about herself, she is unable to be *as* accepting and appreciative of her partner. At her down times, she tends to be overwhelmed or more emotionally reactive. When her wave hits bottom she is more vulnerable and needs more love. It is crucial that her partner understand what she needs at these times, otherwise he may make unreasonable demands.

HOW MEN REACT TO THE WAVE

When a man loves a woman she begins to shine with love and fulfillment. Most men naïvely expect that shine to last forever. But to expect her loving nature to be constant is like expecting the weather never to change and the sun to shine all the time. Life is filled with rhythms—day and night, hot and cold, summer and winter, spring and fall, cloudy and clear. Likewise in a relationship, men and women have their own rhythms and cycles. Men pull back and then get close, while women rise and fall in their ability to love themselves and others.

In relationships, men pull back and then get close,
while women rise and fall in their ability to love
themselves and others.

A man assumes that her sudden change of mood is based solely on his behavior. When she is happy he takes credit, but when she is unhappy he also feels responsible. He may feel extremely frustrated because he doesn't know how to make things better. One minute she seems happy, and so he believes he is doing a good job and then the next minute she is unhappy. He is shocked because he thought he was doing so well.

Don't Try to Fix It

Bill and Mary had been married for six years. Bill had observed this wave pattern in Mary, but because he didn't understand it, he tried to "fix it," which just made matters worse. He thought something was wrong with her tendency to go up and down. He would try explaining to her that she didn't need to be upset. Mary only felt more misunderstood and thus more distressed.

Although he thought he was "fixing it," he was actually preventing her from feeling better. When a woman moves into her well, he needs to learn that this is when she needs him the most, and it is not a problem to be solved or fixed, but an opportunity to support her with unconditional love.

> Bill said, "I can't understand my wife, Mary. For weeks she is the most wonderful woman. She gives her love so unconditionally to me and to everyone. Then suddenly she becomes overwhelmed by how much she is doing for everyone and starts being disapproving of me. It's not my fault she's unhappy. I explain that to her, and we just get into the biggest fights."

Like many men, Bill made the mistake of trying to prevent his partner from "going down" or "bottoming out." He tried to rescue her by pulling her up. He had not learned that when his wife was going down she needed to hit bottom before she could come up.

When his wife, Mary, started to crash, her first symptom was to feel overwhelmed. Instead of listening to her with caring, warmth, and empathy, he would try to bring her back up with explanations of why she shouldn't be so upset.

The last thing a woman needs when she is on her way down is someone telling her why she shouldn't be down. What she needs is someone to be with her as she goes down, to listen to her while she shares her feelings, and to empathize with what she is going through. Even if a man can't fully understand why a woman feels overwhelmed, he can offer his love, attention, and support.

How Men Are Confused

After learning how women are like waves, Bill was still confused. The next time his wife seemed to be in her well, he practiced listening to her. As she talked about some of the things that were bothering her, he practiced not offering suggestions to "fix her" or make her feel better. After about twenty minutes he became very upset, because she wasn't feeling any better.

He told me, "At first I listened, and she seemed to open up and share more. But then she started getting even more upset. It seemed the more I listened the more upset she got. I told her she shouldn't be getting more upset and then we got into a big argument."

Although Bill was listening to Mary, he was still trying to fix her. He expected her to feel better right away. What Bill didn't know is that when a woman goes into her well, if she feels supported she doesn't necessarily feel better right away. She may feel worse. But that is a sign that his support may be helping. His support may actually help her to hit bottom sooner, and then she can and will feel better. To genuinely come up she first needs to hit bottom. That is the cycle.

Bill was confused, because as he listened to her she appeared to get no benefit from his support. To him she just seemed to be going deeper. To avoid this confusion a man needs to remember that sometimes when he is succeeding in supporting a woman she may become even more upset. Through understanding that a wave must hit bottom before it can rise again he can release his expectations that she immediately feel better in response to his assistance.

> **Even when a man is succeeding in supporting a woman she may become even more upset.**

With this new insight, Bill was able to be more understanding and patient with Mary. After becoming much more successful in supporting Mary in her well, he also learned that there was no way to predict how long she would be upset; sometimes her well was deeper than at other times.

RECURRING CONVERSATIONS AND ARGUMENTS

When a woman comes out of the well she becomes her usual loving self again. This positive shift is generally misunderstood by men. A man typically thinks that whatever was bothering her is now completely healed or resolved. This is not the case. It is an illusion. Because she is suddenly more loving and positive he mistakenly thinks all her issues are resolved.

When her wave crashes again, similar issues will arise. When her issues come up again he becomes impatient, because he thinks they have already been resolved. Without understanding the wave, he finds it hard to validate and nurture her feelings while she is in the "well."

When a woman's unresolved feelings recur, he may respond inappropriately by saying:

1. "How many times do we have to go through this?"
2. "I've heard all this before."
3. "I thought we had established that."
4. "When are you going to get off it?"
5. "I don't want to deal with this again."
6. "This is crazy! We are having the same argument."
7. "Why do you have so many problems?"

When a woman goes into her well her deepest issues tend to surface. These issues may have to do with the relationship, but usually they are heavily charged from her past relationships and childhood. Whatever remains to be healed or resolved from her past inevitably will come up. Here are some of the common feelings she may experience as she goes into the well.

WARNING SIGNS FOR MEN THAT SHE MAY BE GOING INTO HER WELL OR WHEN SHE NEEDS HIS LOVE THE MOST

She feels	She may say
Overwhelmed	"There is so much to do."
Insecure	"I need more."
Resentful	"I do everything."
Worried	"But what about…"
Confused	"I don't understand why…"
Exhausted	"I can't do anything more."
Hopeless	"I don't know what to do."
Passive	"I don't care, do what you want."
Demanding	"You should…"
Withholding	"No, I don't want to…"
Mistrustful	"What do you mean by that?"
Controlling	"Well, did you…?"
Disapproving	"How could you forget…?"

As she feels more and more supported at these difficult times, she begins to trust the relationship and is able to journey in and out of her well without conflict in her relationship or struggle in her life. This is the blessing of a loving relationship.

To support a woman when she is in her well is a special gift that she will greatly appreciate. Gradually she will become free from the gripping influence of her past. She will still have her ups and downs, but they will not be so extreme that they overshadow her loving nature.

UNDERSTANDING NEEDINESS

> During my relationship seminar Tom complained, saying, "In the beginning of our relationship, Susan seemed so strong, but then suddenly she became so needy. I remember reassuring her that I loved her and that she was important to me. After a lot of talking we got over that hurdle, but then again a month later she went through the same insecurity. It was as if she had never heard me the first time. I became so frustrated with her that we got in a big argument."

Tom was surprised to see that many other men shared his experience in their relationships. When Tom met Susan she was on the upswing of her wave. As their relationship progressed Susan's love for Tom grew. After her wave peaked, suddenly she started feeling very needy and possessive. She became insecure and demanded more attention.

This was the beginning of her descent into the well. Tom could not understand why she had changed, but after a rather intense discussion that went on for hours, Susan felt much better. Tom had reassured her of his love and support, and Susan was now swinging up again. Inside he felt relieved.

After this interaction Tom thought he had successfully solved this problem in their relationship. But a month later Susan began to crash and began feeling the same way again. This time Tom was much less understanding and accepting of her. He became impatient. He was insulted that she would mistrust him again after he had reassured her of his love a month before. In his defensiveness he negatively judged her recurring need for reassurance. As a result they argued.

Reassuring Insights

By understanding how women are like waves, Tom realized that the recurrence of Susan's neediness and insecurity was natural, inevitable, and temporary. He realized how naïve he had been to think that his loving response to Susan's deepest core issues could permanently heal her.

Tom learning successfully to support Susan when she was in her well not only made it easier for her to do her inner healing but also helped them not to have fights at those times. Tom was encouraged by the three following realizations.

1. A man's love and support cannot instantly resolve a woman's issues. His love, however, can make it safe for her to go deeper into her well. It is naïve to expect a woman to be perfectly loving all the time. He can expect these issues to come up again and again. Each time, however, he can get better at supporting her.

2. A woman going into her well is not a man's fault or his failure. By being more supportive he *cannot* prevent it from happening, but he can help her through these difficult times.

3. A woman has within herself the ability to spontaneously rise up after she has hit bottom. A man does not have to fix her. She is not broken but just needs his love, patience, and understanding.

WHEN A WOMAN DOESN'T FEEL SAFE IN HER WELL

This tendency to be like a wave increases when a woman is in an intimate relationship. It is essential that she feel safe to go through this cycle. Otherwise she works hard at pretending that everything is always all right and suppresses her negative feelings.

When a woman doesn't feel safe to go into her well, her only alternative is to avoid intimacy and sex or to suppress and numb her feelings through addictions like drinking, overeating, overworking, or overcaretaking. Even with her addictions, however, she periodically will fall into her well and her feelings may come up in a most uncontrolled fashion.

You probably know stories of couples who never fight or argue and then suddenly to everyone's surprise they decide to get a divorce. In many of these cases, the woman has suppressed her negative feelings to avoid having fights. As a result she becomes numb and unable to feel her love.

When negative feelings are suppressed positive feelings become suppressed as well, and love dies. Avoiding arguments and fights certainly is healthy but not by suppressing feelings. In chapter 9 we will explore how to avoid arguments without suppressing feelings.

> **When negative feelings are suppressed positive feelings become suppressed as well, and love dies.**

Emotional Housecleaning

When a woman's wave crashes is a time of emotional cleansing or emotional housecleaning. Without this cleansing or emotional catharsis a woman slowly loses her ability to love and to grow in love. Through controlled repression of her feelings her wave nature is obstructed, and she gradually becomes unfeeling and passionless over time.

Some women who avoid dealing with their negative emotions and resist the natural wave motion of their feelings experience premenstrual syndrome (PMS). There is a strong correlation between PMS and the inability to cope with negative feelings in a positive way. In some cases women who have learned successfully to deal with their feelings have felt their PMS symptoms disappear. In chapter 11 we will explore more healing techniques for dealing with negative emotions.

Even a strong, confident, and successful woman will need to visit her well from time to time. Men commonly make the mistake of thinking that if their female partner is successful in the work world then she will not experience these times of emotional house-cleaning. The opposite is true.

When a woman is in the work world she generally is exposed to stress and emotional pollution. Her need for emotional housecleaning becomes great. Similarly, a man's need to pull away like a rubber band may increase when he is under a greater amount of stress at work.

One study revealed that a woman's self-esteem generally rises and falls in a cycle between twenty-one and thirty-five days. No studies have been done on how often a man pulls back like a rubber band, but my experience is that it is about the same. A woman's self-esteem cycle is not necessarily in sync with her menstrual cycle, but it does average out at twenty-eight days.

When a woman puts on her business suit she can detach from this emotional roller coaster, but when she returns home she needs her partner to give the tender loving support that every woman needs and appreciates at these times.

It is important to recognize that this tendency to go into the well does not necessarily affect a woman's competence at work, but it does greatly influence her communication with the people she intimately loves and needs.

How a Man Can Support a Woman in the Well

A wise man learns to go out of his way to help a woman feel safe to rise and fall. He releases his judgments and demands and learns how to give the required support. As a result he enjoys a relationship that increases in love and passion over the years.

He may have to weather a few emotional storms or droughts, but the reward is much greater. The uninitiated man still suffers from storms and droughts, but because he does not know the art of loving her through her time in the well, their love stops growing and gradually becomes repressed.

WHEN SHE'S IN THE WELL AND HE'S IN THE CAVE

> Harris said, "I tried everything I learned in the seminar. It was really working. We were so close. I felt like I was in heaven. Then suddenly my wife, Cathy, started complaining that I watched too much TV. She started treating me like I was a child. We got in a huge argument. I don't know what happened. We were doing so well."

This is an example of what can happen when the wave and the rubber band occur around the same time. After taking the seminar, Harris had succeeded in giving more to his wife and family than ever. Cathy was delighted. She couldn't believe it. They had become closer than ever. Her wave was peaking. This lasted for a couple of weeks, and then Harris decided to stay up late one night and watch TV. His rubber band was starting to droop. He needed to pull away into his cave.

When he pulled away, Cathy was greatly hurt. Her wave began to crash. She saw his pulling away as the end of her new experience of intimacy. The previous couple of weeks had been everything she had wanted, and now she thought she was going to lose it. Ever since she was a little girl this type of intimacy was her dream. His pulling away was a tremendous shock to her. To the vulnerable little girl within her it was an experience of giving candy to a baby and then taking it away. She became very upset.

Martian and Venusian Logic

Cathy's experience of abandonment is hard for a Martian to understand. Martian logic says "I have been so wonderful for the past two weeks. Shouldn't that entitle me to a little time off? I have been giving to you all this time, now it's time for me. You should be more secure and reassured about my love than ever."

Venusian logic approaches the experience differently: "These last two weeks have been so wonderful. I have let myself open up to you more than ever. Losing your loving attention is more painful than ever. I started to really open up and then you pulled away."

How Past Feelings Come Up

By not fully trusting and opening up, Cathy had spent years protecting herself from being hurt. But during their two weeks of living in love she started to open up more than she ever had in her adult life. Harris's support had made it safe for her to get in touch with her old feelings.

Suddenly she began to feel the way she felt as a child when her father was too busy for her. Her past unresolved feelings of anger and powerlessness were projected onto Harris's watching TV. If these feelings had not come up, Cathy would have been able gracefully to accept Harris's wish to watch TV.

Because her past feelings were coming up, she felt hurt when he watched TV. If given the chance to share and explore her hurt, deep feelings would have emerged. Cathy would have hit bottom, and then she would have felt significantly better. Once again, she would have been willing to trust intimacy, even knowing it can be painful when inevitably he temporarily pulls away.

When Feelings Get Hurt

But Harris didn't understand why she would be hurt. He told her she shouldn't be hurt. And the argument began. Telling a woman she shouldn't feel hurt is about the worst thing a man can say. It hurts her even more, like poking a stick into an open wound.

When a woman is feeling hurt, she may sound as if she is blaming him. But if she is given care and understanding, the blame will disappear. Trying to explain to her why she shouldn't be hurt will make matters much worse.

Sometimes when a woman is hurting she may even agree intellectually that she shouldn't be hurting. But emotionally she is still hurting and doesn't want to hear from him that she shouldn't be hurting. What she needs is his understanding of why she is hurting.

Why Men and Women Fight

Harris completely misunderstood Cathy's hurt reaction. He thought she was demanding that he give up TV forever. Cathy wasn't demanding that Harris give up TV. She just wanted him to know how painful it was for her.

Women instinctively know that if only their pain can be heard then they can trust their partner to make whatever changes he can make. When Cathy shared her hurt, she just needed to be heard and then be reassured that he wasn't permanently reverting back to the old Harris, addicted to TV and emotionally unavailable.

Certainly Harris deserved to watch TV, but Cathy deserved the right to be upset. She deserved to be heard, understood, and reassured. Harris was not wrong for watching TV, and Cathy was not wrong for being upset.

> **Men argue for the right to be free while**
> **women argue for the right to be upset.**
> **Men want space while women want understanding.**

Because Harris did not understand Cathy's wave, he thought her reaction was unfair. He thought he had to invalidate her feelings if he wanted to take time to watch TV. He became irritable and thought, I can't be loving and intimate all the time!

Harris felt he had to make her feelings wrong to gain the right to watch TV and live his life and be himself. He argued for his right to watch TV when Cathy just needed to be heard. She argued for the right to be hurt and upset.

RESOLVING CONFLICTS THROUGH UNDERSTANDING

It was naïve for Harris to think that Cathy's anger, resentment, and feelings of powerlessness from being neglected for twelve years were going to go away after two weeks of being in love.

It was equally naïve for Cathy to think that Harris could sustain his focus on her and the family without taking time to pull away and focus on himself.

When Harris started to pull away it triggered Cathy's wave to crash. Her unresolved feelings started coming up. She was not just reacting to Harris watching TV that night but to the years of being neglected. Their argument turned into yelling. After two hours of yelling they weren't talking to each other.

By understanding the bigger picture of what had happened, they were able to resolve their conflict and make up. Harris understood that when he started to pull away it triggered Cathy's time to do some emotional housecleaning. She needed to talk about her feelings and not be made wrong. Harris was encouraged by the realization that she was fighting to be heard, just as he was fighting to be free. He learned that by supporting her need to be heard she could support his need to be free.

> By supporting her need to be heard
> she could support his need to be free.

Cathy understood that Harris did not mean to invalidate her hurt feelings. In addition she understood that though he was pulling away he would be back and they would be able to experience intimacy again. She realized that their increased intimacy had triggered his need to pull away. She learned that her hurt feelings made him feel controlled, and he needed to feel she was not trying to tell him what he could do.

What a Man Can Do When He Can't Listen

Harris asked, "What if I just can't listen and I need to be in my cave? Sometimes, I start to listen and I become furious."

I assured him that this is normal. When her wave crashes and she needs to be heard the most, sometimes his rubber band is triggered and he needs to pull away. He cannot give her what she needs. He emphatically agreed and said, "Yes, that's right. When I want to pull away, she wants to talk."

When a man needs to pull away and a woman needs to talk, his trying to listen only makes matters worse. After a short time he either will be judging her and possibly explode with anger or he will become incredibly tired or distracted, and she will become more upset. When he is not capable of listening attentively with caring, understanding, and respect, these three actions can help:

THREE STEPS FOR SUPPORTING HER WHEN HE NEEDS TO PULL AWAY

1. Accept Your Limitations
The first thing you need to do is accept that you need to pull away and have nothing to give. No matter how loving you want to be, you cannot listen attentively. Don't try to listen when you can't.

2. Understand Her Pain
Next, you need to understand that she needs more than you can give at this moment. Her pain is valid. Don't make her wrong for needing more or for being hurt. It hurts to be abandoned when she needs your love. You are not wrong for needing space, and she is not wrong for wanting to be close. You may be afraid that she will not forgive you or trust. She can be more trusting and forgiving if you are caring and understanding of her hurt.

3. Avoid Arguing and Give Reassurance

By understanding her hurt you won't make her wrong for being upset and in pain. Although you can't give the support she wants and needs, you can avoid making it worse by arguing. Reassure her that you will be back, and then you will be able to give her the support she deserves.

What He Can Say Instead of Arguing

There was nothing wrong with Harris's need to be alone or watch TV, nor was their anything wrong with Cathy's hurt feelings. Instead of arguing for his right to watch TV, he could have told her something like this: "I understand you're upset, and right now I really need to watch TV and relax. When I feel better we can talk." This would give him time to watch TV as well as an opportunity to cool off and prepare himself to listen to his partner's hurt without making her hurt feelings wrong.

She may not like this response, but she will respect it. Of course she wants him to be his usual loving self, but if he needs to pull away, then that is his valid need. He cannot give what he doesn't have. What he can do is avoid making things worse. The solution lies in respecting his needs as well as hers. He should take the time he needs and then go back and give her what she needs.

When a man can't listen to a woman's hurt feelings because he needs to pull away, he can say "I understand you feel hurt and I need some time to think about it. Let's take a time-out." For a man to excuse himself in this way and stop listening is much better than trying to explain away her hurt.

What She Can Do Instead of Arguing

In hearing this suggestion, Cathy said, "If he gets to be in his cave then what about me? I give him space, but what do I get?"

What Cathy gets is the best her partner can give at the time. By not demanding that he listen to her when she wants to talk, she can avoid making the problem much worse by having a huge argument. Second, she gets his support when he comes back–when he is truly capable of supporting her.

Remember, if a man needs to pull away like a rubber band, when he returns he will be back with a lot more love. Then he can listen. This is the best time to initiate conversation.

Accepting a man's need to go into the cave does not mean giving up the need to talk. It means giving up the demand that he listen whenever she wants to talk. Cathy learned to accept that sometimes a man can't listen or talk and learned that at other times he could. Timing was very important. She was encouraged not to give up initiating conversation but to find those other times when he could listen.

When a man pulls away is the time to get more support from friends. If Cathy feels the need to talk but Harris can't listen, then Cathy could talk more with her friends. It puts too much pressure on a man to make him the only source of love and support. When a woman's wave crashes and her partner is in his cave, it is essential that she have other sources of support. Otherwise she can't help but feel powerless and resent her partner.

> It puts too much pressure on a man
> to make him the only source of love and support.

HOW MONEY CAN CREATE PROBLEMS

Chris said, "I am completely confused. When we got married we were poor. We both worked hard and we barely had enough money for the rent. Sometimes my wife, Pam, would complain about how hard her life was. I could understand it. But now we are rich. We both have successful careers. How can she still be unhappy and complain? Other women would give anything to be in her situation. All we do is fight. We were happier when we were poor; now we want a divorce."

Chris did not understand that women are like waves. When he married Pam, from time to time her wave would crash. At those times he would listen and understand her unhappiness. It was easy for him to validate her negative feelings because he shared them. From his perspective she had a good reason to be upset–they didn't have a lot of money.

Money Doesn't Fulfill Emotional Needs

Martians tend to think money is the solution to all problems. When Chris and Pam were poor and struggling to make ends meet, he would listen and empathize with her pain and resolve to make more money so she wouldn't be unhappy. Pam felt that he really cared.

But as their life improved financially she continued to get upset from time to time. He couldn't understand why she still wasn't happy. He thought she should be happy all the time because they were so rich. Pam felt that he didn't care about her.

Chris did not realize that money could not prevent Pam from being upset. When her wave would crash, they fought because he would invalidate her need to be upset. Ironically, the richer they became the more they fought.

When they were poor, money was the major focus of her pain, but as they became more financially secure she became more aware of what she was not getting emotionally. This progression is natural, normal, and predictable.

> As a woman's financial needs are fulfilled
> she becomes more aware of her emotional needs.

A Wealthy Woman Needs More Permission to Be Upset

I remember reading this quote in an article: "A wealthy woman can only get empathy from a wealthy psychiatrist." When a woman has a lot of money, people (and especially her husband) do not give her the right to be upset. She has no permission to be like a wave and crash from time to time. She has no permission to explore her feelings or to need more in any area of her life.

A woman with money is expected to be fulfilled all the time because her life could be so much worse without this financial abundance. This expectation is not only impractical but disrespectful. Regardless of wealth, status, privilege, or circumstances, a woman needs permission to be upset and allow her wave to crash.

Chris was encouraged when he realized he could make his wife happy. He remembered he had validated his wife's feelings when they were poor, and he could do it again even if they were rich. Instead of feeling hopeless, he realized he did know how to support her. He had just gotten sidetracked by thinking his money should make her happy when really his caring and understanding of her had been the source of her contentment.

FEELINGS ARE IMPORTANT

If a woman is not supported in being unhappy sometimes then she can never truly be happy. To be genuinely happy requires dipping down into the well to release, heal, and purify the emotions. This is a natural and healthy process.

If we are to feel the positive feelings of love, happiness, trust, and gratitude, we periodically also have to feel anger, sadness, fear, and sorrow. When a woman goes down into her well is when she can heal these negative emotions.

Men also need to process their negative feelings so that they can then experience their positive feelings. When a man goes into his cave is a time when he silently feels and processes his negative feelings. In chapter 11 we will explore a technique for releasing negative feelings that works equally well for women and men.

When a woman is on the upswing she can be fulfilled with what she has. But on the downswing she then will become aware of what she is missing. When she is feeling good she is capable of seeing and responding to the good things in her life. But when she is crashing, her loving vision becomes cloudy, and she reacts more to what is missing in her life.

Just as a glass of water can be viewed as half full or half empty, when a woman is on her way up she sees the fullness of her life. On the way down she sees the emptiness. Whatever emptiness she overlooks on the way up comes more into focus when she is on her way down into her well.

Without learning about how women are like waves men cannot understand or support their wives. They are confused when things get a lot better on the outside but worse in the relationship. By remembering this difference a man holds the key to giving his partner the love she deserves when she needs it the most.

CHAPTER 8

DISCOVERING OUR DIFFERENT
EMOTIONAL NEEDS

Men and women generally are unaware that they have different emotional needs. As a result they do not instinctively know how to support each other. Men typically give in relationships what men want, while women give what women want. Each mistakenly assumes that the other has the same needs and desires. As a result they both end up dissatisfied and resentful.

Both men and women feel they give and give but do not get back. They feel their love is unacknowledged and unappreciated. The truth is they are both giving love but not in the desired manner.

For example, a woman thinks she is being loving when she asks a lot of caring questions or expresses concern. As we have discussed before, this can be very annoying to a man. He may start to feel controlled and want space. She is confused, because if she were offered this kind of support she would be appreciative. Her efforts to be loving are at best ignored and at worst annoying.

Similarly, men think they are being loving, but the way they express their love may make a woman feel invalidated and unsupported. For example, when a woman gets upset, he thinks he is loving and supporting her by making comments that minimize the importance of her problems. He may say "Don't worry, it's not such a big deal." Or he may completely ignore her, assuming he is giving her a lot of "space" to cool off and go into her cave. What he thinks is support makes her feel minimized, unloved, and ignored.

As we have already discussed, when a woman is upset she needs to be heard and understood. Without this insight into different male and female needs, a man doesn't understand why his attempts to help fail.

THE TWELVE KINDS OF LOVE

Most of our complex emotional needs can be summarized as the need for love. Men and women each have six unique love needs that are all equally important. Men primarily need trust, acceptance, appreciation, admiration, approval, and encouragement. Women primarily need caring, understanding, respect, devotion, validation, and reassurance. The enormous task of figuring out what our partner needs is simplified greatly through understanding these twelve different kinds of love.

By reviewing this list you can easily see why your partner may not feel loved. And most important, this list can give you a direction to improve your relationships with the opposite sex when you don't know what else to do.

The Primary Love Needs of Women and Men

Here are the different kinds of love listed side by side:

Women need to receive	Men need to receive
1. Caring	1. Trust
2. Understanding	2. Acceptance
3. Respect	3. Appreciation
4. Devotion	4. Admiration
5. Validation	5. Approval
6. Reassurance	6. Encouragement

Understanding Your Primary Needs

Certainly every man and woman ultimately needs all twelve kinds of love. To acknowledge the six kinds of love primarily needed by women does not imply that men do not need these kinds of love. Men also need caring, understanding, respect, devotion, validation, and reassurance. What is meant by "primary need" is that fulfilling a primary need is required before one is able fully to receive and appreciate the other kinds of love.

> Fulfilling a primary need is required
> before one is able fully to receive and appreciate
> the other kinds of love.

A man becomes fully receptive to and appreciative of the six kinds of love primarily needed by women (caring, understanding, respect, devotion, validation, and reassurance) when his own primary needs are first fulfilled. Likewise a woman needs trust, acceptance, appreciation, admiration, approval, and encouragement. But before she can truly value and appreciate these kinds of love, her primary needs first must be fulfilled.

Understanding the primary kinds of love that your partner needs is a powerful secret for improving relationships on Earth. Remembering that men are from Mars will help you remember and accept that men have different primary love needs.

It's easy for a woman to give what she needs and forget that her favorite Martian may need something else. Likewise men tend to focus on their needs, losing track of the fact that the kind of love they need is not always appropriate for or supportive of their favorite Venusian.

The most powerful and practical aspect of this new understanding of love is that these different kinds of love are reciprocal. For example, when a Martian expresses his caring and understanding, a Venusian automatically begins to reciprocate and return to him the trust and acceptance that he primarily needs. The same thing happens when a Venusian expresses her trust–a Martian automatically will begin to reciprocate with the caring she needs.

In the following six sections we will define the twelve kinds of love in practical terms and reveal their reciprocal nature.

1. She Needs Caring and He Needs Trust

When a man shows interest in a woman's feelings and heartfelt concern for her well-being, she feels loved and cared for. When he makes her feel special in this caring way, he succeeds in fulfilling her first primary need. Naturally she begins to trust him more. When she trusts, she becomes more open and receptive.

When a woman's attitude is open and receptive toward a man he feels trusted. To trust a man is to believe that he is doing his best and that he wants the best for his partner. When a woman's reactions reveal a positive belief in her man's abilities and intentions, his first primary love need is fulfilled. Automatically he is more caring and attentive to her feelings and needs.

2. She Needs Understanding and He Needs Acceptance

When a man listens without judgment but with empathy and relatedness to a woman express her feelings, she feels heard and understood. An understanding attitude doesn't presume to already know a person's thoughts or feelings; instead, it gathers meaning from what is heard, and moves toward validating what is being communicated. The more a woman's need to be heard and understood is fulfilled, the easier it is for her to give her man the acceptance he needs.

When a woman lovingly receives a man without trying to change him, he feels accepted. An accepting attitude does not reject but affirms that he is being favorably received. It does not mean the woman believes he is perfect but indicates that she is not trying to improve him, that she trusts him to make his own improvements. When a man feels accepted it is much easier for him to listen and give her the understanding she needs and deserves.

3. She Needs Respect and He Needs Appreciation

When a man responds to a woman in a way that acknowledges and prioritizes her rights, wishes, and needs, she feels respected. When his behavior takes into consideration her thoughts and feelings, she is sure to feel respected. Concrete and physical expressions of respect, like flowers and remembering anniversaries, are essential to fulfill a woman's third primary love need. When she feels respected it is much easier for her to give her man the appreciation that he deserves.

When a woman acknowledges having received personal benefit and value from a man's efforts and behavior, he feels appreciated. Appreciation is the natural reaction to being supported. When a man is appreciated he knows his effort is not wasted and is thus encouraged to give more. When a man is appreciated he is automatically empowered and motivated to respect his partner more.

4. She Needs Devotion and He Needs Admiration

When a man gives priority to a woman's needs and proudly commits himself to supporting and fulfilling her, her fourth primary love need is fulfilled. A woman thrives when she feels adored and special. A man fulfills her need to be loved in this way when he makes her feelings and needs more important than his other interests–like work, study, and recreation. When a woman feels that she is number one in his life then, quite easily, she admires him.

Just as a woman needs to feel a man's devotion, a man has a primary need to feel a woman's admiration. To admire a man is to regard him with wonder, delight, and pleased approval. A man feels admired when she is happily amazed by his unique characteristics or talents, which may include humor, strength, persistence, integrity, honesty, romance, kindness, love, understanding, and other so-called old-fashioned virtues. When a man feels admired, he feels secure enough to devote himself to his woman and adore her.

5. She Needs Validation and He Needs Approval

When a man does not object to or argue with a woman's feelings and wants but instead accepts and confirms their validity, a woman truly feels loved because her fifth primary need is fulfilled. A man's validating attitude confirms a woman's right to feel the way she does. (It is important to remember one can validate her point of view while having a different point of view.) When a man learns how to let a woman know that he has this validating attitude, he is assured of getting the approval that he primarily needs.

Deep inside, every man wants to be his woman's hero or knight in shining armor. The signal that he has passed her tests is her approval. A woman's approving attitude acknowledges the goodness in a man and expresses overall satisfaction with him. (Remember, giving approval to a man doesn't always mean agreeing with him.) An approving attitude recognizes or looks for the good reasons behind what he does. When he receives the approval he needs, it becomes easier for him to validate her feelings.

6. She Needs Reassurance and He Needs Encouragement

When a man repeatedly shows that he cares, understands, respects, validates, and is devoted to his partner, her primary need to be reassured is fulfilled. A reassuring attitude tells a woman that she is continually loved.

A man commonly makes the mistake of thinking that once he has met all of a woman's primary love needs, and she feels happy and secure, that she should know from then on that she is loved. This is not the case. To fulfill her sixth primary love need he must remember to reassure her again and again.

> A man commonly makes the mistake of thinking that once he has met all of a woman's primary love needs, and she feels happy and secure, that she should know from then on that she is loved.

Similarly, a man primarily needs to be encouraged by a woman. A woman's encouraging attitude gives hope and courage to a man by expressing confidence in his abilities and character. When a woman's attitude expresses trust, acceptance, appreciation, admiration, and approval it encourages a man to be all that he can be. Feeling encouraged motivates him to give her the loving reassurance that she needs.

The best comes out in a man when his six primary love needs are fulfilled. But when a woman doesn't know what he primarily needs and gives a caring love rather than a trusting love, she may unknowingly sabotage their relationship. This next story exemplifies this point.

THE KNIGHT IN SHINING ARMOR

Deep inside every man there is a hero or a knight in shining armor. More than anything, he wants to succeed in serving and protecting the woman he loves. When he feels trusted, he is able to tap into this noble part of himself. He becomes more caring. When he doesn't feel trusted he loses some of his aliveness and energy, and after a while he can stop caring.

Imagine a knight in shining armor traveling through the countryside. Suddenly he hears a woman crying out in distress. In an instant he comes alive. Urging his horse to a gallop, he races to her castle, where she is trapped by a dragon. The noble knight pulls out his sword and slays the dragon. As a result, he is lovingly received by the princess.

As the gates open he is welcomed and celebrated by the family of the princess and the townspeople. He is invited to live in the town and is acknowledged as a hero. He and the princess fall in love.

A month later the noble knight goes off on another trip. On his way back, he hears his beloved princess crying out for help. Another dragon has attacked the castle. When the knight arrives he pulls out his sword to slay the dragon.

Before he swings, the princess cries out from the tower, "Don't use your sword, use this noose. It will work better."

She throws him the noose and motions to him instructions about how to use it. He hesitantly follows her instructions. He wraps it around the dragon's neck and then pulls hard. The dragon dies and everyone rejoices.

At the celebration dinner the knight feels he didn't really do anything. Somehow, because he used her noose and didn't use his sword, he doesn't quite feel worthy of the town's trust and admiration. After the event he is slightly depressed and forgets to shine his armor.

A month later he goes on yet another trip. As he leaves with his sword, the princess reminds him to be careful and tells him to take the noose. On his way home, he sees yet another dragon attacking the castle. This time he rushes forward with his sword but hesitates, thinking maybe he should use the noose. In that moment of hesitation, the dragon breathes fire and burns his right arm. In confusion he looks up and sees his princess waving from the castle window.

"Use the poison," she yells. "The noose doesn't work."

She throws him the poison, which he pours into the dragon's mouth, and the dragon dies. Everyone rejoices and celebrates, but the knight feels ashamed.

A month later, he goes on another trip. As he leaves with his sword, the princess reminds him to be careful, and to bring the noose and the poison. He is annoyed by her suggestions but brings them just in case.

This time on his journey he hears another woman in distress. As he rushes to her call, his depression is lifted and he feels confident and alive. But as he draws his sword to slay the dragon, he again hesitates. He wonders, Should I use my sword, the noose, or the poison? What would the princess say?

For a moment he is confused. But then he remembers how he had felt before he knew the princess, back in the days when he only carried a sword. With a burst of renewed confidence he throws off the noose and poison and charges the dragon with his trusted sword. He slays the dragon and the townspeople rejoice.

The knight in shining armor never returned to his princess. He stayed in this new village and lived happily ever after. He eventually

married, but only after making sure his new partner knew nothing
about nooses and poisons.

Remembering that within every man is a knight in shining
armor is a powerful metaphor to help you remember a man's primary needs. Although a man may appreciate caring and assistance
sometimes, too much of it will lessen his confidence or turn him off.

HOW YOU MAY BE UNKNOWINGLY TURNING OFF YOUR PARTNER

Without an awareness of what is important for the opposite sex,
men and women don't realize how much they may be hurting their
partners. We can see that both men and women unknowingly communicate in ways that are not only counterproductive but may even
be a turnoff.

Men and women get their feelings hurt most easily when they
do not get the kind of primary love they need. Women generally
don't realize the ways they communicate that are unsupportive and
hurtful to the male ego. A woman may try to be sensitive to a man's
feelings, but because his primary love needs are different from hers,
she doesn't instinctively anticipate his needs.

Through understanding a man's primary love needs, a woman
can be more aware and sensitive to the sources of his discontent.
The following is a list of common communication mistakes women
make in relation to a man's primary love needs.

Mistakes women commonly make	Why he doesn't feel loved
1. She tries to improve his behavior or help him by offering unsolicited advice.	1. He feels unloved because she doesn't *trust* him anymore.
2. She tries to change or control his behavior by sharing her upset or negative feelings. (It is OK to share feelings but not when they attempt to manipulate or punish.)	2. He feels unloved because she doesn't *accept* him as he is.

Mistakes women commonly make	Why he doesn't feel loved
3. She doesn't acknowledge what he does for her but complains about what he has not done.	3. He feels taken for granted and unloved because she doesn't *appreciate* what he does.
4. She corrects his behavior and tells him what to do, as if he were a child.	4. He feels unloved because he does not feel *admired*.
5. She expresses her upset feelings indirectly with rhetorical questions like "How could you do that?"	5. He feels unloved because he feels she has taken away her *approval* of him. He no longer feels like the good guy.
6. When he makes decisions or takes initiatives she corrects or criticizes him.	6. He feels unloved because she does not *encourage* him to do things on his own.

Just as women easily make mistakes when they don't understand what men primarily need, men also make mistakes. Men generally don't recognize the ways they communicate that are disrespectful and unsupportive to women. A man may even know that she is unhappy with him, but unless he understands *why* she feels unloved and *what* she needs he cannot change his approach.

Through understanding a woman's primary needs, a man can be more sensitive to and respectful of her needs. The following is a list of communication mistakes men make in relation to a woman's primary emotional needs.

Mistakes men make	Why she doesn't feel loved
1. He doesn't listen, gets easily distracted, doesn't ask interested or concerned questions.	1. She feels unloved because he is not attentive or showing that he *cares*.

Mistakes men make	**Why she doesn't feel loved**
2. He takes her feelings literally and corrects her. He thinks she is asking for solutions so he gives advice.	2. She feels unloved because he doesn't *understand* her.
3. He listens but then gets angry and blames her for upsetting him or for bringing him down.	3. She feels unloved because he doesn't *respect* her feelings.
4. He minimizes the importance of her feelings and needs. He makes children or work more important.	4. She feels unloved because he is not *devoted* to her and doesn't honor her as special.
5. When she is upset, he explains why he is right and why she should not be upset.	5. She feels unloved because he doesn't *validate* her feelings but instead makes her feel wrong and unsupported.
6. After listening he says nothing or just walks away.	6. She feels insecure because she doesn't get the *reassurance* she needs.

WHEN LOVE FAILS

Love often fails because people instinctively give what they want. Because a woman's primary love needs are to be cared for, understood, and so forth, she automatically gives her man a lot of caring and understanding. To a man this caring support often feels as though she doesn't trust him. Being trusted is his primary need, not being cared for.

Then, when he doesn't respond positively to her caring she can't understand why he doesn't appreciate her brand of support. He, of course, is giving his own brand of love, which isn't what she needs. So they are caught in a loop of failing to fulfill each other's needs.

Beth complained, saying, "I just can't keep giving and not getting back. Arthur doesn't appreciate what I give. I love him, but he doesn't love me."

Arthur complained, saying, "Nothing I do is ever good enough. I don't know what to do. I've tried everything and she still doesn't love me. I love her, but it's just not working."

Beth and Arthur have been married for eight years. They both felt like giving up because they didn't feel loved. Ironically, they *both* claimed to be giving more love than they were getting back. Beth believed she was giving more, while Arthur thought he was giving the most. In truth they were both giving, but neither was getting what they wanted or needed.

They did love each other, but because they didn't understand their partner's primary needs their love wasn't getting through. Beth was giving what she needed to receive while Arthur was giving what he wanted. Gradually they burned out.

Many people give up when relationships become too difficult. Relationships become easier when we understand our partner's primary needs. Without giving more but by giving what is required we do not burn out. This understanding of the twelve different kinds of love finally explains why our sincere loving attempts fail. To fulfill your partner, you need to learn how to give the love he or she *primarily* needs.

LEARNING TO LISTEN WITHOUT GETTING ANGRY

The number one way a man can succeed in fulfilling a woman's primary love needs is through communication. As we have discussed before, communication is particularly important on Venus. By learning to listen to a woman's feelings, a man can effectively shower a woman with caring, understanding, respect, devotion, validation, and reassurance.

One of the biggest problems men have with listening to women is that they become frustrated or angry because they forget that women are from Venus and that they are supposed to communicate differently. The chart below outlines some ways to remember these differences and makes some suggestions about what to do.

HOW TO LISTEN WITHOUT GETTING ANGRY

<u>What to remember</u>	<u>What to do and what not to do</u>
1. Remember anger comes from not understanding her point of view, and this is never her fault.	1. Take responsibility to understand. Don't blame her for upsetting you. Start again trying to understand.
2. Remember that feelings don't always make sense right away, but they're still valid and need empathy.	2. Breathe deeply, don't say anything! Relax and let go of trying to control. Try to imagine how you would feel if you saw the world through her eyes.
3. Remember that anger may come from not knowing what to do to make things better. Even if she doesn't immediately feel better, your listening and understanding are helping.	3. Don't blame her for not feeling better from your solutions. How can she feel better when solutions are not what she needs? Resist the urge to offer solutions.
4. Remember you don't have to agree to understand her point of view or to be appreciated as a good listener.	4. If you wish to express a differing point of view make sure she is finished and then rephrase her point of view before giving your own. Do not raise your voice.
5. Remember you don't fully have to understand her point of view to succeed in being a good listener.	5. Let her know you don't understand but want to. Take responsibility for not understanding; don't judge her or imply she can't be understood.

What to remember	**What to do and what not to do**
6. Remember you are not responsible for how she feels. She may sound as though she is blaming you, but she is really needing to be understood.	6. Refrain from defending yourself until she feels that you understand and care. Then it is OK gently to explain yourself or to apologize.
7. Remember that if she makes you really angry she is probably mistrusting you. Deep inside her is a scared little girl who is afraid of opening up and being hurt and who needs your kindness and compassion.	7. Don't argue with her feelings and opinions. Take time out and discuss things later when there is less emotional charge. Practice the Love Letter technique as described in chapter 11.

When a man can listen to a woman's feelings without getting angry and frustrated, he gives her a wonderful gift. He makes it safe for her to express herself. The more she is able to express herself, the more she feels heard and understood, and the more she is able to give a man the loving trust, acceptance, appreciation, admiration, approval, and encouragement that he needs.

THE ART OF EMPOWERING A MAN

Just as men need to learn the art of listening to fulfill a woman's primary love needs, women need to learn the art of empowerment. When a woman enlists the support of a man, she empowers him to be all that he can be. A man feels empowered when he is trusted, accepted, appreciated, admired, approved of, and encouraged.

Like in our story of the knight in shining armor, many women try to help their man by improving him but unknowingly weaken or hurt him. Any attempt to change him takes away the loving trust, acceptance, appreciation, admiration, approval, and encouragement that are his primary needs.

The secret of empowering a man is never to try to change him or improve him. Certainly you may want him to change—just don't act on that desire. Only if he directly and specifically asks for advice is he open to assistance in changing.

> The secret of empowering a man is
> never to try to change him or improve him.

Give Trust and Not Advice

On Venus, it is considered a loving gesture to offer advice. But on Mars it is not. Women need to remember that Martians do not offer advice unless it is directly requested. A way of showing love is to trust another Martian to solve his problems on his own.

This doesn't mean a woman has to squash her feelings. It's OK for her to feel frustrated or even angry, as long as she doesn't try to change him. Any attempt to change him is unsupportive and counterproductive.

When a woman loves a man, she often begins trying to improve their relationship. In her exuberance she makes him a target for her improvements. She begins a gradual process of slowly rehabilitating him.

Why Men Resist Change

In a myriad of ways she tries to change him or improve him. She thinks her attempts to change him are loving, but he feels controlled, manipulated, rejected, and unloved. He will stubbornly reject her because he feels she is rejecting him. When a woman tries to change a man, he is not getting the loving trust and acceptance he actually needs to change and grow.

When I ask a room filled with hundreds of women and men they all have had the same experience: the more a woman tries to change a man, the more he resists.

The problem is that when a man resists her attempts to improve him, she misinterprets his response. She mistakenly thinks he is not willing to change, probably because he does not love her enough. The truth is, however, that he is resistant to changing because he believes he is not being loved enough. When a man feels loved, trusted, accepted, appreciated, and so forth, automatically he begins to change, grow, and improve.

Two Kinds of Men/One Kind of Behavior

There are two kinds of men. One will become incredibly defensive and stubborn when a woman tries to change him, while the other will agree to change but later will forget and revert back to the old behavior. A man either actively resists or passively resists.

When a man does not feel loved just the way he is, he will either consciously or unconsciously repeat the behavior that is not being accepted. He feels an inner compulsion to repeat the behavior until he feels loved and accepted.

For a man to improve himself he needs to feel loved in an accepting way. Otherwise he defends himself and stays the same. He needs to feel accepted just the way he is, and then he, on his own, will look for ways to improve.

Men Don't Want to Be Improved

Just as men want to explain why women shouldn't be upset, women want to explain why men shouldn't behave the way they do. Just as men mistakenly want to "fix" women, women mistakenly try to "improve" men.

Men see the world through Martian eyes. Their motto is "don't fix it, if it isn't broken." When a woman attempts to change a man, he receives the message that she thinks he is broken. This hurts a man and makes him very defensive. He doesn't feel loved and accepted.

> The best way to help a man grow is to let go of *trying* to change him in any way.

A man needs to be accepted regardless of his imperfections. To accept a person's imperfections is not easy, especially when we see how he could become better. It does, however, become easier when we understand that the best way to help him grow is to let go of *trying* to change him in any way.

The following chart lists ways a woman can support a man in growing and changing by giving up trying to change him in any way:

HOW TO GIVE UP TRYING TO CHANGE A MAN

What she needs to remember

1. Remember: don't ask him too many questions when he is upset or he will feel you are trying to change him.

2. Remember: give up trying to improve him in any way. He needs your love, not rejection, to grow.

3. Remember: when you offer unsolicited advice he may feel mistrusted, controlled, or rejected.

4. Remember: when a man becomes stubborn and resists change he is not feeling loved; he is afraid to admit his mistakes for fear of not being loved.

5. Remember: if you make sacrifices hoping he will do the same for you then he will feel pressured to change.

What she can do

1. Ignore that he is upset unless he wants to talk to you about it. Show some initial concern, but not too much, as an invitation to talk.

2. Trust him to grow on his own. Honestly share feelings but without the demand that he change.

3. Practice patience and trust that he will learn on his own what he needs to learn. Wait until he asks for your advice.

4. Practice showing him that he doesn't have to be perfect to deserve your love. Practice forgiveness. (See chapter 11.)

5. Practice doing things for yourself and not depending on him to make you happy.

What she needs to remember	**What she can do**
6. Remember: you can share negative feelings without trying to change him. When he feels accepted it is easier for him to listen.	6. When sharing feelings, let him know that you are not trying to tell him what to do but that you want him to take your feelings into consideration.
7. Remember: if you give him directions and make decisions for him he will feel corrected and controlled.	7. Relax and surrender. Practice accepting imperfection. Make his feelings more important than perfection and don't lecture or correct him.

As men and women learn to support each other in the ways that are most important for their own unique needs, change and growth will become automatic. With a greater awareness of your partner's six primary needs you can redirect your loving support according to their needs and make your relationships dramatically easier and more fulfilling.

CHAPTER 9
HOW TO AVOID
ARGUMENTS

One of the most difficult challenges in our loving relationships is handling differences and disagreements. Often when couples disagree their discussions can turn into arguments and then without much warning into battles. Suddenly they stop talking in a loving manner and automatically begin hurting each other: blaming, complaining, accusing, demanding, resenting, and doubting.

Men and women arguing in this way hurt not only their feelings but also their relationship. Just as communication is the most important element in a relationship, arguments can be the most destructive element, because the closer we are to someone, the easier it is to bruise or be bruised.

> Just as communication is the most important element in a relationship, arguments can be the most destructive element.

For all practical purposes I strongly recommend that couples not argue. When two people are not sexually involved it is a lot easier to remain detached and objective while arguing or debating. But when couples argue who are emotionally involved and especially sexually involved, they easily take things too personally.

As a basic guideline: never argue. Instead discuss the pros and cons of something. Negotiate for what you want but don't argue. It is possible to be honest, open, and even express negative feelings without arguing or fighting.

Some couples fight all the time, and gradually their love dies. On the other extreme, some couples suppress their honest feelings in order to avoid conflict and not argue. As a result of suppressing their true feelings they lose touch with their loving feelings as well. One couple is having a war while the other is having a cold war.

It is best for a couple to find a balance between these two extremes. By remembering we are from different planets and thus developing good communication skills, it is possible to avoid arguments without suppressing negative feelings and conflicting ideas and desires.

WHAT HAPPENS WHEN WE ARGUE

Without understanding how men and women are different it is very easy to get into arguments that hurt not only our partner but also ourselves. The secret to avoiding arguments is loving and respectful communication.

The differences and disagreements don't hurt as much as the ways in which we communicate them. Ideally an argument does not have to be hurtful; instead it can simply be an engaging conversation that expresses our differences and disagreements. (Inevitably all couples will have differences and disagree at times.) But practically speaking most couples start out arguing about one thing and, within five minutes, are arguing about the way they are arguing.

Unknowingly they begin hurting each other; what could have been an innocent argument, easily resolved with mutual understanding and an acceptance of differences, escalates into a battle. They refuse to accept or understand the content of their partner's point of view because of the way they are being approached.

Resolving an argument requires extending or stretching our

point of view to include and integrate another point of view. To make this stretch we need to feel appreciated and respected. If our partner's attitude is unloving, our self-esteem can actually be wounded by taking on their point of view.

> **Most couples start out arguing about one thing and, within five minutes, are arguing about the way they are arguing.**

The more intimate we are with someone, the more difficult it is objectively to hear their point of view without reacting to their negative feelings. To protect ourselves from feeling worthy of their disrespect or disapproval automatic defenses come up to resist their point of view. Even if we agree with their point of view, we may stubbornly persist in arguing with them.

WHY ARGUMENTS HURT

It is not *what* we say that hurts but *how* we say it. Quite commonly when a man feels challenged, his attention becomes focused on being right and he forgets to be loving as well. Automatically his ability to communicate in a caring, respectful, and reassuring tone decreases. He is aware neither of how uncaring he sounds nor of how hurtful this is to his partner. At such times, a simple disagreement may sound like an attack to a woman; a request turns into an order. Naturally a woman feels resistant to this unloving approach, even when she would be otherwise receptive to the content of what he was saying.

A man unknowingly hurts his partner by speaking in an uncaring manner and then goes on to explain why she should not be upset. He mistakenly assumes she is resisting the content of his point of view, when really his unloving delivery is what upsets her. Because he does not understand her reaction, he focuses more on explaining the merit of what he is saying instead of correcting the way he is saying it.

He has no idea that *he* is starting an argument; he thinks *she* is arguing with him. He defends his point of view while she defends *herself* from his sharpened expressions, which are hurtful to her.

When a man neglects to honor a woman's hurt feelings he invalidates them and increases her hurt. It is hard for him to understand her hurt because he is not as vulnerable to uncaring comments and tones. Consequently, a man may not even realize how much he is hurting his partner and thus provoking her resistance.

Similarly, women don't realize how they are hurtful to men. Unlike a man, when a woman feels challenged the tone of her speech automatically becomes increasingly mistrusting and rejecting. This kind of rejection is more hurtful to a man, especially when he is emotionally involved.

Women start and escalate arguments by first sharing negative feelings about their partner's behavior and then by giving unsolicited advice. When a women neglects to buffer her negative feelings with messages of trust and acceptance, a man responds negatively, leaving the woman confused. Again she is unaware of how hurtful her mistrust is to him.

To avoid arguing we need to remember that our partner objects not to what we are saying but to how we are saying it. It takes two to argue, but it only takes one to stop an argument. The best way to stop an argument is to nip it in the bud. Take responsibility for recognizing when a disagreement is turning into an argument. Stop talking and take a time-out. Reflect on how you are approaching your partner. Try to understand how you are not giving them what they need. Then, after some time has passed, come back and talk again but in a loving and respectful way. Time-outs allow us to cool off, heal our wounds, and center ourselves before trying to communicate again.

THE FOUR F'S FOR AVOIDING HURT

There are basically four stances that individuals take to avoid getting hurt in arguments. They are the four f's: fight, flight, fake, and fold. Each of these stances offers a short-term gain, but in the long run they are all counterproductive. Let's explore each of these positions.

1. Fight. This stance definitely comes from Mars. When a conversation becomes unloving and unsupportive some individuals instinctively begin to fight. They immediately move into an offensive stance. Their motto is "the best defense is a strong offense." They strike out by blaming, judging, criticizing, and making their partner look wrong. They tend to start yelling and express lots of anger. Their inner motive is to intimidate their partner into loving and supporting them. When their partner backs down, they assume they have won, but in truth they have lost.

Intimidation always weakens trust in a relationship.

Intimidation always weakens trust in a relationship. To muscle your way into getting what you want by making others look wrong is a sure way to fail in a relationship. When couples fight they gradually lose their ability to be open and vulnerable. Women close up to protect themselves and men shut down and stop caring as much. Gradually they lose whatever intimacy they had in the beginning.

2. Flight. This stance also come from Mars. To avoid confrontation Martians may retire into their caves and never come out. This is like a cold war. They refuse to talk and nothing gets resolved. This passive-aggressive behavior is not the same as taking a time-out and then coming back to talk and resolve things in a more loving fashion.

These Martians are afraid of confrontation and would rather lie low and avoid talking about any topics that may cause an argument. They walk on eggshells in a relationship. Women commonly complain they have to walk on eggshells, but men do also. It is so ingrained in men that they don't even realize how much they do it.

Rather than arguing, some couples will simply stop talking about their disagreements. Their way of trying to get what they want is to punish their partner by withholding love. They do not come out and directly hurt their partners, like the fighters. Instead they indirectly hurt them by slowly depriving them of the love they deserve. By withholding love our partners are sure to have less to give us.

The short-term gain is peace and harmony, but if issues are not being talked about and feelings are not being heard then resentments will build. In the long run, they lose touch with the passionate and loving feelings that drew them together. They generally use overworking, overeating, or other addictions as a way to numb their unresolved painful feelings.

3. Fake. This stance comes from Venus. To avoid being hurt in a confrontation this person pretends that there is no problem. She puts a smile on her face and appears to be very agreeable and happy with everything. Over time, however, these women become increasingly resentful; they are always giving to their partner but they do not get what they need in return. This resentment blocks the natural expression of love.

They are afraid to be honest about their feelings, so they try to make everything "all right, OK, and fine." Men commonly use these phrases, but for them they mean something completely different. He means "It is OK because I am dealing with it alone" or "It's all right because I know what to do" or "It's fine because I am handling it, and I don't need any help." Unlike a man, when a woman uses these phrases it may be a sign that she is trying to avoid a conflict or argument.

To avoid making waves, a woman may even fool herself and believe that everything is OK, fine, and all right when it really isn't. She sacrifices or denies her wants, feelings, and needs to avoid the possibility of conflict.

4. Fold. This stance also comes from Venus. Rather than argue this person gives in. They will take the blame and assume responsibility for whatever is upsetting their partner. In the short run they create what looks like a very loving and supportive relationship, but they end up losing themselves.

A man once complained to me about his wife. He said, "I love her so much. She gives me everything I want. My only complaint is she is not happy." His wife had spent twenty years denying herself for her husband. They never fought, and if you asked her about her relationship she would say "We have a great relationship. My husband is so loving. Our only problem is me. I am depressed and I don't know why." She is depressed because she has denied herself by being agreeable for twenty years.

To please their partners these people intuitively sense their partners' desires and then mold themselves in order to please. Eventually they resent having to give up themselves for love.

Any form of rejection is very painful because they are already rejecting themselves so much. They seek to avoid rejection at all costs and want to be loved by all. In this process they literally give up who they are.

You may have found yourself in one of these four f's or in many of them. People commonly move from one to the other. In each of the above four strategies our intention is to protect ourselves from being hurt. Unfortunately, it does not work. What works is to identify arguments and stop. Take a time-out to cool off and then come back and talk again. Practice communicating with increased understanding and respect for the opposite sex and you will gradually learn to avoid arguments and fights.

WHY WE ARGUE

Men and women commonly argue about money, sex, decisions, scheduling, values, child rearing, and household responsibilities. These discussions and negotiations, however, turn into painful arguments for only one reason–we are not feeling loved. Emotional pain comes from not feeling loved, and when a person is feeling emotional pain it is hard to be loving.

Because women are not from Mars, they do not instinctively realize what a man needs in order to deal successfully with disagreements. Conflicting ideas, feelings, and desires are a difficult challenge for a man. The closer he is to a woman, the harder it is to deal with differences and disagreements. When she doesn't like something he has done, he tends to take it very personally and feels she doesn't like him.

A man can handle differences and disagreements best when his emotional needs are being fulfilled. When he is deprived of the love he needs, however, he becomes defensive and his dark side begins to emerge; instinctively he draws his sword.

On the surface he may seem to be arguing about the issue (money, responsibilities, and so forth), but the real reason he has drawn his sword is he doesn't feel loved. When a man argues about money, scheduling, children, or any other issue, secretly he may be arguing for some of the following reasons:

THE SECRET REASONS MEN ARGUE

The hidden reason he is arguing	What he needs not to argue
1. "I don't like it when she gets upset over the smallest things I do or don't do. I feel criticized, rejected, and unaccepted."	1. He needs to feel accepted just the way he is. Instead he feels she is trying to improve him.
2. "I don't like it when she starts telling me how I should do things. I don't feel admired. Instead I feel like I am being treated like a child."	2. He needs to feel admired. Instead he feels put down.
3. "I don't like it when she blames me for her unhappiness. I don't feel encouraged to be her knight in shining armor."	3. He needs to feel encouraged. Instead he feels like giving up.

The hidden reason he is arguing	What he needs not to argue
4. "I don't like it when she complains about how much she does or how unappreciated she feels. It makes me feel unappreciated for the things I do for her."	4. He needs to feel appreciated. Instead he feels blamed, unacknowledged, and powerless.
5. "I don't like it when she worries about everything that could go wrong. I don't feel trusted."	5. He needs to feel trusted and appreciated for his contribution to her security. Instead he feels responsible for her anxiety.
6. "I don't like it when she expects me to do things or talk when she wants me to. I don't feel accepted or respected."	6. He needs to feel accepted just the way he is. Instead he feels controlled or pressured to talk and thus has nothing to say. It makes him feel that he can never satisfy her.
7. "I don't like it when she feels hurt by what I say. I feel mistrusted, misunderstood, and pushed away."	7. He needs to feel accepted and trusted. Instead he feels rejected and unforgiven.
8. "I don't like it when she expects me to read her mind. I can't. It makes me feel bad or inadequate."	8. He needs to feel approved of and accepted. Instead he feels like a failure.

Fulfilling a man's primary emotional needs will diminish his tendency to engage in hurtful arguments. Automatically he will be able to listen and speak with much greater respect, understanding, and caring. In this way arguments, differences of opinion, and negative feelings can be resolved through conversation, negotiation, and compromise without escalating into hurtful arguments.

Women also contribute to hurtful arguments but for different reasons. On the surface she may be arguing about finances, responsibilities, or another issue, but secretly inside she is resisting her partner for some of these following reasons:

THE SECRET REASONS WOMEN ARGUE

The hidden reason she is arguing

What she needs not to argue

1. "I don't like it when he minimizes the importance of my feelings or requests. I feel dismissed and unimportant."

1. She needs to feel validated and cherished. Instead she feels judged and ignored.

2. "I don't like it when he forgets to do the things I ask, and then I sound like a nag. I feel like I am begging for his support."

2. She needs to feel respected and remembered. Instead she feels neglected and at the bottom of his list of priorities.

3. "I don't like it when he blames me for being upset. I feel like I have to be perfect to be loved. I am not perfect."

3. She needs him to understand why she is upset and reassure her that she is still loved and that she doesn't have to be perfect. Instead she feels unsafe to be herself.

4. "I don't like it when he raises his voice or starts making lists of why he is right. It makes me feel like I am wrong and he doesn't care about my point of view."

4. She needs to feel understood and respected. Instead she feels unheard, bullied, and pushed down.

5. "I don't like his condescending attitude when I ask questions about decisions we need to make. It makes me feel like I am a burden or that I am wasting his time."

5. She needs to feel that he cares about her feelings and respects her need to gather information. Instead she feels disrespected and unappreciated.

The hidden reason she is arguing

What she needs not to argue

6. "I don't like it when he doesn't respond to my questions or comments. It makes me feel like I don't exist."

6. She needs to feel reassured that he is listening and that he cares. Instead she feels ignored or judged.

7. "I don't like it when he explains why I should not be hurt, worried, angry, or anything else. I feel invalidated and unsupported."

7. She needs to feel validated and understood. Instead she feels unsupported, unloved, and resentful.

8. "I don't like it when he expects me to be more detached. It makes me feel like it is wrong or weak to have feelings."

8. She needs to feel respected and cherished, especially when she is sharing her feelings. Instead she feels unsafe and unprotected.

Though all these painful feelings and needs are valid, they are generally not dealt with and communicated directly. Instead they build up inside and come bursting up during an argument. Sometimes they are directly addressed, but usually they come up and are expressed through facial expression, body posture, and tone of voice.

Men and women need to understand and cooperate with their particular sensitivities and not resent them. You will be addressing the true problem by trying to communicate in a way that fulfills your partner's emotional needs. Arguments can then truly become mutually supportive conversations necessary to resolve and negotiate differences and disagreements.

THE ANATOMY OF AN ARGUMENT

A hurtful argument usually has a basic anatomy. Maybe you can relate to the following example.

My wife and I went on a beautiful walk and picnic. After eating, everything seemed fine until I started talking about possible investments. Suddenly she became upset that I would consider investing a certain portion of our savings in aggressive stocks. From my point of view I was only considering it, but what she heard was that I was planning it (without even considering her point of view). She became upset that I would do such a thing. I became upset with her for being upset with me, and we had an argument.

I thought she disapproved of my investment choices and argued for their validity. My argument however was fueled by my anger that she was upset with me. She argued that aggressive stocks were too risky. But really she was upset that I would consider this investment without exploring her ideas on the subject. In addition she was upset that I was not respecting her right to be upset. Eventually I became so upset that she apologized to me for misunderstanding and mistrusting me and we cooled down.

Later on, after we had made up, she posed this question. She said, "Many times when we argue, it seems that I get upset about something, and then you get upset that I am upset, and then I have to apologize for upsetting you. Somehow I think something is missing. Sometimes I would like you to tell me you are sorry for upsetting me."

Immediately I saw the logic of her point of view. Expecting an apology from her did seem rather unfair, especially when I upset her first. This new insight transformed our relationship. As I shared this experience in my seminars I discovered that thousands of women could immediately identify with my wife's experience. It was another common male/female pattern. Let's review the basic pattern.

1. A woman expresses her upset
feelings about "XYZ."

2. A man explains why she
shouldn't be upset about "XYZ."

3. She feels invalidated and
becomes more upset. (She is
now more upset about being
invalidated than about "XYZ.")

4. He feels her disapproval and becomes upset. He blames her for upsetting him and expects an apology before making up.

5. She apologizes and wonders what happened, or she becomes more upset and the argument escalates into a battle.

With a clearer awareness of the anatomy of an argument, I was able to solve this problem in a fairer way. Remembering that women are from Venus, I practiced not blaming her for being upset. Instead I would seek to understand how I had upset her and show her that I cared. Even if she was misunderstanding me, if she felt hurt by me I needed to let her know that I cared and was sorry.

When she would become upset I learned first to listen, then genuinely to try to understand what she was upset about, and then to say, "I'm sorry that I upset you when I said ——." The result was immediate. We argued much less.

Sometimes, however, apologizing is very difficult. At those times I take a deep breath and say nothing. Inside I try to imagine how she feels and discover the reasons from her point of view. Then I say, "I'm sorry you feel so upset." Although this is not an apology it does say "I care," and that seems to help a lot.

> **Men rarely say "I'm sorry" because on Mars it means you have done something wrong and you are apologizing.**

Men rarely say "I'm sorry" because on Mars it means you have done something wrong and you are apologizing. Women, however, say "I'm sorry" as a way to say "I care about what you are feeling." It doesn't mean they are apologizing for doing something wrong. The men reading this who rarely say "I am sorry" can create wonders by learning to use this aspect of the Venusian language. The easiest way to derail an argument is to say "I'm sorry."

Most arguments escalate when a man begins to invalidate a woman's feelings and she responds to him disapprovingly. Being a man, I've had to learn to practice validating. My wife practiced expressing her feelings more directly without disapproving of me. The result was fewer fights and more love and trust. Without having this new awareness we probably would still be having the same arguments.

> Most arguments escalate when a man begins to invalidate a woman's feelings and she responds to him disapprovingly.

To avoid painful arguments it is important to recognize how men unknowingly invalidate and how women unknowingly send messages of disapproval.

How Men Unknowingly Start Arguments

The most common way men start arguments is by invalidating a woman's feelings or point of view. Men don't realize how much they invalidate.

For example, a man may make light of a woman's negative feelings. He might say "Ah, don't worry about it." To another man this phrase would seem friendly. But to a female intimate partner it is insensitive and hurts.

In another example, a man might try to resolve a woman's upset by saying "It's not such a big deal." Then he offers some practical solution to the problem, expecting her to be relieved and happy. He doesn't understand that she feels invalidated and unsupported. She cannot appreciate his solution until he validates her need to be upset.

A very common example is when a man has done something to upset a woman. His instinct is to make her feel better by explaining why she shouldn't be upset. He confidently explains that he has a perfectly good, logical, and rational reason for what he did. He has no idea that this attitude makes her feel as though she has no right to be upset. When he explains himself, the only message she may hear is that he doesn't care about her feelings.

For her to hear his good reasons, she first needs *him* to hear her good reasons for being upset. He needs to put his explanations on hold and listen with understanding. When he simply starts to care about her feelings she will start to feel supported.

This change in approach takes practice but can be achieved. Generally, when a woman shares feelings of frustration, disappointment, or worry *every* cell in a man's body instinctively reacts with a list of explanations and justifications designed to explain away her upset feelings. A man never intends to make matters worse. His tendency to explain away feelings is just Martian instinct.

By understanding that his automatic gut reactions in this instance are counterproductive, a man can, however, make this shift. Through a growing awareness and his experiences of what works with a woman, a man can make this change.

How Women Unknowingly Start Arguments

The most common way women unknowingly start arguments is by not being direct when they share their feelings. Instead of directly expressing her dislike or disappointment, a woman asks rhetorical questions and unknowingly (or knowingly) communicates a message of disapproval. Even though sometimes this is not the message she wants to give it is generally what a man will hear.

> The most common way women unknowingly start arguments is by not being direct when they share their feelings.

For example, when a man is late, a woman may feel "I don't like waiting for you when you are late" or "I was worried that something had happened to you." When he arrives, instead of directly sharing her feelings she asks a rhetorical question like "How could you be so late?" or "What am I supposed to think when you're so late?" or "Why didn't you call?"

Certainly asking someone "Why didn't you call?" is OK if you are sincerely looking for a valid reason. But when a woman is upset the tone of her voice often reveals that she is not looking for a valid answer but is making the point that there is no acceptable reason for being late.

When a man hears a question like "How could you be so late?" or "Why didn't you call?" he does not hear her feelings but instead hears her disapproval. He feels her intrusive desire to help him be more responsible. He feels attacked and becomes defensive. She has no idea how painful her disapproval is to him.

Just as women need validation, men need approval. The more a man loves a woman the more he needs her approval. It is always there in the beginning of a relationship. Either she gives him the message that she approves of him or he feels confident that he can win her approval. In either case the approval is present.

Even if a woman has been wounded by other men or her father she will still give approval in the beginning of the relationship. She may feel "He is a special man, not like others I have known."

A woman withdrawing that approval is particularly painful to a man. Women are generally oblivious of how they pull away their approval. And when they do pull it away, they feel very justified in doing so. A reason for this insensitivity is that women really are unaware of how significant approval is for men.

A woman can, however, learn to disagree with a man's behavior and still approve of who he is. For a man to feel loved he needs her to approve of who he is, even if she disagrees with his behavior. Generally when a woman disagrees with a man's behavior and she wants to change him, she will disapprove of him. Certainly there may be times when she is more approving and less approving of him, but to be *dis*approving is very painful and hurts him.

Most men are too ashamed to admit how much they need approval. They may go to great lengths to prove they don't care. But why do they immediately become cold, distant, and defensive when they lose a woman's approval? Because not getting what they need hurts.

One of the reasons relationships are so successful in the beginning is that a man is still in a woman's good graces. He is still her knight in shining armor. He receives the blessings of her approval and, as a result, rides high. But as soon as he begins to disappoint her, he falls from grace. He loses her approval. All of a sudden he is cast out into the doghouse.

A man can deal with a woman's disappointment, but when it is expressed with disapproval or rejection he feels wounded by her. Women commonly interrogate a man about his behavior with a disapproving tone. They do this because they think it will teach him a lesson. It does not. It only creates fear and resentment. And gradually he becomes less and less motivated.

To approve of a man is to see the good reasons behind what he does. Even when he is irresponsible or lazy or disrespectful, if she loves him, a woman can find and recognize the goodness within him. To approve is to find the loving intention or the goodness behind the outside behavior.

To treat a man as if he *has* no good reason for what he does is to withhold the approval she so freely gave in the beginning of the relationship. A woman needs to remember that she can still give approval even when she disagrees.

One critical pair of problems from which arguments arise:

1. The man feels that the woman disapproves of his point of view.
2. Or the woman disapproves of the way the man is talking to her.

When He Needs Her Approval the Most

Most arguments occur not because two people disagree but because either the man feels that the woman disapproves of his point of view or the woman disapproves of the way he is talking to her. She often may disapprove of him because he is not validating her point of view or speaking to her in a caring way. When men and women learn to approve and validate, they don't have to argue. They can discuss and negotiate differences.

When a man makes a mistake or forgets to do an errand or fulfill some responsibility, a woman doesn't realize how sensitive he feels. This is when he needs her love the most. To withdraw her approval at this point causes him extreme pain. She may not even realize she is doing it. She may think she is just feeling disappointed, but *he* feels her disapproval.

One of the ways women unknowingly communicate disapproval is in their eyes and tone of voice. The words she chooses may be loving, but her look or the tone of her voice can wound a man. His defensive reaction is to make her feel wrong. He invalidates her and justifies himself.

> **Men are most prone to argue**
> **when they have made a mistake**
> **or upset the woman they love.**

Men are most prone to argue when they have made a mistake or upset the woman they love. If he disappoints her, he wants to explain to her why she should not be so upset. He thinks his reasons will help her to feel better. What he doesn't know is that if she is upset, what she needs most is to be heard and validated.

HOW TO EXPRESS YOUR DIFFERENCES WITHOUT ARGUING

Without healthy role models, expressing differences and disagreements can be a very difficult task. Most of our parents either did not argue at all or when they did it quickly escalated into a fight. The following chart reveals how men and women unknowingly create arguments and suggests healthy alternatives.

In each of the types of arguments listed below I first provide a rhetorical question that a woman might ask and then show how a man might interpret that question. Then I show how a man might explain himself and how a woman could feel invalidated by what she hears. Finally I suggest how men and women can express themselves to be more supportive and avoid arguments.

THE ANATOMY OF AN ARGUMENT

1. When He Comes Home Late

Her rhetorical question

When he arrives late she says "How could you be so late?" or "Why didn't you call?" or "What am I supposed to think?"

The message he hears

The message he hears is "There is no good reason for you to be late! You are irresponsible. I would never be late. I am better than you."

What he explains

When he arrives late and she is upset he explains "There was a lot of traffic on the bridge" or "Sometimes life can't be the way you want" or "You can't expect me to always be on time."

The message she hears

What she hears is "You shouldn't be upset because I have these good and logical reasons for being late. Anyway my work is more important than you, and you are too demanding!"

How she can be less disapproving

She could say "I really don't like it when you are late. It is upsetting to me. I would really appreciate a call next time you are going to be late."

How he can be more validating

He says "I was late, I'm sorry I upset you." Most important is to just listen without explaining much. Try to understand and validate what she needs to feel loved.

2. When He Forgets Something

Her rhetorical question

When he forgets to do something, she says "How could you

The message he hears

The message he hears is "There is no good reason for forgetting. You forget?" or "When will you ever remember?" or "How am I supposed to trust you?"

are stupid and can't be trusted. I give so much more to this relationship."

What he explains

When he forgets to do something and she gets upset he explains "I was real busy and just forgot. These things just happen sometimes" or "It's not such a big deal. It doesn't mean I don't care."

How she can be less disapproving

If she is upset, she could say "I don't like it when you forget." She could also take another effective approach and simply not mention that he has forgotten something and just ask again, saying "I would appreciate it if you would...." (He will know he has forgotten.)

The message she hears

What she hears is "You shouldn't get so upset over such trivial matters. You are being too demanding and your response is irrational. Try to be more realistic. You live in a fantasy world."

How he can be more validating

He says "I did forget.... Are you angry with me?" Then let her talk without making her wrong for being angry. As she talks she will realize she is being heard and soon she will feel very appreciative of him.

3. When He Returns from His Cave

Her rhetorical question

When he comes back from his cave, she says "How could you be so unfeeling and cold?" or "How do you expect me to react?" or "*How am I supposed to know what's going on inside you?*"

The message he hears

The message he hears is "There is no good reason for pulling away from me. You are cruel and unloving. You are the wrong man for me. You have hurt me so much more than I have ever hurt you."

What he explains

When he comes back from his cave and she is upset he explains "I needed some time alone, it was only for two days. What is the big deal?" or "I didn't do anything to you. Why does it upset you so?"

The message she hears

What she hears is "You shouldn't feel hurt or abandoned, and if you do, I have no empathy for you. You are too needy and controlling. I will do whatever I want, I don't care about your feelings."

How she can be less disapproving

If it upsets her she could say "I know you need to pull away at times but it still hurts when you pull away. I'm not saying you are wrong but it is important to me for you to understand what I go through."

How he can be more validating

He says "I understand it hurts when I pull away. It must be very painful for you when I pull away. Let's talk about it." (When she feels heard then it is easier for her to accept his need to pull away at times.)

4. When He Disappoints Her

Her rhetorical question

When he disappoints her, she says "How could you do this?" or "Why can't you do what you say you are going to do?" or "Didn't you say you would do it?" or "When will you ever learn?"

The message he hears

The message he hears is "There is no good reason for disappointing me. You are an idiot. You can't do anything right. I can't be happy until you change!"

What he explains

When she is disappointed with him, he explains "Hey, next time I'll get it right" or "It's not such a big deal" or "But I didn't know what you meant."

The message she hears

What she hears is "If you are upset it is your fault. You should be more flexible. You shouldn't get upset, and I have no empathy for you."

How she can be less disapproving

If she is upset she could say "I don't like being disappointed. I thought you were going to call. It's OK and I need you to know how it feels when you..."

How he can be more validating

He says "I understand I disappointed you. Let's talk about it.... How did you feel?" Again let her talk. *Give her a chance to be heard* and she will feel better. After a while say to her "What do you need from me now to feel my support?" or "How can I support you now?"

5. When He Doesn't Respect Her Feelings and Hurts Her

Her rhetorical question

When he doesn't respect her feelings and hurts her, she says "How could you say that?" or "How could you treat me this way?" or "Why can't you listen to me?" or "Do you even care about me anymore?" or "Do I treat you this way?"

The message he hears

The message he hears is "You are a bad and abusive person. I am so much more loving than you. I will never forgive you for this. You should be punished and cast out. This is all your fault."

What he explains

When he doesn't respect her feelings and she gets even more upset, he explains "Look, I didn't mean that" or "I do listen to you; see I am doing so right now" or "I don't always ignore you" or "I am not laughing at you."

The message she hears

What she hears is "You have no right to be upset. You are not making any sense. You are too sensitive, something is wrong with you. You are such a burden."

How she can be less disapproving

She could say "I don't like the way you are talking to me. Please stop"

How he can be more validating

He says "I'm sorry, you don't deserve to be treated that way."

or "You are being mean and I don't appreciate it. I want to take a time-out" or "This is not the way I wanted to have this conversation. Let's start over" or "I don't deserve to be treated this way. I want to take a time-out" or "Would you please not interrupt" or "Would you please listen to what I am saying." (A man can respond best to short and direct statements. Lectures or questions are counterproductive.)

Take a deep breath and just listen to her response. She may carry on and say something like "You never listen." When she pauses, say "You are right. Sometimes I don't listen. I'm sorry, you don't deserve to be treated that way.... Let's start over. This time we will do it better." Starting a conversation over is an excellent way to keep an argument from escalating. If she doesn't want to start over don't make her feel wrong. Remember, if you give her the right to be upset then she will be more accepting and approving.

6. When He Is in a Hurry and She Doesn't Like It

Her rhetorical question

She complains "Why are we always in a hurry?" or "Why do you always have to rush places?"

The message he hears

The message he hears is "There is no good reason for this rushing! You never make me happy. Nothing will ever change you. You are incompetent and obviously you don't care about me."

What he explains

He explains "It's not so bad" or "This is the way it has always been" or "There is nothing we can do about it now" or "Don't worry so much; it will be fine."

The message she hears

What she hears is "You have no right to complain. You should be grateful for what you have and not be such a dissatisfied and unhappy person. There is no good reason to complain, you are bringing everyone down."

How she can be less disapproving

If she feels upset she can say "It's OK that we are rushing and I don't like it. It feels like we're always rushing" or "I love it when we are not in a hurry and I hate it sometimes when we have to rush, I just don't like it. Would you plan our next trip with fifteen minutes of extra time?"

How he can be more validating

He says "I don't like it either. I wish we could just slow down. It feels so crazy." In this example he has related to her feelings. Even if a part of him likes to rush, he can best support her in her moment of frustration by expressing how some part of himself sincerely relates to her frustration.

7. When She Feels Invalidated in a Conversation

Her rhetorical question

When she feels unsupported or invalidated in a conversation, she says "Why did you say that?" or "Why do you have to talk to me this way?" or "Don't you even care about what I'm saying?" or "How can you say that?"

The message he hears

The message he hears is "There is no good reason for treating me this way. Therefore you do not love me. You do not care. I give you so much and you give back nothing!"

What he explains

When she feels invalidated and gets upset, he explains "But you are not making sense" or "But that is not what I said" or "I've heard all this before."

The message she hears

What she hears is "You have no right to be upset. You are irrational and confused. I know what is right and you don't. I am superior to you. You cause these arguments, not me."

How she can be less disapproving

She could say "I don't like what you are saying. It feels as if you are judging me. I don't deserve that.

How he can be more validating

He says "I'm sorry it's not comfortable for you. What are you hearing me say?" By giving her a

Please understand me" or "I've had a hard day. I know this is not all your fault. And I need you to understand what I'm feeling. OK?" or she can simply overlook his comments and ask for what she wants, saying "I am in such a bad mood, would you listen to me for a while? It will help me feel so much better." (Men need lots of encouragement to listen.)

chance to reflect back what she has heard then he can again say "I'm sorry. I understand why you didn't like it." Then simply pause. This is a time to listen. Resist the temptation to explain to her that she is misinterpreting what you said. Once the hurt is there it needs to be heard if it is to be healed. Explanations are helpful only after the hurt is healed with some validation and caring understanding.

GIVING SUPPORT AT DIFFICULT TIMES

Any relationship has difficult times. They may occur for a variety of reasons, like loss of a job, death, illness, or just not enough rest. At these difficult times the most important thing is to try to communicate with a loving, validating, and approving attitude. In addition we need to accept and understand that we and our partners will not always be perfect. By learning successfully to communicate in response to the smaller upsets in a relationship it becomes easier to deal with the bigger challenges when they suddenly appear.

In each of the above examples I have placed the woman in the role of being upset with the man for something he did or didn't do. Certainly men can also be upset with women, and any of my suggestions listed above apply equally to both sexes. If you are in a relationship, asking your partner how he or she would respond to the suggestions listed above is a useful exercise.

Take some time when you are not upset with your partner to discover what words work best for them and share what works best for you. Adopting a few "prearranged agreed-upon statements" can be immensely helpful to neutralize tension when conflict arises.

Also, remember that no matter how correct your choice of words, the feeling behind your words counts most. Even if you were to use the exact phrases listed above, if your partner didn't feel your love, validation, and approval the tension would continue to in-crease. As I mentioned before, sometimes the best solution for avoiding conflict is to see it coming and lie low for a while. Take a time-out to center yourself so that you can then come together again with greater understanding, acceptance, validation, and approval.

Making some of these changes may at first feel awkward or even manipulative. Many people have the idea that love means "saying it like it is." This overly direct approach, however, does not take into account the listener's feelings. One can still be honest and direct about feelings but express them in a way that doesn't offend or hurt. By practicing some of the suggestions listed above, you will be stretching and exercising your ability to communicate in a more caring and trusting manner. After a while it will become more automatic.

If you are presently in a relationship and your partner is at-tempting to apply some of the above suggestions, keep in mind that they *are* trying to be more supportive. At first their expressions *may* seem not only unnatural but insincere. It is not possible to change a lifetime of conditioning in a few weeks. Be careful to appreciate their every step; otherwise they may quickly give up.

AVOIDING ARGUMENTS THROUGH LOVING COMMUNICATION

Emotionally charged arguments and quarrels can be avoided if we can understand what our partner needs and remember to give it. The following story illustrates how when a woman communicates directly her feelings and when a man validates those feelings an argument can be avoided.

I remember once leaving for a vacation with my wife. As we drove off in the car and could finally relax from a hectic week, I expected Bonnie to be happy that we were going on such a great vacation. Instead she gave a heavy sigh and said, "I feel like my life is a long, slow torture."

I paused, took a deep breath, and then replied, "I know what you mean, I feel like they are squeezing every ounce of life out of me." As I said this I made a motion as if I were wringing the water out of a rag.

Bonnie nodded her head in agreement and to my amazement she suddenly smiled and then changed the subject. She started talking about how excited she was to go on this trip. Six years ago this would not have happened. We would have had an argument and I would have mistakenly blamed it on her.

I would have been upset with her for saying her life was a long, slow torture. I would have taken it personally and felt that she was complaining about me. I would have become defensive and explained that our life was not a torture and that she should be grateful that we were going on such a wonderful vacation. Then we would have argued and had a long, torturous vacation. All this would have happened because I didn't understand and validate her feelings.

This time, I understood she was just expressing a passing feeling. It wasn't a statement about me. Because I understood this I didn't get defensive. By my comment about being wrung out she felt completely validated. In response, she was very accepting of me and I felt her love, acceptance, and approval. Because I have learned to validate her feelings, she got the love she deserved. We didn't have an argument.

CHAPTER

10

SCORING POINTS WITH
THE OPPOSITE SEX

A man thinks he scores high with a woman when he does something very big for her, like buying her a new car or taking her on a vacation. He assumes he scores less when he does something small, like opening the car door, buying her a flower, or giving her a hug. Based on this kind of score keeping, he believes he will fulfill her best by focusing his time, energy, and attention into doing something large for her. This formula, however, doesn't work because women keep score differently.

When a woman keeps score, no matter how big or small a gift of love is, it scores one point; each gift has equal value. Its size doesn't matter; it gets a point. A man, however, thinks he scores one point for one small gift and thirty points for a big gift. Since he doesn't understand that women keep score differently, he naturally focuses his energies into one or two big gifts.

> When a woman keeps score, no matter how big or small
> a gift of love is, it scores one point; each gift has equal value.

177

A man doesn't realize that to a woman the little things are just as important as the big things. In other words, to a woman, a single rose gets as many points as paying the rent on time. Without understanding this basic difference in score keeping, men and women are continually frustrated and disappointed in their relationships.

The following case illustrates this:

> In counseling, Pam said, "I do so much for Chuck and he ignores me. All he cares about is his work."
>
> Chuck said, "But my work pays for our beautiful house and allows us to go on vacations. She should be happy."
>
> Pam replied, "I don't care about this house or the vacations if we are not loving each other. I need more from you."
>
> Chuck said, "You make it sound like you give so much more."
>
> Pam said, "I do. I am always doing things for you. I do the wash, fix the meals, clean the house–everything. You do one thing–you go to work, which does pay the bills. But then you expect me to do everything else."

Chuck is a successful doctor. Like most professionals his work is very time consuming but very profitable. He couldn't understand why his wife, Pam, was so discontent. He earned a "good living" and he provided a "good life" for his wife and family, but when he came home his wife was unhappy.

In Chuck's mind, the more money he made at work, the less he needed to do at home to fulfill his wife. He thought his hefty paycheck at the end of the month scored him at least thirty points. When he opened his own clinic and doubled his income, he assumed he was now scoring sixty points a month. He had no idea that his paycheck earned him only one point each month with Pam–no matter how big it was.

Chuck did not realize that from Pam's point of view, the more he earned, the less she got. His new clinic required more time and energy. To pick up the slack she began to do even more to manage their personal life and relationship. As she gave more, she felt as if she was scoring about sixty points a month to his one. This made her very unhappy and resentful.

Pam felt she was giving much more and getting less. From Chuck's point of view he was now giving more (sixty points) and should get more from his wife. In his mind the score was even. He was satisfied with their relationship except for one thing–she wasn't happy. He blamed her for wanting too much. To him, his increased paycheck equaled what she was giving. This attitude made Pam even more angry.

After listening to my relationship course on tape, both Pam and Chuck were able to let go of their blame and solve their problem with love. A relationship headed for divorce was transformed.

Chuck learned that doing little things for his wife made a big difference. He was amazed at how quickly things changed when he started devoting more time and energy to her. He began to appreciate that for a woman little things are just as important as big things. He now understood why his work scored only one point.

Actually, Pam had good reason to be unhappy. She truly needed Chuck's personal energy, effort, and attention much more than their wealthy life-style. Chuck discovered that by spending less energy making money and devoting just a little more energy in the right direction his wife would be much happier. He recognized that he had been working longer hours in hopes of making her happier. Once he understood how she kept score, he could come home with a new confidence because he knew how to make her happy.

LITTLE THINGS MAKE A BIG DIFFERENCE

There are a variety of ways a man can score points with his partner without having to do much. It is just a matter of redirecting the energy and attention he is already giving. Most men already know about many of these things but don't bother to do them because they don't realize how important the little things are to a woman. A man truly believes the little things are insignificant when compared to the big things he is doing for her.

Some men may start out in a relationship doing the little things, but having done them once or twice they stop. Through some mysterious instinctive force, they begin to focus their energies into doing one big thing for their partners. They then neglect to do all the little things that are necessary for a woman to feel fulfilled in the relationship. To fulfill a woman, a man needs to understand what she needs to feel loved and supported.

The way women score points is not just a preference but a true need. Women need many expressions of love in a relationship to feel loved. One or two expressions of love, no matter how important, will not, and cannot, fulfill her.

This can be extremely hard for a man to understand. One way to look at it is to imagine that women have a love tank similar to the gas tank on a car. It needs to be filled over and over again. Doing many little things (and scoring many points) is the secret for filling a woman's love tank. A woman feels loved when her love tank is full. She is able to respond with greater love, trust, acceptance, appreciation, admiration, approval, and encouragement. Lots of little things are needed to top off her tank.

Following is a list of 101 of the little ways a man can keep his partner's love tank full.

101 WAYS TO SCORE POINTS WITH A WOMAN

1. Upon returning home find her first before doing anything else and give her a hug.
2. Ask her specific questions about her day that indicate an awareness of what she was planning to do (e.g., "How did your appointment with the doctor go?").
3. Practice listening and asking questions.
4. Resist the temptation to solve her problems–empathize instead.

5. Give her twenty minutes of unsolicited, quality attention (don't read the newspaper or be distracted by anything else during this time).
6. Bring her cut flowers as a surprise as well as on special occasions.
7. Plan a date several days in advance, rather than waiting for Friday night and asking her what she wants to do.
8. If she generally makes dinner or if it is her turn and she seems tired or really busy, offer to make dinner.
9. Compliment her on how she looks.
10. Validate her feelings when she is upset.
11. Offer to help her when she is tired.
12. Schedule extra time when traveling so that she doesn't have to rush.
13. When you are going to be late, call her and let her know.
14. When she asks for support, say yes or no without making her wrong for asking.
15. Whenever her feelings have been hurt, give her some empathy and tell her "I'm sorry you feel hurt." Then be silent; let her feel your understanding of her hurt. Don't offer solutions or explanations why her hurt is not your fault.
16. Whenever you need to pull away, let her know you will be back or that you need some time to think about things.
17. When you've cooled off and you come back, talk about what was bothering you in a respectful, nonblaming way, so she doesn't imagine the worst.
18. Offer to build a fire in wintertime.
19. When she talks to you, put down the magazine or turn off the TV and give her your full attention.
20. If she usually washes the dishes, occasionally offer to wash the dishes, especially if she is tired that day.
21. Notice when she is upset or tired and ask what

she has to do. Then offer to help by doing a few of her "to do" items.

22. When going out, ask if there is anything she wants you to pick up at the store, and remember to pick it up.

23. Let her know when you are planning to take a nap or leave.

24. Give her four hugs a day.

Give her four hugs a day.

25. Call her from work to ask how she is or to share something exciting or to tell her "I love you."

26. Tell her "I love you" at least a couple of times every day.

27. Make the bed and clean up the bedroom.

28. If she washes your socks, turn your socks right side out so she doesn't have to.

29. Notice when the trash is full and offer to empty it.

30. When you are out of town, call to leave a telephone number where you can be reached and to let her know you arrived safely.

31. Wash her car.

32. Wash your car and clean up the interior before a date with her.

33. Wash before having sex or put on a cologne if she likes that.

34. Take her side when she is upset with someone.

35. Offer to give her a back or neck or foot massage (or all three).

36. Make a point of cuddling or being affectionate sometimes without being sexual.

37. Be patient when she is sharing. Don't look at your watch.

38. Don't flick the remote control to different channels when she is watching TV with you.

39. Display affection in public.
40. When holding hands don't let your hand go limp.
41. Learn her favorite drinks so you can offer her a choice of the ones that you know she already likes.
42. Suggest different restaurants for going out; don't put the burden of figuring out where to go on her.
43. Get season tickets for the theater, symphony, opera, ballet, or some other type of performance *she* likes.
44. Create occasions when you both can dress up.
45. Be understanding when she is late or decides to change her outfit.
46. Pay more attention to her than to others in public.
47. Make her more important than the children. Let the children see her getting your attention first and foremost.
48. Buy her little presents–like a small box of chocolates or perfume.
49. Buy her an outfit (take a picture of your partner along with her sizes to the store and let them help you select it).
50. Take pictures of her on special occasions.
51. Take short romantic getaways.
52. Let her see that you carry a picture of her in your wallet and update it from time to time.
53. When staying in a hotel, have them prepare the room with something special, like a bottle of champagne or sparkling apple juice or flowers.
54. Write a note or make a sign on special occasions such as anniversaries and birthdays.
55. Offer to drive the car on long trips.
56. Drive slowly and safely, respecting her preferences. After all, she is sitting powerless in the front seat.
57. Notice how she is feeling and comment on it –"You look happy today" or "You look tired"–and then ask a question like "How was your day?"

58. When taking her out, study in advance the directions so that she does not have to feel responsible to navigate.
59. Take her dancing or take dancing lessons together.
60. Surprise her with a love note or poem.
61. Treat her in ways you did at the beginning of the relationship.
62. Offer to fix something around the house. Say "What needs to be fixed around here? I have some extra time." Don't take on more than you can do.
63. Offer to sharpen her knives in the kitchen.
64. Buy some good Super Glue to fix things that are broken.
65. Offer to change light bulbs as soon as they go out.
66. Help with recycling the trash.
67. Read out loud or cut out sections of the newspaper that would interest her.
68. Write out neatly any phone messages you may take for her.
69. Keep the bathroom floor clean and dry it after taking a shower.
70. Open the door for her.
71. Offer to carry the groceries.
72. Offer to carry heavy boxes for her.
73. On trips, handle the luggage and be responsible for packing it in the car.
74. If she washes the dishes or it is her turn, offer to help scrub pots or other difficult tasks.
75. Make a "to fix" list and leave it in the kitchen. When you have extra time do something on that list for her. Don't let it get too long.
76. When she prepares a meal, compliment her cooking.
77. When listening to her talk, use eye contact.
78. Touch her with your hand sometimes when you talk to her.
79. Show interest in what she does during the day, in the books she reads and the people she relates to.

80. When listening to her, reassure her that you are interested by making little noises like ah ha, uh-huh, oh, mmhuh, and hmmmm.
81. Ask her how she is feeling.
82. If she has been sick in some way, ask for an update and ask how she is doing or feeling.
83. If she is tired offer to make her some tea.
84. Get ready to go to sleep together and get in bed at the same time.
85. Give her a kiss and say good-bye when you leave.
86. Laugh at her jokes and humor.
87. Verbally say thank you when she does things for you.
88. Notice when she gets her hair done and give a reassuring compliment.
89. Create special time to be alone together.
90. Don't answer the phone at intimate moments or if she is sharing vulnerable feelings.
91. Go bicycling together, even if it's just a short ride.
92. Organize and prepare a picnic. (Remember to bring a picnic cloth.)
93. If she handles the laundry, bring the clothes to the cleaners or offer to do the wash.
94. Take her for a walk without the children.
95. Negotiate in a manner that shows her that you want her to get what she wants and you also want what you want. Be caring, but don't be a martyr.
96. Let her know that you missed her when you went away.
97. Bring home her favorite pie or dessert.
98. If she normally shops for the food, offer to do the food shopping.
99. Eat lightly on romantic occasions so that you don't become stuffed and tired later.
100. Ask her to add her thoughts to this list.
101. Leave the bathroom seat down.

THE MAGIC OF DOING LITTLE THINGS

It's magic when a man does little things for his woman. It keeps her love tank full and the score even. When the score is even, or almost even, a woman knows she is loved, which makes her more trusting and loving in return. When a woman knows she's loved, she can love without resentment.

Doing little things for a woman is also healing for a man. In fact, those little things will tend to heal his resentments as well as hers. He begins to feel powerful and effective because she's getting the caring she needs. Both are then fulfilled.

What a Man Needs

Just as men need to continue doing little things for a woman, she needs to be particularly attentive to appreciate the little things he does for her. With a smile and a thanks she can let him know he has scored a point. A man needs this appreciation and encouragement to continue giving. He needs to feel he can make a difference. Men stop giving when they feel they are being taken for granted. A woman needs to let him know that what he is doing is appreciated.

This doesn't mean that she has to pretend that everything is now perfectly wonderful because he has emptied the trash for her. But she can simply notice that he has emptied the trash and say "thanks." Gradually more love will flow from both sides.

What a Man Needs a Woman to Accept

A woman needs to accept a man's instinctive tendencies to focus all his energies into one big thing and minimize the importance of the little things. By accepting this inclination, it will not be as hurtful to her. Rather than resenting him for giving less, she can constructively work with him to solve the problem. She can repeatedly let him know how much she appreciates the little things he has done for her and that he works hard and attentively.

She can remember that his forgetting to do the little things doesn't mean he doesn't love her but that he has become too focused on big things again. Instead of fighting him or punishing him, she can encourage his personal involvement by asking for his support. With more appreciation and encouragement a man will gradually learn to value the little things as well as the big. He will become less driven to be more and more successful and begin to relax more and spend more time with his wife and family.

REDIRECTING ENERGY AND ATTENTION

I remember when I first learned to redirect my energies into the little things. When Bonnie and I were first married, I was almost a workaholic. In addition to writing books and teaching seminars, I had a counseling practice for fifty hours a week. In the first year of our marriage, she let me know again and again how much she needed more time with me. Repeatedly she would share her feelings of abandonment and hurt.

Sometimes she would share her feelings in a letter. We call this a Love Letter. It always ends with love and includes feelings of anger, sadness, fear, and sorrow. In chapter 11 we will explore more deeply the methods and importance of writing these Love Letters. She wrote this Love Letter about my spending too much time at work.

Dear John,

I'm writing you this letter to share with you my feelings. I don't mean to tell you what to do. I just want you to understand my feelings.

I am angry that you spend so much time at work. I am angry that you come home with nothing left for me. I want to spend more time with you.

It hurts to feel like you care more about your clients than me. I feel sad that you are so tired. I miss you.

I'm afraid you don't want to spend time with me. I

am afraid of being another burden in your life. I am
afraid of sounding like a nag. I am afraid my feelings
are not important to you.

I'm sorry if this is hard to hear. I know you are
doing your best. I appreciate how hard you work.

I love you, Bonnie

After reading about her feeling neglected I realized that I truly
was giving more to my clients than I was to her. I would give my
undivided attention to my clients and then come home exhausted
and ignore my wife.

When a Man Overworks

I was ignoring her not because I didn't love her or care for her but
because I had nothing left to give. I naïvely thought I was doing the
best thing by working hard to provide a better life (more money) for
her and our family. Once I understood how she felt, I developed a
plan for solving this problem in our relationship.

Instead of seeing eight clients a day I started seeing seven. I pretended that my wife was my eighth client. Every night I came home
an hour earlier. I pretended in my mind that my wife was my most
important client. I started giving her that devoted and undivided
attention I would give a client. When I arrived home I started doing
little things for her. The success of this plan was immediate. Not
only was she happier but I was too.

Gradually, as I felt being loved for the ways I could support her
and our family, I became less driven to be a great success. I started to
slow down, and to my surprise not only our relationship but also
my work flourished, becoming more successful without my having
to work as hard.

I found that when I was succeeding at home, my work reflected
that success. I realized that success in the work world was not
achieved through hard work alone. It was also dependent on my

ability to inspire trust in others. When I felt loved by my family, not only did I feel more confident, but others also trusted and appreciated me more.

How a Woman Can Help

Bonnie's support played a big part in this change. In addition to sharing her honest and loving feelings, she was also very persistent in asking me to do things for her and then giving me a lot of appreciation when I did them. Gradually, I started to realize how wonderful it is to be loved for doing little things. I was relieved from feeling that I had to do great things to be loved. It was a revelation.

WHEN WOMEN GIVE POINTS

Woman possess the special ability to appreciate the little things of life as much as the big things. This is a blessing for men. Most men strive for greater and greater success because they believe it will make them worthy of love. Deep inside, they crave love and admiration from others. They do not know that they can draw that love and admiration to them without having to be a greater success.

> Most men strive for greater and greater success because they believe it will make them worthy of love.

A woman has the ability to heal a man of this addiction to success by appreciating the little things he does. But she may not express appreciation if she doesn't understand how important it is to a man. She may let her resentment get in the way.

HEALING THE RESENTMENT FLU

Women instinctively appreciate the little things. The only exceptions are when a woman doesn't realize a man needs to hear her appreciation or when she feels the score is uneven. When a woman feels unloved and neglected it is hard for her automatically to appreciate what a man does do for her. She feels resentful because she has given so much more than he has. This resentment blocks her ability to appreciate the little things.

Resentment, like getting the flu or a cold, is not healthy. When a woman is sick with resentment she tends to negate what a man has done for her because, according to the way a woman keeps score, she has done so much more.

When the score is forty to ten in favor of the woman, she may begin to feel very resentful. Something happens to a woman when she feels she is giving more than she is getting. Quite unconsciously she subtracts his score of ten from her score of forty and concludes the score in their relationship is thirty to zero. This makes sense mathematically and is understandable, but it doesn't work.

When she subtracts his score from her score he ends up with a zero, and he is not a zero. He has not given zero; he has given ten. When he comes home she has a coldness in her eyes or in her voice that says he is a zero. She is negating what he has done. She reacts to him as if he has given nothing–but he has given ten.

The reason a woman tends to reduce a man's points this way is because she feels unloved. The unequal score makes her feel that she isn't important. Feeling unloved, she finds it very difficult to appreciate even the ten points he can legitimately claim. Of course, this isn't fair, but it is how it works.

What generally happens in a relationship at this point is the man feels unappreciated and loses his motivation to do more. He catches the resentment flu. She then continues to feel more resentful, and the situation gets worse and worse. Her resentment flu gets worse.

What She Can Do

The way of solving this problem is to understand it compassionately from both sides. He needs to be appreciated, while she needs to feel supported. Otherwise their sickness gets worse.

The solution to this resentment is for her to take responsibility.

She needs to take responsibility for having contributed to her problem by giving more and letting the score get so uneven. She needs to treat herself as if she has the flu or a cold and take a rest from giving so much in the relationship. She needs to pamper herself and allow her partner to take care of her more.

When a woman feels resentful, she usually will not give her partner a chance to be supportive, or, if he tries, she will negate the value of what he has done and give him another zero. She closes the door to his support. By taking responsibility for giving too much, she can give up blaming him for the problem and start a new scorecard. She can give him another chance and, with her new understanding, improve the situation.

What He Can Do

When a man feels unappreciated, he stops giving support. A way he can responsibly deal with the situation is to understand that it is hard for her to give points for his support and appreciate him when she is sick with resentment.

He can release his own resentment by understanding that she needs to receive for a while before she can give again. He can remember this as he attentively gives his love and affection in little ways. For a while he should not expect her to be as appreciative as he deserves and needs. It helps if he takes responsibility for giving her the flu because he neglected to do the little things that she needs.

With this foresight he can give without expecting much in return until she recovers from her flu. Knowing that he can solve this problem will help him release his resentment as well. If he continues giving and she focuses on taking a rest from giving and focuses on receiving his support with love, the balance can be quickly restored.

WHY MEN GIVE LESS

A man rarely intends to take more and give less. Yet men are notorious for giving less in relationships. Probably you have experienced this in your relationships. Women commonly complain that their male partner starts out more loving and then gradually becomes passive. Men also feel unfairly treated. In the beginning women are so appreciative and loving, and then they become resentful and demanding. This mystery can be understood when we realize how men and women keep score differently.

There are five major reasons a man stops giving. They are:

1. Martians Idealize Fairness. A man focuses all his energies into a project at work and thinks he has just scored fifty points. Then he comes home and sits back, waiting for his wife to score her fifty points. He does not know that in her experience he has only scored one point. He stops giving because he thinks he has already given more.

In his mind this is the fair and loving thing to do. He allows her to give fifty points worth of support to even the score. He doesn't realize that his hard work at the office scores only one point. His model of fairness can work only when he understands and respects how women give one point for each gift of love. This first insight has practical applications for both men and women. They are:

For Men: Remember that for a woman, big things *and* little things score one point. All gifts of love are equal and equally needed—big and small. To avoid creating resentment, practice doing some of the little things that make a big difference. Do not expect a woman to be satisfied unless she gets an abundance of little expressions of love as well as the big.

For Women: Remember that men are from Mars; they are not automatically motivated to do the little things. They give less not because they do not love you but because they believe they have already given their share. Try not to take it personally. Instead, repeatedly encourage their support by asking for more. Don't wait until you desperately need his support or until the score is greatly uneven to ask. Don't demand his support; trust that he wants to support you, even if he needs a little encouragement.

2. Venusians Idealize Unconditional Love. A woman gives as much as she can and only notices that she has received less when she is empty and spent. Women don't start out keeping score like men do; women give freely and assume men will do the same.

As we have seen, men are not the same. A man gives freely until the score, as he perceives it, gets uneven, and then he stops giving. A man generally gives a lot and then sits back to receive what he has given.

When a woman is happy giving to a man, he instinctively assumes she is keeping score and he must have more points. The last thing he would consider is that he has given less. From his vantage point he would never continue giving when the score became uneven in his favor.

He knows that if he is required to give more when he feels he has already given a greater amount, he will definitely not smile when he gives. Keep this in mind. When a woman continues to give freely with a smile on her face, a man assumes the score must be somewhat even. He does not realize that Venusians have the uncanny ability to give happily until the score is about thirty to zero. These insights also have practical applications for both men and women:

For Men: Remember that when a woman gives with a smile on her face it doesn't necessarily mean the score is close to even.

For Women: Remember that when you give freely to a man, he gets the message the score is even. If you want to motivate him to give more, then gently and gracefully stop giving more. Allow him to do little things for you. Encourage him by asking for his support in little ways and then appreciating him.

3. Martians Give When They Are Asked. Martians pride themselves in being self-sufficient. They don't ask for help unless they really need it. On Mars it is rude to offer help unless you are first asked.

Quite the opposite, Venusians don't wait to offer their support. When they love someone, they give in any way they can. They do not wait to be asked, and the more they love someone the more they give.

When a man doesn't offer his support a woman mistakenly assumes he doesn't love her. She may even test his love by definitely not asking for his support and waiting for him to offer it. When he doesn't offer to help, she resents him. She does not understand that he is waiting to be asked.

As we have seen, keeping the score even is important to a man. When a man feels he has given more in a relationship, he will instinctively begin to ask for more support; he naturally feels more entitled to receive and starts asking for more. On the other hand, when he has given less in a relationship, the last thing he is going to do is ask for more. Instinctively he will not ask for support but will look for ways that he might give more support.

When a woman doesn't ask for support, a man mistakenly assumes the score must be even or that he must be giving more. He does not know that she is waiting for him to offer his support.

This third insight has practical applications for both men and women.

For Women: Remember that a man looks for cues telling him when and how to give more. He waits to be asked. He seems to get the necessary feedback only when she is asking for more or telling him he needs to give more. In addition, when she asks, he knows what to give. Many men don't know what to do. Even if a man senses he is giving less, unless she specifically asks for support in the little ways, he may devote even more of his energy to big things like work, thinking that greater success or more money will help.

For Men: Remember that a woman instinctively does not ask for support when she wants it. Instead, she expects you to offer it if you love her. Practice offering to support her in little ways.

4. Venusians Say Yes Even When the Score Is Uneven. Men don't realize that when they ask for support, a woman will say yes even if the score is uneven. If they can support their man, they will. The concept of keeping score is not on her mind. Men have to be careful not to ask for too much. If she feels she is giving more than she is getting, after a while she will resent that you do not offer to support her more.

Men mistakenly assume that as long as she says yes to his needs and requests, she is receiving equally what she wants. He mistakenly assumes the score is even when it isn't.

I remember taking my wife to the movies about once a week for the first two years of our marriage. One day she became furious with me and said, "We always do what you want to do. We never do what I want to do."

I was genuinely surprised. I thought that as long as she said yes and continued to say yes that she was equally happy with the situation. I thought she liked the movies as much as I did.

Occasionally she would suggest to me that the opera was in town or that she would like to go to the symphony. When we drove by the local playhouse, she would make a remark like "That looks like fun, let's see that play."

But then later in the week I would say, "Let's go to this movie, it's got a great review."

And she would happily say, "OK."

Mistakenly, I got the message that she was as happy as I was about going to the movies. In truth she was happy to be with me, the movie was OK, but what *she* wanted was to go to the local cultural events. That is why she kept mentioning them to me. But because she kept saying yes to the movies, I had no idea that she was sacrificing her wants to make me happy.

This insight has practical applications for both men and women.

For Men: Remember that if she says yes to your requests, it doesn't mean the score is even. The score may be twenty to zero in her mind and she will still happily say "Sure I'll pick up your clothes at the cleaners" or "OK, I'll make that call for you."

Agreeing to doing what you want doesn't mean that it is what she wants. Ask her what she wants to do. Collect information about what she likes, and then offer to take her to those places.

For Women: Remember that if you immediately say yes to a man's requests, he gets the idea that he has given more or that the score is at least even. If you are giving more and getting less, stop saying yes to his requests. Instead, in a graceful way, begin asking him to do more for you.

5. Martians Give Penalty Points. Women don't realize that men give penalty points when they feel unloved and unsupported. When a woman reacts to a man in an untrusting, rejecting, disapproving, or unappreciative way, he gives minus or penalty points.

For example, if a man feels hurt or unloved because his wife has failed to appreciate something he's done, he feels justified in taking away the points she has already earned. If she has given ten, when he feels hurt by her, he may react to her by taking away her ten points. If he is more hurt he may even give her a negative twenty. As a result she now owes him ten points, when a minute before she had ten points.

This is very confusing to a woman. She may have given the equivalent of thirty points, and then in one angry moment he takes them away. In his mind he feels justified in not giving anything because she owes him. He thinks it is fair. This may be fair mathematically, but it is not really fair.

Penalty points are destructive to relationships. They make a woman feel unappreciated and a man less giving. If he negates in his mind all the loving support she has given, when she does express some negativity, which is bound to happen occasionally, he then loses his motivation to give. He becomes passive. This fifth insight has practical applications for both men and women.

For Men: Remember that penalty points are not fair and do not work. At moments when you feel unloved, offended, or hurt, forgive her and remember all the good she has given rather than penalize her by negating it all. Instead of punishing her, ask her for the support you want, and she will give it. Respectfully let her know how she has hurt you. Let her know how she has hurt you and then give her an opportunity to apologize. Punishment does not work! You will feel much better by giving her a chance to give you what you need. Remember she is a Venusian–she doesn't know what you need or how she hurts you.

For Women: Remember that men have this tendency to give penalty points. There are two approaches to protect yourself from this abuse.

The first approach is to recognize that he is wrong in taking away your points. In a respectful way let him know how you feel. In the next chapter we will explore ways to express difficult or negative feelings.

The second approach is to recognize he takes away points when he feels unloved and hurt and he immediately gives them back when he feels loved and supported. As he feels more and more loved for the little things he does, he will gradually give penalty points less and less. Try to understand the different ways he needs love so that he doesn't get hurt as much.

When you are able to recognize how he has been hurt, let him know that you are sorry. Most important, then give him the love he didn't get. If he feels unappreciated, give him the appreciation he needs; if he feels rejected or manipulated, give him the acceptance he needs; if he feels mistrusted, give him the trust he needs; if he feels put down, give him the admiration that he needs; if he feels disapproval, give him the approval he needs and deserves. When a man feels loved he will quit using penalty points.

The most difficult part of the above process is knowing what hurt him. For the most part, when a man withdraws into his cave, he doesn't know what hurt him. Then, when he comes out, he generally doesn't talk about it. How is a woman supposed to know what actually hurts his feelings? Reading this book and understanding how men need love differently is a good beginning and gives you an edge that women have never had before.

The other way a woman can learn what happened is through communication. As I have mentioned before, the more a woman is able to open up and share her feelings in a respectful way, the more a man is able to learn to open up and share his hurt and pain.

HOW MEN GIVE POINTS

Men give points differently from women. Every time a woman appreciates what a man has done for her, he feels loved and gives her a point in return. To keep the score even in a relationship, a man really doesn't require anything but love. Women don't realize the power of their love and many times unnecessarily seek to earn a man's love by doing more things for him than they want to do.

When a woman appreciates what a man does for her, he gets much of the love he needs. Remember, men primarily need appreciation. Certainly a man also requires equal participation from a woman in doing the domestic duties of day-to-day life, but if he is not appreciated, then her contribution is nearly meaningless and completely unimportant to him.

> Certainly a man also requires equal participation from a woman in doing the domestic duties of day-to-day life, but if he is not appreciated, then her contribution is nearly meaningless and completely unimportant to him.

Similarly, a woman cannot appreciate the big things a man does for her unless he is also doing a lot of little things. Doing a lot of little things fulfills her primary needs to feel cared for, understood, and respected.

A major source of love for a man is the loving reaction that a woman has to his behavior. He has a love tank too, but his is not necessarily filled by what she does for him. Instead it is mainly filled by how she reacts to him or how she feels about him.

When a woman prepares a meal for a man, he gives her one point or ten points, depending on how she is feeling toward him. If a woman secretly resents a man, a meal she may cook for him will mean very little to him–he may even give minus points because she was resenting him. The secret to fulfilling a man lies in learning to express love through your feelings, not necessarily through your actions.

Philosophically speaking, when a woman feels loving, her behavior will automatically express that love. When a man expresses himself in loving behavior, automatically his feelings will follow and become more loving.

Even if a man is not feeling his love for a woman, he can still decide to do something loving for her. If his offering is received and appreciated, then he will begin to feel his love for her again. "Doing" is an excellent way to prime a man's love pump.

However, women are very different. A woman generally does not feel loved if she doesn't feel cared about, understood, or respected. Making a decision to do something more for her partner will not help her feel more loving. Instead it may actually fuel her resentment. When a woman is not feeling her loving feelings, she needs to focus her energies directly on healing her negative feelings and definitely not on doing more.

A man needs to prioritize "loving behavior," for this will ensure that his partner's love needs are met. It will open her heart and also open his heart to feel more loving. A man's heart opens as he succeeds in fulfilling a woman.

A woman needs to prioritize "loving attitudes and feelings," which will ensure that her partner's love needs are fulfilled. As a woman is able to express loving attitudes and feelings toward a man, he feels motivated to give more. This then assists her in opening her heart even more. A woman's heart opens more as she is able to get the support she needs.

Women are sometimes unaware of when a man really needs love. At such times a woman can score twenty to thirty points. These are some examples:

HOW WOMEN CAN SCORE BIG WITH MEN

What happens	Points he gives her
1. He makes a mistake and she doesn't say "I told you so" or offer advice.	10-20
2. He disappoints her and she doesn't punish him.	10-20
3. He gets lost while driving and she doesn't make a big deal out of it.	10-20

What happens	**Points he gives her**
4. He gets lost and she sees the good in the situation and says "We would never have seen this beautiful sunset if we had taken the most direct route."	20-30
5. He forgets to pick up something and she says "It's OK. Would you do it next time you are out?"	10-20
6. He forgets to pick up something again and she says with trusting patience and persistence "It's OK. Would you still get it?"	20-30
7. When she has hurt him and she understands his hurt, she apologizes and gives him the love he needs.	10-40
8. She asks for his support and he says no and she is not hurt by his rejection but trusts that he would if he could. She does not reject him or disapprove of him.	10-20
9. Another time she asks for his support and he again says no. She does not make him feel wrong but accepts his limitations at that time.	20-30
10. She asks for his support without being demanding when he assumes the score is somewhat even.	1-5
11. She asks for support without being demanding when she is upset or he knows she has been giving more.	10-30

What happens	**Points he gives her**
12. When he withdraws she doesn't make him feel guilty.	10-20
13. When he comes back from his cave she welcomes him and doesn't punish him or reject him.	10-20
14. When he apologizes for a mistake and she receives it with loving acceptance and forgiveness. The bigger the mistake he makes the more points he gives.	10-50
15. When he asks her to do something and she says no without giving a list of reasons why she can't do it.	1-10
16. When he asks her to do something and she says yes and stays in a good mood.	1-10
17. When he wants to make up after a fight and starts doing little things for her and she starts appreciating him again.	10-30
18. She is happy to see him when he gets home.	10-20
19. She feels disapproving and instead of expressing it she goes in another room and privately centers herself and then comes back with a more centered and loving heart.	10-20
20. On special occasions she overlooks his mistakes that might normally upset her.	20-40
21. She really enjoys having sex with him.	10-40

What happens	Points he gives her
22. He forgets where he put his keys and she doesn't look at him as though he was irresponsible.	10-20
23. She is tactful or graceful in expressing her dislike or disappointment about a restaurant or movie when on a date.	10-20
24. She doesn't give advice when he is driving or parking the car and then appreciates him for getting them there.	10-20
25. She asks for his support rather than dwelling on what he has done wrong.	10-20
26. She shares her negative feelings in a centered way without blaming, rejecting, or being disapproving of him.	10-40

When a Woman Can Score More Points

Each of the above examples reveals how men score points differently from women. But a woman is not required to do all of the above. This list reveals those times when he is most vulnerable. If she can be supportive in giving him what he needs he will be very generous in giving points.

As I mentioned in chapter 7, a woman's ability to give love at difficult times fluctuates like a wave. When a woman's ability to give love is increasing (during the upswing of her wave) is the time when she can score many bonus points. She should not expect herself to be as loving at other times.

Just as a woman's ability to give love fluctuates, a man's need for love fluctuates. In each of the above examples, there is no fixed amount for how many points a man gives. Instead there is an approximate range; when his need for her love is greater he tends to give her more points.

For example, if he has made a mistake and feels embarrassed, sorry, or ashamed, then he needs her love more; therefore he gives more points if she responds by being supportive. The bigger the mistake, the more points he gives her for her love. If he doesn't receive her love he tends to give her penalty points according to how much he needed her love. If he feels rejected as the result of a big mistake he may give a lot of penalty points.

> If a man has made a mistake and feels embarrassed,
> sorry, or ashamed, then he needs her love more....
> The bigger the mistake, the more points he gives.

WHAT MAKES MEN DEFENSIVE

A man may become so angry at a woman when he has made the mistake and the woman is upset. His upset is proportional to the size of his mistake. A little mistake makes him less defensive, while a big mistake makes him much more defensive. Sometimes women wonder why a man doesn't say he is sorry for a big mistake. The answer is he is afraid of not being forgiven. It is too painful to acknowledge that he has failed her in some way. Instead of saying he is sorry he may become angry with her for being upset and give *her* penalty points.

> When a man is in a negative state,...
> treat him like a passing tornado and lie low.

When a man is in a negative state, if she can treat him like a passing tornado and lie low, after the tornado has passed he will give her an abundance of bonus points for not making him wrong or for not trying to change him. If she tries to stop the tornado it will create havoc, and he will blame her for interfering.

This is a new insight for many woman because on Venus when someone is upset the Venusians.never ignore her or even consider lying low. Tornadoes don't exist on Venus. When someone is upset everyone gets involved with one another and tries to understand what is bothering her by asking a lot of questions. When a tornado passes on Mars everyone finds a ditch and lies low.

WHEN MEN GIVE PENALTY POINTS

It helps greatly when women understand that men score points differently. That men give penalty points is very confusing to women and doesn't make it safe for women to share their feelings. Certainly, it would be wonderful if all men could see how unfair penalty points are and change overnight–but change takes time. What can be reassuring for a woman, however, is to know that just as a man quickly gives out the penalty points he also takes them back.

A man giving penalty points is similar to a woman feeling resentful when she gives more than he does. She subtracts his score from hers and gives him a zero. At such times a man can just be understanding that she is sick with the resentment flu and give her some extra love.

Similarly, when a man is giving penalty points, a woman can realize that he has his own version of resentment flu. He needs some extra love so he can get better. As a result, he immediately gives her bonus points to even the score again.

Through learning how to score big with a man, a woman has a new edge for supporting her man when he seems distant and hurt. Instead of doing little things for him (from the list 101 Ways to Score Points with a Woman, page 180), which is what she would want, she can more successfully focus her energies in giving him what he wants (as listed in How Women Can Score Big with Men, page 199).

REMEMBERING OUR DIFFERENCES

Both men and women can benefit greatly by remembering how differently we keep score. Improving a relationship takes no more energy than we are already expending and doesn't have to be terribly difficult. Relationships are exhausting until we learn how to direct our energies into the ways that our partner can fully appreciate.

CHAPTER 11

HOW TO COMMUNICATE
DIFFICULT FEELINGS

When we are upset, disappointed, frustrated, or angry it is difficult to communicate lovingly. When negative emotions come up, we tend momentarily to lose our loving feelings of trust, caring, understanding, acceptance, appreciation, and respect. At such times, even with the best intentions, talking turns into fighting. In the heat of the moment, we do not remember how to communicate in a way that works for our partner or for us.

At times like these, women unknowingly tend to blame men and make them feel guilty for their actions. Instead of remembering that her partner is doing the best he can, a woman could assume the worst and sound critical and resentful. When she feels a surge of negative feelings, it is especially difficult for a woman to speak in a trusting, accepting, and appreciative way. She doesn't realize how negative and hurtful her attitude is to her partner.

When men become upset, they tend to become judgmental of women and women's feelings. Instead of remembering that his partner is vulnerable and sensitive, a man may forget her needs and sound mean and uncaring. When he feels a surge of negative feelings, it is especially difficult for him to speak in a caring, understanding, and respectful way. He doesn't realize how hurtful his negative attitude is to her.

These are the times when talking does not work. Fortunately, there is another alternative. Instead of verbally sharing your feelings with your partner, write him or her a letter. Writing letters allows you to listen to your own feelings without worrying about hurting your partner. By freely expressing and listening to your own feelings, you automatically become more centered and loving. As men write letters they become more caring, understanding, and respectful; as women write letters they become more trusting, accepting, and appreciative.

Writing out your negative feelings is an excellent way to become aware of how unloving you may sound. With this greater awareness you can adjust your approach. In addition, by writing out your negative emotions their intensity can be released, making room for positive feelings to be felt again. Having become more centered, you can then go to your partner and speak to him or her in a more loving way—a way that is less judgmental or blaming. As a result, your chances of being understood and accepted are much greater.

After writing your letter you may no longer feel a need to talk. Instead you could become inspired to do something loving for your partner. Whether you share the feelings in your letter or you just write a letter to feel better, writing down your feelings is an important tool.

> **Whether you share the feelings in your letter**
> **or you just write a letter to feel better,**
> **writing down your feelings is an essential tool.**

Instead of writing down your feelings you may also choose to do the same process in your mind. Simply refrain from talking and review what happened in your mind. In your imagination imagine you are saying what you feel, think, and want—without editing yourself in any way. By carrying on an inner dialogue expressing the complete truth about your inner feelings, you will suddenly become free from their negative grip. Whether you write down your feelings or do it mentally, by exploring, feeling, and expressing your negative feelings they loose their power and positive feelings reemerge. The Love Letter Technique increases the power and effectiveness of this process tremendously. Although it is a writing technique, it can also be done mentally as well.

THE LOVE LETTER TECHNIQUE

One of the best ways to release negativity and then communicate in a more loving fashion is to use the Love Letter Technique. Through writing out your feelings in a particular manner, the negative emotions automatically lessen and the positive feelings increase. The Love Letter Technique enhances the letter writing process. There are three aspects or parts to the Love Letter Technique.

1. Write a Love Letter expressing your feelings of anger, sadness, fear, regret, and love.

2. Write a Response Letter expressing what you want to hear from your partner.

3. Share your Love Letter and Response Letter with your partner.

The Love Letter Technique is quite flexible. You may choose to do all three steps, or you may only need to do one or two of them. For example, you might practice steps one and two in order to feel more centered and loving and then have a verbal conversation with your partner without being overwhelmed with resentment or blame. At other times you may choose to do all three steps and share your Love Letter and Response Letter with your partner.

To do all three steps is a powerful and healing experience for both of you. However sometimes doing all three steps is too time consuming or inappropriate. In some situations, the most powerful technique is to do just step one and write a Love Letter. Let's explore a few examples of how to write a Love Letter.

STEP 1: WRITING A LOVE LETTER

To write a Love Letter, find a private spot and write a letter to your partner. In each Love Letter express your feelings of anger, sadness, fear, regret, and then love. This format allows you fully to express and understand all your feelings. As a result of understanding all your feelings you will then be able to communicate to your partner in a more loving and centered way.

When we are upset we generally have many feelings at once. For example, when your partner disappoints you, you may feel *angry* that he is being insensitive, angry that she is being unappreciative; *sad* that he is so preoccupied with his work, sad that she doesn't seem to trust you; *afraid* that she will never forgive you, afraid that he doesn't care as much about you; *sorry* that you are secretly withholding your love from him or her. But at the same time you *love* that he or she is your partner and you want his or her love and attention.

To find our loving feelings, many times we need first to feel all our negative feelings. After expressing these four levels of negative feelings (anger, sadness, fear, and regret), we can fully feel and express our loving feelings. Writing Love Letters automatically lessens the intensity of our negative feelings and allows us to experience more fully our positive feelings. Here are some guidelines for writing a basic Love Letter:

1. Address the letter to your partner. Pretend that he or she is listening to you with love and understanding.

2. Start with anger, then sadness, then fear, then regret, and then love. Include all five sections in each letter.

3. Write a few sentences about each feeling; keep each section approximately the same length. Speak in simple terms.

4. After each section, pause and notice the next feeling coming up. Write about that feeling.

5. Do not stop your letter until you get to the love. Be patient and wait for the love to come out.

6. Sign your name at the end. Take a few moments to think about what you need or want. Write it in a P.S.

To simplify writing your letters you may wish to make copies of page 211 to use as a guide in writing your own Love Letters. In each of the five sections a few helpful lead-in phrases are included to help you express your feelings. You may use just a few of these phrases or all of them. Generally the most releasing expressions are: "I am angry," "I am sad," "I am afraid," "I am sorry," "I want," and "I love." However, any phrases that assist you in expressing your feelings will work. It usually takes about twenty minutes to complete a Love Letter.

A Love Letter

Dear _____   Date _____

I am writing this letter to share my feelings with you.

1. For Anger
- I don't like it...
- I feel frustrated...
- I am angry that...
- I feel annoyed...
- I want...

2. For Sadness
- I feel disappointed...
- I am sad that...
- I feel hurt...
- I wanted...
- I want...

3. For Fear
- I feel worried...
- I am afraid...
- I feel scared...
- I do not want...
- I need...
- I want...

4. For Regret
- I feel embarrassed...
- I am sorry...
- I feel ashamed...
- I didn't want...
- I want...

5. For Love
- I love...
- I want...
- I understand...
- I forgive...
- I appreciate...
- I thank you for...
- I know...

P.S. The response I would like to hear from you:

Here are some typical situations and some sample Love Letters that will help you understand the technique.

A Love Letter About Forgetfulness

When Tom napped longer than he'd planned and forgot to take his daughter Hayley to the dentist, his wife, Samantha, was furious. Instead of confronting Tom with her anger and disapproval, however, she sat down and wrote the following Love Letter. Afterward she was able to approach Tom in a more centered and accepting way.

Because she wrote this letter, Samantha did not feel an urge to lecture or reject her husband. Instead of having an argument they enjoyed a loving evening. The next week Tom made sure Hayley got to the dentist.

This is Samantha's Love Letter:

Dear Tom,

1. Anger: I am furious that you forgot. I am angry that you overslept. I hate it when you take naps and forget everything. I am tired of feeling responsible for everything. You expect me to do everything. I am tired of this.

2. Sadness: I am sad that Hayley missed her appointment. I am sad that you forgot. I am sad because I feel like I can't rely on you. I am sad that you have to work so hard. I am sad that you are so tired. I am sad that you have less time for me. I feel hurt when you are not excited to see me. I feel hurt when you forget things. I feel like you don't care.

3. Fear: I am afraid I have to do everything. I am afraid to trust you. I am afraid that you don't care. I am afraid I will have to be responsible next time. I don't want to do everything. I need your help. I am afraid to need you. I am afraid you will never be responsible. I am afraid you are working too hard. I am afraid you may get sick.

4. Regret: I feel embarrassed when you miss appointments. I feel embarrassed when you are late. I am sorry that I am so demanding. I am sorry that I am not more accepting. I feel ashamed that I am not more loving. I don't want to reject you.

5. Love: I love you. I understand that you were tired. You work so hard. I know you are doing your best. I forgive you for forgetting. Thank you for making another appointment. Thank you for wanting to take Hayley to the dentist. I know you really do care. I know you love me. I feel so lucky to have you in my life. I want to have a loving evening with you.

Love, Samantha

P.S. I need to hear that you will be responsible to take Hayley next week to the dentist.

A Love Letter About Indifference

Jim was leaving the next morning for a business trip. That evening, his wife, Virginia, attempted to create some intimacy. She brought a mango into their bedroom and offered him some. Jim was preoccupied reading a book in bed and briefly commented that he wasn't hungry. Virginia felt rejected and left. Inside she was hurt and angry. Instead of coming back and complaining about his rudeness and insensitivity, she wrote a Love Letter.

After writing this letter, Virginia, feeling more accepting and forgiving, went back into the bedroom and said, "This is our last night before you leave, let's spend some special time together." Jim put down his book and they had a delightful, intimate evening. Writing a Love Letter gave Virginia the strength and love to persist more directly in getting her partner's attention. She did not even need to share her Love Letter with her partner.

This is her letter:

Dear Jim,

1. Anger: I am frustrated that you want to read a book and this is our last evening together before you leave. I am angry that you ignore me. I am angry that you do not want to spend this time with me. I am angry that we don't spend more time together. There is always something more important than me. I want to feel you love me.

2. Sadness: I am sad that you don't want to be with me. I am sad that you work so hard. I feel like you wouldn't even notice if I wasn't here. I am sad that you are always so busy. I am sad that you don't want to talk with me. I feel hurt that you do not care. I don't feel special.

3. Fear: I am afraid you don't even know why I am upset. I am afraid you don't care. I am afraid of sharing my feelings with you. I am afraid you will reject me. I am afraid we are drifting further apart. I am scared that I can't do anything about it. I am afraid that I am boring to you. I am afraid that you don't like me.

4. Regret: I feel so embarrassed wanting to spend time with you when you don't even care. I feel embarrassed getting so upset. I am sorry if this sounds demanding. I

am sorry that I am not more loving and accepting. I
am sorry that I was cold when you didn't want to
spend time with me. I am sorry that I didn't give you
another chance. I am sorry that I stop trusting your love.

5. *Love:* I do love you. That's why I brought the mango.
I wanted to do something to please you. I wanted to
spend some special time together. I still want to have a
special evening. I forgive you for being so indifferent to
me. I forgive you for not responding right away. I
understand that you were in the middle of reading
something. Let's have a loving intimate evening.

I love you, Virginia

P.S. The response I would like to hear: "I love you,
Virginia, and I also want to spend a loving evening
with you. I am going to miss you."

A Love Letter About Arguing

Michael and Vanessa disagreed about a financial decision. Within a
few minutes they got into an argument. When Michael noticed that
he was starting to yell he stopped yelling, took a deep breath, and
then said, "I need some time to think about this and then we will
talk." Then he went into another room and wrote out his feelings in
a Love Letter.

After writing the letter he was able to go back and discuss the
matter in a more understanding way. As a result they were able lovingly to resolve their problem.

This is his Love Letter:

Dear Vanessa,

1. *Anger:* I am angry that you get so emotional. I am angry that you keep misunderstanding me. I am angry that you can't stay calm when we talk. I am angry that you are so sensitive and easily hurt. I am angry that you mistrust and reject me.

2. *Sadness:* I am sad that we are arguing. It hurts to feel your doubts and mistrust. It hurts to lose your love. I am sad that we fought. I am sad that we disagree.

3. *Fear:* I am afraid of making a mistake. I am afraid I can't do what I want to do without upsetting you. I am afraid to share my feelings. I am afraid you will make me wrong. I am afraid of looking incompetent. I am afraid you do not appreciate me. I am afraid to talk with you when you are so upset. I don't know what to say.

4. *Regret:* I am sorry I hurt you. I am sorry I don't agree with you. I am sorry that I became so cold. I am sorry that I am so resistant to your ideas. I am sorry that I am in such a hurry to do what I want. I am sorry that I make your feelings wrong. You do not deserve to be treated that way. I am sorry that I judged you.

5. Love: I love you and I want to work this out. I think I could listen to your feelings now. I want to support you. I understand I hurt your feelings. I am sorry I was so invalidating of your feelings. I really love you so much. I want to be your hero and I don't want to just agree with everything. I want you to admire me. I need to be me and I support you in being you. I love you. This time when we talk I will be more patient and understanding. You deserve that.

I love you, Michael

P.S. The response I would like to hear: "I love you, Michael. I really appreciate what a caring and understanding man you are. I trust we can work this out."

A Love Letter About Frustration and Disappointment

Jean left a message for her husband, Bill, saying that she wanted him to bring some important mail home. Somehow, Bill never got the message. When he arrived home without the mail, Jean's reaction was strong frustration and disappointment.

Although Bill was not at fault, when Jean continued making comments about how much she needed that mail and how frustrated she was, he started to feel blamed and attacked. Jean did not realize that Bill was taking personally all her feelings of frustration and disappointment. Bill was about to explode and make her wrong for being so upset.

Instead of dumping his defensive feelings on her and ruining their evening, he wisely decided to take ten minutes and write a Love Letter. When he finished writing, he came back more loving and gave his wife a hug, saying, "I am sorry you didn't get your mail. I wish I had gotten that message. Do you still love me anyway?" Jean responded with a lot of love and appreciation, and they had a wonderful evening instead of a cold war.

This is Bill's Love Letter:

Dear Jean,

1. *Anger:* I hate when you get so upset. I hate when you blame me. I am angry that you are so unhappy. I am angry that you are not happy to see me. It feels like nothing I do is ever enough. I want you to appreciate me and be happy to see me.

2. *Sadness:* I am sad that you are so frustrated and disappointed. I am sad that you are not happy with me. I want you to be happy. I am sad that work is always getting in the way of our love life. I am sad that you don't appreciate all the wonderful things we have in our lives. I am sad I didn't come home with the mail you needed.

3. *Fear:* I am afraid I can't make you happy. I am afraid you will be unhappy all evening. I am afraid to be open with you or be close to you. I am afraid of needing your love. I am afraid I am not good enough. I am afraid you will hold this against me.

4. *Regret:* I am sorry that I didn't bring home the mail. I am sorry you are so unhappy. I am sorry that I didn't think to call you. I didn't want to upset you. I wanted you to be happy to see me. We have a four-day holiday and I want it to be special.

5. *Love:* I love you. I want you to be happy. I understand that you are upset. I understand that you need some time to just be upset. I know that you are not trying to make me feel bad. You just need a hug and some empathy. I am sorry. Sometimes I don't know what to do and I start making you be in the wrong. Thank you for being my wife. I love you so much. You don't have to be perfect and you don't have to be happy. I understand that you are upset about the mail.

I love you, Bill

P.S. The response I would like to hear: "I love you, Bill. I appreciate how much you do for me. Thank you for being my husband."

STEP 2: WRITING A RESPONSE LETTER

Writing a Response Letter is the second step in the Love Letter Technique. Once you have expressed both your negative and positive feelings, taking an additional three to five minutes to write a Response Letter can be a healing process. In this letter, you will write the kind of response you would like to have from your partner.

It works like this. Imagine that your partner is able to respond lovingly to your hurt feelings–the ones you expressed in your Love Letter. Write a short letter to yourself pretending it is your partner writing to you. Include all the things you would like to hear from your partner about the hurts you have expressed. The following lead-in phrases can get you started:

- Thank you for...
- I understand...
- I am sorry...
- You deserve...
- I want...
- I love...

Sometimes writing a Response Letter is even more powerful than writing a Love Letter. Writing out what we actually want and need increases our openness to receiving the support we deserve. In addition, when we imagine our partners responding lovingly, we actually make it easier for them to do so.

Some people are very good at writing out their negative feelings but have a hard time finding the feelings of love. It is especially important for these people to write Response Letters and explore what they would want to hear in return. Be sure to feel your own resistance about letting your partner support you. This gives you an added awareness about how difficult it must be for your partner to deal lovingly with you at such times.

How We Can Learn About Our Partner's Needs

Sometimes women object to writing Response Letters. They expect their partners to know what to say. They have a hidden feeling that says "I don't want to tell him what I need; if he really loves me he will know." In this case a woman needs to remember men are from Mars and don't know what women need; they need to be told.

A man's response is more a reflection of his planet than a mirror of how much he loves her. If he were a Venusian, he would know what to say, but he is not. Men really don't know how to respond to a woman's feelings. For the most part, our culture doesn't teach men what women need.

If a man has seen and heard his father respond with loving words to his mother's upset feelings, then he would have a better idea about what to do. As it is, he doesn't know because he's never been taught. Response Letters are the best way to teach a man about a woman's needs. Slowly, but surely, he will learn.

> Response Letters are the best way
> to teach a man about a woman's needs.

Sometimes women ask me "If I tell him what I want to hear, and he starts saying it, how do I know he is not *just* saying it? I'm afraid he may not really mean it."

This is an important question. If a man doesn't love a woman he will not even bother to give her what she needs. If he even attempts to give a response similar to her request, then most likely he is really trying to respond.

If he doesn't sound fully sincere it's because he is learning something new. Learning a new way of responding is awkward. To him it may feel weak. This is a critical time. He needs lots of appreciation and encouragement. He needs feedback telling him he's on the right track.

If his attempts to support her seem somewhat insincere, it is usually because he is afraid his efforts will not work. If a woman appreciates his attempt, the next time he will feel more secure and thus be able to be more sincere. A man is not a fool. When he feels that a woman is receptive to him and that he can respond in a way that makes a positive difference, he will do it. It just takes time.

Women as well can learn a lot about men and what they need by hearing a man's Response Letter. A woman is generally perplexed by a man's reactions to her. She has no idea why he rejects her attempts to support him. She misunderstands what he needs. Sometimes she resists him because she thinks he wants her to give up herself. In most cases, however, he really wants her to trust, appreciate, and accept him.

To receive support we not only have to teach our partners what we need but we also have to be willing to be supported. Response Letters ensure that a person is open to being supported. Otherwise communication cannot work. To share hurt feelings with an attitude that says "Nothing you say can make me feel better" is not only counterproductive but also hurtful to your partner. It is better not to talk at these times.

Here is an example of a Love Letter and its Response Letter. Notice that the response is still under the P.S., but it's a bit longer and more detailed than those above.

A Love Letter and Response Letter About His Resistance

When Theresa asks her husband, Paul, for support, he resists her and appears burdened by her requests.

Dear Paul,

1. *Anger:* I am angry that you resist me. I am angry that you do not offer to help me. I am angry that I always have to ask. I do so much for you. I need your help.

2. *Sadness:* I am sad that you don't want to help me. I am sad because I feel so alone. I want to do more things together. I miss your support.

3. Fear: I am afraid to ask for your help. I am afraid of your anger. I am afraid you will say no and then I will be hurt.

4. Regret: I am sorry that I resent you so much. I am sorry that I nag you and criticize you. I am sorry I don't appreciate you more. I am sorry I give too much and then demand you do the same.

5. Love: I love you. I understand you are doing your best. I know you do care about me. I want to ask you in more loving ways. You are such a loving father to our children.

I love you, Theresa

P.S. The response I would like to hear is:

Dear Theresa,

Thank you for loving me so much. Thank you for sharing your feelings. *I understand* that it hurts you when I act as if your requests are too demanding. I understand that it hurts when I resist you. *I am sorry* that I don't offer to help you more often. *You deserve* my support and *I want* to support you more. *I do love you* and I feel so happy that you are my wife.

I love you, Paul

STEP 3: SHARING YOUR LOVE LETTER AND RESPONSE LETTER

Sharing your letters is important for the following reasons:

- It gives your partner an opportunity to support you.
- It allows you to get the understanding you need.

- It gives your partner necessary feedback in a loving and respectful way.
- It motivates change in a relationship.
- It creates intimacy and passion.
- It teaches your partner what is important to you and how successfully to support you.
- It helps couples to start talking again when communication breaks down.
- It teaches us how to hear negative feelings in a safe way.

There are five ways to share your letters outlined below. In this case, it is assumed that *she* wrote the letter, but these methods work just as well if *he* wrote the letter.

1. He reads her Love Letter and Response Letter out loud while she is present. Then he holds her hands and gives his own loving response with a greater awareness of what she needs to hear.

2. She reads her Love Letter and Response Letter out loud while he is listening. Then he holds her hands and gives his own loving response with a greater awareness of what she needs to hear.

3. First he reads her Response Letter out loud to her. Then he reads her Love Letter out loud. It is much easier for a man to hear negative feelings when he already knows how to respond to those feelings. By letting a man know what is required of him, he doesn't panic as much when he is hearing negative feelings. After he reads her Love Letter he then holds her hands and gives his own loving response with a greater awareness of what she needs to hear.

4. First she reads her Response Letter to him. Then she reads her Love Letter out loud. Finally he holds her hands and gives her a loving response with a greater awareness of what she needs.

5. *She gives her letters to him and he reads them privately within twenty-four hours.* After he has read the letters, he thanks her for writing them and holds her hands and gives her a loving response with a greater awareness of what she needs.

What to Do If Your Partner Can't Respond Lovingly

Based on their past experiences some men and women have great difficulty hearing Love Letters. In this case they should not be expected to read one. But even when your partner chooses to hear a letter, sometimes they are unable to respond right away in a loving manner. Let's take Paul and Theresa as an example.

If Paul is not feeling more loving after he has heard his partner's letters, then it is because he can't respond with love at that time. But after time his feelings will change.

When reading the letters, he may feel attacked by the anger and hurt and become defensive. At such times he needs to take a time-out to reflect on what was said.

Sometimes when a person hears a Love Letter they only hear the anger and it will take a while before they can hear the love. It helps if, after a bit, he rereads the letter, especially the regret and love sections. Sometimes before I read a Love Letter from my wife, I read the love section first and then I read the full letter.

If a man is upset after reading a Love Letter, he could also respond with his own Love Letter, which would allow him to process the negative feelings that came up when he read her Love Letter. Sometimes I don't know what is bothering me until my wife shares a Love Letter with me, and then suddenly I have something to write about. By writing my letter I am able to find again my loving feelings and reread her letter and hear the love behind her hurt.

If a man cannot immediately respond with love, he needs to know that it's OK and not be punished. His partner needs to understand and accept his need to think about things for a while. Perhaps, to support his partner, he can say something like "Thank you for writing this letter. I need some time to think about it and then we can talk about it." It is important that he not express critical feelings about the letter. Sharing letters needs to be a safe time.

All of the above suggestions for sharing Love Letters also apply when a woman has difficulty responding to a man's letter in a loving way. I generally recommend that couples read out loud the letters they have written. It is helpful to read your partner's letter out loud because it helps them feel heard. Experiment with both, and see what fits you.

MAKING IT SAFE FOR LOVE LETTERS

Sharing Love Letters can be scary. The person writing their true feelings will feel vulnerable. If their partner rejects them it can be very painful. The purpose of sharing the letter is to open up feelings so that partners can become closer. It works well as long as the process is done in safety. The person receiving the Love Letter needs to be particularly respectful of the writer's expression. If they cannot give true, respectful support, then they shouldn't agree to listen until they can.

Sharing letters needs to be done with the correct intention. Sharing a letter needs to be done in the spirit of the following two statements of intent:

Statement of Intent for Writing and Sharing a Love Letter

I have written this letter in order to find my positive feelings and to give you the love you deserve. As part of that process I am sharing with you my negative feelings, which are holding me back.

Your understanding will help me to open up and let go of my negative feelings. I trust that you do care and that you will respond to my feelings in the best way you can.

I appreciate your willingness to listen and support me.
In addition I hope that this letter will assist you in
understanding my wants, needs, and wishes.

The partner who is hearing the letter needs to listen in the spirit
of the following statement of intent.

Statement of Intent for Hearing a Love Letter

I promise to do my best to understand the validity of
your feelings, to accept our differences, to respect your
needs as I do my own, and to appreciate that you are
doing your best to communicate your feelings and love.
I promise to listen and not correct or deny your feelings. I promise to accept you and not try to change you.
I am willing to listen to your feelings because I do
care and I trust that we can work this out.

The first few times you practice the Love Letter Technique it will
be much safer if you actually read these statements out loud. These
statements of intent will help you remember to respect your partner's feelings and respond in a loving, safe way.

MINI LOVE LETTERS

If you are upset and you don't have twenty minutes to write a Love
Letter, you can try writing a mini Love Letter. It only takes three to
five minutes and can really help. Here are some examples:

Dear Max,

1. I am so angry that you are late!

2. I am sad that you have forgotten me.

3. I am afraid you don't really care about me.

4. I am sorry that I am so unforgiving.

5. I love you and I forgive you for being late. I know you really love me. Thank you for trying.

Love, Sandie

Dear Henry,

1. I am angry that you are so tired. I am angry that you just watch TV.

2. I am sad that you don't want to talk to me.

3. I am afraid that we are growing apart. I am afraid of making you angry.

4. I am sorry that I rejected you at dinner. I am sorry I blame you for our problems.

5. I miss your love. Would you schedule an hour with me tonight or sometime soon just for me to share with you what's going on in my life?

Love, Lesley

P.S. What I would like to hear from you is:

Dear Lesley,

Thank you for writing me about your feelings. I understand that you miss me. Let's schedule special time tonight between eight and nine.

Love, Henry

WHEN TO WRITE LOVE LETTERS

The time to write a Love Letter is whenever you are upset and you want to feel better. Here are some common ways Love Letters can be written:

1. Love Letter to an intimate partner.
2. Love Letter to a friend, child, or family member.
3. Love Letter to business associate or client. Instead of saying "I love you" at the end you may choose to use "I appreciate" and "I respect." In most cases I don't recommend sharing it.
4. Love Letter to yourself.
5. Love Letter to God or Higher Power. Share your upset feelings about your life with God and ask for support.
6. Role reversal Love Letter. If it is hard to forgive someone, pretend that you are them for a few minutes and write a Love Letter from them to you. You will be amazed at how quickly you become more forgiving.
7. Monster Love Letter. If you are really upset and your feelings are mean and judgmental, vent them in a letter. Then burn the letter. Do not expect your partner to read it unless you both can handle negative feelings and are willing to do so. In that case even monster letters can be very helpful.
8. Displacement Love Letter. When present events upset you and remind you of unresolved feelings from childhood, imagine you can go back in time and write a letter to one of your parents, sharing your feelings and asking for their support.

WHY WE NEED TO WRITE LOVE LETTERS

As we have explored throughout this book, it is vastly important for women to share their feelings and feel cared for, understood, and respected. It is equally important for men to feel appreciated, accepted, and trusted. The biggest problem in relationships occurs when a woman shares her upset feelings and, as a result, a man feels unloved.

To him, her negative feelings may sound critical, blaming, demanding, and resentful. When he rejects her feelings, she then feels unloved. The success of a relationship is solely dependent on two factors: a man's ability to listen lovingly and respectfully to a woman's feelings, and a woman's ability to share her feelings in a loving and respectful way.

A relationship requires that partners communicate their changing feelings and needs. To expect perfect communication is certainly too idealistic. Fortunately, between here and perfection there is a lot of room for growth.

Realistic Expectations

To expect communication always to be easy is unrealistic. Some feelings are very difficult to communicate without hurting the listener. Couples who have wonderful and loving relationships will sometimes agonize over how to communicate in a way that works for both people. It is difficult truly to understand another person's point of view, especially when he or she is not saying what you want to hear. It is also hard to be respectful of another when your own feelings have been hurt.

Many couples mistakenly think that their inability to communicate successfully and lovingly means they don't love each other enough. Certainly love has a lot to do with it, but communication *skill* is a much more important ingredient. Fortunately, it's a learnable skill.

How We Learn to Communicate

Successful communication would be second nature if we grew up in families that were already capable of honest and loving communication. But in previous generations, so-called loving communication generally meant avoiding negative feelings. It was often as if negative feelings were a shameful sickness and something to be locked away in the closet.

In less "civilized" families what was considered loving communication might include acting out or rationalizing negative feelings through physical punishment, yelling, spanking, whipping, and all kinds of verbal abuse–all in the name of trying to help the children learn right from wrong.

Had our parents learned to communicate lovingly, without suppressing negative feelings, we as children would have been safe to discover and explore our own negative reactions and feelings through trial and error. Through positive role models we would have learned successfully how to communicate–especially our difficult feelings. As a result of eighteen years of trial and error in expressing our feelings, we would have gradually learned to express our feelings respectfully and appropriately. If this had been the case, we would not need the Love Letter Technique.

If Our Past Were Different

Had our past been different, we would have watched our father successfully and lovingly listen to our mother expand and express her frustrations and disappointments. Daily we would have experienced our father giving our mother the loving caring and understanding that she needed from her loving husband.

We would have watched our mother trusting our father and sharing her feelings openly, without disapproving or blaming him. We would have experienced how a person could be upset without pushing someone away with mistrust, emotional manipulation, avoidance, disapproval, condescension, or coldness.

Throughout our eighteen years of growing up we would gradually be able to master our own emotions just as we have mastered walking or math. It would be a learned skill, like walking, jumping, singing, reading, and balancing a checkbook.

But it didn't happen that way for most of us. Instead we spent eighteen years learning unsuccessful communication skills. Because we lack education in how to communicate feelings, it is a difficult and seemingly insurmountable task to communicate lovingly when we are having negative feelings.

To come to understand how difficult this is, consider your answers to these following questions:

1. When you are feeling angry or resentful, how do you express love if, while you were growing up, your parents either argued or conspired to avoid arguing?

2. How do you get your kids to listen to you without yelling or punishing them if your parents yelled and punished you to maintain control?

3. How do you ask for more support if, even as a child, you felt repeatedly neglected and disappointed?

4. How do you open up and share your feelings if you are afraid of being rejected?

5. How do you talk to your partner if your feelings say "I hate you"?

6. How do you say "I am sorry" if, as a child, you were punished for making mistakes?

7. How can you admit your mistakes if you are afraid of punishment and rejection?

8. How can you show your feelings if, as a child, you were repeatedly rejected or judged for being upset and crying?

9. How are you supposed to ask for what you want if, as a child, you were repeatedly made to feel wrong for wanting more?

10. How are you even supposed to know what you are feeling if your parents didn't have the time, patience, or awareness to ask you how you were feeling or what was bothering you?

11. How can you accept your partner's imperfections if, as a child, you felt you had to be perfect to be worthy of love?

12. How can you listen to your partner's painful feelings if no one listened to yours?

13. How can you forgive if you were not forgiven?

14. How are you supposed to cry and heal your pain and grief if, as a child, you were repeatedly told "Don't cry" or "When are you going to grow up?" or "Only babies cry"?

15. How can you hear your partner's disappointment if, as a child, you were made to feel responsible for your mother's pain long before you could understand that you were *not* responsible?

16. How can you hear your partner's anger if, as a child, your mother or father took their frustrations out on you through yelling and being demanding?

17. How do you open up and trust your partner if the first people you trusted with your innocence betrayed you in some way?

18. How are you supposed to communicate your feelings lovingly and respectfully if you haven't had eighteen years of practice without the threat of being rejected and abandoned?

The answer to all these eighteen questions is the same: it is possible to learn loving communication, but we need to work at it. We have to make up for the eighteen years of neglect. No matter how perfect our parents were, nobody is really perfect. If you have problems communicating, it is neither a curse nor all your partner's fault. It is simply a lack of having the correct training and the safety to practice.

In reading the above questions, you may have had some feelings come up. Don't waste this special opportunity to heal yourself. Take twenty minutes right now and write one of your parents a Love Letter. Simply get a pen and some paper and begin expressing your feelings, using the Love Letter format. Try it now, and you will be amazed at the outcome.

TELLING THE COMPLETE TRUTH

Love Letters work because they assist you in telling the complete truth. Merely to explore a part of your feelings does not bring about the desired healing. For example:

1. Feeling your anger may not help you at all. It may just make you more angry. The more you dwell on just your anger, the more upset you will become.

2. Crying for hours may leave you feeling empty and spent, if you never move past the sadness.

3. To feel only your fears may make you even more fearful.

4. To feel sorry, without moving through it, may just make you feel guilty and ashamed and may even be harmful to your self-esteem.

5. Trying to feel loving all the time will force you to suppress all your negative emotions, and after a few years, you will become numb and unfeeling.

Love Letters work because they guide you in writing out the complete truth about *all* your feelings. To heal our inner pain, we must feel each of the four primary aspects of emotional pain. They are anger, sadness, fear, and regret.

Why Love Letters Work

By expressing each of the four levels of emotional pain, our pain is released. Writing only one or two negative feelings does not work as well. This is because many of our negative emotional reactions are not real feelings but defense mechanisms we unconsciously use to avoid our true feelings.

For example:

1. People who get angry easily generally are trying to hide from their hurt, sadness, fear, or regret. When they feel their more vulnerable feelings, the anger goes away and they become more loving.

2. People who cry easily generally have a hard time getting angry, but when they are helped to express anger they feel much better and more loving.

3. People who are fearful generally need to feel and express their anger; the fear then goes away.

4. People who often feel sorry and guilty generally need to feel and express their hurt and anger before they can feel the self-love they deserve.

5. People who always feel loving but wonder why they are depressed or numb generally need to ask themselves this question: "If I were angry and upset about something, what would it be?" and write out the answers. This will help them get in touch with the feelings hidden behind the depression and numbness. Love Letters can be used in this fashion.

How Feelings Can Hide Other Feelings

Following are some examples of how men and women use their negative emotions to avoid or suppress their true pain. Keep in mind that this process is automatic. We are often not aware that it is happening.

Consider for a moment these questions:

- Do you ever smile when you are really angry?
- Have you acted angry when deep inside you were afraid?

- Do you laugh and make jokes when you are really
  sad and hurt?
- Have you been quick to blame others when you felt
  guilty or afraid?

The following chart shows how men and women commonly deny their true feelings. Certainly not all men will fit the male description just as not all women will fit the female description. The chart gives us a way to understand how we may remain strangers to our real feelings.

WAYS WE COVER UP OUR REAL FEELINGS

How men hide their pain (This process is generally unconscious)

1. Men may use anger as a way of avoiding the painful feelings of sadness, hurt, sorrow, guilt, and fear.

2. Men may use indifference and discouragement as a way of avoiding the painful feelings of anger.

3. Men may use feeling offended as a way of avoiding feeling hurt.

4. Men may use anger and righteousness as a way to avoid feeling afraid or uncertain.

5. Men may feel ashamed to avoid anger and grieving.

How women hide their pain (This process is generally unconscious)

1. Women may use concern and worry as a way of avoiding the painful feelings of anger, guilt, fear, and disappointment.

2. Women may fall into confusion as a way of avoiding anger, irritation, and frustration.

3. Women may use feeling bad as a way of avoiding embarrassment, anger, sadness, and regret.

4. Women may use fear and uncertainty as a way of avoiding anger, hurt, and sadness.

5. Women may use grieving to avoid feeling angry and afraid.

How <u>men</u> <u>hide</u> <u>their</u> <u>pain</u> (This process is generally unconscious)	How <u>women</u> <u>hide</u> <u>their</u> <u>pain</u> (This process is generally unconscious)
6. Men may use peace and calm as a way to avoid anger, fear, disappointment, discouragement, and shame.	6. Women may use hope as a way to avoid anger, sadness, grief, and sorrow.
7. Men may use confidence to avoid feeling inadequate.	7. Women may use happiness and gratitude to avoid feeling sadness and disappointment.
8. Men may use aggression to avoid feeling afraid.	8. Women may use love and forgiveness as a way to avoid feeling hurt and angry.

HEALING NEGATIVE FEELINGS

Understanding and accepting another's negative feelings are difficult if your own negative feelings have not been heard and supported. The more we are able to heal our own unresolved feelings from childhood the easier it is responsibly to share our feelings and to listen to our partner's feelings without being hurt, impatient, frustrated, or offended.

The more resistance you have to feeling your inner pain, the more resistance you will have to listening to the feelings of others. If you feel impatient and intolerant when others express their childlike feelings, then this is an indicator of how you treat yourself.

To retrain ourselves we must reparent ourselves. We must acknowledge that there is an emotional person inside us who gets upset even when our rational adult mind says there is no reason to be upset. We must isolate that emotional part of our self and become a loving parent to it. We need to ask ourselves "What's the matter? Are you hurt? What are you feeling? What happened to upset you? What are you angry about? What makes you sad? What are you afraid of? What do you want?"

When we listen to our feelings with compassion, our negative feelings quite miraculously are healed, and we are able to respond to situations in a much more loving and respectful way. By understanding our childlike feelings we automatically open a door for loving feelings to permeate what we say.

If as children our inner emotions had been repeatedly heard and validated in a loving way, then as adults we wouldn't get stuck in negative emotions. But most of us weren't supported this way as children, so we have to do it for ourselves.

How Your Past Affects You Today

Certainly you've had the experience of feeling gripped by negative emotions. These are some common ways our unresolved emotions from childhood may affect us today as we encounter the stresses of being adults:

1. When something has been frustrating, we remain stuck feeling angry and annoyed, even when our adult self says we should feel calm, loving, and peaceful.

2. When something has been disappointing, we remain stuck feeling sad and hurt, even when our adult self says we should feel enthusiastic, happy, and hopeful.

3. When something has been upsetting, we remain stuck feeling afraid and worried, even when our adult self says we should feel assured, confident, and grateful.

4. When something has been embarrassing, we remain stuck feeling sorry and ashamed, even when our adult self says we should feel secure, good, and wonderful.

Silencing Your Feelings Through Addictions

As adults we generally try to control these negative emotions by avoiding them. Our addictions can be used to silence the painful cries of our feelings and unfulfilled needs. After a glass of wine, the pain is gone for a moment. But it will come back again and again.

Ironically, the very act of avoiding our negative emotions gives them the power to control our lives. By learning to listen to and nurture our inner emotions, they gradually lose their grip.

> Ironically, the very act of avoiding our negative emotions
> gives them the power to control our lives.

When you are very upset, it certainly is not possible to communicate as effectively as you want to. At such times the unresolved feelings of your past have come back. It is as though the child that was never allowed to throw a tantrum now throws one, only to be exiled once again into the closet.

Our unresolved childhood emotions have the power to control us by gripping our adult awareness and preventing loving communication. Until we are able lovingly to listen to these seemingly irrational feelings from our past (which seem to intrude into our life when we most need our sanity), they will obstruct loving communication.

The secret of communicating our difficult feelings lies in having the wisdom and the commitment to express our negative feelings in writing so that we can become aware of our more positive feelings. The more we are able to communicate to our partners with the love they deserve, the better our relationships will be. When you are able to share your upset feelings in a loving way, it becomes much easier for your partner to support you in return.

SECRETS OF SELF-HELP

Writing Love Letters is an excellent self-help tool, but if you don't immediately get in the habit of writing them you may forget to use it. I suggest that at least once a week when something is bothering you, sit down and write a Love Letter.

Love Letters are helpful not only when you feel upset with your partner in a relationship but also whenever you are upset. Writing Love Letters help when you are feeling resentful, unhappy, anxious, depressed, annoyed, tired, stuck, or simply stressed. Whenever you want to feel better, write a Love Letter. It may not always completely improve your mood, but it will help move you in the direction you want to go.

In my first book, *What You Feel You Can Heal*, the importance of exploring feelings and writing Love Letters is more fully discussed. In addition, in my tape series, *Healing the Heart*, I share healing visualizations and exercises based on the Love Letter Technique for overcoming anxiety, releasing resentment, and finding forgiveness, loving your inner child, and healing past emotional wounds.

In addition, many more books and workbooks have been written on this subject by other authors. Reading these books is important to help you get in touch with your inner feelings and heal them. But remember, unless you are letting that emotional part of you speak out and be heard, it cannot be healed. Books can inspire you to love yourself more, but by listening to, writing out, or verbally expressing your feelings you are actually doing it.

> Books can inspire you to love yourself more, but by listening to, writing out, or verbally expressing your feelings you are are actually doing it.

As you practice the Love Letter Technique you will begin to experience the part of you that needs love the most. By listening to your feelings and exploring your emotions, you will be helping this part of you to grow and develop.

As your emotional self gets the love and understanding it needs, you will automatically begin to communicate better. You will become capable of responding to situations in a more loving manner. Even though we have all been programmed to hide our feelings and react defensively and not lovingly, we can retrain ourselves. There is great hope.

To retrain yourself you need to listen to and understand the unresolved feelings that have never had a chance to be healed. This part of you needs to be felt, heard, and understood and then it is healed.

Practicing the Love Letter Technique is a safe way to express unresolved feelings, negative emotions, and wants without being judged or rejected. By listening to our feelings we are in effect wisely treating our emotional side like a little child crying in a loving parent's arms. By exploring the complete truth of our feelings we are giving ourselves full permission to have these feelings. Through treating this childlike part of us with respect and love, the unresolved emotional wounds of our past can be gradually healed.

Many people grow up too quickly because they reject and suppress their feelings. Their unresolved emotional pain is waiting inside to come out to be loved and healed. Although they may attempt to suppress these feelings, the pain and unhappiness continue to affect them.

Most physical diseases are now widely accepted as being directly related to our unresolved emotional pain. Suppressed emotional pain generally becomes physical pain or sickness and can cause premature death. In addition, *most* of our destructive compulsions, obsessions and addictions are expressions of our inner emotional wounds.

A man's common obsession with success is his desperate attempt to win love in hopes of reducing his inner emotional pain and turmoil. A woman's common obsession with being perfect is her desperate attempt to be worthy of love and reduce her emotional pain. Anything done to excess can become a means to numb the pain of our unresolved past.

Our society is filled with distractions to assist us in avoiding our pain. Love Letters, however, assist you in looking at your pain, feeling it and then healing it. Every time you write a Love Letter you are giving your inner emotional and wounded self the love, understanding, and attention it needs to feel better.

The Power of Privacy

Sometimes, by privately writing out your feelings, you will discover deeper levels of feelings that you could not feel with another person present. Complete privacy creates the safety to feel more deeply. Even if you are in a relationship and you feel you can talk about anything, I still recommend privately writing down your feelings sometimes. Writing Love Letters in private is also healthy because it provides a time for you to give to yourself without depending on anyone else.

I recommend keeping a journal of your Love Letters or keeping them together in a file. To make writing Love Letters easier, you may wish to refer to the sample Love Letter format given earlier in this chapter. This Love Letter format can assist you in remembering the different stages of a Love Letter and offer some lead-in phrases when you may be stuck.

If you have a personal computer then type in the Love Letter format and use it over and over again. Simply open to that file whenever you want to write a Love Letter, and when you are finished save it by the date. Print it out if you wish to share it with someone.

In addition to writing letters, I suggest that you keep a private file for your letters. Occasionally reread these letters when you are not upset because that is when you can review your feelings with a greater objectivity. This objectivity will help you to express upset feelings at a later time in a more respectful way. Also if you write a Love Letter and you are still upset, by rereading the letter you may begin to feel better.

The Power of Intimacy

Privately writing Love Letters is very healing in itself, but it does not replace our need to be heard and understood by others. When you write a Love Letter you are loving yourself, but when you share a letter you are receiving love. To grow in our ability to love ourselves we need to receive love as well. Sharing the truth opens the door of intimacy through which love can enter.

> To grow in our ability to love ourselves
> we need to receive love as well.

To receive more love we need to have people in our life with whom we can openly and safely share our feelings. It is very powerful to have some select people in your life with whom you can share your every feeling and trust that they will still love you and not hurt you with criticism, judgment, or rejection.

When you can share who you are and how you feel, then you can fully receive love. If you have this love, it is easier to release negative emotional symptoms like resentment, anger, fear, and so forth. This does not mean that you need to share everything you feel and discover in private. But if there are feelings that you are afraid to share, then gradually these fears need to be healed.

A loving therapist or close friend can be a tremendous source of love and healing if you can share your inner and deepest feelings. If you don't have a therapist, then having a friend read your letters from time to time is very helpful. Writing in private will make you feel better, but occasionally sharing your Love Letters with another person who cares and can be understanding is essential.

The Power of the Group

The power of group support is something that cannot be described but has to be experienced. A loving and supportive group can do wonders to help us more easily get in touch with our deeper feelings. To share your feelings with a group means there are more people available to give you love. The potential for growth is magnified by the size of the group. Even if you do not speak out in a group, by listening to others speak openly and honestly about their feelings, your awareness and insight expand.

When I lead group seminars around the country I repeatedly experience deeper parts of myself that need to be heard and understood. When someone stands up and shares their feelings, suddenly I begin to remember something or feel something myself. I gain valuable new insights about myself and others. At the end of each seminar I generally feel much lighter and more loving.

Everywhere small support groups on almost every topic meet each week to give and receive this support. Group support is especially helpful if as children we did not feel safe to express ourselves in groups or in our family. While any positive group activity is empowering, speaking or listening in a loving and supportive group can be personally healing.

I meet regularly with a small men's support group, and my wife, Bonnie, meets regularly with her women's support group. Getting this outside support greatly enhances our relationship. It frees us from looking to each other as the sole source of support. In addition, by listening to others share their successes and failures our own problems tend to shrink.

Taking Time to Listen

Whether you are privately writing down your thoughts and feelings on your computer or sharing them in therapy, in your relationships, or in a support group, you are taking an important step for yourself. When you take the time to listen to your feelings you are in effect saying to the little feeling person inside "You matter. You deserve to be heard and I care enough to listen."

> When you take the time to listen to your feelings you are
> in effect saying to the little feeling person inside "You matter.
> You deserve to be heard and I care enough to listen."

I hope you will use this Love Letter Technique because I have witnessed it transform the lives of thousands of people, including my own. As you write more Love Letters it becomes easier and works better. It takes practice, but it is worth it.

HOW TO ASK
FOR SUPPORT AND GET IT

If you are not getting the support you want in your relationships a significant reason may be that you do not ask enough or you may ask in a way that doesn't work. Asking for love and support is essential to the success of any relationship. If you want to G-E-T then you have to A-S-K.

Both men and women have difficulty asking for support. Women, however, tend to find it much more frustrating and disappointing to ask for support than men do. For this reason, I will be addressing this chapter to women. Of course, men will deepen their understanding of women if they too read this chapter.

WHY WOMEN DON'T ASK

Women make the mistake of thinking they don't have to ask for support. Because *they* intuitively feel the needs of others and give whatever they can, they mistakenly expect men to do the same. When a woman is in love, she instinctively offers her love. With great delight and enthusiasm, she looks for ways to offer her support. The more she loves someone, the more motivated she is to offer her love. Back on Venus, everyone automatically gives support, so there was no reason to ask for it. In fact, not needing to ask is one of the ways they show their love for one another. On Venus their motto is "Love is never having to ask!"

**On Venus their motto is
"Love is never having to ask!"**

Because this is her reference point, she assumes that if her partner loves her, he will offer his support and she won't have to ask. She may even purposefully *not ask* as a test to see if he really loves her. To pass the test, she requires that he anticipate her needs and offer his unsolicited support!

This approach to relationships with men doesn't work. Men are from Mars, and on Mars if you want support you simply have to ask for it. Men are not instinctively motivated to *offer* their support; they need to be asked. This can be very confusing because if you ask a man for support in the wrong way he gets turned off, and if you don't ask at all you'll get little or none.

In the beginning of a relationship, if a woman doesn't get the support she wants, she then assumes that he is not giving because he has nothing more to give. She patiently and lovingly continues to give, assuming that sooner or later he'll catch up. He assumes, however, he is giving enough, because she continues giving to him.

He doesn't realize she is expecting him to give back. He thinks that if she needed or wanted more she would stop giving. But since she is from Venus, she not only wants more but also expects him to *offer* his support without being asked. But he is waiting for her to start asking for support if she wants it. If she is not asking for support he assumes he is giving enough.

Eventually, she may ask for his support, but by this time she has given so much more and feels so much resentment that her request is really a demand. Some women will resent a man simply because they have to ask for his support. Then, when they do ask, even if he says yes and gives her some support, she will still resent that she had to ask. She feels "If I have to ask, it doesn't count."

Men do not respond well to demands and resentment. Even if a man is willing to give support, her resentment or demands will lead him to say no. Demands are a complete turnoff. Her chances of getting his support are dramatically reduced when a request becomes a demand. In some cases he will even give less for a while if he senses that she is demanding more.

> **If a woman is not asking for support
> a man assumes he is giving enough.**

This pattern makes relationships with men very difficult for the unaware women. Though this problem may feel insurmountable, it can be solved. By remembering that men are from Mars you can learn new ways to ask for what you want–ways that work.

In my seminars I have trained thousands of women in the art of asking, and they repeatedly have had immediate success. In this chapter we will explore the three steps involved in asking for and getting what you want. They are: (1) Practice asking correctly for what you're already getting; (2) Practice asking for more, even when you know he will say no, and accept his no; (3) Practice assertive asking.

STEP 1: ASKING CORRECTLY FOR WHAT YOU ARE ALREADY GETTING

The first step in learning how to get more in your relationships is to practice asking for what you are already getting. Become aware of what your partner is already doing for you. Especially the little things, like carrying boxes, fixing things, cleaning up, making calls, and other little chores.

The important part of this stage is to begin asking him to do the little things he already does and not to take him for granted. Then when he does those things give him a lot of appreciation. Temporarily give up expecting him to offer his support unsolicited.

In step 1, it is important not to ask for more than what he is

used to giving. Focus on asking him to do little things that he normally does. Allow him to become used to hearing you ask for things
in a nondemanding tone.

When he hears a demanding tone, no matter how nicely you
phrase your request, all he hears is that he is not giving enough. This
makes him feel unloved and unappreciated. His tendency is then to
give less until you appreciate what he is already giving.

> When a man hears a demanding tone,
> no matter how nicely you phrase your request,
> all he hears is that he is not giving enough.
> His tendency is then to give less until you
> appreciate what he is already giving.

He may be conditioned by you (or his mother) immediately to
say no to your requests. In step 1 you will be reconditioning him to
respond positively to your requests. When a man gradually realizes
that he is appreciated and not taken for granted and that he pleases
you, he will want to respond positively to your requests when he
can. Then he will begin automatically offering his support. But this
advanced stage shouldn't be expected in the beginning.

But there's another reason to start by asking him for what he's
already giving. You need to be sure you're asking in a way he can hear
you and respond. That's what I mean when I say "asking correctly."

Tips for Motivating a Man

There are five secrets of how to correctly ask a Martian for support.
If they are not observed, he may be easily turned off. They are:
appropriate timing, nondemanding attitude, be brief, be direct, and
use correct wording.

Let's look at each more closely:

1. *Appropriate Timing.* Be careful not to ask him to do
something that he is obviously just planning to do. For example, if

he is about to empty the trash, don't say "Could you empty the trash?" He will feel you are telling him what to do. Timing is crucial. Also if he is fully focused on something don't expect him immediately to respond to your request.

2. Nondemanding Attitude. Remember, a request is not a demand. If you have a resentful or demanding attitude, no matter how carefully you choose your words, he will feel unappreciated for what he has already given and probably say no.

3. Be Brief. Avoid giving him a list of reasons why he should help you. Assume that he doesn't have to be convinced. The longer you explain yourself the more he will resist. Long explanations validating your request make him feel as though you don't trust him to support you. He will start to feel manipulated instead of free to offer his support.

> **When asking a man for support,
> assume that he doesn't have to be convinced.**

Just as a woman who is upset doesn't want to hear a list of reasons and explanations about why she shouldn't be upset, a man doesn't want to hear a list of reasons and explanations about why he should fulfill her request.

Women mistakenly give a list of reasons to justify their needs. They think it will help him see that her request is valid and therefore motivate him. What a man hears is "This is why you have to do it." The longer the list, the more he may resist supporting you. If he asks you "why?" then you can give your reasons, but then again, be cautiously brief. Practice trusting that he will do it, if he can. Be as brief as possible.

4. Be Direct. Women often think they are asking for support when they are not. When she needs support, a woman may present the problem but not directly ask for his support. She expects him to offer his support and neglects directly to ask for it.

An indirect request *implies* the request but does not directly say it. These indirect requests make a man feel taken for granted and unappreciated. Occasionally using indirect statements is certainly OK, but when they are repeatedly used, a man becomes resistant to giving his support. He may not even know why he is so resistant. The following statements are all examples of indirect requests and how a man might respond to them:

WHAT HE MAY HEAR WHEN SHE IS NONDIRECT

What she should say (brief and direct)	What she should not say (indirect)	What he hears when she is indirect
"Would you pick up the kids?"	"The kids need to be picked up and I can't do it."	"If you can pick them up you should, otherwise I will feel very unsupported and resent you" (demand).
"Would you bring in the groceries?"	"The groceries are in the car."	"It's your job to bring them in, I went shopping" (expectation).
"Would you empty the trash?"	"I can't fit anything else in the trash can."	"You haven't emptied the trash. You shouldn't wait so long" (criticism).
"Would you clean up the backyard?"	"The backyard is really a mess."	"You didn't clean up the yard again. You should be more responsible, I shouldn't have to remind you" (rejection).
"Would you bring in the mail?"	"The mail hasn't been brought in."	"You forgot to bring in the mail. You should remember" (disapproval).

What she should say (brief and direct)	What she should not say (indirect)	What he hears when she is indirect
"Would you take us out to eat tonight?"	"I have no time to make dinner tonight."	"I have done so much, the least you could do is take us out tonight" (dissatisfaction).
"Would you take me out this week?"	"We haven't gone out in weeks."	"You are neglecting me. I'm not getting what I need. You should take me out more often" (resentment).
"Would you schedule some time to talk with me?"	"We need to talk."	"It is your fault we don't talk enough. You should talk with me more" (blame).

5. Use Correct Wording. One of the most common mistakes in asking for support is the use of *could* and *can* in place of *would* and *will*. "*Could* you empty the trash?" is merely a question gathering information. "*Would* you empty the trash?" is a request.

Women often use "could you?" indirectly to imply "would you?" As I mentioned before, indirect requests are a turnoff. When used occasionally they certainly may go unnoticed, but persistently using *can* and *could* begins to irritate men.

When I suggest to women that they begin asking for support, sometimes they panic because their partners have already made comments many times such as:

- "Don't nag me."
- "Don't ask me to do things all the time."
- "Stop telling me what to do."
- "I already know what to do."
- "You don't have to tell me that."

In spite of how it sounds to a woman, when a man makes this kind of comment, what he really means is "I don't like the way you ask!" If a woman doesn't understand how certain language can affect men, she will get even more snarled. She becomes afraid to ask and starts saying "Could you..." because she thinks she is being more polite. Though this works well on Venus, it doesn't work at all on Mars.

On Mars it would be an insult to ask a man *"Can you empty the trash?"* Of course he can empty the trash! The question is not *can* he empty the trash but *will* he empty the trash. After he has been insulted, he may say no just because you have irritated him.

What Men Want to Be Asked

When I explain this distinction between the *c* words and the *w* words in my seminars, women tend to think I am making a big deal over nothing. To women there is not much difference—in fact, "could you?" may even seem more polite than "would you?" But to many men it is a big difference. Because this distinction is so important, I'm including comments by seventeen different men who attended my seminars.

> 1. When I am asked *"Could you clean up the back-yard"* I really take it literally. I say, "I could do it, sure it's possible." But I am not saying "I will do it," and I certainly don't feel like I am making a promise to do it. On the other hand, when I am asked *"Would you clean up the backyard"* I begin to make a decision, and I am willing to be supportive. If I say yes, the chances of my remembering to do it are much greater because I have made a promise.

> 2. When she says "I need your help. *Could* you please help?" it sounds critical, like somehow I have already failed her. It doesn't feel like an invitation to be the

good guy I want to be and support her. On the other hand, "I need you help. *Would* you please carry this?" sounds like a request and an opportunity to be the good guy. I want to say yes.

3. When my wife says "*Can* you change Christopher's diaper?" I think inside, Sure I can change it. I am capable, and a diaper is a simple thing to change. But then if I don't feel like doing it I might make some excuse. Now, if she asked "*Would* you change Christopher's diaper?" I would say "Yeah, sure," and do it. Inside I would feel, I like to participate and I enjoy helping raise our children. I want to help!

4. When I am asked "*Would* you help me please?" it gives me an opportunity to help, and I am more than willing to support her, but when I hear "*Could* you help me please?" I feel backed up against the wall, as if I have no choice. If I have the ability to help then I am expected to help! I don't feel appreciated.

5. I resent being asked "*could* you." I feel like I have no choice but to say yes. If I say no she will be upset with me. It is not a request but a demand.

6. I keep myself busy or at least pretend to be busy so that the woman I work with doesn't ask me the "could you" question. With "would you" I feel I have a choice, and I want to help.

7. Just this last week my wife asked me, "Could you plant the flowers today?" and without hesitation I said yes. Then when she came home she asked, "Did you plant the flowers?" I said no. She said, "Could you do it tomorrow?" and again, without hesitation, I said

yes. This happened every day this week, and the flowers are still not planted. I think if she had asked me "Would you plant the flowers tomorrow?" I would have thought about it, and if I had said yes I would have done it.

8. When I say "Yes, I *could* do that" I am not committing myself to doing it. I am just saying that I *could* do it. I have not promised to do it. If she gets upset with me I feel like she doesn't have a right. If I say I *will* do it, then I can understand why she is upset if I don't do it.

9. I grew up with five sisters, and now I am married and have three daughters. When my wife says "Can you bring out the trash?" I just don't answer. Then she asks "why?" and I don't even know. Now I realize why. I feel controlled. I can respond to "would you?"

10. When I hear a "could you" I'll immediately say yes, and then over the next ten minutes I will realize why I'm not going to do it and then ignore the question. But when I hear a "will you" a part of me comes up saying "Yes, I want to be of service," and then even if objections come up later in my mind, I will still fulfill her request because I have given my word.

11. I will say yes to a "can you," but inside I resent her. I feel that if I say no she will throw a fit. I feel manipulated. When she asks "would you," I feel free to say yes or no. It is then my choice, and then I want to say yes.

12. When a woman asks me "Would you do this?" I feel assured inside that I am going to get a point for this. I feel appreciated and happy to give.

13. When I hear a "would you" I feel I am being trusted to serve. But when I hear a "can you" or "could you" I hear a question behind the question. She is asking me if I can empty the trash when it is obvious that I could. But behind her question is the request, which she doesn't trust me enough to directly ask.

14. When a woman asks "would you" or "will you" I feel her vulnerability. I am much more sensitive to her and her needs; I definitely don't want to reject her. When she says "could you" I am much more apt to say no because I know it is not a rejection of her. It is simply an impersonal statement saying I can't do it. She won't take it personally if I say no to a "Could you do this?"

15. For me, "would you" makes it personal, and I want to give, but "could you" makes it impersonal, and I will give if it is convenient or if I don't have anything else to do.

16. When a woman says "Could you please help me?" I can feel her resentment and I will resist her, *but* if she says "Would you please help me" I can't hear any resentment, even if there is some. I am willing to say yes.

17. When a woman says "Could you do this for me?" I get kind of honest and say "I'd rather not." The lazy part of me comes out. But when I hear a "Would you please?" I become creative and start thinking of ways to help.

One way women are sure to relate to the significant difference between *would* and *could* is to reflect for a moment on this romantic scene. Imagine a man proposing marriage to a woman. His heart is full, like the moon shining above. Kneeling before her, he reaches out to hold her hands. Then he gazes up into her eyes and gently says, "*Could* you marry me?"

Immediately the romance is gone. Using the *c* word he appears weak and unworthy. In that moment, he reeks of insecurity and low self-esteem. If instead he said "*Would* you marry me?" then both his strength and vulnerability are present. That is the way to propose.

Similarly, a man requires that a woman propose her requests in this manner. Use the *w* words. The *c* words sound too untrusting, indirect, weak, and manipulative.

When she says "*Could* you empty the trash?" the message he receives is "If you *can* empty it then you should do it. I would do it for you!" From his point of view he feels it is obvious that he *can* do it. In neglecting to ask for his support he feels she is manipulating him or taking him for granted. He doesn't feel trusted to be there for her if he can.

I remember one woman in a seminar explaining the difference in Venusian terms. She said, "At first I couldn't feel the difference between these two ways of asking. But then I turned it around. It feels very different to me when he says 'No, I *can't* do it' versus 'No, I *will* not do it.' The 'I *will* not do it' is a personal rejection. If he says 'I can't do it' then it is no reflection on me, it is just that *he* can't do it."

Common Mistakes in Asking

The hardest part of learning to ask is remembering how to do it. Try using the *w* words whenever possible. It will take a lot of practice.

To ask a man for support:

1. Be direct.
2. Be brief.
3. Use "would you" or "will you" phrases.

It's best not to be too indirect, too lengthy, or to employ phrases such as "could you" or "can you." Let's look at some examples.

Do say	**Don't say**
"Would you empty the trash?"	"This kitchen is a mess; it really stinks. I can't fit anything else into the trash bag. It needs to be emptied. Could you do it?" (This is too long and uses *could*.)
"Would you help me move this table?"	"I can't move this table. I need to rearrange it before our party tonight. Could you please help?" (This is too long and uses *could*.)
"Would you please put this away for me?"	"I can't put all of this away." (This is an indirect message.)
"Would you bring the groceries in from the car?"	"I have four bags of groceries left in the car. And I need that food to make dinner. Could you bring them in?" (This is too long, indirect, and uses *could*.)
"Would you pick up a bottle of milk on your way home?"	"You'll be going by the store. Lauren needs a bottle of milk. I just can't go out again. I am so tired. Today was a bad day. Could you get it?" (This is too long, indirect, and uses *could*.)
"Would you pick up Julie from school?"	"Julie needs a ride home and I can't pick her up. Do you have time? Do you think you could pick her up?" (This is too long, indirect, and uses *could*.)

<u>Do</u> <u>say</u>	**<u>Don't</u> <u>say</u>**
"Would you take Zoey to the vet today?"	"It's time for Zoey to get her shots. Would you like to take her to the vet?" (This is too indirect.)
"Would you take us out to dinner tonight?"	"I am too tired to make dinner. We haven't gone out in a long time. Do you want to go out?" (This is too lengthy and indirect.)
"Would you zip me up?"	"I need your help. Could you zip me up?" (This is indirect and uses *could.*)
"Would you build a fire for us tonight?"	"It's really cold. Are you going to build a fire?" (This is too indirect.)
"Would you take me to a movie this week?"	"Do you want to go to a movie this week?" (This is too indirect.)
"Would you help Lauren put on her shoes?"	"Lauren still hasn't put on her shoes! We are late. I can't do this all by myself! Could you help?" (This is too long, indirect, and uses *could.*)
"Would you sit down with me now or sometime tonight and talk about our schedule?"	"I have no idea of what's going on. We haven't talked and I need to know what you are doing." (This is too long and indirect.)

As you have probably noticed by now, what you think has been asking is not asking to Martians–they hear something else. It takes a conscious effort to make these little but significant changes in the way you ask for support. I suggest practicing at least three months correcting the way you ask for things before moving on to step two. Other request statements that work are "Would you please...?" and "Would you mind...?"

Start out in step 1 by being aware of how many times you don't ask for support. Become aware of how you do ask when you do. With this increased awareness, then practice asking for what he is already giving you. Remember to be brief and direct. Then give him lots of appreciation and thanks.

Common Questions About Asking for Support

This first step can be difficult. Here are some common questions, which give clues to both the objections and the resistance that women may have.

1. Question. A woman might feel, Why should I have to ask him when I don't require him to ask me?

Answer: Remember, men are from Mars; they are different. By accepting and working with his differences you will get what you need. If, instead, you try to change him he will stubbornly resist. Although asking for what you want is not second nature to Venusians, you can do it without giving up who you are. When he feels loved and appreciated he will gradually become more willing to offer his support without being asked. That is a later stage.

2. Question. A woman may feel, Why should I appreciate what he does when I am doing more?

Answer: Martians give less when they do not feel appreciated. If you want him to give more, then what he needs is more appreciation. Men are motivated by appreciation. If you are giving more it may, of course, be hard to appreciate him. Gracefully begin to give less so that you can appreciate him more. By making this change, not only are you supporting him in feeling loved, but you will also get the support you need and deserve.

3. *Question*. A woman may feel, If I have to ask him for support, he may think he is doing me a favor.

Answer: This is how he should feel. A gift of love is a favor. When a man feels he is doing you a favor, he is then giving from his heart. Remember, he's a Martian and doesn't keep score the way you do. If he feels that you are telling him he is obligated to give, his heart closes and he gives less.

4. *Question*. A woman may feel, If he loves me he should just offer his support, I shouldn't have to ask.

Answer: Remember men are from Mars; they are different. Men wait to be asked. Instead of thinking, If he loves me he will offer his support, consider this thought, If he were a Venusian he would offer his support, but he's not, he's a Martian. By accepting this difference, he will be much more willing to support you, and gradually he will begin to offer his support.

5. *Question*. A woman may feel, If I have to ask for things he will think I am not giving as much as he is. I am afraid–he may feel like he doesn't have to give me more!

Answer: A man is more generous when he feels as though he doesn't have to give. In addition, when a man hears a woman asking for support (in a respectful way), what he also hears is that she feels entitled to that support. He does not assume she has given less. Quite the contrary, he assumes she must be giving more or at least as much as he is, and that is why she feels good about asking.

6. *Question*. A woman may feel, When I ask for support, I am afraid to be brief. I want to explain why I need his help. I don't want to appear demanding.

Answer: When a man hears a request from his partner, he trusts she has good reasons for asking. If she gives him a lot of reasons why he should fulfill her request, he feels as though he can't say no, and if he can't say no then he feels manipulated or taken for granted. Let him give you a gift instead of taking his support for granted.

If he needs to understand more he will ask why. Then it is OK to give reasons. Even when he asks, be careful not to be too lengthy. Give one, or at most, two reasons. If he still needs more information, he'll let you know.

STEP 2: PRACTICE ASKING FOR MORE (EVEN WHEN YOU KNOW HE MAY SAY NO)

Before attempting to ask a man for more, make sure he feels appreciated for what he is already giving. By continuing to ask for his support without expecting him to do more than he has been doing he will feel not only appreciated but also accepted.

When he is used to hearing you ask for his support without wanting more, he feels loved in your presence. He feels he doesn't have to change to get your love. At this point he will be willing to change and stretch his ability to support you. At this point you can risk asking for more without giving him the message that he is not good enough.

The second step of this process is to let him realize that he can say no and still receive your love. When he feels that he can say no when you ask for more, he will feel free to say yes or no. Keep in mind that men are much more willing to say yes if they have the freedom to say no.

> Men are much more willing to say yes
> if they have the freedom to say no.

It's important that women learn both how to ask and how to accept no for an answer. Women usually intuitively feel what their partner's response will be even before they ask. If they sense that he will resist their request, they won't even bother asking. Instead, they will feel rejected. He, of course, will have no idea what happened–all this has gone on in her head.

In step 2, practice asking for support in all those situations where you would want to ask but don't because you feel his resistance. Go ahead and ask for support even if you sense his resistance; even if you know he will say no.

For example, a wife might say to her husband, who is focused on watching the news, "Would you go to the grocery store and pick up some salmon for dinner?" When she asks this question, she is already prepared for him to say no. He is probably completely surprised because she has never interrupted him with a request like this before. He will probably make some excuse like "I am right in the middle of watching the news. Can't you do it?"

She may feel like saying "Sure I could do it. But I am always doing everything around here. I don't like being your servant. I want some help!"

When you ask and sense you will get a rejection, prepare yourself for the no and have a ready answer like "OK." If you want to be really Martian in your response, you could say "no problem"–that would be music to his ears. A simple "OK" is fine, however.

It is important to ask and then act as if it is perfectly OK for him to say no. Remember, you're making it safe for him to refuse. Use this approach only for situations that are really OK if he says no. Pick situations where you would appreciate his support but rarely ask for it. Make sure you will feel comfortable if he says no.

These are some examples of what I mean:

When to ask	What to say
He is working on something and you want him to pick up the kids. Normally you wouldn't bother him, and so you do it yourself.	You say "Would you pick up Julie, she just called?" If he says no, then graciously and simply say "OK."

When to ask

What to say

He normally comes home and expects you to make dinner. You want him to make dinner, but you never ask. You sense he resists cooking.

You say "Would you help me cut the potatoes?" or "Would you make dinner tonight?"

If he says no, then graciously and simply say "OK."

He normally watches TV after dinner while you wash the dishes. You want him to wash them, or at least help, but you never ask. You sense he hates doing dishes. Maybe you don't mind it as much as he does, so you go ahead and do it.

You say "Would you help me with the dishes tonight?" or "Would you bring in the plates?" or wait for an easy night and say "Would you do the dishes tonight?"

If he says no then graciously and simply say "OK."

He wants to go to a movie and you want to go dancing. Normally you sense his desire to see the movie and you don't bother asking to go dancing.

You say "Would you take me dancing tonight? I love to dance with you."

If he says no, then graciously and simply say "OK."

You are both tired and ready to go to bed. The trash is collected the next morning. You sense how tired he is, so you don't ask him to bring the trash out.

You say "Would you take the trash out?"

If he says no, then graciously and simply say "OK."

He is very busy and preoccupied with an important project. You don't want to distract him because you sense how focused he is, but you also want to talk with him. Normally you would sense his resistance and not ask for some time.

You say "Would you spend some time with me?"

If he says no, then graciously and simply say "OK."

When to ask

What to say

He is focused and busy, but you need to pick up your car, which has been in the shop. Normally you anticipate how difficult it will be for him to rearrange his schedule and you don't ask him for a ride.

You say "Would you give me a ride today to pick up my car? It's being repaired."

If he says no, then graciously and simply say "OK."

In each of the above examples, be prepared for him to say no and practice being accepting and trusting. Accept his no and trust that he would offer support if he could. Each time you ask a man for support and he isn't made wrong for saying no, he gives you between five and ten points. Next time you ask he will be more responsive to your request. In a sense, by asking for his support in a loving way, you are helping him stretch his ability to give more.

I first learned this from a woman employee years ago. We were working on a nonprofit project and needed volunteers. She was about to call Tom, who was a friend of mine. I told her not to bother because I already knew he would not be able to help this time. She said she would call anyway. I asked her why, and she said, "When I call I will ask for his support, and when he says no I will be very gracious and understanding. Then next time, when I call for a future project, he will be more willing to say yes. He will have a positive memory of me." She was right.

When you ask a man for support and you do not reject him for saying no, he will remember that, and next time he will be much more willing to give. On the other hand, if you quietly sacrifice your needs and don't ask, he won't have any idea how many times he is needed. How could he know if you don't ask?

> When you ask a man for support and you do not reject him
> for saying no, he will remember that,
> and next time he will be much more willing to give.

As you gently continue to ask for more, occasionally your partner will be able to stretch his comfort zone and say yes. At this point it has become safe to ask for more. This is one way healthy relationships are built.

Healthy Relationships

A relationship is healthy when both partners have permission to ask for what they want and need, and they both have permission to say no if they choose.

For example, I remember standing in the kitchen with a family friend one day when our daughter Lauren was five years old. She asked me to lift her up and do tricks, and I said, "No, I can't today. I am real tired."

She persisted, asking playfully, "Please, Daddy, please, Daddy, just one flip."

The friend said, "Now, Lauren, your father is tired. He has worked hard today. You shouldn't ask."

Lauren immediately responded by saying, "I am just asking!"

"But you know your father loves you," my friend said. "He can't say no to you."

(The truth is, if he can't say no, that's his problem, not hers.)

Immediately my wife and all three daughters said, "Oh yes he can!"

I was proud of my family. It has taken a lot of work, but gradually we have learned to ask for support and also to accept no.

STEP 3: PRACTICE ASSERTIVE ASKING

Once you have practiced step 2 and you can graciously accept a no, you are ready for step 3. In this step you assert your full power to get what you want. You ask for his support, and if he starts making excuses and resists your request, you don't say "OK" as in step 2. Instead you practice making it OK that he resists but continue waiting for him to say yes.

Let's say he is on his way to bed, and you ask him, "Would you go to the store and get some milk." In his response, he says "Oh, I'm really tired, I want to go to bed."

Instead of immediately letting him off the hook by saying "OK," say nothing. Stand there and accept that he is resisting your request. By not resisting his resistance there is a much greater chance he will say yes.

The art of assertive asking is to remain silent after you have made a request. After you have asked, expect him to moan, groan, scowl, growl, mumble, and grumble. I call the resistance men have to responding to requests the grumbles. The more focused a man is at the time, the more he will grumble. His grumbles have nothing to do with his willingness to support; they are a symptom of how focused he is at the time when asked.

A woman will generally misinterpret a man's grumbles. She mistakenly assumes that he is unwilling to fulfill her request. This is not the case. His grumbles are a sign that he is in the process of considering her request. If he was not considering her request then he would very calmly say no. When a man grumbles it is a good sign–he is trying to consider your request versus his needs.

> When a man grumbles it is a good sign–
> he is trying to consider your request versus his needs.

He will go through internal resistance at shifting his direction from what he's focusing on to your request. Like opening a door with rusty hinges, the man will make unusual noises. By ignoring his grumbles they quickly go away.

Often when a man grumbles he is in the process of saying yes to your request. Because most women misunderstand this reaction, they either avoid asking him for support or they take it personally and reject him in return.

In our example, where he is headed for bed and you ask him to go to the store for milk, he is likely to grumble.

"I'm tired," he says with an annoyed look. "I want to go to bed."

If you misunderstand his response as a rejection, you might

reply with "I made you dinner, I washed the dishes, I got the kids ready for bed, and all you did was plant yourself on this couch! I don't ask for much, but at least you could help now. I am so exhausted. I feel like I do everything around here."

The argument starts. On the other hand, if you know that grumbles are just grumbles and are often his way of starting to say yes, your response will be silence. Your silence is a signal that you trust that he is stretching inside and about to say yes.

Stretching is another way to understand a man's resistance to your requests. Whenever you ask for more, he has to stretch himself. If he is not in shape, he can't do it. That is why you have to prepare a man for step 3 by moving through steps 1 and 2.

In addition, you know that it is more difficult to stretch in the morning. Later in the day you can stretch much farther and easier. When a man grumbles, just imagine that he is stretching in the morning. Once he has finished stretching he will feel great. He just needs to grumble first.

Programming a Man to Say Yes

I first became conscious of this process when my wife asked me to buy some milk at the store when I was on my way to bed. I remember grumbling out loud. Instead of arguing with me, she just listened, assuming that eventually I would do it. Then finally I made a few banging noises on my way out, got in my car, and went to the store.

Then something happened, something that happens to all men, something that women don't know about. As I now moved closer to my new goal, the milk, my grumbles went away. I started feeling my love for my wife and my willingness to support. I started feeling like the good guy. Believe me, I liked that feeling.

By the time I was in the store, I was happy to be getting the milk. When my hand reached the bottle, I had achieved my new goal. Achievement always makes men feel good. I playfully picked up the bottle in my right hand and turned around with a look of pride that said "Hey, look at me. I'm getting the milk for my wife. I am one of those great generous guys. What a guy."

When I returned with the milk, she was happy to see me. She gave me a big hug and said, "Thank you so much. I'm so glad I didn't have to get dressed."

If she had ignored me, I probably would have resented her. Next time she asked me to buy the milk I would have probably grumbled even more. But she didn't ignore me, she gave me lots of love.

I watched my reaction and heard myself think, What a wonderful wife I have. Even after I was so resistant and grumbly she is still appreciating me.

The next time she asked me to buy the milk, I grumbled less. When I returned she was again appreciative. The third time, automatically I said, "Sure."

Then a week later, I noticed that she was low on milk. I offered to get it. She said she was already going to the store. To my surprise a part of me was disappointed! I wanted to get the milk. Her love had programmed me to say yes. Even to this day whenever she asks me to go to the store and get milk a part of me happily says yes.

I personally experienced this inner transformation. Her acceptance of my grumbles and appreciation of me when I returned healed my resistance. From that time on, as she practiced assertive asking, it was much easier for me to respond to her requests.

The Pregnant Pause

One of the key elements of assertive asking is to remain silent after you have asked for support. Allow your partner to work through their resistance. Be careful not to disapprove of his grumbles. As long as you pause and remain silent, you have the possibility of getting his support. If you break the silence you lose your power.

Women unknowingly break the silence and lose their power by making comments like:

- "Oh, forget it."
- "I can't believe you are saying no. I do so much for you."

- "I don't ask you for much."
- "It will only take you fifteen minutes."
- "I feel disappointed. This really hurts my feelings."
- "You mean you won't do this for me."
- "Why can't you do it?"

Etc., etc., etc. You get the idea. When he grumbles, she feels the urge to defend her request and mistakenly breaks her silence. She argues with her partner in an attempt to convince him that he should do it. Whether he does it or not, he will be more resistant next time she asks for his support.

> One of the key elements of assertive asking is to remain silent after you have asked for support.

To give him a chance to fulfill your requests, ask and pause. Let him grumble and say things. Just listen. Eventually he will say yes. Don't mistakenly believe that he will hold this against you. He can't and won't hold it against you as long as you don't insist or argue with him. Even if he walks off grumbling, he will let go of it, if both of you feel it is his choice to do or not to do it.

Sometimes, however, he may not say yes. Or he may try to argue his way out by asking you some questions. Be careful. During your pause he may ask questions like:

- "Why can't you do it?"
- "I really don't have time. Would you do it?"
- "I am busy, I don't have time. What are you doing?"

Sometimes these are just rhetorical questions. So you can remain quiet. Don't speak unless it is clear that he is really looking for an answer. If he wants an answer, give him one, but be very brief, and then ask again. Assertive asking means asking with a sense of confidence and trust that he will support you if he can.

If he questions you or says no, then respond with a brief answer giv-

ing the message that your need is just as great as his. Then ask again.
Here are some examples:

What he says in resistance to her request	How she can respond with assertive asking
"I don't have time. Can't you do it?"	"I'm also rushed. Would you please do it?" Then remain silent again.
"No, I don't want to do that."	"I would really appreciate it. Will you please do it for me?" Then remain silent again.
"I'm busy, what are you doing?"	"I'm busy too. Will you please do it?" Then remain silent again.
"No, I don't feel like it."	"I don't feel like it either. Would you please do it?" Then remain silent again.

Notice that she is not trying to convince him but is simply matching his resistance. If he is tired, don't try to prove that you are more tired and therefore he should help you. Or if he thinks he is too busy don't try to convince him that you are more busy. Avoid giving him reasons why he should do it. Remember, you are just asking and not demanding.

If he continues to resist then practice step two and graciously accept his rejection. This is not the time to share how disappointed you are. Be assured that if you can let go at this time, he will remember how loving you were and be more willing to support you next time.

As you progress you will experience greater success in asking for and getting his support. Even if you are practicing the pregnant pause of step three, it is still necessary to continue practicing steps one and two. It is always important that you continue to ask correctly for the little things as well as graciously accept his rejections.

WHY MEN ARE SO SENSITIVE

You may be asking yourself why men are so sensitive about being asked for support. It is not because men are lazy but because men have so much need to feel accepted. Any request to be more or to give more might instead give the message that he is not accepted just the way he is.

Just as a woman is more sensitive about being heard and feeling understood when she is sharing her feelings, a man is more sensitive about being accepted just the way he is. Any attempt to improve him makes him feel as though you are trying to change him because he is not good enough.

On Mars, the motto is "Don't fix it unless it is broken." When a man feels a woman wanting more, and that she is trying to change him, he receives the message that she feels he is broken; naturally he doesn't feel loved just the way he is.

By learning the art of asking for support, your relationships will gradually become greatly enriched. As you are able to receive more of the love and support you need, your partner will also naturally be quite happy. Men are happiest when they feel they have succeeded in fulfilling the people they care about. By learning to ask correctly for support you not only help your man feel more loved but also ensure you'll get the love you need and deserve.

In the next chapter we will explore the secret of keeping the magic of love alive.

CHAPTER

KEEPING THE MAGIC OF
LOVE ALIVE

One of the paradoxes of loving relationships is that when things are going well and we are feeling loved, we may suddenly find ourselves emotionally distancing our partners or reacting to them in unloving ways. Maybe you can relate to some of these examples:

    1. You may be feeling a lot of love for your partner, and then, the next morning, you wake up and are annoyed and resentful of him or her.

    2. You are loving, patient, and accepting, and then, the next day, you become demanding or dissatisfied.

    3. You can't imagine not loving your partner, and then, the next day, you have an argument and suddenly begin thinking about divorce.

    4. Your partner does something loving for you, and you feel resentful for the times in the past when he or she ignored you.

5. You are attracted to your partner, and then suddenly you feel numb in his or her presence.

6. You are happy with your partner and then suddenly feel insecure about the relationship or powerless to get what you need.

7. You feel confident and assured that your partner loves you and suddenly you feel desperate and needy.

8. You are generous with your love, and then suddenly you become withholding, judgmental, critical, angry, or controlling.

9. You are attracted to your partner, and then when he or she makes a commitment you lose your attraction or you find others more attractive.

10. You want to have sex with your partner, but when he or she wants it, you don't want it.

11. You feel good about yourself and your life and then, suddenly, you begin feeling unworthy, abandoned, and inadequate.

12. You have a wonderful day and look forward to seeing your partner, but when you see him or her, something that your partner says makes you feel disappointed, depressed, repelled, tired, or emotionally distant.

Maybe you have noticed your partner going through some of these changes as well. Take a moment to reread the above list, thinking about how your partner may suddenly lose his or her ability to give you the love you deserve. Probably you have experienced his or her sudden shifts at times. It is very common for two people who are madly in love one day to hate each other or fight the very next day.

These sudden shifts are confusing. Yet they are common. If we don't understand why they happen we may think we are going crazy, or we may mistakenly conclude that our love has died. Fortunately there is an explanation.

Love brings up our unresolved feelings. One day we are feeling loved, and the next day we are suddenly afraid to trust love. The painful memories of being rejected begin to surface when we are faced with trusting and accepting our partner's love.

Whenever we are loving ourselves more or being loved by others, repressed feelings tend to come up and temporarily overshadow our loving awareness. They come up to be healed and released. We may suddenly become irritable, defensive, critical, resentful, demanding, numb, or angry.

Feelings that we could not express in our past suddenly flood our consciousness when we are safe to feel. Love thaws out our repressed feelings, and gradually these unresolved feelings begin to surface into our relationship.

It is as though your unresolved feelings wait until you are feeling loved, and then they come up to be healed. We are all walking around with a bundle of unresolved feelings, the wounds from our past, that lie dormant within us until the time comes when we feel loved. Then, when we feel safe to be ourselves, our hurt feelings come up.

If we can successfully deal with those feelings, then we feel much better and enliven more of our creative, loving potential. If, however, we get into a fight and blame our partner instead of healing our past, we just get upset and then suppress the feelings again.

How Repressed Feelings Come Up

The problem is that repressed feelings don't come up saying "Hi, I am your unresolved feelings from the past." If your feelings of abandonment or rejection from childhood start coming up, then you will feel you are being abandoned or rejected by your partner. The pain of the past is projected onto the present. Things that normally would not be a big deal hurt a lot.

For years we have suppressed our painful feelings. Then one day we fall in love, and love makes us feel safe enough to open up and become aware of our feelings. Love opens us up and we start to feel our pain.

Why Couples May Fight During Good Times

Our past feelings suddenly come up not just when we fall in love but at other times when we are feeling really good, happy, or loving. At these positive times, couples may unexplainably fight when it seems as though they should be happy.

For example, couples may fight when they move into a new home, redecorate, attend a graduation, a religious celebration, or a wedding, receive presents, go on a vacation or car ride, finish a project, celebrate Christmas or Thanksgiving, decide to change a negative habit, buy a new car, make a positive career change, win a lottery, make a lot of money, decide to spend a lot of money, or have great love making.

At all of these special occasions one or both partners may suddenly experience unexplained moods and reactions; the upset tends to be either before, during, or right after the occasion. It may be very insightful to review the above list of special occasions and reflect on how your parents might have experienced these occasions as well as reflect on how you have experienced these occasions in your relationships.

THE 90/10 PRINCIPLE

By understanding how past unresolved feelings periodically surface, it is easy to understand why we can become so easily hurt by our partners. When we are upset, about 90 percent of the upset is related to our past and has nothing to do with what we think is upsetting us. Generally only about 10 percent of our upset is appropriate to the present experience.

Let's look at an example. If our partner seems a little critical of us, it may hurt our feelings a little. But because we are adults we are capable of understanding that they don't mean to be critical or maybe we see that they had a bad day. This understanding prevents their criticism from being too hurtful. We don't take it personally.

But on another day their criticism is very painful. On this other day our wounded feelings from the past are on their way up. As a result we are more vulnerable to our partner's criticism. It hurts a lot because as a child we were criticized severely. Our partner's criticism hurts more because it triggers our past hurt as well.

As a child we were not able to understand that we were innocent and that our parents' negativity was their problem. In childhood we take all criticism, rejection, and blame personally.

When these unresolved feelings from childhood are coming up, we easily interpret our partner's comments as criticism, rejection, and blame. Having adult discussions at these times is hard. Everything is misunderstood. When our partner seems critical, 10 percent of our reaction relates to their effect on us and 90 percent relates to our past.

Imagine someone poking your arm a little or gently bumping into you. It doesn't hurt a lot. Now imagine you have an open wound or sore and someone starts poking at it or bumps into you. It hurts much more. In the same way, if unresolved feelings are coming up, we will be overly sensitive to the normal pokes and bumps of relating.

In the beginning of a relationship we may not be as sensitive. It takes time for our past feelings to come up. But when they do come up, we react differently to our partners. In most relationships, 90 percent of what is upsetting to us would not be upsetting if our past unresolved feelings were not coming up.

How We Can Support Each Other

When a man's past comes up, he generally heads for his cave. He is overly sensitive at those times and needs a lot of acceptance. When a woman's past comes up is when her self-esteem crashes. She descends into the well of her feelings and needs tender loving care.

This insight helps you to control your feelings when they come up. If you are upset with your partner, before confronting him or her first write out your feelings on paper. Through the process of writing Love Letters your negativity will be automatically released and your past hurt will be healed. Love Letters help center you in present time so that you can respond to your partner in a more trusting, accepting, understanding, and forgiving way.

Understanding the 90/10 principle also helps when your partner is reacting strongly to you. Knowing that he or she is being influenced by the past can help you to be more understanding and supportive.

Never tell your partner, when it appears as though their "stuff" is coming up, that they are overreacting. That just hurts them more. If you poked someone right in the middle of a wound you wouldn't tell them they were overreacting.

Understanding how the feelings of the past come up gives us a greater understanding of why our partners react the way they do. It is part of their healing process. Give them some time to cool off and become centered again. If it is too difficult to listen to their feelings, encourage them to write you a Love Letter before you talk about what was so upsetting.

A Healing Letter

Understanding how your past affects your present reactions helps you heal your feelings. If your partner has upset you in some way, write them a Love Letter, and while you are writing ask yourself how this relates to your past. As you write you may find memories coming up from your past and discover that you are really upset with your own mother or father. At this point continue writing but now address your letter to your parent. Then write a loving Response Letter. Share this letter with your partner.

They will like hearing your letter. It feels great when your partner takes responsibility for the 90 percent of their hurt that comes from the past. Without this understanding of our past we tend to blame our partners, or at least they feel blamed.

If you want your partner to be more sensitive to your feelings, let them experience the painful feelings of your past. Then they can understand your sensitivities. Love Letters are an excellent opportunity to do this.

YOU ARE NEVER UPSET FOR THE REASON YOU THINK

As you practice writing Love Letters and exploring your feelings you will begin to discover that generally you are upset for different reasons than you first think. By experiencing and feeling the deeper reasons, negativity tends to disappear. Just as we suddenly can be gripped by negative emotions we can also suddenly release them. These are a few examples:

1. One morning Jim woke up feeling annoyed with his partner. Whatever she did disturbed him. As he wrote her a Love Letter he discovered that he was really upset with his mother for being so controlling. These feelings were just coming up, so he wrote a short Love Letter to his mother. To write this letter he imagined he was back when he was feeling controlled. After he wrote the letter suddenly he was no longer upset with his partner.

2. After months of falling in love, Lisa suddenly became critical of her partner. As she wrote a Love Letter she discovered that she was really feeling afraid that she was not good enough for him and afraid he was no longer interested in her. By becoming aware of her deeper fears she started to feel her loving feelings again.

3. After spending a romantic evening together, Bill and Jean got in a terrible fight the next day. It started when Jean became a little angry with him for forgetting to do

something. Instead of being his usual understanding self, suddenly Bill felt like he wanted a divorce. Later as he wrote a Love Letter he realized he was really afraid of being left or abandoned. He remembered how he felt as a child when his parents fought. He wrote a letter to his parents, and suddenly he felt loving toward his wife again.

4. Susan's husband, Tom, was busy meeting a deadline at work. When he came home Susan felt extremely resentful and angry. One part of her understood the stress he was under, but emotionally she was still angry. While writing him a Love Letter she discovered that she was angry with her father for leaving her alone with her abusive mother. As a child she had felt powerless and abandoned, and these feelings were again coming up to be healed. She wrote a Love Letter to her father and suddenly she was no longer angry with Tom.

5. Rachel was attracted to Phil until he said he loved her and wanted to make a commitment. The next day her mood suddenly changed. She began to have a lot of doubts and her passion disappeared. As she wrote him a Love Letter she discovered that she was angry with her father for being so passive and hurting her mother. After she wrote a Love Letter to her father and released her negative feelings, she suddenly felt attracted again to Phil.

As you begin practicing Love Letters, you may not always experience past memories and feelings. But as you open up and go deeper into your feelings, it will become clearer that when you are really upset it is about something in your past as well.

THE DELAYED REACTION RESPONSE

Just as love may bring up our past unresolved feelings, so does getting what you want. I remember when I first learned about this. Many years ago I had wanted sex from my partner, but she wasn't in the mood. In my mind I accepted that. The next day I hinted around, and she still was not interested. This pattern continued every day.

By the end of two weeks I was beginning to feel resentful. But at that time in my life I didn't know how to communicate feelings. Instead of talking about my feelings and my frustration I just kept pretending as if everything were OK. I was stuffing my negative feelings and trying to be loving. For two weeks my resentment continued to build.

I did everything I knew to please her and make her happy, while inside I was resenting her rejection of me. At the end of two weeks I went out and bought her a pretty nightgown. I brought it home and that evening I gave it to her. She opened the box and was happily surprised. I asked her to try it on. She said she wasn't in the mood.

At this point I gave up. I just forgot about sex. I buried myself in work and gave up my desire for sex. In my mind I made it OK by suppressing my feelings of resentment. About two weeks later, however, when I came home from work, she had prepared a romantic meal and was wearing the nightgown I had bought her two weeks before. The lights were low and soft music was on in the background.

You can imagine my reaction. All of a sudden I felt a surge of resentment. Inside I felt "Now you suffer for four weeks." All of the resentment that I had suppressed for the last four weeks suddenly was coming up. After talking about these feelings I realized that her willingness to give me what I wanted released my old resentments.

When Couples Suddenly Feel Their Resentment

I began to see this pattern in many other situations. In my counseling practice, I also observed this phenomenon. When one partner was finally willing to make a change for the better, the other would become suddenly indifferent and unappreciative.

As soon as Bill was willing to give Mary what she had been asking for, she would have a resentful reaction like "Well, it is too late" or "So what."

Repeatedly I have counseled couples who have been married for over twenty years. Their children have grown up and left home. Suddenly the woman wants a divorce. The man wakes up and realizes that he wants to change and get help. As he starts to make changes and give her the love she has been wanting for twenty years, she reacts with cold resentment.

It is as though she wants him to suffer for twenty years just as she did. Fortunately that is not the case. As they continue to share feelings and he hears and understands how she has been neglected, she gradually becomes more receptive to his changes. This can also go the other way; a man wants to leave and the woman becomes willing to change, but he resists.

The Crisis of Rising Expectations

Another example of the delayed reaction occurs on a social level. In sociology it is called the crisis of rising expectations. It occurred in the sixties during the Johnson administration. For the first time minorities were given more rights than ever before. As a result there were explosions of anger, rioting, and violence. All of the pent-up racial feelings were suddenly released.

This is another example of repressed feelings surfacing. When the minorities felt more supported they felt an upsurge of resentful and angry feelings. The unresolved feelings of the past started coming up. A similar reaction is occurring now in countries where people are finally gaining their freedom from abusive government leaders.

WHY HEALTHY PEOPLE MAY NEED COUNSELING

As you grow more intimate in your relationships, love increases. As a result, deeper, more painful feelings will come up that need to be healed–deep feelings like shame and fear. Because we generally do not know how to deal with these painful feelings, we become stuck.

To heal them we need to share them, but we are too afraid or ashamed to reveal what we are feeling. At such times we may become depressed, anxious, bored, resentful, or simply exhausted for no apparent reason at all. These are all symptoms of our "stuff" coming up and being blocked.

Instinctively you will want to either run away from love or increase your addictions. This is the time to work on your feelings and not run away. When deep feelings come up you would be very wise to get the help of a therapist.

When deep feelings come up, we project our feelings onto our partner. If we did not feel safe to express our feelings to our parents or a past partner, all of a sudden we cannot get in touch with our feelings in the presence of our *present* partner. At this point, no matter how supportive your partner is, when you are with your partner you will not feel safe. Feelings will be blocked.

It is a paradox: because you feel safe with your partner, your deepest fears have a chance to surface. When they surface you become afraid and are unable to share what you feel. Your fear may even make you numb. When this happens the feelings that are coming up get stuck.

> It is a paradox: because you feel safe with your partner,
> your deepest fears have a chance to surface. When they surface you
> become afraid and are unable to share what you feel.

This is when having a counselor or therapist is tremendously helpful. When you are with someone you are not projecting your fears on, you can process the feelings that are coming up. But if you are only with your partner, you may feel numb.

This is why people with even very loving relationships may inevitably need the help of a therapist. Sharing in support groups also has this liberating effect. Being with others whom we don't know intimately but who are supportive creates an opening for our wounded feelings to be shared.

When our unresolved feelings are being projected on our intimate partner, he or she is powerless to help us. All our partner can do is encourage us to get support. Understanding how our past continues to affect our relationships frees us to accept the ebb and flow of love. We begin to trust love and its healing process. To keep the magic of love alive we must be flexible and adapt to the ongoing changing seasons of love.

THE SEASONS OF LOVE

A relationship is like a garden. If it is to thrive it must be watered regularly. Special care must be given, taking into account the seasons as well as any unpredictable weather. New seeds must be sown and weeds must be pulled. Similarly, to keep the magic of love alive we must understand its seasons and nurture love's special needs.

The Springtime of Love

Falling in love is like springtime. We feel as though we will be happy forever. We cannot imagine not loving our partner. It is a time of innocence. Love seems eternal. It is a magical time when everything seems perfect and works effortlessly. Our partner seems to be the perfect fit. We effortlessly dance together in harmony and rejoice in our good fortune.

The Summer of Love

Throughout the summer of our love we realize our partner is not as perfect as we thought, and we have to work on our relationship. Not only is our partner from another planet, but he or she is also a human who makes mistakes and is flawed in certain ways.

Frustration and disappointment arise; weeds need to be uprooted and plants need extra watering under the hot sun. It is no longer easy to give love and get the love we need. We discover that we are not always happy, and we do not always feel loving. It is not our picture of love.

Many couples at this point become disillusioned. They do not want to work on a relationship. They unrealistically expect it to be spring all the time. They blame their partners and give up. They do not realize that love is not always easy; sometimes it requires hard work under a hot sun. In the summer season of love, we need to nurture our partner's needs as well as ask for and get the love we need. It doesn't happen automatically.

The Autumn of Love

As a result of tending the garden during the summer, we get to harvest the results of our hard work. Fall has come. It is a golden time—rich and fulfilling. We experience a more mature love that accepts and understands our partner's imperfections as well as our own. It is a time of thanksgiving and sharing. Having worked hard during summer we can relax and enjoy the love we have created.

The Winter of Love

Then the weather changes again, and winter comes. During the cold, barren months of winter, all of nature pulls back within itself. It is a time of rest, reflection, and renewal. This is a time in relationships when we experience our own unresolved pain or our shadow self. It is when our lid comes off and our painful feelings emerge. It is a time of solitary growth when we need to look more to ourselves than to our partners for love and fulfillment. It is a time of healing. This is the time when men hibernate in their caves and women sink to the bottom of their wells.

After loving and healing ourselves through the dark winter of love, then spring inevitably returns. Once again we are blessed with the feelings of hope, love, and an abundance of possibilities. Based on the inner healing and soul searching of our wintery journey, we are then able to open our hearts and feel the springtime of love.

SUCCESSFUL RELATIONSHIPS

After studying this guide for improving communication and getting what you want in your relationships, you are well prepared for having successful relationships. You have good reason to feel hopeful for yourself. You will weather well through the seasons of love.

I have witnessed thousands of couples transform their relationships–some literally overnight. They come on Saturday of my weekend relationship seminar and by dinnertime on Sunday they are in love again. By applying the insights you have gained through reading this book and by remembering that men are from Mars and women are from Venus you will experience the same success.

But I caution you to remember that love is seasonal. In spring it is easy, but in summer it is hard work. In autumn you may feel very generous and fulfilled, but in winter you will feel empty. The information you need to get through summer and work on your relationship is easily forgotten. The love you feel in fall is easily lost in winter.

In the summer of love, when things get difficult and you are not getting the love you need, quite suddenly you may forget everything you have learned in this book. In an instant it is all gone. You may begin to blame your partner and forget how to nurture their needs.

When the emptiness of winter sets in, you may feel hopeless. You may blame yourself and forget how to love and nurture yourself. You may doubt yourself and your partner. You may become cynical and feel like giving up. This is all a part of the cycle. It is always darkest before the dawn.

To be successful in our relationships we must accept and understand the different seasons of love. Sometimes love flows easily and automatically; at other times it requires effort. Sometimes our hearts are full and at other times we are empty. We must not expect our partners to always be loving or even to remember how to be loving. We must also give ourselves this gift of understanding and not expect to remember everything we have learned about being loving.

The process of learning requires not only hearing and applying but also forgetting and then remembering again. Throughout this book you have learned things that your parents could not teach you. They did not know. But now that you know, please be realistic. Give yourself permission to keep making mistakes. Many of the new insights you have gained will be forgotten for a time.

Education theory states that to learn something new we need to hear it two hundred times. We cannot expect ourselves (or our partners) to remember all of the new insights in this book. We must be patient and appreciative of their every little step. It takes time to work with these ideas and integrate them into your life.

Not only do we need to hear it two hundred times but we also need to unlearn what we have learned in the past. We are not innocent children learning how to have successful relationships. We have been programmed by our parents, by the culture we have grown up in, and by our own painful past experiences. Integrating this new wisdom of having loving relationships is a new challenge. You are a pioneer. You are traveling in new territory. Expect to be lost sometimes. Expect your partner to be lost. Use this guide as a map to lead you through uncharted lands again and again.

Next time you are frustrated with the opposite sex, remember men are from Mars and women are from Venus. Even if you don't remember anything else from this book, remembering that we are supposed to be different will help you to be more loving. By gradually releasing your judgments and blame and persistently asking for what you want, you can create the loving relationships you want, need, and deserve.

You have a lot to look forward to. May you continue to grow in love and light. Thank you for letting me make a difference in your life.

Mars AND Venus

IN THE Bedroom

A Guide to Lasting Romance and Passion

John Gray, Ph.D.

CONTENTS

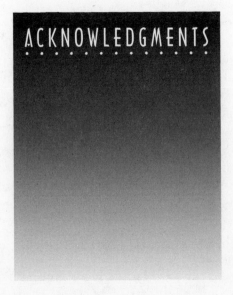

ACKNOWLEDGMENTS

I thank my wife, Bonnie, for once again sharing the journey of developing a book with me. I thank her for her continued patience and creative support in helping me to be successful as a loving partner. I also thank her for allowing me to share our stories and especially for continuing to expand my understanding and ability to honor the female perspective. Her insightful suggestions and comments have provided an important and necessary balance.

I thank my agent, Patti Breitman, for her helpful assistance, brilliant creativity, and enthusiasm, which have guided this book from its conception to its completion. She is a special angel in my life. I thank Carole Bidnick who connected Patti and me for the beginning of our first project, *Men Are from Mars, Women Are from Venus*.

I thank Nancy Peske for her persistent editorial expertise

and creativity throughout the whole process. I thank Jack McKeown for his interest and committed support of this project since its beginning and for the support of the entire staff at HarperCollins for their continued responsiveness to my needs.

I thank Michael Najarian and his wife, Susan, for the successful organization of so many seminars. I thank Michael for the many extra hours of creative planning, plus the important and insightful feedback he has given me in developing this material. I thank the many different promoters and organizers who have put their hearts and souls into producing and supporting seminars for me to teach and develop the material in this book: Elly and Ian Coren in Santa Cruz; Ellis and Consuelo Goldfrit in Santa Cruz; Sandee Mac in Houston; Richi and Debra Mudd in Honolulu; Garry Francell of Heart Seminars in Honolulu; Bill and Judy Elbring of *Life Partners* in San Francisco; David Farlow and Julie Ricksacker in San Diego; David and Marci Obstfeld in Detroit; Fred Kleiner and Mary Wright in Washington, D.C.; Clark and Dotti Bartells in Seattle; Earlene and Jim Carillo in Las Vegas; Bart and Merril Berens in L.A.; and Grace Merrick of the Dallas Unity Church.

I thank John Vestman at Trianon Studios for his expert audio recordings of my seminars. I thank Dave Morton and the staff of Cassette Express for their continued appreciation of this material and their quality service. I thank Bonnie Solow for her competence and gentle support in producing the audio version of this book, as well the staff at HarperAudio.

I thank Ramy El-Batrawi of Genesis-Nuborn Productions and his wife, Ronda, for the successful creation and ongoing production of television infomercials making available audio and video presentations of my seminars.

I thank my executive assistants, Ariana Husband and

Susie Harris, for their hard work, devotion, and efficient managing of my schedule and office.

I thank my chiropractor, Terry Safford, for the incredible support he provided twice a week during the most intensive six months of this project. I thank Raymond Himmel for his many acupuncture sessions at the end of this project that miraculously healed me of dizziness and exhaustion. I thank my friend Renee Swisko for her amazing and powerful healing sessions with me and the rest of my family.

I thank my friends and associates for their open, honest, and supportive sharing of ideas and feedback: Clifford McGuire, Jim Kennedy and Anna Everest, John and Bonnie Grey, Reggie and Andrea Henkart, Lee and Joyce Shapiro, Gabriel Grunfeld, Harold Bloomfield and Sirah Vittese, Jordan Paul, Lenny Eiger, Charles Wood, Jacques Earley, Chris Johns, Mike Bosch and Doug Aarons.

I thank Oprah for her warm and personal support and the opportunity to share freely my ideas on her show before 30 million viewers.

I thank the thousands of participants of my relationship seminars who shared their stories and encouraged me to write this book. Their positive and loving support along with the thousands of calls and letters I have received from readers continues to support me in developing and validating the principles of this book.

Particularly for the enormous success of my previous books I wish to thank the millions of readers who not only have shared my books with others but continue to benefit from these ideas in their lives and relationships.

I give thanks to God for the opportunity to make a difference in this world and the simple but effective wisdom that comes to me and is presented in this book.

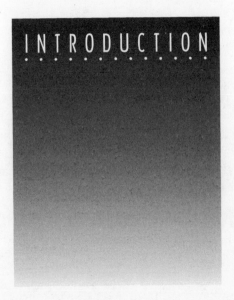

INTRODUCTION

He wants sex. She wants romance. Sometimes it seems as if our partners are from different planets, as if he's from Mars and she's from Venus. In the bedroom, it is obvious that men and women are different, but we may not realize just how different we are. It is only through understanding and accepting our obvious and less obvious differences that we can achieve true intimacy and great sex.

Why Sex Is So Important

We're all aware that sex tends to be more important to men while romance is more important to women, but we generally don't understand why. Without a deeper understanding of this fundamental difference, women commonly underestimate the importance of sex for men and many times judge them as superficial for wanting only one thing.

A woman's judgments begin to soften when she discovers the real reasons that some men seem to want only sex. With a deeper understanding of our sexual differences based on our historical development and social conditioning, she can begin to understand why, for many men, sexual arousal is the key for helping them connect with and realize their loving feelings.

For many men, sexual arousal is the key for helping them connect with and realize their loving feelings.

It is through sex that a man's heart opens, allowing him to experience both his loving feelings and his hunger for love as well. Ironically, it is sex that allows a man to feel his needs for love, while it is receiving love that helps a woman to feel her hunger for sex.

Sex allows a man to feel his needs for love, while receiving love helps a woman to feel her hunger for sex.

A man often misunderstands a woman's real need for romance and may feel instead that she is withholding sex. When he wants sex and she is not readily in the mood, he easily misunderstands and feels rejected. He does not instinctively realize that a woman generally needs to feel loved and romanced before she can feel her hunger for sex.

Just as a woman needs good communication with her partner to feel loved and loving, a man needs sex. Certainly, a man can feel loved in other ways, but the most powerful way a woman's love can touch his soul and open his heart is through great sex.

What Makes Sex Great

Ideally, for sex to be great there must be loving and supportive communication in the relationship. This is the first step. When communication works, all the bedroom skills in this book can be most easily applied.

If communication in a relationship is OK, hearing and using the ideas in this book will dramatically increase the passion and quality of sex. When sex gets better, suddenly the whole relationship gets better. Through great sex, the man begins to feel more love, and, as a result, the woman starts getting the love she may have been missing. Automatically, communication and intimacy increase.

> **When sex gets better, suddenly the whole relationship automatically gets better.**

When a couple is experiencing relationship problems, sometimes, instead of focusing on the problems, taking a shortcut and creating great sex immediately reduces the problems and makes them easier to solve. To most effectively solve relationship problems and ensure lasting intimacy and better communication, I recommend that you read my other books, *What Your Mother Couldn't Tell You & Your Father Didn't Know* and *Men Are from Mars, Women Are from Venus*. Sometimes, however, the most effective way to jumpstart a relationship is to first learn the bedroom skills for creating great sex.

Great sex is the most powerful way to open a man's heart and help him to feel his love and express it to a woman. Great sex softens a woman's heart and helps her to relax and receive her partner's support in other areas of the relationship. This softening of her feelings dramatically improves her ability to communicate in a manner that her partner can hear without becoming defensive. This improved communication in turn provides a basis for sex to remain passionate.

> Great sex is the most powerful way to open a man's heart and help him to feel his love and express it to a woman.

Why Another Book on Sex?

While many useful books address the mechanics of sex, this book addresses the mechanics of making sure you have sex. Through new approaches for communicating, you will learn how to initiate sex in ways that assure that both your sexual needs and your partner's are satisfied. In addition, we will explore the psychological differences between men and women in a way that will help you understand what works best for your partner.

Most books focus on what men and women physically need, but few address their unique psychological needs as well. This book leads men and women toward sexual fulfillment both physically and emotionally. Not only are men grateful when women learn this information, but women experience greater happiness in and out of the bedroom. I receive so many letters from couples after they take my seminars saying that they are now enjoying the best sex they ever had. Sometimes these couples have been married only a few years, but some of them have been married for more than thirty years.

Advanced Bedroom Skills

Women today expect more from sex than ever before. It used to be that sex was primarily a way a woman fulfilled her husband. For many of our mothers, sex was something she did for him and not for herself. But now that birth control is more reliable and available and society is much more accepting of women's sexual needs and desires, women have greater permission to explore and enjoy their sensual side. For many women, a growing interest in sex also reflects their need to find balance within themselves by reconnecting with their feminine side.

Having spent most of the day in a traditionally male job, she too wants a "wife" to greet *her* with love when she gets home. She too wants to enjoy the release that sex brings. Great sex fulfills her as much as it fulfills him. To cope with the stress of the modern workplace, not only does he need her support, but she needs his as well. Through learning new relationship skills, men and women can solve this problem together.

Advanced bedroom skills are required if a man is to provide his partner with the sexual fulfillment that she now requires. The more traditional bedroom skills men and women have used for centuries are outdated. It is not enough for a man to have his way with a woman. She wants more. She wants her orgasm too. He must learn her way as well.

Just as women want more, men also want more. Men don't want to give up passion in their relationships. More and more, both men and women would rather get a divorce than stay in a passionless marriage.

Neither sex is willing to put up with the old system of a man having discreet affairs to fulfill his sexual passion while a woman sacrifices her need for passion in favor of maintaining the family unit. AIDS and other sexually transmitted diseases make extramarital affairs far more dangerous than they were in the past. A modern man wants his partner to value sex in a way that allows him to stay passionately connected to her and their relationship. To achieve this end, advanced bedroom skills are required for both men and women.

In the first twelve chapters of *Mars and Venus in the Bedroom*, we will explore how to create great sex in bed, and then, in chapter 13, we will explore the importance of romance outside the bedroom to keep the passion alive.

Why Couples Stop Having Sex

Quite commonly, after being married for several years, one of the partners stops wanting sex. Although the partner feels as if he or she has simply lost interest in sex, the disinterest is really caused because certain conditions for wanting sex are not being met. Throughout *Mars and Venus in the Bedroom*, we will explore these different needs in much detail. Many times men and women do not clearly know what their needs are or how to have them met. Rather than feel frustrated all the time, they just lose interest.

Surprisingly, at my seminars it is mostly the women who come up to me during the breaks and mention that their husbands just aren't interested in sex anymore. Certainly, it is not unusual for men to want sex more than their partners do, but no matter which partner loses interest, passion can be rekindled with advanced bedroom skills.

How to Share This Book with Your Partner

This is a fun book and not too technical. I purposely made many of the chapters very short so that you can put the book down and enjoy practicing some of these new bedroom skills.

If a woman suggests to a man that he read this book, it is important that she not give him the message that he needs it or that she wants to improve their sex life. It may sound too serious to him and convey the message that *he* is not good enough or that *he* needs to be improved; he'll easily feel insulted by this approach.

Instead, she should say, "Let's read this book about sex. It is really fun," or "This is really a sexy book. Let's take turns reading it together." He'll respond much more positively if he sees that she wants to try something new along with him.

When a man approaches a woman to read this book, he should use the same approach but also be careful not to insist. If she resists, he can read it on his own and begin to use many of the techniques involved. As he succeeds in applying these techniques, she will be much more willing to read the book.

In each case, if your partner resists, gracefully say OK and read the book yourself. Eventually, the man will become interested in what the woman is reading if he sees that she is working on making sex great. Likewise, the woman will be more interested in sharing the book when the man begins applying new skills.

If your partner does not seem interested, just leave the book around the bedroom or put it in the bathroom, and curiosity will motivate him or her without you having to do anything more.

Reading this book out loud with your partner can

assist you in expressing feelings about sex in an easy manner. By making a simple sound of enthusiasm or delight as a certain passage is read, you can give your partner a very important message. In a positive way, you can share ideas that you have avoided expressing for fear that they might sound critical or controlling. Seeing something in print makes it much easier to accept.

Another approach is for both partners to read the book alone and then start using it. Eventually, it is helpful to improve communication if they read it out loud together or at least read their favorite parts.

Many times a woman is hesitant to describe what she likes in sex because she doesn't want her partner to follow her instructions mechanically. Reading about various skills in sex will certainly give both men and women plenty of new approaches to experiment with. This newness can assist couples in experiencing new passion. The purpose of this book is not just to educate, but also to inspire.

Men sometimes tell me that they already know what I am telling them about sex, but it is certainly great to be reminded in such a positive way. Just talking about sex or reading about it in a book can release new passion.

I recommend that, after trying out some of these approaches, a couple continue to talk occasionally about each of their unique preferences. Some of these skills or approaches may be desirable to you but not to your partner. In some cases, over time your partner may change and begin to like certain things and not like other things.

It is important that you do not demand something that makes your partner uncomfortable and do not do something to your partner that he or she doesn't want. Sex is a precious gift that two people can give to each other when they love each other.

It is best to just take in this information and then use whatever you like, as if choosing from a buffet. What some people like, others don't like. You would never want to convince your partner that she should like potatoes if she doesn't, nor would you judge your partner if he likes potatoes and you don't.

For sex and passion to grow over time, it is important that we not feel the possibility of being judged or criticized for our wishes and desires. We should always try to approach sex in a nonjudgmental manner.

I offer this book as a reminder of many of the things you probably already know intuitively. I personally have benefited tremendously from each of the ideas I present, as have thousands of people I've counseled or who have attended my seminars. I hope you enjoy this book and continue to enjoy its insights for the rest of your days and nights.

Great sex is God's gift to those who are committed to creating loving and supportive relationships. Great sex is your reward, and you deserve it.

John Gray
April 29, 1994

Special Note

This book is for couples who are in a committed, monogamous relationship. If you are not in a committed, monogamous relationship, or if you are not absolutely one-hundred-percent sure that your partner is HIV negative, for your own safety and self-respect, you must practice safe sex. Many books explain how to practice safe sex without sacrificing spontaneity and pleasure, and I urge you to learn how to protect yourself from the AIDS virus as well as other sexually transmitted diseases.

It is especially important for women to take precautions. In a heterosexual relationship, women are at a higher risk than men are to be exposed to the AIDS virus, because during intercourse the virus, if it is present in the man's semen, can enter her bloodstream through tiny tears in her vagina, tears that commonly occur during intercourse. Some women find it very difficult to insist that a man use a condom every time they have sex to protect her. Women need to remember that their lives and their health are far too important to risk just because he doesn't want to reduce his sensitivity by wearing a condom. Many brands of condoms and lubricants will limit the loss of sensitivity, and there are many enjoyable ways of incorporating condoms into sex. Also, when a man's sensitivity is reduced by wearing a condom, he may have an easier time holding back from ejaculating too early before she is satisfied, and by holding back, as I explain in greater detail in chapter 9, his orgasm may be even stronger.

Men need to remember that it is extremely difficult for a woman to relax, trust her partner, and truly enjoy sex when she is worried about being infected by HIV or another sexually transmitted disease, or when she is worried about getting pregnant. In the heat of the moment, it is easy for a man to forget the consequences of unsafe sex, but if he takes responsibility for remembering to protect her *every* time, she will appreciate him greatly and be even more open and intimate during sex because she will feel safe.

If you are in a committed, monogamous partnership and have been for at least six months, you can be accurately tested for the HIV virus (it often does not show up in the blood until six months after exposure). Ask your doctor or a public health clinic to test you and your partner.

Advanced Bedroom Skills for Great Sex

One of the special rewards for learning and applying advanced bedroom skills is that sex gets better and better. Like a fabulous vacation after working hard, or a sensual walk through the forest on a sunny spring day, or the exhilaration of climbing to the top of a mountain, great sex is not just a reward but something that can rejuvenate the body, mind, and soul. It brightens our days and strengthens our relationship in the most basic ways.

A great sex life is not just the symptom of a passionate relationship, but is also a major factor in creating it. Great sex fills our hearts with love and can fulfill almost all our emotional needs. Loving sex, passionate sex, sensual sex, long sex, short sex, quickie sex, gourmet sex, playful sex, tender sex, rough sex, soft sex, hard sex, romantic sex, goal-oriented sex, erotic sex, simple sex, cool sex, and hot sex are all an important part of keeping the passion of love alive.

> A great sex life is not just the symptom of a passionate relationship, but is also a major factor in creating it.

Great Sex for Women

Great sex softens a woman and opens her to experience the love in her heart and to remember her partner's love for her in a most definite way. Her partner's skillful and knowing touch leaves no doubt in her mind that she is important to him. The hunger for love within her soul is fulfilled with her partner's passionate and fully present attention. An ever-present tension is momentarily released as she surrenders once again to the deepest long-ings of her feminine being. Her passion to love and be loved can be fully felt and fulfilled.

Great Sex for Men

Great sex releases a man from all his frustrations and allows him to rekindle his passion and commitment to the relationship. In a most immediate way, he experiences the results of his efforts. Her fulfillment is his ultimate quest and victory. Her warm and wet responsiveness excites, electrifies, and awakens the deepest fibers of his masculine being. Heaven's gates are opened, and he has arrived! Through her fulfillment, he feels he has made his mark and his love is appreciated. His sometimes hidden but all-consuming and ever-present desire to love and be loved is both felt and satisfied as he returns to his world yet remains deep within her.

Great Sex for the Relationship

Great sex reminds both men and women of the tender and highest love that originally drew them together. The alchemy of great sex generates the chemicals in the brain and body that allow the fullest enjoyment of one's partner. It increases our attraction to each other, stimulates greater energy, and even promotes better health.* It leaves us not only with the sparkle of youthful vitality, but with a heightened sense of beauty, wonder, and appreciation not only for each other, but for the world around us. Great sex is God's special gift to those who work hard to make love a priority in their lives.

The one major characteristic that makes a marriage more than just a loving friendship is sex. Sex directly nurtures our male and female sides more than any other activity a couple can share. Great sex is soothing to a woman and helps keep her in touch with her feminine side, while it strengthens a man and keeps him in touch with his masculine side. Sex has a tremendous power to bring us closer or push us apart.

To create great sex, it is not enough for men or women to follow their ancient instincts. As times have changed, the quality of sex has become much more important. Our mothers couldn't tell us and our fathers

*In his book, *The Power of Five*, Harold Bloomfield, M.D., reveals that regular sex is vital for maintaining higher estrogen levels in women. Higher estrogen has been associated with better bones, better cardiovascular health, and a feeling of joy in life. Men who experience regular sex have a higher testosterone level, which leads to greater confidence, vitality, strength, and energy.

didn't know the secrets of great sex. Just as the skills for relating and communicating have changed, so also have the skills for sex. To fulfill our partners in bed, new skills are required.

Without a clear understanding of our different requirements in sex, after a few years—sometimes only months— sex becomes routine and mechanical. By making a few but significant shifts, we can completely overcome this pattern.

Women Love Great Sex

Great sex requires a positive attitude about sex. For a man to continue feeling attracted to his partner, he needs to feel that she likes sex as much as he does. Quite often a man will feel defeated in sex because he mistakenly gets the message that his partner is not as interested in sex. Without a deeper understanding of how we are wired differently for sex, it is very easy to feel discouraged.

Women love great sex as much as men. The difference between a woman and a man is that she doesn't feel her strong desire for sex unless her need for love is first satisfied. Most important, she first needs to feel loved and special to a man. When her heart is opened in this way, her sexual center begins to open, and she feels a longing equal to or greater than what any man feels. To her, love is much more important than sex, but as the need for love is fulfilled, the importance of sex dramatically increases.

> **Women love great sex as much as men,
> but to feel turned on, women have
> many more requirements.**

Even if a woman doesn't feel loved but feels the possibility of being loved, she can begin to feel her deep desires for sex. Generally speaking, however, a man needs only the opportunity and the place to become aroused. In the beginning of a relationship, sexual arousal is much more automatic and quick for a man.

> **In the beginning of a relationship,**
> **sexual arousal is much more automatic**
> **and quick for a man.**

Different Chemistry

This difference is reflected physiologically. The hormones in a man's body that are responsible for arousal quickly build up and then are quickly released after orgasm. For a woman, the pleasure builds up much more slowly and remains long after orgasm.

For a woman, arousal slowly builds long before it becomes a physical desire for sex. Before longing for sexual stimulation, a woman first feels warm, sensual, and attractive. She feels drawn to a man and enjoys sharing time together. It could be days before she wants to have sex.

> **For a woman, arousal slowly builds long**
> **before it becomes a physical desire for sex.**
> **It is hard for a man to understand**
> **her different requirements because**
> **they are not his experience.**

When a man becomes aroused, it is immediately sexual. To wait days requires enormous restraint on his part.

It is hard for him to understand her different requirements because they are not his experience.

When a man returns home from a trip, he might want to have sex immediately, while his wife wants to take some time to get reacquainted and talk. Without an understanding of this difference, it would be very easy for him to feel unnecessarily rejected or for her to feel used.

In the beginning of a relationship, a man is more understanding of a woman's need to wait before she has sex. But once they are having sex, he doesn't realize that she still requires emotional support first before she wants to have sex. In a very real sense, emotional support is the price of admission. He does not understand the importance of fulfilling her emotional needs first because his requirements are less.

"Men Only Want One Thing"

Women commonly think men only want one thing: sex. The truth is, however, that men really want love. A man wants love just as much as a woman, but before he can open his heart and let in his partner's love, sexual arousal is a prerequisite. Just as a woman needs love to open up to sex, a man needs sex to open up to love.

> Just as a woman needs love to open up to sex,
> a man needs sex to open up to love.

As a general guideline, a woman needs to be emotionally fulfilled *before* she can long for sexual contact. A man, however, gets much of his emotional fulfillment *during* sex.

Women do not understand this about men. The hidden reason a man is so much in a hurry to have sex is that through sex, a man is able to feel again. Throughout the day, a man becomes so focused on his work that he loses touch with his loving feelings. Sex helps him to feel again. Through sex, a man's heart begins to open up. Through sex, a man can give and receive love the most.

When a woman begins to understand this difference, it changes her whole perspective on sex. Instead of a man's desire for sex being something crude and divorced from love, she can begin to see it as his way of eventually finding love. A woman's feelings about a man's preoccupation with sex can dramatically shift when she understands why a man needs sex.

Why Men Need Sex

Men need sex to feel. For thousands of years, men adapted to their primary job as protector and provider by shutting down their sensitivities, emotions, and feelings. Getting the job done was more important than taking the time to explore feelings. More feeling or sensitivity would just hold them back or get in the way.

Men need sex to feel.

To go out into the wild or into battle, men needed to put their feelings aside. To provide for and protect their families, men were required to risk their lives while enduring the discomforts of scorching sun and freezing cold. Men gradually adapted to this requirement by becoming desensitized. In fact, this difference shows up dramatically in skin sensitivity. Women's skin is ten times more sensitive than men's skin.

To cope with pain, men learned to turn off their feelings. When they stopped feeling pain, however, they also lost their ability to feel pleasure and love. For many men, other than hitting their finger with a hammer or watching a football game, sex is one of the only ways they can feel! It is definitely the way they can feel most intensely. When a man is aroused, he rediscovers the love hidden in his heart. Through sex, a man can feel, and through feeling, he can come back to his soul again.

Why Women Don't Understand

Women don't understand this difference because they have different requirements to fully feel. A woman primarily needs the emotional security to talk about her feelings. When she feels supported in a relationship, she can rediscover the love in her heart. When her emotional needs are met in this way, her sexual needs become more important.

It is confusing to her when he wants sex and they are not even talking or he has ignored her for days. To her, it seems as if he doesn't care if they have much of a relationship. She has no idea that when he begins to hunger for sex it is because he wants to reconnect and share love. Just as communication is so important to women, sex is important to men.

A woman's sexual responsiveness is the most powerful way he can hear that he is loved. Sex can be the most powerful means to rekindle a man's feelings of love.

When Mom said that the way to a man's heart was through his stomach, she was about four inches too high. Sex is the direct line to a man's heart.

....

When Mom said that the way to a man's heart was through his stomach, she was about four inches too high.

....

What Men Need

A man is empowered and nurtured most when he feels appreciated, accepted, and trusted. When a woman is aroused, she is actually giving a man megadoses of what he needs most.

When a woman is longing to have sex with a man, she is most open and trusting. In a very dramatic way, she is willing to surrender her defenses and not only reveal her nakedness, but bring him into her body and being as well. By desiring a man in this way, she makes him feel very accepted. Then, when his every touch creates a pleasurable response, he feels greatly appreciated. In the most tangible and physical way possible, he feels and experiences that he is making a difference.

Even if he is stressed from the day, if his wife is feeling loved and supported and enjoys sex with him, he can be immediately rejuvenated. Although it seems as if sex makes him feel better, it is really that he is feeling again and able to let in her love. He is no longer cut off from his feeling self but can move into that deserted part of his being again. He can feel whole again. Like a thirsty man wandering in the desert, he can finally relax and take a drink from the oasis of his feelings.

....
Like a thirsty man wandering in the desert, during sex he can finally relax and take a drink from the oasis of his feelings.
....

Through touching her softness and entering the warmth of her loving body, he is able to remain hard and masculine but also experience his own softness and warmth. Through skillfully restraining his sexual passions, he is able to gradually open up not just to pleasurable sensations, but to the deeper joy of loving his partner and being loved in return.

What Makes Sex Great

It was about the fifth year of my marriage with Bonnie when I began to understand consciously what really makes sex great.

One time after having really great sex, I said, "Wow, that was great. I loved it. I loved every little moment. That was as good as it was in the beginning . . . "

I looked at Bonnie, expecting her to nod in agreement or say something like, "Yes, that was spectacular." Instead, she looked a little puzzled.

I said, "Well, wasn't it as good for you?"

She said matter-of-factly, "I thought it was much better."

I suddenly had ambivalent feelings. I thought, "What do you mean, this was better? Were you just faking it in the beginning? How could you say this was better? Wasn't it great then too?"

She continued, "When we first had sex, it was wonderful, but you didn't really know me and I didn't really know you. It takes years to really get to know someone. Now when you make love to me, you know who I am. You know the best of me and you know the worst of me, and you still desire me and love me. That is what makes sex great for me now."

From that moment on, I began to realize the truth of what she said. What makes sex really great is love. The more you get to know someone and continue to grow in intimacy and love, the more the sexual experience has a chance to thrive.

Over the years, my sexual experience had also changed. It had been so gradual that I hadn't even noticed until she pointed it out. This awareness allowed me to focus my attention on how to make sex even better. In the next chapter, we will explore how sex can continue to improve.

CHAPTER 2

Sex and Passion

Without passion, sex becomes routine and boring. With the assistance of advanced bedroom skills and love, a couple can continue to experience great passion and fulfillment. Instead of becoming less passionate over the years, a man who sees and touches his wife's naked body can be more turned on than ever. Not only can he be excited by the pleasure of arousal and increasing sexual intensity, but he can also be aware of how much more love, warmth, passion, and sensual affection he will be able to experience as well as provide for her. This awareness elevates sex to an even higher level of passion and excitement.

When she feels his passion for her, she can rejoice in his continued desire to connect with her and provide her with pleasure. She also recognizes sex as an opportunity to share love in a way that nurtures him the most. Sex becomes a beautiful expression of her love for him and an opportunity to receive in the deepest fibers of her femininity his love for her.

After practicing advanced bedroom skills, he will be much more aware that he is not only loving her, but also is getting the love he needs. He will be turned on to her not just because he is horny, but because he loves her and wants to get close. Without depending on some fantasy woman to be turned on, he will truly know who he is loving.

Sex is great when it is shared in love and the love keeps growing. For a woman to grow in sexual fulfillment, she primarily needs to feel emotionally supported in the relationship, but it is also important for the man to skillfully understand her different sexual needs.

For a man to grow in sexual fulfillment, he primarily needs to feel successful in fulfilling his partner sexually. This requires that he practice new skills not only in the relationship, but also in bed.

> **For a woman to grow in sexual fulfillment, she primarily needs to feel emotionally supported in the relationship, but it is also important for the man to skillfully understand her different sexual needs.**

How Sex Can Get Better

Sex can always get better, but like anything else, it requires new information and the opportunity to practice. Most men are never taught how to have sex. Once they can get turned on or can masturbate, they are some-how expected to be sexual experts. Sure, they know where to put it and how to have an orgasm in two min-utes, but the art of giving a woman an orgasm is a differ-ent story altogether. How are men supposed to know what makes women happy when they are not women? For great sex, a man needs to understand a woman's body and what turns her on.

> **How are men supposed to know what makes
> women happy when they are not women?**

It is hard for men to find out what makes women really happy in bed because we are expected to already know. In most cases, a man actually thinks he does know. He mistakenly assumes that what makes him happy will make her happy. When a woman isn't satisfied, he thinks something is wrong with her instead of with his tech-niques. He doesn't understand that a woman's needs are dramatically different from his in bed.

> **A man doesn't instinctively understand
> that a woman's sexual needs are dramatically
> different from his in bed. He mistakenly
> assumes that what makes him happy
> will make her happy.**

Having Sex the First Time

I remember when I first had sex. My partner and I had talked about it and were going to go all the way. I was so excited. I immediately and instinctively began to run around the bases as quick as possible to score. First base, I kissed her. Second base, I felt her up. Third base, I entered her, and then I scored a home run with an orgasm.

Before I had reached my destination, I noticed that she was following another tactic. She didn't go right to my erogenous zone. It was as though she was purposely striking out. She was moving her hands slowly up and down my body. Down my thighs and then back up to my chest. Up and down my arms and then up and down my chest and back. She was touching me everywhere I didn't want to be touched. Since we were planning to go all the way, I reached down to her hand and put it between my legs. I said, "There!"

Women Slow Up While Men Speed Up

I didn't understand at the time what she was doing. I thought she was trying to torture me. I didn't care about being touched all over my body. I just wanted to be touched in one place. Later on, as I learned about a woman's body, I discovered that she was doing to me what she would have liked me to do to her.

Men don't instinctively know what women like, and even when they hear about it, they tend to forget. Every song and book about sex says the same thing. A woman likes a man with a slow hand. Yet once he gets excited, he speeds up. He assumes she wants it speeded up because he does. He doesn't have a clue how much more exciting he can make it for her by restraining himself again and again.

> **A woman likes a man with a slow hand.**

When he gets excited, he gives the kind of stimulation that he would like but not what she needs. To make sex great over time, a man needs to open his awareness to the different needs a woman has while a woman has to help her man be successful in fulfilling her sexually.

How Sex Is Different for Men and Women

Sex is a very different experience for women and men. A man experiences pleasure primarily as a *release* of sexual tension. A woman experiences sex in an opposite way. For her, the great joys of sex correspond to a gradual *buildup* of tension. The more she can feel her desire for sex, the more fulfilling it is.

> **A man experiences pleasure primarily
> as a *release* of sexual tension. A woman's
> pleasure corresponds to a gradual *buildup*
> of sexual tension.**

For a man, sex instinctively is a testosterone drive toward the ultimate release of climax. When he becomes aroused, he automatically seeks release. His fulfillment in sex is mainly associated with the release of tension leading to and including the orgasm.

Biologically, in a man's body there is actually an inner sac of semen already waiting and seeking release. Unlike a woman, whose fluids are generated through arousal, when a man is aroused, he is already seeking release. In a sense, he is trying to empty out while she is seeking to be filled up.

A man's immediate desire to touch and be touched in his sensitive zones is a given. He does not need much help in getting excited. He needs help in releasing or letting go of his excitement. In a sense, he seeks to *end* his excitement, while a woman seeks to *extend* her excitement to feel more deeply her inner longing.

She relishes his ability to slowly build up her desire to

be touched in her most sensitive zones. As one layer at a time is stripped away, she longs for the deeper layers of her sensual soul to be revealed. As much as he wants to immediately satisfy his desire for sexual stimulation, she hungers and loves to feel her desire increase.

Why Men Crave Release

When the man touches the softness of a woman's bare breast, the smoothness of her inner thigh, or the warmth of her wet vagina, he begins to feel his own inner link to experiencing pleasure and love. Through touching her soft femininity, he can connect with his own softness and yet remain hard, focused, and masculine.

Sensuality is a part of his being, but he primarily experiences it through touching her body and feeling her pleasurable response. Many times after having great sex with my wife, I realize that I had forgotten how beautiful the trees are in our neighborhood. I go outside and breathe in the fresh air and feel alive again.

It is not that I didn't feel alive in my work, but by connecting with my wife through great sex, I can reawaken and bring to life my more sensual feelings that are easily forgotten in the focused pursuit of achieving my goals at work. In a sense, great sex helps me to stop and smell the flowers.

The more a man in his daily life is disconnected from his feelings, the more he will crave sexual stimulation and release. The intense pleasure of release at every stage of the sexual unfolding allows him to connect momentarily with his feelings and open his heart. For him, sexual hunger is not only for the experience of pleasure, but also for the experience of love.

Although he may not be aware of it, his persistent

sexual longing is really his soul seeking wholeness. The barren landscape of living only in his mind seeks union with the rich, sensuous, colorful, and sweet-smelling terrain of his heart.

> **A man's persistent sexual longing is really his soul seeking wholeness. The barren landscape of living only in his mind seeks union with the rich, sensuous, colorful, and sweet-smelling terrain of his heart.**

As his need to touch and be touched sexually is satisfied, his ability to *feel* automatically increases. As his feeling self is awakened, a tremendous energy is released. He can experience again his feelings of joy, love, and peace.

The Pleasure of Intercourse

Before intercourse, a man longs to enter a woman's body. His penis, hard and erect, is fully focused and extended to make contact with her most feminine sacred chamber. When he moves into her, penetrating her vagina, his pleasure is greatly intensified. This pleasure results from the releasing of his sexual tension.

As his penis is momentarily held and massaged on all sides by her warm and wet vagina, his whole being is nourished. Suddenly, he is teleported out of the dry domain of his intellectual detachment into the moist caverns of sensitive and sensuous feeling.

> **During intercourse, a man is teleported out of the dry domain of his intellectual detachment into the moist caverns of sensitive and sensuous feeling.**

A man's penis is his most sensitive organ; when it is touched, all of him is touched, soothed, excited, and electrified with pleasure. The feelings of love and attachment that are so easily dismissed by his rational mind are suddenly awakened by the intensity of sexual fulfillment.

After entering her welcoming vagina, he feels the intense satisfaction of arriving at his goal. When his tension is released, he automatically experiences a wave of increased feeling.

After this momentary release of tension, he pulls back to experience the tension again and then plunges forward to release it. This back and forth pumping action increases the tension and thus increases the feeling that results from his release. In this way, the tension builds up until he experiences a final release.

How a Man Feels Love

A man is free to feel when he has achieved his goal. When his male side has done its work successfully, he swings over to his female side and fully feels. When he can satisfy his own desires and also fulfill his partner, he can relax and feel a greater sense of peace, love, and joy.

In a way, when he and his partner experience an orgasm, he feels he has completed his job and has been richly rewarded by her deeply felt appreciation and love for him.

By providing her orgasm first, a man opens a woman up to fully respond to his orgasm. After she has experienced her orgasm, she can best share the fullness of her love and receptivity. At the moment of his climax, he is able to fully join with her and receive the love she has for him. To whatever extent his partner loves him, at this precious moment, he is able to let it in the most.

To whatever extent his partner loves him, at
the precious moment of orgasm, a man is able
to receive her love the most.

Particularly when he knows she is fulfilled and appreciative of him, he can fully thrive in that moment. More than at any other time, he can let her love in and can feel the love deep in his heart and reaffirm his commitment to her.

As a man's heart opens during orgasm, he is
able to feel the depth of his love and reaffirm
his commitment to her.

The Therapy of Great Sex

Any resentments building up in a man are easily washed away when he experiences great sex. There is no therapy better for a man than great sex. Sometimes therapy or counseling is needed to get to that place where a man and woman can experience great sex, but once a couple is there and they know how to keep getting there, for a man great sex keeps him going and keeps the magic of passionate love alive.

Without the regular experience of great sex, it is very easy for a man to forget how much he loves his partner. He may wish her well and be congenial or civil in the relationship, but he will not feel the deep connection that they felt in the beginning.

Without great sex, her little imperfections will begin to get bigger and bigger in his eyes. Unlike a woman, who needs to talk about feelings to feel more loving, a man can feel more loving through great sex.

Although good communication is essential in a relationship and will lead to great sex, when a woman in a relationship doesn't experience great sex over time, she can easily harden under the weight of all her responsibilities. She feels responsible not only for herself, but also for her partner. She forgets her own sensual and sexual feminine desires. Without the romantic support of her loving companion, she doesn't feel she has time for herself.

Why Women Relish Desire

The more a woman is focused throughout her day on caring for and giving to others, the less aware she is of herself and her own sensual desires. She may be in touch with other people's feelings but out of touch with her own.

Just as a man forgets feelings, a woman forgets her sensual desires and longings. The practicalities of day-to-day survival and living take precedence over her deeper and more sensual desires. The more pressured or overwhelmed she is, the harder it is for her to relax and enjoy life's simple pleasures.

> **Just as a man forgets feelings, a woman forgets her sensual desires and longings. The practicalities of day-to-day survival and living take precedence over her deeper and more sensual desires.**

When a man focuses on a woman in a caring and attentive way, he frees her to experience herself again. When a woman feels temporarily relieved of her pressure to care for others, she can begin to feel her sexual desires. A man's romantic attention to details designed to please her automatically begins to open her up.

By receiving the caring, nurturing, and sensuous support her female side craves, she begins to consciously feel her sexual yearnings. It is as though she doesn't even know she wants this stimulation until she gets it. The act of skillfully giving a woman what she needs helps her to discover her needs, and then she begins to long for more.

For example, when a man touches a woman close to her erogenous zones and then pulls away, back and forth in a rhythmic manner, a woman can begin to feel her desire to be touched more intensely. A skillful man moves his touch in the direction that she will eventually want him to touch, and then just as he gets close, he pulls away. This has the effect of increasing her desire for him to touch her there. He teases her by giving a little and then taking it away.

As a man touches her body in the nonerogenous zones bordering the places where she is not usually touched, she automatically begins to feel her need to be touched in the erogenous zones.

During great sex, a woman's desire gradually increases. In the beginning she may only feel a little or faint desire, but as that desire is fulfilled and tension is released, a greater desire follows. As desire continues to be fulfilled, a new and more intense desire is generated. In this way, through the gradual buildup and release of tension, she can feel her maximum desire for union and release it with an orgasm.

A secret of great sex is for the man to slowly tease a woman to increase her sexual desire. In the next chapter, we will explore the art of teasing.

CHAPTER 3

How to Drive a Woman Wild with Pleasure

Women enjoy conversation most when they are not required to get to the point right away. Many times, to relax or to get closer to someone, they like to circle around for a while and gradually discover what they want to say. This is a perfect metaphor for how a woman enjoys sex. She loves it when a man takes time to get to the point and circles around for a while.

Until her desire and arousal is intense, a woman enjoys being touched in a nondirect manner. For example, before moving his fingers or the palms of his hands to touch her breasts, a man should circle them for a while, getting closer and closer. Then, when he is about to touch, he should move somewhere else and start again.

Instead of being directly stimulated in her most sensitive places, as a man likes, a woman wants to be teased or gradually led to the place where she is longing to be touched. For example, when taking off her bra, instead of just taking it off each time, sometimes a man should slowly move his finger along the inner lining, then slowly pull down the bra strap, allowing the breast to be exposed, and then cover it up again.

**A woman wants to be teased
or gradually led to the place where
she is longing to be touched.**

A man can tease a woman by giving a little and then backing up to start over again. Repeating this process generates more desire in her. Her increased longing provides great pleasure for her as well as for him. Once he realizes what is really turning her on, he begins to feel the power of restraining his own passion to drive her wild with pleasure.

A Woman's Need to Relax

A man generally doesn't understand a woman's need to relax and get into sex slowly. He starts out ready to go. He does not readily understand a woman's need to relax first because sometimes he may want to have an orgasm so that he can relax. Unlike men, most women need to relax first before they can enjoy great sex.

Teasing and foreplay give her the time to relax and gradually let go of her inhibitions. Slow, rhythmic, and unpredictable physical touching, stroking, and rubbing of the nonerogenous zones gradually awaken a more intense longing to be touched in her erogenous zones. Before a man can fulfill a woman, she first needs time to relax and feel the part of her that needs to be filled up.

A piece of good advice commonly found in books about sex is for women to prepare for sex by taking a long warm bubble bath with the lights down low. Before I understood the differences between men and women, I could never understand this. If I took a long warm bath, I would probably fall asleep. Now, however, it makes sense to me that a woman could greatly benefit from a long warm bath.

Relaxation and gentle stimulation are the basis for a woman's arousal. By slowly tracing her body with his fingers and tender kisses, a man will awaken her more erogenous zones, which will long to be touched.

A Lover with a Slow Hand

When I interview women about what they want most from a man, again and again they tell me they want a lover with a slow hand. This slow process increases her pleasure so that when his fingers and tongue eventually move to touch her breasts, her nipples are erect and longing to be touched. When he moves to her inner thighs, vulva, labia, clitoris, and vagina, she is already wet, warm, and ready to be touched. When she is stimulated in this way, her pleasure wells up from deep inside her being.

A man is different. Directly touching his penis dramatically increases his pleasure. Many women don't realize this and frustrate a man by waiting too long to touch and rub his genitals. If such touching seems too direct for her, a woman can relieve much of his frustration with the weight of her body pressing against his groin.

**A woman needs to remember that
direct stimulation provides
maximum pleasure for a man.**

Because men are different in this way, a man needs to practice going slow. When he begins to consciously experience how wonderful it makes her feel, gradually it becomes more instinctive. A man needs to remember that to increase a woman's pleasure, he needs to delay direct stimulation. It will take longer and sometimes it will seem as if nothing is working, but eventually her pleasure will be much greater. If he takes this extra time, not only will she be happier, but he will also experience greater pleasure.

> A man needs to remember that to increase
> a woman's pleasure, he needs to delay
> direct stimulation.

Circumambulating the Temple

Certain ancient temples are dedicated to worshipping the female aspect of God. According to one ritual associated with these temples, you have to circumambulate the temple three times before entering it. This same principle applies to loving and adoring a woman during sex.

Before directly touching or entering a very delicate spot, a man should prepare her first. For example, when a man is kissing a woman, abruptly putting his tongue in her mouth can be too sudden. Instead, he should kiss her lightly several times, and then as she begins to open up, he can place his tongue in her mouth. One wonderful sensation is to first circle around inside her mouth before plunging more deeply.

When touching her breast and eventually the nipples, he should also circle first. For example, instead of directly touching her breast and then her nipple, he should first slowly move down toward the breast and then come back up. Then, with a slow rhythmic back and forth movement, he can get closer.

Once he begins to touch her breast, he can gracefully move his hand back and forth, cupping his hand around her breast in much the way her bra would. He could move his hand back and forth in a gentle rocking motion. Eventually, he can move all around the breast. Then he may squeeze and release it again and again. All these motions are designed to slowly and repetitively increase and then decrease stimulation.

One little tip that any man can easily learn is the art of taking off her bra. Years ago when I would take off my partner's bra, I would practically wrestle with the fasteners. Sex suddenly became very clumsy and awkward. How is a guy supposed to know how to take off a bra when he doesn't wear one?

This problem can be easily solved. One day when your wife is not around, find her bra drawer and take five minutes to examine her different bras. In a few minutes, you can become an expert. There are basically three kinds of fasteners: the up and down kind, the back and forth ones, and the ones in the front. Practice opening them so you can do it effortlessly with one hand. Then, with your eyes closed, practice doing it with one hand.

The next time you have sex, she will be greatly impressed as you coolly and confidently release her bra. Women like men to have confidence. This is one area in which a man can definitely know what to do. As he releases her bra with one hand, she will begin to melt and surrender to his knowledgeable and masterful touch.

How to Increase Desire

To increase her desire, a man may choose to touch her somewhere else and then come back to her breast and start all over. When he comes back this time, he may choose to get closer to the nipple. Instead of going directly, he should graze over it as if his touch is unintentional. This gives her a chance to feel her nipple's sensitivity and long for more.

When he comes back, he should circle the breast for a while. In this case, circling three times is not enough. Ten times longer than he would normally wait will probably do the trick.

Once he is touching the nipple, he can gently stroke it back and forth, back and forth, back and forth. The approach should be as though he has all the time in the world. Once the nipple is erect, he can gently lick it or begin to suck it. A woman will be particularly aroused when a man sucks on her nipple while he is stroking her clitoris.

Taking Off Her Panties

A man should begin to touch between her legs only when he thinks she is already wet. Sometimes it is good to first touch around the lining of her panties and gradually explore her vulva.

It is very exciting for her if he doesn't just suddenly pull down her panties. Instead, he may start to pull them down and then pull them back up a little higher.

Instead of taking them off, he can begin touching her on the inside edge of her panties across the back, then the front, then along the edge down the front. Then he can put his fingers inside the edge between her legs and feel the moist hairs and flesh around her vagina.

Once he has checked with a gentle probing finger that she is wet, he can take off her panties. Or, instead of immediately pulling them off, he can once again delay pulling them down to convey the message that he is in control of his passions.

Even if his passion is mounting, he can take a long time. This restraint and control allow her to feel freer to release her inhibitions and let go of control. Instead of taking off her panties, he can reach around her buttocks and pull her panties into her crack to expose her bare bottom. After turning her panties into a G string, he can begin to touch and stroke her buttocks and her inner thigh from behind.

Eventually, he can take off her panties and begin stroking her inner thighs and circling her whole vulva to touch her clitoris.

Touching Her Clitoris

Many times men forget to touch the clitoris. In my counseling, I've often heard a woman complain that her partner doesn't touch her there, or that when he tries to, he misses the spot much of the time, or that even when he gets it right, he doesn't stay long enough. Many women see this as a sign that he doesn't really care about her.

That judgment is generally not true. A man forgets to touch the clitoris because he doesn't instinctively understand how important it is. Here are some findings that will help a man to remember. In my own interviews and in most sexual studies, women report that ninety-eight percent of the orgasms they experience are directly the result of stimulation of the clitoris.

> A man forgets to touch the clitoris not because
> he doesn't care about her fulfillment, but
> because he doesn't instinctively understand
> that almost *all* female orgasms result from the
> stimulation of her clitoris.

Men, imagine having sex without having your penis stimulated. It would certainly not be very much fun. In a similar way, for a woman to enjoy great sex, stimulation of the clitoris for five to fifteen minutes is necessary if he wants her to have an orgasm.

Quite commonly in counseling, a man will tell me he touches his wife's clitoris for five or ten minutes. His wife, however, will privately tell me he rarely touches her there, and when he does, it is only for a minute or two.

I assure her that he really thinks he is taking more time and then teach her advanced skills for getting what she wants. By first accepting a man's tendencies to forget her needs, a woman can begin to get what she wants. If she is angry with him, it is hard for him to hear her legitimate requests.

Taking More Time for Her

If a man is not touching a woman's clitoris for a long enough time, I suggest that she reach down and continue touching herself. In this way, he gets the message loud and clear but doesn't feel criticized, corrected, or controlled. When he experiences how much she is enjoying it, he will then automatically begin taking more time for her.

When there is another way she would like him to touch her, instead of patiently and silently bearing what he is doing, she can reach down and make the moves on herself that she wants him to make. At those times, the man should grab a pillow and go down there to watch and learn.

One very effective way a man can learn to give a woman a longer interlude in sex is to time it. It doesn't sound romantic, but it sure works. I recommend that the man discreetly put a clock by the bed. While he is touching her vulva and clitoris, he can occasionally glance over and time himself.

Men are often surprised to discover that when they are aroused, they truly are living in a different time zone. What feels like ten or fifteen minutes of stimulation is really only one or two minutes by the clock.

By setting himself up to take a full five to fifteen minutes, he can begin to give her the stimulation she really needs. When she is prepared in this way, she can more fully receive him when they begin intercourse.

Skillful Stimulation

A skillful female lover directly stimulates a man's most sensitive and erogenous area, his penis and testicles. As these areas are stimulated, the rest of his body gradually wakes up and wants to be touched, licked, and stimulated as well. She can then successfully begin to use on him all the teasing techniques that would excite her. The trick with a man is to first stimulate his most pressing and sensitive organ.

A skillful male lover first stimulates a woman's least sensitive and least erogenous areas. First he might touch her hair, kiss her lips without yet inserting his tongue, wrap his arms around her, touch her legs but not her inner thighs, touch her back, or touch her buttocks. Then he might gently press his body against her, up and down, rubbing her with his groin back and forth in a circular motion.

By gradually moving around her body or rhythmically going back and forth on a certain area next to an erogenous zone, he wakes up her more sensitive areas and makes them want to be touched. Then, again in an indirect fashion, he can approach her more sensitive areas to provide repetitive stimulation.

A skillful male lover first stimulates a woman's least sensitive and least erogenous areas. A skillful female lover first stimulates a man's most pressing and sensitive organ.

By mastering the art of slowly increasing her desire, a man can be confident that he knows what to do to drive his partner wild with pleasure. This confidence alone is very exciting to a woman. In the next chapter, we will explore how to increase sexual confidence.

CHAPTER 4

*S*exual Confidence

Sexual confidence is the ultimate turn-on for both men and women. A woman is turned on when she feels her partner is confident that he knows how to fulfill her. His confidence assures her that he knows what to do, can be flexible if something isn't working, and has staying power. A man is turned on when a woman has confidence as well, but in a different way.

Sexual confidence is the ultimate turn-on.

When he senses her confidence in him, he is even more turned on. When her eyes give the message that she feels assured that she is going to have a good time, that he can do no wrong, and that she wants him to make love to her, he is very excited.

If a woman seems too confident that she knows what to do to drive him wild, it can possibly be intimidating. He may begin to wonder if he can do as much for her; he may begin to doubt that he can last long enough to satisfy her. Certainly, it is good for her to be confident in her abilities to satisfy him, but as with all advanced relationship skills, her greatest ability to fulfill him is through helping him be successful in fulfilling her.

A woman's greatest ability to fulfill a man in sex is through helping him be successful in fulfilling her.

Learning About Sex

Before I began teaching seminars on sex, I had been a celibate monk for nine years. As a monk, I had been a teacher of spiritual philosophy and meditation. When I reached the age of twenty-seven, my life radically changed. I ceased being a monk, returned to the world, and started having sex again.

For the first year after nine years of abstinence, I was like a hungry man eating after a long fast. I felt a great need to make up for what I had missed. All I could think about was women, love, and sex. I had sex for breakfast, lunch, and dinner. Sometimes after a few hours of sex, I was so sore that I would walk as if I had bowling balls between my legs.

I read all I could about sex and had as much sex as possible. I wanted to learn as much as I could. Eventually, I began a Ph.D. program in sex and psychology.

When I was with a woman, I would explain to her that I had been a monk for nine years and was just learning about sex. I would ask her to teach me about her body and tell me what made her sexual experience the most fulfilling.

This approach had a tremendous effect. Somehow, women didn't mind my not knowing about sex because I had been a monk. Not only would they get really turned on telling me about what they liked in sex, but I really learned a lot.

After about two years of intense sexual experimentation according to various ancient traditions of the world, my sexual partner at the time and I started teaching workshops on sex and spirituality. Together we facilitated discussions about what made sex great for both men and women. Throughout the seminar, many participants talked openly about what made sex memorable.

Everyone benefited from this process of talking about male and female likes and dislikes. Although I was leading the discussions, I was clearly a student as well. I was taking notes and then trying things out with my partner at home.

Why Talking Doesn't Always Work

Most men have never been monks and thus feel uncomfortable asking a woman the details of what she likes in sex. Not only does a man think he should already be a sexual expert, but a woman also wants her man to know what he is doing. She expects him to know intuitively what to do. She may also resist telling him what she likes because she doesn't want sex to be a pat formula but something they discover together.

Secretly, a woman may feel that if he is the right man or if he really loves her, he will know what to do. These feelings are food for romantic fantasy, but they don't create great sex. In addition, a woman is commonly afraid to let her wishes be known for fear that she may be judged in some way or that her partner won't do what she wants. For a variety of reasons, it just takes some of the romance out of sex if she has to tell him what to do.

> Secretly, a woman may feel that if he is the
> right man or if he really loves her,
> he will know what to do.
> These feelings are food for romantic fantasy,
> but they don't create great sex.

While most books on sexuality say that it is important to talk about sexual likes and dislikes, couples generally don't do it. People in our society commonly are very inhibited when it comes to talking about sex, so we generally only discuss sex when it is not working. A partner who is dissatisfied begins to talk about what he or she wants, but by then the other partner has trouble hearing about these needs. Instead of talking being a fun experience, it sounds like criticism or blame, and usually to some degree it is.

Men are particularly sensitive about hearing feedback. When a woman tells him what she would like or doesn't like, he hears her saying, "You are not good enough. Other men know how to do it, why don't you? What's wrong with you?"

Ironically, a man is expected to know about sex, and because he is supposed to know, he can't ask her questions about what she likes and take time to learn about her. Just as women sometimes feel a need to fake orgasm to please him, men have to fake confidence to please her. Many men want to know more but don't know how to talk about sex without sounding as if they don't know all about it.

Just as women sometimes feel a need to fake
orgasm to please him, men have to fake
confidence to please her.

Easy Ways to Talk About Sex

One way to overcome this lack of communication is to
read books together that describe sex and then discuss
them. It is a lot easier to approach the subject of sex if
your partner doesn't feel blamed for doing it wrong.
When you hear something that feels good to you,
responding to it with a little "ummm" or a bigger
"ummm" gives your partner the hint or reminder he or
she needs.

No matter how much we know about sex, understanding differences between men and women adds a
whole new slant. We are much more motivated to give
our partners what they need when we understand the differences.

Sometimes when I speak about sex, I ask my audience
to clap when they really like what I am saying, to empha-
size to their partners that the point I am making rings true
for them. Men are surprised at the times when the women
clap the hardest, and vice versa. A husband doesn't take
it so personally when his wife claps because almost all
the women are clapping, and besides, she is just clapping
at what she likes, not complaining about him. She doesn't
need to tell him directly what she needs because he can
observe her reaction.

Through directly experiencing feedback in this non-
threatening way, many couples who had even stopped
having sex suddenly started to enjoy great sex. By learning about their differences in this way, men and women

are more able to remember them and are thus more motivated to do what it takes to create great sex for themselves and their partners.

Every Woman Is Different

Not only are men and women different, but every woman is different. For a man to truly understand what a woman needs, a simple discussion at some point can make a big and lasting difference. To complicate matters more, not only are women different, but over time they change and then may change back. While general techniques and approaches can be discussed in a book or seminar, your partner's unique preferences cannot.

> Every woman is different. For a man to truly
> understand what she needs, a simple
> discussion at some point can make
> a big and lasting difference.

For Sam, touching a woman's clitoris was a hit or miss process. When she was getting all aroused, he knew he was doing something right, but didn't exactly know what. So that he could become more confident, I suggested that he ask his partner, Ellen, to take a few minutes to teach him about her body. I recommended that they talk about it in a casual and detached manner without trying to get turned on.

In a very matter-of-fact way rather than some sexy conversation, she explained briefly what she liked most. At first, Ellen was a little shy about it, but Sam assured her that it would really help. Years later, Sam can still remember every word she said.

With a clear understanding of what a woman likes

most, a man can relax. While he doesn't have to be mechanical about it and follow her suggestions to the letter every time they make love, an awareness of her preferences gives him the confidence to create a new sexual experience each time. When something does not seem to be working, he knows he can always come back to what she likes the most. This kind of confidence helps a man to relax in sex and actually be more creative and spontaneous.

> A man feels free to try new things
> when he knows he can always come back
> to the tried and true.

The Book of Love

In response to Sam's request, Ellen said, "You want the book on how to make love to me?" Sam smiled and agreed.

In the privacy of their bedroom, Ellen first talked for a while about some of the ways she liked to be touched and where. He then asked her to show him how she liked to be touched between the legs. In a kind of clinical way, she began to show him. She was not really trying to stimulate herself but was just showing him her favorite moves.

After watching for a while, Sam looked very closely and repeated her moves just to get them right. He tried to remember clearly what her vulva looked like when she touched herself so that he could make the same motions with the same accuracy without looking.

To practice, they used a mirror. He lay down beside her and reached down to her vulva and began touching her with one hand while holding the mirror with the other hand. As he touched her genitals, he also watched his movements in the mirror. Later, when they were really having sex and she was moaning with excitement, he knew what was pleasing her because he could clearly visualize what his hands were doing and where they were touching.

During their talk, Sam carefully studied the terrain of her sexual organs, particularly the clitoris. Because he knew precisely where her clitoris was, Ellen was assured of always getting the stimulation she needed, but most importantly, Sam knew exactly what he was doing down there.

While this worked wonders to improve their sex life, I also suggested to Sam that when sex was exceptionally great, he could again ask Ellen what she liked most. At those times, I explained to Ellen, she should be careful to focus on what she liked so as not to sound critical.

If Sam asked specifically about something and she didn't like it, instead of going into great detail, I told Ellen, she should just pause for a while as if to say she was thinking of a nice way to say that she didn't like it. This consideration makes negative feedback much easier to hear.

Sometimes she might say, "It was nice," or "It was all right," but without much enthusiasm. Sam would get the clear message that it didn't go over big. If something was displeasing to her, she might say, "I'm not really into that." These kind, gentle comments make it easy for Sam to ask again in the future.

By asking her from time to time what she likes, Sam allows her to share any new discoveries or shifts in her awareness of what she likes in sex. Likewise, Sam would almost always let her know when she did something that he really liked.

When to Talk About Sex

It is just not romantic to ask a woman what she wants while you are having sex. It is best done either after sex or at another time when you are not immediately planning to have sex. During sex, she doesn't want to think about her needs; instead, she wants to *feel* more and let it all gradually unfold.

To gather information about what a woman likes in bed, a man should listen carefully to how she responds during sex. A man needs to hear a woman verbally express her pleasure. That way, he gets the feedback he needs to know what is working to fulfill her. A woman may even enjoy sex more when she expresses her feelings verbally.

To more directly get feedback, a man can ask, but ideally he should do it when it seems as if sex has been rather good. Another good time to ask is in response to a comment in a book you are reading, or a lecture or movie scene.

This kind of conversation needs to be casual and not too direct. For example, a man should not take notes and then say, "OK, first you want this and then you want that, then after this I should do that."

This approach is too mechanical for her. She needs to feel that when he is having sex with her, he is expressing his feelings and not following a formula.

Giving Hot and Cold Feedback During Sex

Men are particularly sensitive about sexual feedback. When a man hears a woman's suggestions or requests, sometimes he feels he is being corrected or criticized, and this is hard for many men to handle.

Giving "hot" and "cold" messages can help your partner tremendously. At some time in your life, you have probably played the game of finding something that was hidden. The way to help the person looking, without directly telling, was to give hot and cold messages.

When the searcher was getting closer you'd say, "Warmer," and when the searcher was getting farther away, you would say, "Cooler." In a similar fashion, a woman can make sounds during sex that say, "You are getting warmer," or sounds that say, "You are getting cooler."

These responses are very important. It is as though he is wearing a blindfold and needs her responses to find his way. With every touch, he needs to know whether it is hot or cold. Feedback is very important for him to learn about her body over time.

Sometimes a woman may be enjoying the relaxing phase of sex, and making no sounds is a natural expression of her inner calm and relaxation. This is confusing because at other times, no sounds could mean he is not stimulating her the right way and she is not getting into it. The solution is for her to verbally let him know if she is quietly enjoying the relaxation.

She could say, "This feels so good. I like just cuddling for a while," or "It feels so good to just relax for a while and enjoy your touch," or simply, "Umm, I like this." This will give him the patience and understanding he needs to proceed.

How to Give Positive Direction

When a man is doing something that is uncomfortable for her or that she doesn't want, the best technique is to move him in the direction that will be more pleasurable. As with other advanced relationship skills, the approach that works best is to help him be successful rather than focus on his mistakes.

In sex, she can just move his hand where she would like it and make a pleasurable response. He will quickly get the message. For example, if she wants to verbally say something, she should ideally say, "I like this," instead of "I don't like that."

Ten Sexual Turnoffs

When a woman doesn't understand a man's sensitivities in this area, she will tend to unintentionally turn him off saying things like this:

1. "You're not doing it right."
2. "I don't like that."
3. "Ouch! That hurts!"
4. "Don't touch me like that."
5. "That tickles."
6. "Not like that."
7. "Not yet."
8. "Not there."
9. "I'm not ready."
10. "What are you doing?"

This kind of feedback can simply shut a man off immediately. One minute he is aroused, and the next he is not.

Why a Man Shuts Down

Many times during sex, a man's one goal is to please his partner. At those times, he is more sensitive to negative feedback. If he makes a mistake and feels criticized,

sometimes the only thing a woman can do is accept that
his feelings have been hurt and he just needs a little time
before he can become aroused again.

**When a man is seeking to please his partner, he
is most sensitive to negative feedback.**

Here's an example of how a woman can unintentionally cause a man to shut down. During sex with Jake,
Annie kept saying things like, "Not like that," "I don't
like that," and "That tickles." Well, after three strikes,
Jake was out. Suddenly, he stopped. In an instant, all his
feelings were gone. He lost all his attraction to her and
was simply turned off.

She said, "What's wrong?"

He didn't answer.

After waiting a few moments, she said, "Weren't we
just having sex?"

He said, "Yes."

She said, "Well, are we going to continue having sex?"

He said, "No," and then rolled over and went to
sleep.

In counseling, I advised Jake to discuss with Annie
what had happened. He told her, "During sex, I think I
am very sensitive to certain comments. I would rather
you move my hand where you want it than tell me you
don't like it. If I am tickling you, then I would rather you
just pull my hand away and try not to laugh, particularly
if I happen to be in a serious mood. If my touch tickles,
you could also just apply pressure to my fingers to give
me a message to press harder and not continue tickling
you with a feather touch."

To Jake's surprise, Annie was very open to his comments, and he greatly appreciated that. Afterward, when

Annie occasionally would say something that he felt was a turnoff, Jake did his best to dodge and let it pass.

Even if a man's arousal goes away for a little while, if he just pretends that everything is fine, with a little time it comes back. To stop and discuss why he shut down is generally not effective in returning him to a state of arousal.

> **Even if a man's arousal goes away for a little while, if he just pretends that everything is fine, with a little time it comes back.**

Sounds Verses Sentences

To give feedback in sex, it is best for women to make little noises and not use complete sentences. When a woman uses complete sentences, it can be a turnoff. Using complete sentences is a subtle clue to him that she is still in her head and not fully in her body.

Sometimes a woman will say things she read in a romance novel, such as "Your touch makes me long for you to enter my body." To a man, this can sound as stilted as "My, how big your hard member is." It just doesn't sound as if it's coming from her feelings. To give him the same message much more effectively, she can make deep sounds like "uumph" or high sounds like "ohhh." A woman's feeling responses to a man's touch give him all the feedback he needs.

> **A woman's responses to a man's touch give him all the feedback he needs.**

If a woman is using complete sentences, it may be because she is turned on when a man uses them. It is very impressive to a woman when a man can be hard and aroused and also talk to her.

A man tends to be silent as his arousal is building. Although he has the ability to talk in complete sentences, he doesn't do it; he doesn't like her to talk in complete sentences and so he doesn't realize that she will love it.

Talking to her in complete sentences not only increases her arousal but can raise her self-esteem and help her to love her body.

Twenty Sexual Turn-on Phrases

These are some phrases he can use to increase her pleasure if they express his true feelings. He should not use these phrases just to turn her on. It is important that they be genuine expressions of what is true inside him that perhaps he didn't realize were important to say. Here is a list of twenty:

1. "You are so beautiful."
2. "You are my dream come true."
3. "I love you so much."
4. "I love sharing my life with you."
5. "You turn me on so much."
6. "Your breasts turn me on."
7. "I love touching your soft skin."
8. "I love holding you in my arms."
9. "I love your breasts."
10. "I love your legs."
11. "Your breasts are perfect."
12. "Your lips are perfect."
13. "You feel so good."
14. "You feel so hot."
15. "You are so delicious."

16. "You are so wet."
17. "I am all yours."
18. "All my love is for you."
19. "I love having sex with you."
20. "I long for you."

These messages clearly expressed or whispered in her ear help her to feel loved, which in turn opens her up to her more intense sexual desires. With all the media and magazines focusing on women with perfect bodies, it is difficult for a woman to accept that her partner truly adores her body.

I always get lots of applause from women when I recount this list of things to say. The comments about the breasts especially get big applause. Men don't realize that women love and need to hear such things again and again. A man will feel during sex that his partner's breasts are perfect, but he doesn't realize that she needs to hear it. He mistakenly thinks it is enough that he wants to touch them.

The manager of a women's lingerie store told me this story. While a group of women over age sixty were shopping, one of them was trying on a very sexy outfit. The other women were shaking their heads and telling her that she couldn't wear it. With great confidence, she responded, "When you are the only naked woman in the room, to him you are a million dollars." This comment revealed an insight that most women do not know about men. When a man loves you, the more aroused he becomes, the more perfect your body becomes to him. The last thing on a man's mind during sex is how fat your thighs are.

When you are the only naked woman in the room, to him you are a million dollars.

When Men Look at Other Women

When every man's head turns in a trance as a woman with a "10" body walks by, all the other women in the room are reminded that they don't have "10" bodies. This can be hard on a woman's self-image. Expressing love to a woman using complete sentences when she is open and naked in his arms not only turns her on but also helps her to feel really good about herself and grateful to be with such a loving man.

> When every man's head turns in a trance as a woman with a "10" body walks by, all the other women in the room are reminded that they don't have "10" bodies. This can be hard on a woman's self-image.

A woman doesn't instinctively understand that the same man who stares at the "10" body, when in love and turned on by her, is also totally entranced by the feminine beauty of her body, regardless of where the media would rank it on a scale of one to ten.

When a man loves a woman and she is expressing her femininity in their relationship, he is attracted to her, not just to her body. The more he is attracted to her, the more beautiful her body is to him. Attraction that is only skin deep cannot last a long time. Quite commonly, an attraction that is only physical is quickly burned out, like a match.

Men Are Attracted Visually

It is important for women to understand that men are first attracted to a woman visually. A man sees a beautiful woman and instinctively wants to look at her body.

When a woman sees a handsome man, she may want to get to know him but not just because of his looks. She is not immediately concerned about his body.

A woman commonly misunderstands and assumes that a man is superficial if he is attracted primarily to the physical. She does not realize that he too wants to get to know her, but the place he starts is the body.

At first, men are most turned on visually while a woman is most interested in getting to know the person. Gradually, as the relationship unfolds, a man becomes more and more turned on to the inner person. As a woman loves the inner man gradually over time, she is increasingly attracted and turned on to his body as well.

Even if at times in the beginning of a relationship, a man is not sure he is fully satisfied with his partner's body, over time, as he grows to know her and love her, he will begin to experience the perfection of her body for him. It is quite easy for a single man to be hypnotized by the media about what makes a woman beautiful. He compares a woman to what he sees on TV and in magazines. Fortunately, when he is aroused and growing in love with a woman, the spell of the media is broken, and he can fully appreciate her beauty.

At these times in sex, he should reassure her by saying sweet nothings about how beautiful her body is to him. This not only frees him from the influence of the media but frees her as well.

A Simple Solution

Without an awareness of how men are attracted visually, a woman begins to feel unattractive when her partner looks at another woman, and begins to resent him as well. The solution to this problem can be simple.

A woman needs to accept a man's natural visual

appreciation of other women, and when a man looks, he needs to look appropriately. Once Bonnie and I were in an elevator with another older couple and a nineteen-year-old female model in a string bikini. This time, it was even difficult for the women not to look. When we got out of the elevator, the other woman said to her husband, "George, it's OK to look, but don't drool!"

> **A woman needs to accept a man's natural visual appreciation of other women, and when a man looks, he needs to look appropriately.**

Appropriateness and a sensitivity to your partner's feelings is the answer. When I happen to notice another woman and enjoy looking at her, I will out of consideration for my wife turn back around and give her some special attention. It is my way of saying, "Yes, that was a beautiful woman. Oh, how I like beautiful women. I am such a lucky guy to be married to such a beautiful woman. You are the one I want to be with."

By turning back to her and being a little affectionate, I assure her that she is the one I want to be with. Instead of being turned off, she is able to warm up to me instead.

Time, Time, and More Time

If we want confidence to grow and passion to last over time, we must take more time in sex. While a man may need only a few minutes of stimulation to have an orgasm, a woman generally needs much more. With this understanding, a man can remain confident that he is doing the right things even though his partner is taking much longer to become aroused and orgasmic.

Timing is one of the biggest sexual differences between

men and women. A man is biologically wired to become fully aroused very quickly, like a blow torch, while a woman is wired to become aroused slowly and gradually.

How Much Time?

Basically, a man needs about two or three minutes of stimulation to have an orgasm. It is generally a very simple process, as easy as shaking up a can of beer and then letting it pop!

If a woman is to have an orgasm, she generally needs about ten times that amount of time. She needs twenty to thirty minutes of foreplay and stimulation of her genitals.

If a man wants to give a woman an orgasm, he should remember this: For her to experience the big "O," he needs to place the "O" after his two to three minutes, making it twenty to thirty minutes.

> For a woman to experience the big "O,"
> a man needs to place the "O" after
> his two to three minutes, making it
> twenty to thirty minutes.

Many times a man will be done with his orgasm after a few minutes and truly assume that she was just as happy and fulfilled.

He says, "Did you come?"

She feels like saying, "I didn't even start."

Sexual Versus Emotional Fulfillment

Intercourse feels so good to him, he can't imagine that it wasn't as wonderful for her. When she tells him that she didn't come, he is easily confused or frustrated. Without understanding that she needs ten times more time than he does, he can easily feel powerless to turn her on.

During intercourse, she may also be making noises of pleasure and fulfillment. This does not always mean that she is getting the stimulation she needs. Many times the pleasure she feels is her emotional response to his pleasure. It feels good to connect to him emotionally and provide him with such pleasure, and it increases her desire, but emotional fulfillment does not stimulate her sexually. She needs the touch and the time if she is to have the orgasm.

> **Emotional fulfillment is not enough.**
> **A woman needs touch and more time**
> **if she is to have the orgasm.**

In real estate, there is a saying to help us understand the value of a property: "Location, location, location." In sex, it is "Time, time, and more time."

When a woman gets the time she needs, she can feel confident that she will get the fulfillment she is looking for. When a man understands that it is not so much what he does but how long he takes to do it that makes the difference, his confidence is also increased.

A man instinctively feels confident when his partner has regular orgasms. If she doesn't have an orgasm each time, he begins to worry. In the next chapter, we will explore how sometimes a woman can be fulfilled in sex without having an orgasm.

Women Are Like the Moon, Men Are Like the Sun

Women are like the moon in that their sexual experience is always waxing or waning. Sometimes, regardless of what a great lover he is, she will not have an orgasm. She is not only unable to have an orgasm, but she may not even want one. This difference between men and women is very important for men to understand.

In her sexual cycle, which tends to last approximately twenty-eight days, sometimes she really wants an orgasm and her body is ripe and ready, while at other times she would rather cuddle and be close. She could have sex at these times and even be aroused, but her body doesn't care to have an orgasm.

....

Sometimes a woman really wants an orgasm and her body is ripe and ready,

**while at other times she would rather
cuddle and be close.**

Sometimes she is in the full-moon stage of her cycle, sometimes she is in the half-moon stages, and sometimes she is in the new-moon stage. In each of these phases and all the many phases in between, her sexual longings will vary. There is no way to predict which stage she is in. Even from month to month, the length of the cycle varies.

Men do not instinctively understand this difference because they are not like the moon in this regard. Men are like the sun. Every morning, it rises with a big smile!

When a man gets turned on, his body generally wants a release. He wants his orgasm, and he is generally quite capable of having one. If he gets all hot and turned on and then doesn't have a release, not only will he feel emotionally dissatisfied, but he may also experience the physical discomfort of "blue balls." This is why it is hard for him to imagine his partner not wanting or needing orgasmic release every time she has sex. She may enjoy the closeness of sex but not want an orgasm. When she is not interested or doesn't have an orgasm, he mistakenly assumes something is wrong.

How Men Measure Success in Sex

Men tend to measure their success in sex by a woman's orgasm. If she doesn't come, he may pout for hours. This is why a woman feels pressured to perform in sex even if she doesn't feel like it. She may fake sexual pleasure and orgasm just to satisfy him.

This pressure on her to perform prevents sex from being completely fulfilling for her. It also prevents her from experiencing the natural ebb and flow of her sexual experience. If she has to be equally responsive or orgasmic for him each time, she can't relax and discover where sex will naturally take her.

**Pressure on a woman to have an orgasm
prevents sex from being
completely fulfilling for her.**

Once a woman feels she has to fake orgasms or perform, it can prevent her from having real orgasms. It is said that many of the great "sex goddesses" as proclaimed by the media were actually nonorgasmic in their real personal relationships. Quite commonly, prostitutes pretend to enjoy sex tremendously and be orgasmic but are incapable of having a real orgasm.

The pressure to have an orgasm each time can prevent a woman from having orgasms at those times when her body really can have one. One of the requirements for great sex is that a woman not feel pressured to perform in any way. This can be easily accomplished through an understanding of how men and women are different.

A great sex life means that sometimes sex will be a super fantastic memory never to be forgotten, while at other times it is may not be so intense, but it is loving and both partners get what they want; the man gets his orgasm, and whether or not she's in the mood to have an orgasm, she gets the physical affection she wants.

Memorable Sex

One time while getting undressed before bed, I looked over at my wife while she was also getting undressed. I suddenly began thinking about the possibility of having sex that night.

I said, "Did we have sex this morning?"

She smiled and said, "Yeah, it was real memorable, wasn't it?"

I laughed.

This exchange best describes for me the difference between regular sex and memorable sex. A great sex life includes both regular sex *and* regular memorable sex.

Although one may know the skills of memorable sex, it is easy to forget to use them and settle for a routine of regular sex. Men particularly forget how to create memorable sex. It is not that they don't care, but they just forget what is important to the woman.

Men are more driven to be efficient. When twenty minutes of foreplay works, a subconscious impulse emerges saying, "Let's see if ten minutes can create the same effect." Quite automatically, he forgets her need for *more* time.

Why Men Forget

Having a great sex life doesn't mean you experience fireworks every time, but it does require you to persist in being aware of your partner's different needs. Ideally, each time both the man and the woman should feel they are getting what they need.

Men commonly tend to forget what a woman needs to be fulfilled in sex. In the beginning, he may go very slow in sex because he is not sure of what she likes or he is not sure that she is willing to let him touch her. But once they are having sex regularly, he doesn't realize that it was his slow and tentative movements that were so arousing to her. Even when a man has read about these differences, because they are not his instinctive experience, he may easily forget them in the heat of his passion.

....

**Once they are having sex regularly
a man doesn't realize that it was**

**his slow and tentative movements
that were so arousing to her.**

Commonly, a woman will feel as if he doesn't care about her. Even if a man cares deeply, he can still forget and not even know he is forgetting. I remember a surprising experience in the first year of our marriage. After giving an evening lecture on sex, while driving home I asked Bonnie if she had liked my talk.

She said, "I love hearing you talk about sex. That's why I always come to your sex lectures. You describe it so clearly."

I said rather proudly and confidently, "When I describe great sex, is that what I do?" I was expecting her to say, "Oh yes."

Instead, she hesitantly said, "Well . . . you used to do it more."

I said, "You mean I don't do all those things?"

She said, "Well, recently you've kind of been in a hurry."

I said, "Well, tonight we will have lots of time."

She said, "Ummm, that sounds good."

Her noncritical tone of voice helped me not to feel defensive. That night we did have a great time. I share this story to make the point that even when I regularly used to teach audiences about great sex, I could forget the very basics of taking more time for her.

When a man doesn't take the time a woman needs, one skill for slowing him down is to make a brief, well-chosen comment like this:

"Oh, this feels so good. Let's go real slow."
"Let's make sure we have plenty of time."
"Tonight I want to take a long time."

These kinds of comments are informative but not corrective or controlling.

What Makes Sex Memorable

While listening to men and women share stories of memorable sex in my early seminars, I began to notice a common theme. A man would tell stories about how a woman responded to him. He was proud of how he had driven her wild or taken her to higher states of ecstasy.

Women, on the other hand, described more how they felt and what he did for her. The buildup was more important to her than the end result. Women would proudly describe what the man did to provide for her fulfillment. This different theme is very significant.

The bottom line of what makes sex fulfilling and memorable for a man is a woman's fulfillment. When a man is successful in fulfilling her, he feels most fulfilled.

What makes sex fulfilling and memorable for a man is a woman's fulfillment.

What makes sex fulfilling and memorable for a woman is the same, her fulfillment. Certainly, she wants him to be fulfilled, but his fulfillment is not a primary cause of her pleasure. It doesn't give her the physical stimulation she needs for orgasm. Women do not commonly say things like, "Sex was really great because he had such a great orgasm." When a man is successful in fulfilling her, sex is great for her.

For sex to be memorable from both the male and female perspectives, the woman needs to be fulfilled. I have never heard a man complain, "She had a great time and I didn't. All she cared about was herself and her own pleasure. She had her way with me and then left."

When Her Pleasure Becomes His Pleasure

The more emotionally connected to a woman a man is, the more her pleasure becomes his pleasure. Through physically moving inside her being, he also emotionally moves inside her and can actually experience her fulfillment as his own.

If a woman has a great time, the man tends to take credit, and it excites him even more. His fulfillment and pleasure are ensured by her fulfillment. As we have discussed, his fulfillment in sex is determined or measured by her maximum fulfillment. If she doesn't have an orgasm, he mistakenly thinks that she was not fulfilled. This tendency can be overcome when he understands that she can be just as fulfilled without always having an orgasm.

> **Sometimes a woman can be just as fulfilled without having an orgasm.**

It is such a relief for both partners when the man finally understands that a woman can be fulfilled sometimes without an orgasm. He can stop measuring the success of sex by whether she had an orgasm, and she can stop feeling the pressure to have an orgasm when her body is not responding in that way. Instead, he can measure success by her fulfillment, and she can relax and enjoy the sex without the pressure. Men need to remember that women are like the moon and sometimes can be fulfilled even without an orgasm.

Women I've counseled have expressed this truth in different ways:

> "I don't need to have an orgasm each time. If I don't have an orgasm, it doesn't mean something is wrong."

"Sometimes to be fulfilled, I just want to be held. I am
   happy if he gets off and has an orgasm, but I don't
   really want one. It is just not there. At other times,
   it is there and I definitely want to have one."
"I like having orgasms sometimes, but at other times,
   what I like most is the touching and cuddling."
"Sometimes sex is too much about getting to the
   orgasm. I find myself trying to have one, and all
   the fun is gone. I want it to be OK with him if I
   don't have one. It's OK with me."

When a man doesn't understand that women are like
the moon, it is not only very frustrating for him, but also
puts a lot of pressure on women to perform.

Why Women Are Surprised

When I talk in groups about how men want a woman to
be fulfilled, it is clearly a surprise to most of the women.
They feel in response, "If he is so concerned with my fulfillment, then why is he in such a hurry to fulfill his own
passions?" With an understanding of how we are different, it becomes easy to answer this question.

Men want a woman to be fulfilled but mistakenly
assume that what makes him happy makes her happy.
Just as he is turned on and fulfilled through her pleasure,
he assumes she will be just as happy with his pleasure.
He does not instinctively know that she needs more time,
nor does he realize all the other requirements that women
have for great sex.

As I have mentioned repeatedly, a woman's sexual fulfillment is much more complex than a man's. She
requires a man with a skillful touch, lots of time, and a
loving attitude. For a man, once he is aroused, it is generally a given that he will have an orgasm.

His problem, which we will discuss a little later, is that he may have an orgasm too soon; from his side, she takes too long and from her side, he is too quick. This problem is easily solved as men begin to understand how to prolong the sexual experience to fulfill her basic needs. Once she is fulfilled, then at other times she can be more supportive of occasions when he doesn't want to take a long time.

Men and women are actually very compatible. For those times when a woman is like the full moon, needing an orgasm, a man can greatly enjoy taking her to higher levels of pleasure and fulfillment. At those times when she is a half-moon or less, her need to be touched can be fulfilled while he gets to enjoy sex freely without having to hold back. In the latter case he can quickly have an orgasm in a few minutes, the way he was biologically wired to.

Sometimes they can choose to take a long time so that she gets her orgasm, and at other times, when she is not in the mood for an orgasm, he can enjoy the unrestrained freedom of just going for his orgasm. At these times, he is like a sprinter running to his goal. At other times, he is like a long distance runner and is required to pace himself to last as long as it takes.

When a Woman Doesn't Want an Orgasm

Sometimes when a woman begins sex, she doesn't know whether her body wants to have an orgasm or not. She doesn't know if she is in the full-moon or half-moon phase of her cycle. She may feel romanced by her partner and want to have sex, but as sex progresses, she may discover that her body doesn't want to have an orgasm.

When the man is taking a lot of time trying to give her an orgasm and she is trying to have one but her body is just not responding, it can be very frustrating to them both. He feels as if something is wrong and blames her or himself. Without understanding her moon phases, she may feel that something is wrong with her. She will try to perform and respond for him, but it is not real. This can minimize sexual confidence for them both and leave a disturbing memory that minimizes their desire to have sex.

Once both partners understand the woman's sexual cycle, these old frustrations disappear. When the partners have greater confidence, their sexual juices can begin to flow freely. Repeatedly, women tell me that by just hearing that they are like the moon, they are released to become orgasmic. A woman who has difficulty opening up in sex begins to open up when she doesn't feel the pressure to have an orgasm. Not having to respond leads her to the place where her responses are more natural. By not trying to have an orgasm one day, she is freed to have an orgasm at another time.

> A woman who has difficulty opening up in sex begins to open up when she doesn't feel the pressure to have an orgasm.

During sex, if a woman begins to realize that she is not going to have an orgasm, instead of continuing to try, she can say, "Let's just have a quickie." This little phrase can make a world of difference. He has no problem shifting from trying to give her an orgasm to suddenly going for his own orgasm.

Her not having an orgasm is only difficult when they don't share an understanding that he has not failed her. When she says, "Let's just have a quickie," a part of him feels let off the hook. It reminds him that it is not his fault or hers; it is just not the time for her to have an orgasm. He can successfully fulfill her just by being affectionate and holding her while he goes for it.

Just as a man needs to take a long time for the woman to be fulfilled in sex, sometimes he needs her to not take a long time. In the next chapter, we will explore the joy of quickies for men, and women can be assured of getting what they need as well.

CHAPTER 6

The Joy of Quickies

While many books talk about taking time for the woman to have a pleasurable experience, none seem to talk about the man's legitimate need to *not* take a lot of time.

Although most men are happy to please their partners, sometimes a man can feel that he just wants to skip all the foreplay and, as the slogan goes, just do it. Something deep inside him wants to cut loose and completely let go without any restraint or worry about lasting longer or what he should do to make his partner happy. It's not that he doesn't want her to be happy, it's that he doesn't want to hold himself back.

To be patient and regularly take the time a woman needs in sex, a man needs to enjoy an occasional quickie. When he can follow his instincts once in a while to fulfill his need to "go for it" without all the buildup and fore-play, he can more easily take the time she needs on other occasions. Just as a car needs to run occasionally at high speeds on the highway to clean out the carburetor, some part of a man just needs to attain his sexual expression without any slowing down.

> **To be patient and regularly take the time a woman needs in sex, a man needs to enjoy an occasional quickie.**

Feeling this need inside and acting on it are too differ-ent things. For example, even when James and Lucy did have quickies, James always felt a little guilty because it was clear that Lucy didn't get what she needed.

James felt that having sex without foreplay for her was selfish and he was not being a good lover. To try to solve this problem, he would wait till he was almost late for work and then initiate sex with Lucy.

He would say, "Well, I only have a few minutes because I need to leave for work. Let's have sex before I go." She was very cooperative, and he would experience the joy of having a quickie guilt-free.

After a while, this didn't feel right. James didn't want to have to be late in order to enjoy an occasional quickie. To more effectively solve this problem, I suggested that James and Lucy negotiate.

Quickies for Cuddles

James said to Lucy, "Sometimes I would just like to have sex without all the foreplay. I know it doesn't give you what you want, but it would sure feel good to me." I asked Lucy, "What could James do to support you so that you would feel good about supporting him with quickies?"

She said, "I'm not sure. I guess I have a lot of considerations. I'm worried that if I willingly have quickies with James, that's all I will get."

He said, "OK, that makes sense. What if I promise to have more leisurely sex with you just as much as we are having now?"

She said, "That's good. What about really special sex or a romantic getaway for an evening at least once a month?"

James agreed. In return for an occasional quickie, or "fast food sex," they would have leisurely or "healthy home-cooked sex" once or twice a week, and at least once a month they would schedule a special time with no interruptions for "gourmet sex." I asked Lucy, "Is there anything else you need James to do so that you will be comfortable indulging him in quickies?"

She said, "It all sounds great, but I still don't feel completely comfortable with the idea of quickie sex." She turned to James and said, "When we have a quickie, it is sometimes over in three or four minutes. By the time you are done, I am just getting started. I feel like you expect me to be all excited and responsive. I can't in that short time period."

James said, "That's OK. I can give that to you. If you are OK with occasional quickies, I promise to never expect you to respond. It will just be your gift to me. I don't expect you to get anything out of it. You can lie there like a dead log!"

She laughed and said, "OK, but there is more." Lucy realized that in this moment she had great negotiating power. She had the moon and she was going for the stars as well, and James was glad to go with her.

She said, "If you are going to have regular quickies, then I want cuddles. I want to feel your willingness to cuddle with me for a few minutes without you getting turned on and wanting sex."

He said, "No problem. Just tell me that you want to cuddle and that's it. I'll restrain myself and just be warm and affectionate." He paused. "Is that it?"

She said, "I think that's it."

The Four Conditions

I thought this was a terrific deal, and so did James and Lucy. To make sure that their quickies would be guilt-free, I suggested that they summarize their deal.

James said to Lucy, "So given these four conditions: regular healthy home-cooked sex, gourmet sex once a month, no expectations during the quickie, and regular cuddles, you will then be happy to have fast food sex with me."

She said, "It sounds good. But still if I'm just too tired or I'm bloated with my period or for whatever reason, I don't want to feel like I have to say yes."

James happily agreed.

In our next session, James shared that while having a quickie, Lucy really did lie there like a dead log, and he didn't mind at all.

How to Increase Sexual Attraction

This new deal completely improved James and Lucy's sex life in ways that they couldn't imagine. James's sexual attraction for Lucy began to increase dramatically.

James described it this way: "For the first time in my sexual history, I felt completely free. I was suddenly free to skip foreplay and go right to intercourse. For the first time, I was not at all concerned about my performance or having to please. It was strictly for me, and there was no sinking guilty feeling that she wasn't getting what she needed. We both feel good about it because we know she will get hers at another time."

For James and most men, the freedom to have guilt-free quickies is as liberating as going into a store and knowing that you can buy anything you want, or being able to drive your car without any speed limits; it is like riding a motorcycle without having to wear a helmet. It is definitely a very adolescent feeling, but it also brings new life into a man's life and into the relationship. After all, it is in adolescence that a young man is in his sexual prime. No wonder this newfound sexual freedom greatly recharges a man's sex life.

In addition, after James and Lucy made this agreement, he was never hesitant to initiate sex because there was no possibility of feeling rejected. On most occasions, when he initiated sex, if she was not in the mood, instead of saying no, which would make him feel rejected, she would simply say yes to a quickie.

Interestingly, after a few years of guilt-free quickies, they were not so important to James. Many times when he initiates sex and she is not in the mood, rather than have a quickie, he will happily wait until she too wants sex.

Knowing that he can almost always have a quickie and that she is happy to give him one, when she is not in the mood for more leisurely sex, he doesn't feel in the slightest way rejected. This feeling that he will not be rejected is essential for a man to continue to be passionately attracted to his partner. Once this agreement is made and the man doesn't feel rejected, it is still a great feeling for a man just to go for it sometimes without having to put on the brakes.

How to Safely Initiate Sex Even When She's Not in the Mood

By making quickies guilt-free, a woman automatically supports a man in feeling free to initiate sex. These are some common phrases for initiating sex and common answers a woman can give instead of just saying no.

1. He says, "I'm feeling really turned on to you. Let's have sex." — She says, "I'm not in the mood for sex, but we could have a quickie."

2. He says, "I've missed you. Let's find some time to have sex." — She says, "Um, that sounds like a good idea. I don't have a lot of time right now, but we could have a quickie."

3. He says, "I have some time. Would you like to have sex?" — She says, "We could have a quickie now and then maybe tomorrow we could schedule more time to have sex."

4. He says, "Would you like to go upstairs and spend some intimate time together?" — She says, "We could have a quickie. Maybe that will help me relax a little, and then we could talk."

5. He says, "Let's schedule some time today to make love." — She says, "Well, I'm not in the mood for a lot of foreplay, but a quickie would be nice. Sometimes I just want to feel you moving inside me even though I don't feel like an orgasm."

6. He says, "I'm feeling so turned on. I would love to have sex."

She says, "I would love that too. We don't have much time, so why don't we have a quickie?"

7. He says, "Let's have sex tonight."

She says, "I've really got a bad headache. Maybe we could have sex tomorrow. I could give a you a hand job right now."

8. He says nothing but gently reaches over in bed and begins making the moves.

She whispers, "Um, this feels good. Don't worry about me tonight. Just go for it."

9. They are having sex, he is touching her clitoris, and she realizes that she is not going to have an orgasm.

She pulls his hand up and says, "Just come inside me. I just want to feel you in me. I love to feel your pleasure." This is a code phrase for "You don't have to pleasure me. A quickie is fine because tonight my body is not in the mood for an orgasm."

10. He is spending a lot of time on foreplay, and she really isn't in the mood for sex and just wants to feel close to him while he enjoys getting off.

She can take his erect penis and put it inside her, saying, "Let's have a quickie tonight."

Adding guilt-free quickies to your sex life provides an unexpected relief for both partners. Until a man experiences the freedom of never feeling the possibility of rejection, he won't know how it has been affecting him and holding back his passions. Using these new communication skills also frees a woman from having to perform or fake orgasm at those times when she discovers that she just isn't in the mood.

Why Men Stop Initiating Sex

Each time a man initiates sex and is rejected, he's a little more hurt, his ego is a little more bruised. After being burned and spurned again and again, he hesitates to initiate sex and may even begin to lose touch with his desire to have sex. He may begin desiring other women who have not yet rejected him, or he may just lose interest. If he is attracted to other women, he may mistakenly assume that he is no longer attracted to his wife. If he just loses interest in sex, he thinks it is because he is getting older.

> When a man feels repeatedly rejected in sex,
> he begins to lose touch with his desire
> to have sex. He may begin desiring
> other women who have not yet
> rejected him, or he may just lose interest.

In the beginning of a relationship, couples often have sex almost anytime they have the opportunity. Then as the practicalities of work and home come back into focus, naturally there is less sex. Then with children, they have to schedule time or wait for an available moment.

When a man tries to initiate sex by saying, "Let's have sex," quite commonly a woman will unknowingly give any of the following rejecting messages:

"I can't right now. I need to make dinner."
"I can't right now. I have to return my calls."
"I can't. I have to go shopping."
"I don't have time."
"I can't. I already have too much to do."
"I'm not in the mood right now."
"This really isn't a good time."
"I have a headache."
"I can't think about sex right now."
"I have my period and I'm feeling crampy."

Each time this happens, a man will try to be understanding, but at a more primal emotional level, he finds it gets harder and harder to not feel rejected, and over time he may stop initiating sex. He may still want sex, but after being burned so often, he will hold back and wait for some clear sign from her that she is in the mood.

He may spend a lot of time trying to figure out when she seems open to sex, wondering, "Is this a good time to pursue?" Although he may not realize it consciously, every time he is in the mood and holds back from initiating sex, he ends up feeling more rejected.

All Is Not As It Seems

Jake and Annie had been married for seven years. After about the first three years, they started having marital problems and sought help. They had started out passionately attracted to each other, and then over time the passion was gone. In counseling, Annie told Jake, "I miss having more sex with you. Is it something I did? Are you upset with me?"

He seemed surprised. "It seems to me like I always want sex and you don't. A lot of times when I want sex, I don't say anything because I know you are not in the mood."

She said, "How do you know if I am in the mood unless you ask?"

He said, "I can tell. I have been rejected enough."

She said, "That's really not fair. Sometimes if I am not in the mood, just by you mentioning that you want sex, I may discover that I am in the mood. Even if I don't feel in the mood right away, it helps me to move in that direction. I really appreciate when you initiate sex."

After Jake and Annie learned about guilt-free quickies, the passion came back into their relationship.

Why Men Feel Rejected

When Annie and Jake talked about sexual rejection, she didn't readily understand why he would feel so rejected if she was not in the mood. She felt that because she truly loved having sex with him, he shouldn't feel rejected.

Intellectually, he agreed with that, but emotionally, it was very different. There are a variety of reasons that sexual rejection is one of the most sensitive and vulnerable areas for a man.

Biologically and hormonally, men are much more driven to be sexual than women are. Quite naturally, it is on their minds more of the time. Because a man is wanting it so much, he will feel rejected more of the time when he is not getting it.

> **Because a man is wanting sex so much,
> he will feel rejected more of the time
> when he is not getting it.**

As we discussed before, it is primarily through sexual arousal that men begin to feel the most. A man's heart begins to open as he is turned on. When a man is aroused and about to initiate sex, he is most vulnerable. It is then that he can most deeply feel the pain of rejection. If he is already feeling hurt and rejected by his partner, arousal will make him feel that pain again. He may feel aroused and begin to feel angry and not even know why.

> **If a man is already feeling hurt and rejected by his partner, arousal will make him feel that pain again. He may feel aroused and begin to feel angry and not even know why.**

When a man doesn't know how to avoid feeling rejected, it just increases his frustration and pain. As a result, he stops feeling attracted to his partner. If he doesn't consciously know how to solve this problem, to avoid feeling rejected, he unconsciously stops feeling turned on to his partner. This loss of attraction is not a choice but an automatic reaction.

In some cases, his sexual attraction is directed elsewhere to a fantasy woman who will not reject him or to a woman whom he doesn't care for. He is not risking a painful rejection if he doesn't care for the woman. This explains why a man can be turned on to a stranger but lose his attraction to the woman he loves most.

Women Love Sex

Women love sex, but before they can feel their desire for it, they have more requirements than men. A man doesn't readily understand this because throughout his life, he gets many messages that women don't like sex. To sustain passion and attraction in a relationship over the years, a man needs clear messages that she loves sex with him.

**To sustain passion and attraction in a
relationship over the years, a man needs clear
messages that she loves sex with him.**

As a general rule, men peak in their sexual interest
when they are seventeen or eighteen years old. A woman
reaches her prime when she is thirty-six to thirty-eight
years old. It is similar to the pattern that men and women
experience during sex. The man gets excited very quickly
with little foreplay—except the opportunity to have
sex—while a woman requires more time. Quite naturally,
he feels that women don't like sex as much as he does.

His mother's attitude about sex may also influence
him. If, as an adolescent, he was afraid of having his
mother find out about his growing interest in sex and
girls, he might have gotten the message that it is not OK
to want sex. Later in life when he is with a woman that
he cares about, these subconscious feelings can begin to
emerge as little voices or faint feelings saying, "I can't be
sexual around her or I will be rejected."

These past experiences may not directly cause a man
to lose interest, but they certainly make him more sensitive to feeling rejected when she seems disinterested in
sex. When she is not in the mood, subconsciously he
begins to feel, "I knew it. She doesn't want to have sex."

One of the ways to counteract this tendency is for a
woman to give the man repeated subtle messages that she
likes sex. Her acceptance of occasional quickies is the
strongest message of support she can give. Another pow-
erfully positive message is to be very supportive whenever
he initiates sex.

**A woman's acceptance of occasional quickies and
a positive message whenever her partner initiates
sex ensures lasting attraction and passion.**

How Men Unnecessarily Feel Rejected

Many times a woman is potentially in the mood for sex, but a man just doesn't realize it. He ends up feeling rejected when she might really want to have sex.

Sometimes a man will ask her any of the following questions:

"Would you like to have sex?"
"Do you want to have sex?"
"Are you in the mood for sex?"

To any of these requests, if she responds, "I'm not sure," or "I don't know," he will generally misunderstand and mistakenly hear rejection. He thinks she is politely saying no when she is really saying she doesn't know. This is hard for men to understand, because men are like the sun and not like the moon. When a man is asked if he wants sex, he has a definite response. The sun is either up or down. He generally knows for certain if he wants to have sex.

When a woman is unsure about wanting sex, it means that she needs a little time, attention, and talking to find out. With this new awareness, a man can easily overcome his tendency to immediately feel rejected and give up his pursuit.

Is There a Part of You That Wants to Have Sex?

When a man's partner seems uncertain about having sex, instead of giving up, he should say, "Is there a part of you that wants to have sex with me?"

Almost always she will say yes. He may be surprised sometimes by how quickly she will respond by saying,

"Sure, a part of me always wants to have sex with you." This will be music to his ears.

She may, however, then proceed to talk about all the reasons she doesn't want to have sex. She might say, "I don't know if we have enough time. I still have to do laundry and some errands." Or she might say, "I'm not sure how I am feeling. I have so much on my mind right now. I feel like I should devote time to finishing this project."

As she continues to talk, he should remind himself that she is not saying no. She just needs to talk, verbally sort things out, and then she can find her desire. Many times after sharing several reasons why she is not in the mood, she will then turn around and say, "Let's do it."

Without understanding how a woman is different, a man can easily feel turned off while she is talking about the reasons she doesn't know if she wants to have sex. But as long as he hears that a part of her wants to have sex, it is much easier for him to hear about the parts of her that don't want to have sex. Even if she finally discovers that she doesn't want sex, she can say, "We could have a quickie if you want and then sometime soon we can have (more leisurely) sex."

A woman can also use this insight. When a man wants to have sex and she is not sure, she can make it a lot easier for him to patiently discover with her what she would like. Let's take an example:

He says, "Would you like to have sex?"

She says, "A part of me would love to have sex, but I'm not sure. I still have to buy groceries and then run some errands. I still haven't . . . etc."

Through first letting him know that a part of her wants to have sex, she makes it much easier for him to listen and accept the other reasons she may not be in the mood.

Is It Sex or Making Love?

Another way a man may get the message that his partner doesn't like sex is if she never uses the word "sex." Eric said, "I remember in one relationship, my partner refused to call sex, sex. She always wanted to call it 'making love.' When I called it 'sex,' she would say no and become a little judgmental. She didn't even want me to use the term. I could understand that she liked the term 'making love,' but I felt shamed by her. Certainly, my heart and mind wanted to make love, but my body wanted sex. After a while, I lost interest in sex with her. Eventually, we broke up." This little semantics difference eventually created big problems.

When Eric went on to get involved with Trish, he noticed that she often used the term "making love" and not "sex." Having already had some experience with this, he decided to clear things up right from the beginning.

Eric told Trish that he really liked calling sex, sex. He also told her that he understood that she liked the term "making love." They made a deal that she would be happy for him to use the word "sex" as long as when they had sex they would "make love," meaning that sex was always loving.

Occasionally, Trish would use the phrase "making love," which was OK with Eric, but it was very validating to him when she referred to it as "sex." Since they made their deal, when he uses the word "sex," he feels assured that she is completely OK with it.

Eric said, "If I had to say 'making love' instead of 'sex,' it would make me feel like I was somehow trying to fool her, or that in some way I had to hide that I wanted sex." Just this small difference in the way they referred to sex improved their sexual relationship.

Code Words for Sex

For some couples, the word "sex" has certain negative or painful connotations. If using the word "sex" is not comfortable, you can create secret code phrases. Even if the word "sex" is comfortable, you might like to do this anyway for fun.

One couple shared their code phrase with me in an interview. For them, the word "sailing" meant sex. Sometimes when the husband initiates sex, he says, "It's a sunny day. Would you like to go sailing?"

When she initiates sex, she says, "The weather looks really good today. Maybe we should go . . . " and he says, "Sailing?" They both smile and are ready to have a good time.

If "sailing" is your code word, then for long gourmet sex, you could say, "How about going for a long cruise?"

When he initiates sex and she is not in the mood, she could suggest a quickie by saying, "Let's use the speedboat instead." Be creative. See what fun code words you can share together.

Sex and the Media

The media have a big effect on why men are so sensitive to rejection. A modern man is sensitive to feeling rejected sexually because each day he is bombarded with media advertisements featuring alluring sexual women whose bodies are saying, "Yes, I want you. I am ready for you. I long for you. I am yours. I want sex and more sex. Come and get me."

While this message is very exciting to a man, when he is caught up in this fantasy world, or when he is in the real world and thinking about his fantasy, he feels as if he is the only one not having hot and passionate sex. Even if he is in a relationship, he may feel that something is wrong when his sexual partner doesn't seem to be in the mood. The grass on the other side of the picture tube definitely seems greener.

A man does not realize that a woman really does want sex, but sometimes before she can feel her desires, she first needs his emotional support. When his partner doesn't want sex as much as he does, he begins to feel as if he has to jump through hoops to get it. He feels at a disadvantage because she doesn't want it as much.

She, however, does love sex but just needs to feel romanced and loved before her sexual needs can be just as strong as his. Sometimes awakening her sexual desires could be as simple as bringing home flowers for her or cleaning up the kitchen. (Don't laugh, men—in my seminars, women always clap loudly at this point!)

A man does not realize that a woman really does want sex, but sometimes before she can feel her desires, she first needs his emotional support.

The irony of modern times is that sex is everywhere in the media, and yet more and more I hear women complaining that their husbands are not interested in sex. The more sex men see in the media, the more rejected they begin to feel at home, and the more they lose attraction for their partners. A man loses attraction not because his partner doesn't measure up to the flawless silicone-breasted female bodies he sees on TV or in magazines, but because he feels sexually rejected and frustrated.

It is vitally important for women to understand that it is not primarily the bodies men are attracted to but the message that these women are definitely open to having sex. To keep a man attracted to her, a woman does not need to compete with the fantasy women of the media and strive to create a perfect body. Instead, she needs to work toward communicating positive and nonrejecting messages about sex.

> To keep a man attracted to her,
> a woman does not need to compete
> with the fantasy women of the media and
> strive to create a perfect body. Instead, she
> needs to work toward communicating positive
> and nonrejecting messages about sex.

Why Men Feel at a Disadvantage

Without this understanding of the differences between men and women's sexual needs, a man feels at a disadvantage. He wants sex, but he feels that he has to convince the woman to want it as well.

He does not realize that she has a similar disadvantage. Women hunger for intimacy and good communication, and men don't seem that interested. A woman can better understand a man's sexual sensitivities by comparing them to her sensitivities about feelings, communication, and intimacy.

> A woman can better understand a man's
> sexual sensitivities by comparing them to her
> sensitivities about feelings, communication,
> and intimacy.

It is a painful experience when a woman wants to talk but feels repeatedly rejected. Women can readily relate to this sensitivity. Without an understanding of the differences between men and women and the use of advanced skills to create better communication, his emotional withdrawing into his cave can be very painful for her. After a while, she doesn't even feel her needs to share and be open with him.

Just as a woman can apply new skills to draw her partner out of the cave (see my book *What Your Mother Couldn't Tell You & Your Father Didn't Know*), a man can apply skills to open a woman up to sex. When we understand our differences, we realize that we are not trying to convince our partners to love us more or have sex with us on our terms, but rather we are supporting our partners by applying advanced skills. By successfully loving them, we enable them to give us the love we need.

Without these skills, after three or four years couples automatically lose the strong physical attraction they felt in the beginning. In the next chapter, we will explore why couples today are having less sex.

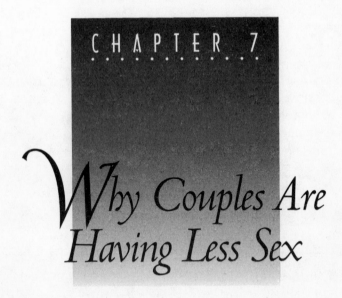

CHAPTER 7

Why Couples Are Having Less Sex

Couples today are having much less sex than the media suggest. Yes, a lot of hungry men and women are out there wanting sex, but once they are married, after a few years other things become more important and sex is overlooked.

The primary reason for this loss of interest is that men feel rejected and women don't feel romanced and understood in the relationship. A woman does not instinctively realize how sensitive a man is when she isn't in the mood for sex. A man does not instinctively realize how much a woman needs romance and good communication to open up and feel in the mood.

....

**The primary reason for loss of interest
is that men feel rejected and women**

> **don't feel romanced and understood
> in the relationship.**

For men not to feel rejected, couples need to create free, positive, and easy communication about sex, particularly about initiating sex. When a man repeatedly gets the message and truly believes that his partner loves sex with him, his sexual desires can remain healthy and strong.

> **When a man repeatedly gets the message
> and truly believes that his partner loves sex
> with him, his sexual desires can remain
> healthy and strong.**

When a woman feels a man is skilled in sex and he supports her in the relationship, her sexual desire can remain fresh. Good communication and loving support in the relationship, however, are most important for a woman. For a man, a good relationship is certainly important, but many times what makes the big difference is his sexual success with her.

> **When a woman feels a man is skilled in sex
> and he supports her in the relationship, her
> sexual desire can remain fresh.**

Initiating Sex Versus Conversation

When a man is confident of his partner's positive feelings about sex, he will generally keep initiating sex. If he feels that he is repeatedly rejected or that he has to convince her to have sex, he will stop initiating. Eventually, he will become sexually passive and less interested.

For a man to grow in passion, he needs to feel free to initiate sex. Just as a woman needs to feel that her partner will listen to her feelings in a positive way without rejecting her, a man needs to feel he can initiate sex without being rejected.

When a man is not in the mood for conversation, he needs to say so gracefully. He can say, "I want to understand your feelings, but first I need some time alone, and then we can talk." When a man works to show he is interested in his partner's feelings and cares enough to come back and initiate conversation, she feels loved.

In a similar way, when a woman is not in the mood for sex, but is careful to let him know that she loves sex with him, a man feels loved. When a woman is not in the mood, a man needs to hear that soon she will be back, ready and happy to have sex with him.

With this awareness, a woman automatically becomes more responsive to his sensitivity and is more motivated to find ways for him to feel free to initiate sex. Just as great communication opens a woman up to enjoy great sex, the possibility of great sex directly helps a man to be more loving in the relationship.

> **Just as great communication opens a woman up to enjoy great sex, the possibility of great sex directly helps a man to be more loving in the relationship.**

When a Woman Wants More Sex

When a man doesn't initiate sex because he might get burned by rejection, he has to wait for her. When he feels he always has to wait for his partner to initiate sex, he eventually loses his desire and doesn't even know why. When this happens, the pendulum swings the other way, and he wants sex less than she does. Quite commonly, the woman begins to panic a bit.

She begins to miss sex and want it more. The more she wants it, however, the more he seems to lose his desire for it. Her desire for more becomes a message that he is not measuring up. Whatever desire he still has is quickly turned off.

Sex is a very delicate balance, and men are more vulnerable than women to an imbalance. If a man wants sex more than a woman does and can patiently persist in initiating sex respectfully, he will gradually win a woman over and sweep her off her feet, and automatically she will want to have sex.

When a woman consistently wants sex more than he does and expresses her unhappy feelings about it, a man can start to feel really turned off. He begins to feel as if he is obligated to have sex and has to perform for her.

Women already understand how performance pressure can numb their own arousal. With men, the effect of performance pressure is ten times greater.

A man cannot fake his arousal as a woman can. If he is not getting hard and erect, it is clear that he is not getting into it. A woman can easily hide her lack of arousal and pretend that everything is fine. A man cannot.

This increased sensitivity makes the pressure greater on a man. This greater pressure can immediately prevent him from getting aroused. If he feels he has to perform or become erect, nothing, and I mean nothing, happens down there.

Because a man cannot fake his arousal as a woman can, he feels a greater pressure to perform.

What She Can Do When He's Not in the Mood

Many couples just give up at this point. The woman senses the embarrassment he feels and backs off. She doesn't know what to do. If she talks about it, he feels blamed, and if she makes sexual moves, he just feels tired or not in the mood.

Fortunately, there are solutions to this problem. Just as a man can share a quickie with his partner when she is not in the mood for sex, a woman can apply certain skills when her partner is not in the mood.

> **Just as a man can share a quickie with his partner when she is not in the mood for sex, a woman can apply certain skills when her partner is not in the mood.**

At one point in their relationship, David and Sue found that she began to want sex a lot more than he did. Sue was frequently in the mood, and David happily responded when she initiated sex. For several weeks, everything worked great. They had sex several times a week and sometimes twice a day. Eventually, though, David began to wear out. This was a new experience for him. He had never felt a woman wanting it more than he did.

At first, he didn't know how to say no and would go ahead and have sex even if he didn't want to. This was not a good idea. Quite quickly, he began to feel pressure to perform. Sex was no longer fun. It was some kind of duty or obligation, and that just didn't feel good. To prevent feeling that way again, he decided he would have to say no.

It still wasn't clear to him how he could say no without rejecting Sue or hurting her feelings. When he came home from the office one evening, she cuddled up next to him on the couch while he was watching the news. After a few minutes, she started to gently stroke his thighs.

Trying not to be rude, he put his hand on hers to stop her movement and said, "I am so tired tonight. I really need to watch the news." Then, not wanting to sound too rejecting, he added without thinking, "Why don't you go upstairs and start, and then I'll join you later?"

David went back to watching TV and gradually forgot all about the exchange. He was tired and about ready to fall asleep when, forty-five minutes later, he heard a little voice from upstairs saying, "David, I'm ready."

It was like a miracle. Suddenly, from the waist down he was immediately awake. He said, "I'll be right up!"

When he got into bed, Sue was already prepared for an orgasm because she'd just spent the last forty-five minutes becoming more and more aroused, fantasizing about David making love to her while she caressed herself. It was no wonder that after about two minutes of penetration, she had an orgasm. A few seconds later, he had his. She was happy getting the sex she wanted, and it was a heavenly experience for David, even better than a quickie, because he didn't have to perform in any way and he still got to do the honors and give her an orgasm.

Taking Responsibility for Our Own Pleasure

Instead of resenting that David was not in the mood, Sue just took responsibility for satisfying herself. This sense of responsibility is very healthy. Ideally, in all areas of a relationship, we should not make our partners responsible for our unhappiness, but particularly with sex it is very hard to satisfy our sexual needs without betraying our partners. This is why masturbation is so important.

Sue's creativity freed her from feeling dependent on David when he couldn't be there for her the way she would have preferred. She made the best of the situation and got into bed and imagined him making love to her. Taking a long time to touch herself in a sensual way and masturbate herself, she slowly built up her sexual tension so that when he entered her, she was already about to have an orgasm.

Afterward, he told her how much fun it was for him and that any time he was not in the mood, this was a great way to turn him on. This little conversation gave her permission to be much freer in her sexual expression and also ensured that she could have sex whenever she wanted it.

If a man is tired and not in the mood for sex, and she acts as if everything is fine, he really appreciates her easy acceptance. Otherwise, he might begin to feel the weight of performance pressure. If she wants an orgasm and he's not in the mood, as he drifts off to sleep, she can just get into bed and begin to touch herself sensually and masturbate herself.

After about twenty minutes, she can then turn on her side and gently but firmly rub up against his side. When he wakes up feeling her wet vagina pressing on him, he can then move over to do the honors. In this way, they will both be happy. She never has to feel as if she can't get the sexual fulfillment she is looking for. This is why it's good for her to masturbate when he's around instead of just when she is alone.

If her partner travels a lot, she may occasionally want to masturbate while he is away. Knowing she can't wait may even turn him on more. Maybe he'll even start shortening his trips. I strongly recommend that couples should let each other know when they are masturbating so the partner can at least have the opportunity to join in.

Couples should let each other know when they are masturbating so the partner can at least have the opportunity to join in.

Getting Back to Sex

Many times when a couple stops having sex, it is hard to get back to it. The interruption could be a due to sickness, an argument, or a particularly stressful period of time, but after a couple loses the rhythm of sex, they may have a hard time getting back into the swing of things. It can be difficult to start again when you haven't had sex in a long while. If you use advanced skills, it won't be difficult to get back into the rhythm.

Jim had been out of work for several months and was feeling rather depressed. Julie, his wife of thirteen years, was frustrated not only that he was in his cave all the time, but also because they weren't having sex. Understanding his need for space, she worked hard at being very patient. Eventually, he got a new job and started feeling much better. Everything got better—except there was no sex.

I gave them a new approach to having sex again. I recommended that when she wanted sex, she say to him something along these lines: "I have been feeling really turned on today, and I can see that you're really tired. It's OK if you don't want to have sex, but I thought I would masturbate thinking about you. As I get closer to having an orgasm, if you want to join in at any time, that will be fine with me. If you don't feel like it, that's OK too."

The next day, Julie called me and left a happy message on my machine. After many thanks, she said the new approach had worked like a charm. Jim also was very grateful. Sometimes it just takes one good experience, and a man is back in the saddle. There is no better aphrodisiac than sex itself. The easier it is to have sex, the more you want it.

The Indirect Approach

Another secret for helping a man shift gears from not being interested in sex to feeling arousal is for a woman to be clear but indirect in her approach. Once you ask a man if he wants to have sex and he says no, it is much harder for him to shift and change his mind. As we have discussed, for women it is just the opposite. When you give her a chance to say no and talk about her feelings, she may start to become aroused and discover that she has changed her mind and does want sex.

Men tend to be very different. Once a man verbally says he doesn't want to have sex, to a certain extent it is written in stone. If she persists in her attempts to initiate sex, he feels controlled or pressured to perform.

> Once a man verbally says he doesn't want to
> have sex, to a certain extent it is written in
> stone. If she persists in her attempts to
> initiate sex, he feels controlled or
> pressured to perform.

If, however, she can initiate sex in an indirect manner, he has time to silently overcome any resistance to having sex and possibly become aroused. To initiate sex in an indirect manner, a woman can develop various sexual signals. Even if he is in the mood and doesn't need time to gradually become aroused, he will still appreciate her signals, because they make it so much easier for him to initiate sex.

While these particular messages are very personal and may vary among women, here are some ways women can send sexual messages, particularly through what they wear to bed. The interpretations I give seem to be true for many, but, of course, every woman is ultimately unique and special.

BLACK LACE OR GARTERS

Wearing black lace or garters is one very clear signal that she wants sex. A revealing silky black outfit says she knows what she wants, and what she wants is hot, lusty, and intense sex; not only does she want sex but she longs for it.

WHITE SILKY SATIN

When she wears white silky satin, she signals that she would like sensitive, gentle, and loving sex. It is as though she is a virgin and wants him to go slow and be tenderly affectionate with her.

SILKY PINK OR LACE

When she wears silky pink or lace, she is ready to surrender to sex as a romantic expression of loving vulnerability and eventually wild abandon. She wants to feel his strength and surrender to his love. There is a deeper passion within her waiting to be drawn out that just needs to be ignited by his passionate longing and devotion to her.

SENSUOUS PERFUMES AND EXOTIC SMELLS

When she wears certain perfumes, she may want to be breathed in and savored in a sensuous way. For many men, a woman's sensuous perfumes and exotic smells can make sex much more lustful. He must be careful to control his passions and proceed slowly in sex, savoring each stage, occasionally pausing and repeating his previous actions before moving on to the next way of stimulating and pleasuring her.

BLACK BRA AND BLACK PANTIES

When she wears a black bra and black panties, she wants to be seductive, arousing, and more aggressive than usual. Although she begins strong, inside she wants him to dance with her but eventually end up on top and in control of his passions as she lets go and surrenders to his love.

A SHORT AND LOOSE NIGHTGOWN WITH NO PANTIES

When she wears a short feminine cotton T-shirt and matching panties or a short and loose nightgown with no panties, it may mean she doesn't need a lot of foreplay tonight and she may or may not be in the mood for an orgasm. Maybe she just wants to feel him moving inside her through intercourse and is happy and satisfied by feeling his orgasm inside her.

GETTING INTO BED NAKED

When she gets into bed naked, after he initiates sex, she is open to discovering what kind of sex she is in the mood for, or she is simply open to whatever happens.

EARRINGS AND JEWELRY

When she wears earrings and other jewelry to bed, she feels beautiful and wants to be adored with lots of kisses. It may mean she wants very leisurely and sensual sex. He should remember to express verbally how beautiful she is many times.

OLD COTTON FLANNELS

When she wears old cotton flannels, clearly she is not in the mood! This is a particularly good time for cuddling. He can simply move closer and be physically affectionate and loving without becoming sexual.

Dressing for Sex

Through expressing her sexual feelings and moods in her dress, a woman greatly assists a man in feeling sexually wanted and welcomed. The messages listed above certainly are not exact for every woman, but they do provide a reference point for men to begin reading a woman's sexual signals. These examples may also assist women in becoming more conscious of the importance of dressing for sex in a way that is pleasing to him, but it must be pleasing and comfortable to her as well.

I personally became more aware of the messages my wife was sending me through the way she dressed for bed after a certain incident. After being affectionate for some time in bed, she got up, saying that she wanted to change. As she walked to the closet, I said, "Why bother changing? I am just going to take it off." She responded with a smile, "Yes, but I want you to take off the right outfit. This one really doesn't express how I feel today." From that point on, I become much more observant of what she wore and how it expressed her feelings and wishes in sex.

More Sexual Signals

There are many more ways a woman can signal to a man that she is in the mood for sex without being too direct. Let's explore a few easy examples of how some women give their husbands a clear but indirect message when they are in the mood and open to sex.

Some of these messages may work for you, while others won't. Pick and choose as if you were in a store trying on outfits. They may even give you ideas to create your own messages as well.

RELAXING BATHS

Mary takes a long bath to let her partner, Bill, know she's in the mood. She brings in the portable CD player and plays the music that best fits her mood. Soft and gentle music means soft and gentle sex. Hard rock means she is in the mood for intense sex. Music with lots of drumbeats means she feels really sexy and wants it to last a long time.

CANDLES

Susan lights a candle by the bed or some incense when she is in the mood. Rachel lights candles for dinner when she is in the mood.

CHOCOLATES

When Sharon asks Tim to buy her a chocolate bar at the movies, he knows, "Tonight's the night." His wife tends to crave chocolate at those times when her body is desiring a big orgasm.

BUILDING FIRES

When she is in the mood, Carol lights a fire in the bedroom fireplace or asks her husband to build one. When he is building it, she sits and watches him and clearly lets him know how much she appreciates his taking the time.

STAYING UP

Usually when Grant arrives home late from a trip, Theresa has already gone to bed. Sometimes, however, she will stay up for him and be reading in bed when he gets home. If she clearly puts away her book when he walks into the room, he knows that she is in the mood.

MAKING HIS FAVORITE DINNER

Karen makes her husband's favorite salmon dinner with mashed potatoes when she is in the mood.

PISTACHIO NUTS

After a conversation during which Tom told Joyce that fresh pistachio nuts worked on him like an aphrodisiac, Joyce lets him know she is in the mood by bringing home fresh pistachio nuts from the market. Sometimes she just leaves them out on the table early in the day. This gives him a lot of time to get turned on thinking about what a great time they are going to have.

SPECIAL WINES

Margaret brings out a special wine that she and her husband really love. Sometimes she asks him to buy a bottle of it on his way home from work.

SNUGGLING

When Cheryl snuggles up to her husband while they are walking, he gets a clear message that she's in the mood.

THREE KISSES

When Maggie gives her husband a hello kiss, if she is in the mood, she will give him another two kisses. Three little kisses in a row, and he begins to feel the tingle that she is in the mood.

FOOT MASSAGE

Evelyn asks her husband for a foot massage when she is in the mood. Leslie signals that she is in the mood by offering to give her partner a foot massage. Either approach works.

Putting Up the Flag

My favorite example of sexual signals came from a movie I watched about a Mongolian family. When the wife was in the mood for sex, she would put out a flag. When her husband came home, he would see the flag and know that she was in the mood. He would then race to get his flag and hoop while she got on her horse and rode away. He would then get on his horse and chase after her, lasso her with his hoop, pull her off her horse, and wrestle with her. Then they would have sex. This little ritual definitely made for passionate sex. With her indirect but clearly stated permission, he would pursue her and take her. Although clearly in control, she could feel as if she were being pursued and eventually surrender herself in sexual passion and ecstasy.

Positioning for Sex

Even where a woman gets undressed and ready for bed can be a very clear signal. If she undresses discreetly in front of her closet, she is generally not in the mood. But if she lays out her nightclothes on his side of the bed and undresses on his side of the bed so that he can clearly see her, it can be a definite message that she is in the mood.

When a woman positions herself to have sex by undressing in front of him, she may or may not get a response. If he is not in the mood, she is successfully preparing him to be aroused the next time.

If he is tired, instead of having to say, "I'm not in the mood" (which can be awkward for many men), he can just turn his head away into his pillow and let out a sigh, saying, "Ahhh, I am so glad to get into bed. I am so tired." This is a clear message that he is not in the mood.

She is spared from directly being rejected, and he is spared from having to say he doesn't want to have sex. The last thing he wants is for her to interrogate him with a series of questions expressing her concern.

When Questions Are a Turnoff

Asking a man a series of questions about why he is not in the mood is not only an immediate turnoff, but can prevent him from being in the mood in the future. These are some questions not to ask if he doesn't respond to your sexually inviting signals.

"What's wrong?"
"Don't you want to have to sex with me anymore?
"You used to always want sex."
"Do you think I am getting fat?"
"Are you still attracted to me?"
"Aren't you turned on to me?"
"Do you still love me?"
"Maybe we should talk about it."
"Maybe we should get some help."
"Are we ever going to have sex again?"
"You were looking at other women tonight. Don't you want to be with me anymore?"
"Would you rather be with someone else?"
"Did I do something to turn you off?"
"Why don't you want to have sex?"
"What's the matter, is something wrong?"

Certainly there may be appropriate times she can ask these questions, but they are definitely not recommended when she has just undressed in front of him and he is tired and turning away from her. Instead, she should respond at this most sensitive moment as if everything is fine and OK. This is not the time for her to seek his reassurance.

By being neutral and indirect, she can more successfully maintain the nondemanding message that she is welcoming him if he happens to be in the mood.

If he is not in the mood, she can go to bed knowing that they will have sex soon. If, however, she is really in the mood, she can just masturbate herself. It is very important that a man support a woman's need to masturbate so that she doesn't ever feel deprived of having an orgasm if her body happens to be wanting one when he is not in the mood.

This mutual understanding works like a charm. If he knows he is welcome to join in at any time or simply go to sleep, he will tend to wait till she is almost about to have her orgasm and then join in. This method works because there is no pressure on him.

After hearing about this approach, a man may decide to reassure his partner that it's fine with him if she wakes him up and includes him right before she is about to have her orgasm.

When Men Stop Initiating Sex

One of the major reasons a couple stops having sex is that a man stops initiating sex or a woman initiates sex too much. When a woman does all the initiating, not only does she gradually become frustrated, but after a while a man will begin to lose interest in sex with her.

Women generally do not understand that if they pursue a man more than he pursues her, the man will eventually become more passive. A little pursuing energy is fine to let him know when it is a good time for him to pursue her, but when she does it all, he loses interest and doesn't even know why.

When a woman feels too responsible for initiating sex, a man slowly begins to feel less motivated. When she expresses her masculine pursuing side, he moves too far to his feminine receptive side. This imbalance slowly erodes the passion in a marriage.

Quite commonly, he doesn't even know what happened to his passionate feelings for his partner, and he may even mistakenly assume that he simply is no longer attracted to her. When a women initiates sex in an indirect manner, as I have pointed out, she ensures that her partner can find his masculine side that desires her and seeks to pursue her.

> **When a women initiates sex in an indirect manner, she ensures that her partner can find his masculine side that desires her and seeks to pursue her.**

Most men have no idea that too much assertiveness and sexual aggression on her part can eventually turn him off. Some men like a woman's assertiveness very much at first but then have no idea why they are no longer attracted to her or suddenly find other women more attractive. In the beginning, a sexually assertive woman may feel great for him because he feels relieved that he doesn't have to risk rejection, but over time, his passion will lessen.

Women commonly complain that they don't want to always initiate sex. My suggestion is that instead of initiating sex, a woman can focus on giving a man the message that it is safe for him to initiate sex.

**Instead of initiating sex, a woman can focus
on giving a man the message that it is safe
for him to initiate sex.**

There is no problem with a woman initiating sex *some* of the time. It becomes a problem when she initiates sex *more* of the time. Gradually, he will initiate sex less and lose interest.

When Women Aren't Interested in Sex

Men feel discouraged when they feel that their wives don't seem to make sex as important as they do. Without consistent clear messages from her that she enjoys sex, he may lose his attraction to her. Suddenly, women he doesn't know, who haven't yet rejected him, become more attractive.

Historically, men have been much more sexually active outside a marriage than women. Without good communication and romantic skills, couples lose a great degree of their sexual interest in each other. While women might have sought fulfillment in their fantasies, men acted out their frustrated feelings and fantasies through having affairs.

In the past, women could more easily give up the need for sex in favor of the routine requirements of creating a home and family. The survival of the family was more important than the fulfillment of sexual passions. Sexual fulfillment was a luxury women couldn't afford. Men coped with the lessening of women's sexual interest by discreetly finding sex elsewhere.

Unfortunately, as soon as a man directs his energies elsewhere, it is much harder for his partner to feel emotionally fulfilled enough to direct her sexual passions toward him. As a result, the family unit was preserved, but romance was lost.

> **The major reason men would resort to affairs is that they did not understand that they had the power to reawaken their partner's sexuality.**

The major reason men would resort to affairs is that they did not understand that they had the power to reawaken their partner's sexuality. They did not have the skills that we can now apply. With a deeper understanding of the opposite sex, we can now rekindle the flame of passion even when it has blown out. In the next chapter, we will explore how to rekindle the passion in a relationship.

How to Rekindle the Passion

Many times a couple may feel sexually attracted to each other during the day when they're apart, but when they get home, they lose the feeling. For example, a husband at work may miss his wife and feel aroused, but when he gets home, he loses the attraction. A woman may feel as if she also wants more romance, but when she gets home, the feeling is gone.

This occurrence may be due to a variety of reasons. It could simply be that the domestic responsibilities of managing the home or children overshadow the romantic feelings. Too much routine can lessen the passion.

It may also be that some little unresolved feelings linger after an uncomfortable conversation or argument. To a great extent, the issue may have been resolved, but it wasn't resolved in an ideal way. The disagreement is easily forgotten outside the home, but when the couple is at home, it comes back in a vague way, and suddenly the attraction is gone. When you rekindle the passion in your relationship, the love shared while having sex can wash away these little stains and smooth out rough edges.

Although as a general rule of thumb the relationship comes first before sex can be enjoyed, sometimes having loving sex can dramatically improve the relationship. A woman's openness to having sex can open up a man's love for her. Sometimes even if she is feeling cold, having sex with him and feeling his love for her in sex can open her up again.

> **Although as a general rule of thumb the relationship comes first before sex can be enjoyed, sometimes having loving sex can dramatically improve the relationship.**

Perhaps the partners are simply out of the habit of having sex regularly. Outside the home, they are free to feel their sexual desires, but in the home, the old routine of not having sex takes over. Once sex gets put on a back burner, it becomes harder to bring back without advanced relationship skills. With a greater awareness of what skills are needed, even when the passion is gone, it is often very easy to rekindle.

Romantic Getaways

One of the simplest and most powerful ways to rekindle passion is to get out of the house on a romantic getaway. Spend the night at a hotel. Enjoy a change of scenery. Get away from the routine and familiar. Temporarily leave all domestic responsibilities behind. The more beautiful the new environment is, the better.

Try to get away at least one night once a month. If you can't visit a vacation spot or a neighboring town, go to a local hotel. Sometimes just getting into a different bed can do the trick.

Women particularly often need a change of environment to be aroused. This change frees the woman from feeling responsible for the family and the home. When the environment is beautiful, it awakens her to her inner beauty.

> **Women particularly often need a change of environment to be aroused.**

When to Get Away

Quite commonly, a man will make the mistake of waiting until his partner gives clear messages that she wants sex before he plans a little getaway. This is a big mistake. The getaway helps her to get in the mood. If he waits for her to feel sexy before planning a getaway, then he may just wait and wait, and things will just get worse.

If, for a long time, a woman has not been able to get away and feel free to be romantic and sexual, her mood may become increasing asexual. To reignite the passion and to feel like a beautiful and loved woman, she needs to get away from the daily responsibilities and routine. Just by scheduling the getaway, it may begin to bring back her romantic feelings.

A man needs to remember that sometimes before a woman can feel romantic, she needs to talk. If it is a long drive to the vacation spot, she can talk the whole way.

Women particularly need to talk to let go of stress and leave it behind.

After this kind of long drive in which she can unwind, she's likely to arrive at your vacation spot and your new bedroom in a great mood. Suddenly, a whole new feeling emerges that could not have come up at home. She might want sex right away, or she might want to go for a walk or enjoy eating out. But once she starts feeling taken care of, she can stop feeling as if she has to take care of others. In this way, her inner passions are awakened.

Another way to help her relax is to take her shopping, if that is something she enjoys. Although this can be very tiring for men, most women's stores now have chairs for a man to sit in while she tries on outfits. Just the act of exploring a store and gently reflecting on what she likes and what she wants helps her to shift from being concerned about others to feeling her own needs. Even if she doesn't buy anything she can still be happy.

A woman directly benefits from the process of exploring what she wants. This helps her understand her likes, wishes, and desires, and directly prepares her for experiencing intense sexual passion and desire. A little shopping can greatly add to the joys of getting away.

If she is enjoying herself and appreciating everything, a man will probably be easily aroused as well. When she enjoys the new environment, an emotional part of him takes credit for her happiness. This feeling of success can awaken his feelings of arousal. Leaving their problems behind in this way, they can enjoy each other more fully.

While spontaneous getaways can rekindle the romantic spirit, sometimes we are just too busy or responsible to others to get away easily. When getaways are scheduled, a woman can stay more in touch with her sexual desires. That part of her can look forward with certainty to being fulfilled.

Writing a Sex Letter

Another secret for bringing back sexual feelings is to write a sex letter to your partner. If you find that when you are away from your partner, you are getting turned on, but when you are home you are not turned on, practice writing down your sexual feelings when they arise. As I mentioned, domestic stresses can easily overshadow and lessen sexual feelings. The sexual feelings may be inside us, but they need a little extra help to come out in the home.

When you are away from your partner, feel your aroused mood and imagine a romantic scene acting out those sexual feelings with your partner. In a letter to your partner, describe what you want to do and then describe the scene and your feelings as if it is really happening. Here is an example of a letter from a man to his wife.

Dear _____,

I really miss you. I feel really turned on, and I can't wait to see and touch you. I love touching your beautiful naked body. Your graceful curves and beautiful breasts drive me wild with pleasure and longing. I love to hold and suck on your erect nipples.

Right now, I am imagining holding you in my arms. I feel the warm softness of your body pressed against mine. I love holding you tight to me. I breathe in your sweet smells, and my love for you increases. I kiss your sweet lips, and my whole body tingles. Gradually, we kiss harder, and then you open your lips to me. My tongue enters your mouth, and your wetness arouses me more.

I hold your head in my hands, and I stroke your beautiful hair. I love to explore your body with my fingers, knowing how aroused you are getting. I love to feel your fingers tracing over my body. Just as you give me such great pleasure with your every touch, I know you are enjoying my touch.

I love taking off your bra and feeling the softness of your breasts and the hardness of your nipples. I know you are wanting me as I am wanting you. I surrender my love to you in response. You are all I want. I am consumed in my passion to unite with you, to be close to you, to enter your warm and wet vagina.

As my fingers first touch your wet vagina, more excitement surges through my body. Slowly and rhythmically, I began to circle around and around till I begin to gently stroke your clitoris. With an ever-increasing pace, as you begin to pant I increase the speed and pressure.

I can feel you reaching for more of me as I long to unite with you more deeply. After touching you everywhere, I hear your breathing change and your sweet responsive sounds. My hard and fully erect penis longing to enter you is finally relieved. What heavenly bliss to enter your sacred chamber, what love fills my heart, what passion builds within me. I begin to slowly move deeper.

Time stands still. At last we are connected. As I gently push through and fill you up, I hear your loud cry and feel you surrender to my presence. I continue to move in and out, in and out, my penis getting harder and harder. Every movement in soothes the more delicate fibers of my soul. I feel as if I want to burst, and then my pressure is momentarily relieved with your delicious moans of pleasure.

Together we rise in feelings of love, pleasure, and ecstasy. All of my love goes to you as you begin to climax. Your panting moans of pleasure reach their peak, and a lightning bolt of orgasmic pleasure explodes within me as I come to you. As we sink into blissful union, clinging to each other, our naked bodies entwined together, I am at peace. My life is at peace, and I feel once again whole and complete. I thank God for you and the special gift it is to love and be loved by you.

As we lie together, I gently stroke your hair and look into your beautiful eyes. I say, "That was wonderful," and you give me a sweet smile. Once again, I am reminded of how lucky I am.

I love you always,
(Sign your name)

When You Are Not a Writer

Of course, many people are not writers, and expressing these delicate sentiments may be difficult. That does not mean the feelings don't exist; it just means that you are not gifted in expressing them in words. Women particularly love to hear these emotions in words. That is one reason women spend billions of dollars buying romance novels.

A man who has difficulty verbalizing his passion might want to buy a greeting card that poetically expresses how he feels. It is perfectly normal to have loving feelings and not know how to articulate them and do justice to them. Picking the right card to express your feelings is just as good as writing the words yourself.

> **Picking the right card to express your feelings is just as good as writing the words yourself.**

This same principle holds true with sex letters. Feel free to borrow many of the words and expressions from the above sex letter or from romance novels to get yours going. It is more important to capture your feelings and express them in words than to be original.

After you have written your sex letter, tell your partner

you have a special letter to share. Schedule some special time—at least forty-five minutes without any interruptions—so that you can read the letter or your partner can read it (either aloud or silently). Quite automatically, those feelings will come back as the letter is read, and you can then enjoy great sex again.

This technique has helped me and my wife many times to rekindle our sexual feelings for each other. I did not realize how important it was to Bonnie until once she shared with me that she kept these letters in a very special spot, and when she didn't feel loved by me, she would bring them out and read them again.

Sexual letters are not only good for getting sex going but can also help your partner understand how you feel when you are having sex. Without these letters, Bonnie would have never known so definitely the depth of my passion for her during great sex.

Phone Sex

If a couple is physically separated, with one partner away on a business trip, or if two people are carrying on a long distance relationship, they may get very horny and want to masturbate. Sometimes an empty hotel room or bedroom can be very lonely, and strong sexual feelings come up. Instead of just releasing the sexual tension by masturbating, why not call your partner and have telephone sex?

This is very similar to writing a sex letter. First tell your partner how turned on you are and how much you wish he or she were there. Ask your partner to touch himself or herself, with eyes closed, as if you were doing the touching. As you touch yourself, imagine your partner touching you. Take turns talking and responding.

Describe occasionally how you feel and what you imagine your partner is doing to you or you are doing to your partner.

Eventually, in this way a couple can get to imagining intercourse, and with the help of a little lubricant such as KY jelly (the hand lotion that hotels always provide will do nicely) they can masturbate together and have orgasms.

Although this isn't the same as great sex, it is definitely close to it. Just be sure you aren't talking on a cellular phone, which can transmit over some radios. This is your private moment, not the neighbors'!

In the Middle of the Night

A combination of great sex and the quickie is doing it in the middle of the night. It is a wonderful feeling for a man to have his wife wake him up in the middle of the night by pressing her warm and wet vagina against his leg as she presses her bare breasts against his chest.

A woman who is feeling in the mood might want to take twenty to thirty minutes touching herself and masturbating herself until she is almost about to have an orgasm, then move over to his side of the bed and climb onto him. He'll find this a particularly wonderful way to wake up.

Since he only needs a few minutes to be aroused and she has taken twenty minutes to stimulate herself, they both get to have an orgasm. If a man wants sex with his partner in the middle of the night, however, it is not the same, because she doesn't wake up ready to go in a few minutes.

It is, however, an incredibly liberating experience for him to feel free sometimes to reach over and have sex with her. This kind of freedom is wonderful, but certain conditions need to be met first. There must be openness to regular sex and regular loving communication before you try this technique.

He needs to ask her at another time if she is open to being awakened. She may not want to be awakened unless she is on vacation and is very rested or can sleep late.

Even with her consent, when a man wakes up his partner, he must be less aggressive about it than she would be in waking him up. If he is horny in the night, he can gently begin to move over to his wife, slowly touching her, holding her and rubbing against her. If she opens herself to him, it is OK, but she must also feel that it is also perfectly OK for her to say, "Not tonight."

If a man can hear, "Not tonight" without feeling rejected, it is safe for her to say it. If she doesn't feel safe to say no to sex, she automatically loses her ability to really say yes to sex. There is no greater way to lessen sexual attraction than to have sex when you don't want to.

If a woman doesn't feel safe to say no to sex, she automatically loses her ability to really say yes to sex.

Through respecting each other's unique sexual needs, both partners can give and receive the support they need. In the next chapter, we will explore an approach to sex that ensures that both partners are always satisfied.

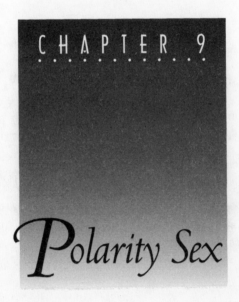

CHAPTER 9

Polarity Sex

Another secret for great sex and keeping the passion alive is understanding and working with our different sexual polarities. Just as the negative pole of a magnet strongly attracts the positive pole of another magnet, by expressing our opposite sexual polarities, we can increase attraction, desire, and pleasure.

There are two sexual polarities, giving pleasure and receiving pleasure. When one partner is giving and the other partner is receiving, the sexual pleasure can easily build. In polarity sex, partners take turns consciously using these polarities to increase desire and pleasure. One partner gives while the other receives. Then, later on, they switch, and the giver stops giving and just receives.

Polarity sex has two stages. In the first stage, the man

takes and the woman gives. Then, in the second stage, he attends to her needs while she relaxes and focuses on receiving.

While practicing the first stage of polarity sex, the man starts out receiving. He is not primarily concerned with spending a lot of time providing her with pleasure. Certainly, he wants her to enjoy it, but he is really focused on his own pleasure. Likewise, she is not expecting herself to get turned on right away and keep up with him.

In the second stage, it is her turn to receive while he focuses on giving. She has done all her giving, and now she can just receive. In this way, both people eventually get everything they want.

Developing Polarity Sex

I first developed the idea of polarity sex because I know a man doesn't *always* want to take a long time giving his sexual partner the foreplay she may need to have an orgasm. It is not that he doesn't care about her pleasure, just that his body wants to get on with it and get to intercourse and then orgasm. This difference in time needed for foreplay sometimes creates a big problem.

Going for it without giving her the foreplay she needs only builds resentment on her part. Yet waiting for her might create frustration for him. If he just goes for it, after his orgasm his energy will be spent, and his partner will be left with very little of what she needs. After a while, he'll stop wanting sex because he doesn't want to take the time for foreplay. Sometimes a man is just tired at the end of the day and doesn't have the patience. The thought of having to do all that foreplay can be a turnoff.

In a similar way, many times a woman doesn't want

to have sex because she doesn't want her partner to be frustrated as he tries to quickly get her off. For the thought of sex to be a welcome idea, a woman needs to feel that she doesn't have to get turned on right way. She doesn't always know how long it will take or if it will even happen that time.

> **For the thought of sex to be a welcome idea, a woman needs to feel that she doesn't have to get turned on right way. Polarity sex is the solution to this problem.**

Polarity sex is the solution to this problem, and as we will see, it has many other advantages as well. Instead of feeling frustrated that he has to wait for his partner's sexual pleasure to build up, a man can at first just go for it and do whatever turns him on. Then, before he is about to have an orgasm, he should stop and start over to give her all the foreplay she needs to build up her desire. Then, after giving her an orgasm, he can easily have his.

Practicing Polarity Sex

Polarity sex often starts with the man feeling aroused and aggressive about releasing his sexual tension, and the woman simply enjoying his arousal. He may hold his lover, kiss her, touch her, rub her, undress her, and become increasingly excited by her. She might just lie there enjoying being so desirable to him, or she might begin to touch him in ways that excite him.

She does not feel that she has to match his level of excitement. Instead, she just supports him in being excited. She can get involved in stimulating him, particularly by touching, holding, rubbing, squeezing, and stroking his penis, and perhaps by doing oral sex on him. All this is to build up the man's sexual excitement. In a very clear way, he is receiving or taking pleasure, and she is giving it to him.

After about five minutes, as his excitement begins to peak and he can tell that orgasm is approaching, he signals for her to stop stimulating him. He might signal that he is getting close to an orgasm by making a strong sound like "ooohhh" or taking a deep breath, relaxing on the exhale and gently pulling away from her touch to change positions.

To signal that he is ready to switch the polarity, he can simply move her hands back and place them over her shoulders. In addition, he may also gently switch sides of the bed.

Each of these signals says clearly to her that now he is ready to give back all the pleasure she has given him. She can relax and begin to focus on her body and her pleasure as he slowly begins to arouse her body. Although he might only need two or three minutes of stimulation, he needs to remind himself that she needs twenty to thirty minutes.

> **Although a man might only need two or three minutes of stimulation to approach orgasm, he needs to remind himself that a woman needs twenty to thirty minutes.**

Shifting the Polarity

In the beginning, it may be hard for him to stop and shift polarities by moving to stage two. He might get so excited that he will just go for it. This particularly happens when she gives him oral sex or they are having intercourse in stage one. By understanding her need for him to be aroused when she has her orgasm, he can find the control he needs.

> **By understanding her need for him to be aroused when she has her orgasm, he can find the control he needs.**

Women and men are biologically wired to have a different experience after orgasm. After a woman has an orgasm, she is still aroused and can enjoy penetration even more. After her orgasm, her pleasure hormones* stay at a very high level. After his orgasm, a man generally loses his arousal and erection quickly. When he is done, he is done. His pleasure hormones to a great extent dissipate and disappear.

If he comes first, his energy is not there for her when she is ready to have an orgasm. If she has her orgasm first, not only is she still sexually aroused, but she can enjoy his orgasm more.

Timing Orgasms: Ladies First

Many times couples will try to schedule their orgasms to occur at the same time. This kind of timing can actually make sex less fulfilling. It is very distracting for a woman to be concerned about when she is going to have an orgasm. It is best for her to feel free to discover it when it comes without having to adjust herself and try to control it. After she's had her orgasm, he can then have his right away or wait a little.

When a man and woman come together, both individ-

---

*Endorphins, catecholamine, and neurotransmitters.

uals are so absorbed with their intense pleasure that in a way the partner is momentarily gone, and the intimacy suddenly disappears.

When a man and woman come to orgasm together, sometimes it can be less fulfilling.

One minute a woman is enjoying the full extent of his attention, and the next minute it is gone. Likewise, when a man feels the pleasure of his own orgasm, he misses experiencing the full extent of her pleasure. Until his orgasm suddenly comes, he fully experiences her increasing pleasure. When his orgasm comes, he is too caught up in the intensity of his own experience of pleasure to feel the full development and expression of her pleasure and her love for him.

If he times it so that she can have an orgasm first, because he remains in control, he helps her to go further out of control. When she has her orgasm, he can fully be there with her to completely enjoy her pleasure. Then, once she has had her orgasm, she is free to fully experience his. It is like having two orgasms instead of just one. Both partners fully experience her orgasm, and then both partners fully experience his orgasm.

If he has an orgasm first, to fully experience his pleasure, she is distracted from her own gradual buildup and then, if she does eventually have an orgasm, he is definitely unable to fully feel her orgasm because he is no longer completely aroused. Through following the general guidelines of polarity sex, a woman is assured each time that she will at least have the opportunity to have an orgasm. Sometimes she may discover that she is not going to have one, but because he has spent the time without burdening her with expectations, she is quite fulfilled.

Through following the general guidelines of
polarity sex, a woman is assured each time
that she will at least have the opportunity to
have an orgasm.

Bonus Benefits of Polarity Sex

A bonus benefit of polarity sex is that after a man has
taken his pleasure in phase one, when it is her turn a
woman naturally feels more entitled to receive her pleasure. Without this extra feeling of entitlement, some
woman find it difficult to achieve orgasm.

Many times, when a women is particularly good at
giving to others, she has a difficult time receiving. In sex,
she may be so busy thinking about her partner's need or
so concerned for him that she doesn't give herself permission to focus on her own needs. This tendency can be
completely unconscious. Once when I was describing this
point in one of my seminars, a woman suddenly became
very animated and exclaimed, "I can't believe it. . . .
That's it." Everyone could tell she had had an "ah ha"
experience and wondered what it was.

I stopped and asked her what had happened. This is
her story:

I just realized why I had my only orgasm. I am forty-
two years old, and I have never had an orgasm with a
partner except once. I never could understand why,
and now I know. About six years ago, my partner
wanted to have sex with me. However, I was feeling
resentful. I felt I had given much more in our relationship. After he persisted, I decided to have sex but
planned to only receive and enjoy being touched.

When we had sex, he did everything for me, but
for the first time in my life, I did nothing for my sexual partner. I told myself this was for me and really
had the time of my life. Now I understand why I had
an orgasm—because I wasn't focusing on giving him
pleasure, I could focus on myself, and it worked.
Even though I did nothing to please him, he also was
quite happy as well.

As this example points out, when a woman can fully
receive, she can really enjoy sex. Polarity sex helps her to
receive because after she clearly gives to him she can then
shift to receiving. By having the mutual understanding of
polarity sex and a clear signal that phase two has begun,
a woman can more fully relax and enjoy the gradual
buildup of her sexual fulfillment.

When a Man Is in Control

When a man is in control of his pleasure so that it doesn't
become so great that he has an orgasm before she does, a
woman can enjoy sex even more. She does not have to be
concerned with having to hurry up so she can achieve
orgasm before he is done.

The more she knows he is in control and not going to
come before she does, the more she can fully relax and let
go. This is another advantage of polarity sex. In phase
one, he gets his pleasure but doesn't come. Then, in phase
two, she knows the rest of the time is for her. She can
relax, knowing that he will be there for her.

> **The more she knows he is in control and not
> going to come before she does, the more she
> can fully relax and let go.**

Sometimes in sex a man feels a strong urge to come before a woman does. At these times, he must not allow her to stimulate his penis. He needs to pull back from stimulation and calm down. This calming down is done in two ways.

First, he needs to pull away from being stimulated before it is too late. Then he can begin to increase stimulation of her. Increasing her pleasure to the level of his pleasure will actually allow him to regain control.

Sometimes a woman really loves it if he gives her an orgasm before he penetrates her. This means that he gets excited in phase one, then in phase two he brings her to orgasm, and then they have intercourse, and he can have his orgasm. When he enters her after her orgasm, he is very, very welcome.

After a Woman's Orgasm

After a woman has had her orgasm, she can actually enjoy his penetration the most because she is not only more open to being stimulated, but she can enjoy his pleasure more. She has had her release, and now she can focus on receiving and loving him. For her at this point, it is a different kind of stimulation. Before orgasm, she experiences a mounting pleasure, but after orgasm, it is as if she has climbed the mountain and is dancing on top of the world with her partner.

In addition, after he gives her an orgasm through stimulating her whole body and her clitoris, her vagina contracts and longs to be filled up with his penis. What better time for him to make his entrance?

Not only does she enjoy this, but he is free to move in and out of her without any performance pressure. He could come in one minute or in ten, and she will be completely happy. To a woman, it doesn't matter how long a man lasts if he first satisfies her. Sometimes men misunderstand a woman's need and mistakenly assume longer is better. Generally speaking, intercourse longer than thirty minutes will make a woman very sore and can lead to vaginal infections.

Men feel a great deal of pressure to last a long time so that she will get the stimulation she needs. By practicing polarity sex, she is always assured that she will get the time she needs before he comes.

> **To a woman, it doesn't matter how long a man lasts if he first satisfies her.**

Increasing a Woman's Pleasure

A man tends to think in a very goal-oriented way. He wants to provide increased pleasure for a woman in the most efficient way possible. Once she is getting close to orgasm, he continues stimulating her to push her over the edge and achieve the goal. The secret of giving her more pleasure is to bring her close to orgasm and then pull back, slow down, lessen stimulation, and then start over.

To most effectively build a woman's pleasure, a man should bring her to the point of orgasm and then let her energy settle down, then bring her back up, and then let her settle down. When he brings her to the verge of orgasm two or three times and then finally gives her an orgasm, a woman's orgasm is much bigger and more fulfilling.

Each time she gets closer, her longing and desire for orgasm increases. Her body also gets a chance to fully prepare for the orgasm. By extending foreplay in this way, not only does she experience a bigger orgasm, but his orgasm is much more intense as well.

In polarity sex, a man should first build his energy toward his orgasm. Then when he pauses and focuses on her, his energy will relax. Later on, when it is his turn to have an orgasm, his pleasure will be much greater because he has waited.

One way a woman can signal to a man that she is about to have an orgasm is to use the code word, "Please." The word has a double meaning: "Please stop or I will have an orgasm," and "You are pleasing me so much." When he gets the signal, he can choose to continue and give her an orgasm or lessen direct stimulation of the clitoris for thirty seconds to a few minutes before he brings her up again.

When he pauses, it is not as if everything has to stop. He can continue touching her all over her body in a very erotic way without directly touching her clitoris. This gives her a chance to let her energy settle down a bit before he takes it even higher.

Expanding Our Pleasure Potential

Each time we allow the energy to settle down before building it up, we are expanding the body's ability to enjoy pleasure. I once did an experiment that is analogous to this point.

A friend of mine had a pain clinic. To lessen chronic pain, the doctor would first place a needle in the patient's body at a certain key point. Then a current of electricity would be sent into the patient's body through the needle. Over a one-hour period, the current flow would be dramatically increased. It was amazing how much more electric current the body could accept if the flow was slowly increased. Although I was not experiencing chronic pain, I wanted to see what this treatment felt like.

They put the needle in my arm then slowly turned up the electricity until I felt a burning pain. At that point, I signaled that it was too much, and they reduced it a little and then left it at that more comfortable level.

After ten minutes, a nurse came and turned a knob that immediately doubled the intensity. I could feel a difference, but it didn't burn at all.

Because the electricity flow was first at my maximum tolerance, then was decreased a little and kept at that point for ten minutes, my body had time to adjust and open up to receive more current. In just ten minutes, I could receive twice as much electric current. I was amazed.

After another ten minutes, the nurse came back and again increased the flow by the original amount. After just twenty minutes, I was easily able to accept three times the original amount.

Every ten minutes for an hour, the flow was increased. After an hour, I could receive without shock or pain six times the original amount. By slowly adapting to the current, my body could take six times more current. This was a typical response.

The next day, I returned to the pain clinic and started with the same amount that I had begun with the day before. Then I decided to turn the current up further anyway and doubled the amount right away instead of waiting ten minutes. I ended up shocking and burning myself. I was able to clearly experience the body's ability to adapt and receive more current if given the time.

In a similar way in sex, if we take the time to build up the energy and then get used to it and then build again, the ability to experience pleasure dramatically increases.

By building up the energy and then pausing, we are actually expanding our container of pleasure so that we can experience greater enjoyment and have bigger and more fulfilling orgasms.

> **By building up the energy and then pausing, we are actually expanding our container of pleasure so that we can experience greater enjoyment and have bigger and more fulfilling orgasms.**

When you take the time to build up pleasure again and again, you have a full body orgasm. If you just get excited and go straight for a quick orgasm, it is generally more concentrated in the genitals and not nearly as grand.

Healthy Home-Cooked Sex and Gourmet Sex

Unless they are having a quickie, a man should bring his partner up at least two or three times before giving her an orgasm. This is a dietary staple of great sex and takes about thirty minutes.

Healthy home-cooked sex takes about thirty minutes. Five minutes for him, twenty minutes for her to build to orgasm, and then, after he comes, five minutes to enjoy the afterglow of lying together in love.

It is good to know clearly that sex can be mutually satisfying for both partners in a relatively short period of time. If sex takes hours and hours, the passion will eventually die out. We begin to associate sex with a lot of time, and in our busy schedules, it is too difficult to find that much time. But even in a busy schedule, a half hour is easy to schedule at least once or twice a week.

In addition to home-cooked sex, it is important to create a window of privacy when you have at least two hours to enjoy gourmet sex. During gourmet sex, you can take turns bringing each other up to the point of orgasm. For example, she might start by bringing him up, then he takes her up a few times, then she can take him up again. Going back and forth, they can extend the foreplay until, eventually, she can't hold back anymore.

For a man, not only is gourmet sex wonderful, but it trains him to control his sexual energy. Not only is it more pleasurable, but it also gives him the new experience of slowing down and being more in the moment.

After you go up several times, the urgency for climax lessens, and you can begin to savor every moment, every taste, every smell, every breath, every little sound, every sensation. In addition, you can more fully experience the flow or current of love to and from your partner.

During gourmet sex, however, a couple will spend more time in phase one. The man might come close to climax several times. Then they will shift to phase two, and she will come close to orgasm again and again. Then they might move back into phase one. Eventually, as their bodies gradually open up to receive more sexual electricity, they can enjoy giving and receiving at the same time. Although you don't have to follow the guidelines of polarity sex rigidly, do make sure that the woman has her orgasm first.

Quickie Sex

Quickie sex takes about three to five minutes. It is basically just phase one of polarity sex and is all for his pleasure. A woman is generally open to occasional quickie sex when she feels emotionally supported in the relationship and knows that at other times she will experience regular healthy home-cooked sex and occasional gourmet sex.

> A woman is generally open to occasional
> quickie sex when she feels emotionally
> supported in the relationship and knows
> that at other times she will experience regular
> healthy home-cooked sex
> and occasional gourmet sex.

Regular quickie sex may appeal only to him, but it has extra benefits for her as well. Although she doesn't experience the physical stimulation of longer sex, emotionally it can be very fulfilling for a woman for a variety of reasons.

Since I began teaching how and why to incorporate quickies into a couple's sex life, not only men have thanked me but women as well. These are some examples of what women have told me:

"Now when we are having sex and I discover I am not in the mood, I don't have to fake it, I can just say, 'Let's have a quickie.' He doesn't get bummed out, and I don't have to explain that there is nothing wrong."

"It's great because sometimes I just want to be close and cuddle, but I also want him to be satisfied as well. I get to be close, but I don't have to try and get into it."

"Finally he understands that sometimes I just like to have intercourse and I don't care about having an orgasm."

"Quickies are great. I don't have to worry about how turned on I have to get. Sometimes we start out in a quickie and I start getting really turned on. I just tell him I want him to touch me, and he is very happy to shift gears and give me an orgasm. I would have never known I was in the mood if we hadn't started out in a quickie."

"I used to tell him that I didn't have to have an orgasm, but I did like having sex if he was in the mood. He used to get upset, like something was wrong. Then when he heard your tapes on sex, everything changed. Somehow, because someone else told him, he could really hear. Now, without feeling pressured to perform each time, I have started enjoying sex much more, and now I feel like having an orgasm much more often."

"Sometimes I don't want sex to be this long process. I want to get it over with. Instead of having to fake an orgasm to finish up, I can just tell him, 'Let's have a quickie,' and in a few minutes we are done."

"Sometimes when we go out, there are a lot of younger women around. Even if I am not in the mood for sex, I do enjoy feeling that I still turn my partner on. I will initiate sex at those times with some clear signals. Then as we start, I let him know he doesn't need to stimulate me much. It feels good to feel my man wanting and desiring me."

These kinds of comments add a new awareness to the importance of quickies.

How Many Orgasms Are Enough?

Many books today talk about achieving more and more orgasms. Although these books are certainly helping some couples, many women just feel more pressure to perform. With our busy schedules, it is enough to think about having one orgasm. Now in the nineties, women are expected to have many.

Many women are completely satisfied with one orgasm. Sometimes more of something is not better. When a woman is satisfied with one orgasm, the man giving her that one orgasm is also very satisfied. In a way, he can feel, "I did that. I completely satisfied her."

Some women go on and on, one orgasm after another. Although a man might find this very exciting, after a while he may feel as if he has to keep giving her orgasms, as if nothing will satisfy her. Gradually, sex can become a time-consuming duty for both men and women and lose its magic charm.

Sometimes women in my seminars have told me that they are multiorgasmic, but after ten or so orgasms, they still want more. When they finish sex and the man has his orgasm, the woman doesn't feel satisfied. This is dissatisfying not only for her but for the man as well. He wants to feel that he has given her the ultimate orgasm or at least fulfilled her hunger.

If a woman is generally multiorgasmic, I suggest that instead of having lots of orgasms, she have one big orgasm. She can signal her partner right before her orgasm so that he can lessen stimulation and build her back up. If he builds her up several times, when she finally does have an orgasm, she may happily find that one *is* enough, and she doesn't feel a hunger for more. She is truly satisfied.

Now, when I talk about what works for great sex, I run the risk of sounding as if one approach is the best approach. This is a very male attitude. Men like to find a formula and stick to it. While consistently using one approach may work for men, it generally doesn't work for women. In the next chapter, we will explore the differences between mechanical sex and spontaneous sex.

CHAPTER 10

Mechanical Sex Versus Spontaneous Sex

Another secret of great sex is variety. Women want sex to be a little different every time. Men don't instinctively understand this because they are so goal-oriented. A man seeks to find a formula that will get him where he wants to go, and if it works once, he tends to repeat it over and over. His guiding principle is "If it ain't broke, don't fix it."

Many men find it frustrating to think that each time they have to risk trying something new. A man wants to find a formula that will work each time so he can relax in sex, feeling confident that he knows what he is doing. He feels comfortable with specific formulas. A woman, however, feels most excited when she doesn't know what he is going to do next. Predictability is a turnoff.

A woman feels most excited in sex when she doesn't know what her partner is going to do next. Predictability is a turnoff.

No matter how good a sexual formula is, after it is used a few times in a row, it becomes predictable, routine, and eventually boring. When a man is touching her breasts or nipples, unless she is at a peak moment of stimulation, the same stroke over and over can become a little boring. Shifting rhythms and movements may seem unimportant to a man, but to a woman it makes a big difference.

Shifting rhythms and movements may seem unimportant to a man, but to a woman it makes a big difference.

Variation in the movement of the body also helps to arouse her more. Sometimes he can lie on top of her, sometimes she can be on top. Sometimes they can switch sides. All this movement helps her to stop thinking and just feel the sensations. While following his lead, she doesn't question why he is gently moving her from time to time, because she feels the thrill of wondering, "Where are we going next?" This anticipation is very exciting to a woman.

Sex and Baseball

To convey a sense of what excites women in sex in terms that most men can really understand, I compare sex to baseball. When a man watches a baseball game, it is the anticipation of what will happen that makes it most exciting. Who will get on base? Will the ball be caught? Who will strike out? Who will score, and who will win?

While he watches the game, his tension builds and releases with every inning. Each time a player gets on base, he feels increasing excitement and tension. This tension is released with hoots of enthusiasm when his team's player moves to another base or scores.

No matter how exciting a game is the first time, if you watch a recording of the exact same game over and over, it will become predictable and boring. In a similar way, when a man follows the same formula in sex, it becomes boring and predictable to his partner.

Sometimes a man will find a formula that works in sex and change it by making it more efficient. Instead of taking the time for foreplay, he skips ahead to intercourse. This is like tuning in the sports report to find out who won, instead of watching the game itself. Briefly seeing the highlights of a game in a sports summary is certainly fun, but it doesn't come close to the building excitement of being there or watching the whole game.

Watching the entire game makes the conclusion much more exciting. In a similar way, foreplay makes sex and orgasm very exciting to a woman. It is not just scoring that makes her happy, but the buildup as well.

First Batter Up

To carry the metaphor further, when a man begins gently stroking his forefinger above her breast in foreplay, it is like first batter up. Then, as he begins to move closer to the breast, he hits a line drive. The crowd is excited. She wonders, "Will he get on base?" Then as he approaches her breast, he teases her by pulling back and starting over. Our first batter is out of there, and the crowd moans. Suddenly, the thrill of anticipation arises again as the next batter steps up to the plate.

This time, instead of repeating the stroking motion the same way, he can use two fingers instead of one. This little shift will increase her excitement. It is like having another batter come up. Will he get on base?

Eventually, as he builds up the stimulation, he may be touching one of her breasts, licking or sucking on the other. Then he might slowly move his other hand down to her vagina. Having all this happen gradually is as exciting as having a tie game, with two outs in the ninth inning, bases loaded, and a new batter up. Then when he scores a home run and penetrates her for intercourse, the crowd goes wild as four runs are scored in one play.

The Magic of Foreplay

If he remembers this example of baseball and sex, foreplay will take on a whole new dimension for a man. He can begin to truly understand why foreplay is so important to her. It is as though God gave a woman a circular body to remind a man to move his hands and fingers in circles over her body instead of getting right to the point!

**God gave a woman a circular body
to remind a man to move his
hands and fingers in circles over her body
instead of getting right to the point!**

She has three major erogenous zones, the two breasts and the vagina, to remind a man that there is not just one "point." Her three major zones are also good reminders for him to use both his hands and his tongue.

When using his right hand, sometimes he can use one

finger, sometimes three. Sometimes he can trace over her body with straight lines and sometimes with wiggly lines. Sometimes his touch can be strong and firm, sometimes extra gentle. Sometimes he may circle his fingers to the right, and then he can go to the left. He can go up and down. Every little variation fulfills her need for variety.

> **Every little variation in his touch fulfills a woman's need for variety.**

By taking the time to build her up in foreplay, he increases her pleasure. Don't forget that, as a general rule, a woman needs about ten times more foreplay than a man. As a man gets older, he may need a little more foreplay to become fully aroused, while a woman may sometimes require less. As a general guideline, a man should remember that it is not what he does but how long he takes to do it that ensures her fulfillment.

> **A man should remember that it is not what he does but how long he takes to do it that ensures a woman's fulfillment.**

If foreplay has lasted thirty minutes and she hasn't gotten close to orgasm, it's probably safe to say she is not going to have one. Sometimes, however, if he keeps going longer, she will have one. To assist a man in knowing what to do, it is very helpful for a woman to give him some clear feedback.

> **To assist a man in knowing what to do, it is very helpful for a woman to give him some clear feedback.**

If it seems as if he has been stimulating her for a long time and the result is not in sight but she really wants him to continue, she can say something like:

"I really like this a lot."
"I know it's taking a long time, but this really feels good."
"I don't want you to come yet. I am loving this."

Also, if he is touching her body and she just needs to silently soak it up and melt into his touch, he may not realize this and begin to panic because he thinks nothing is happening. She can help tremendously by making a comment like:

"I know I'm really quiet, but I really like this."
"I really like what you are doing. It is helping me to relax and begin to really open up."
"Oh, this is just what I needed."

With a little reassuring comment like this, he can keep going without worry that he is doing the wrong things. He needs her positive feedback.

> **With a little reassuring comment from her, a man can keep going without worry that he is doing the wrong things.**

How a Man Can Become More Spontaneous

As we have discussed, it is hard for some men to relax in sex without being able to rely on a formula. A man can solve this problem by having lots of formulas that he rotates using. His favorite pat formula will work if at other times he uses other formulas.

In this way, a man can use formulas but at the same time give the woman the variety she needs. As he picks and chooses from a variety of patterns and skills, she gets to wonder what he is going to do next, and he gets to feel secure that he knows what to do. By alternating techniques in this way, he will automatically begin to create more techniques and approaches. In this way, mechanical sex slowly becomes more and more spontaneous and creative over time.

How a Woman's Sexual Mood Changes

When a man is less mechanical and thus nonpredictable in sex, the woman has the opportunity to explore and express her unique sexual moods or feelings that day. She is more able to be spontaneous and responsive in differing ways. When a woman feels free to change each time, and over time, like the weather, her sexual expression changes. If sex is to remain exciting, her natural changes are important.

Sexual Seasons

Just as the seasons change, so also will sex change and continue to be interesting. For this change to occur naturally, a woman must feel supported in discovering the different expression of her sexual feelings.

The sexual act for a woman is a process of discovering what feels good that day. She does not want her partner to follow any premeditated rigid plan. She would rather that sex be a spontaneous creation each time, appropriate to how both partners are feeling.

This requires a new skill. As we have already discussed, a man instinctively prefers a tried and tested formula because he is then assured that he will fulfill his partner. A woman also wants him to know what to do, but in a different way.

She wants him to know that each time her mood may be different. She wants him to know how to discover with her what she wants. She wants him to be sensitive to her feedback that will assist him in leading her to higher states of fulfillment and pleasure.

To do this, a man needs to know the basics of great sex and to be willing to experiment by rotating his various skills. Like an artist, he needs to be very familiar with the basic colors of sex and then experiment with how they combine to create a new work of art. Like a musician, he needs to know the basic notes and chord combinations to create a beautiful piece of music.

> **Like an artist, he needs to be very familiar with the basic colors of sex and then experiment with how they combine to create a new work of art.**

Following His Lead

When a man can take the lead in sex, he frees his partner to think less and feel more. This does not mean that she just lies there passively. The freedom to relax and stop thinking about what "should" happen allows her to flow in the currents and undulating rhythms of her sensual and sexual nature. Like dancing to a particular type of music, she can move and dance with him to the rhythm of her mood that day.

Sometimes she might feel like a snake wrapping up next to his body, entwining him and seducing him with her naked flesh. At other times, she might feel like an innocent virgin experiencing his touch for the first time. Or she might start out cool and reserved but then gradually, as he touches her body, be taken over by her hot inner passions. She might feel assertive and tell him to lie there as she does with him what she will to drive him wild, or she may peacefully cuddle up to him and melt into a deeply relaxing place as he gently touches her. These different expressions of her sexual nature are not planned or thought out, but instead are discovered in the moment.

> **Different expressions of her sexual nature are not planned or thought out, but instead are discovered in the moment.**

When a woman has the freedom to be spontaneous, these different expressions and others will naturally come up and be expressed. When a man carefully takes the time to stimulate a woman with no expectations of how she is supposed to respond, over time she feels safer and safer in sex to do and express whatever she feels. This uninhibited sexual expression frees her to experience new heights of sexual ecstasy.

Communicating About Sex

Both men and women need clear and positive feedback to know what brings their partners the greatest fulfillment. I recommend that you take a half hour sometime, particularly when you are not feeling negative about sex, and talk about your sexual experience. In fact, it's a good idea to have an update on this conversation every few years in your relationship.

Here is a list of questions to stimulate an informative conversation.

What do you like about having sex with me?

How did you feel when I did that?

Would you like more sex?

About how much sex would you like each week?

Would you like more time in foreplay sometimes?

Would you like less time in foreplay sometimes?

Is there something specific you would like me to do in the next month during sex?

Is there a new way you would like me to touch you? If yes, would you show me?

Is there anything new you would like me to try?

Is there anything you would like to try sexually that we've never done?

Is there anything I used to do that you would like me to do more of?

If you are not having sex or are not completely satisfied, it is OK to have this kind of conversation, but be very careful to put aside any negative feelings, complaints, and criticisms. Talking about sex is very, very delicate.

What makes it difficult to talk about our needs in bed is that we don't want to feel that we are in any way disappointing our partners, but at the same time, we don't want to be expected to do what doesn't feel comfortable or natural to us. When answering these questions, it is important that you make it clear that you are not demanding more.

You should not do things that do not feel right to you.

When your partner does not seem open to things you favor, it is critically important to be nonjudgmental and accept your partner's feelings. At the same time, if your partner wants something that doesn't seem important to you or seems unpleasant at first, keep an open mind. You can always say, "At this point, that feels like too big a stretch for me, but I am definitely considering it."

A way to let your partner know something is really important to you is to gently and persistently bring it up in a friendly and nondemanding way each time you occasionally have this kind of conversation about sex. A secret of great sex is to build on the strengths you have and not focus on the problems or what you are missing. Many men and women have shared with me that after hearing my tapes on sex, they were able to automatically release some "prudish" ideas about sex and really begin to enjoy the pleasures of sex with someone they love.

> **A secret of great sex is to build on the strengths you have and not focus on the problems or what you are missing.**

In the next chapter, we explore how monogamy helps to keep sex passionate and alive.

CHAPTER 11

Passionate Monogamy

For some people, the thought of having sex with one person all their life seems too boring. They want more excitement. When you learn how to make sex spontaneous and not mechanical, it doesn't have to become boring. Over time the feeling of sex can continue to change and passion can continue to grow.

There is no doubt in my mind that the secret of success in my marriage is the sexual commitment we have to each other. Many men don't realize why monogamy is so important. They don't instinctively understand that monogamy ensures that a woman continues to feel special and loved. If she is not feeling loved in this way, she cannot continue to open herself to him. Trust is essential for a woman to continue getting turned on to her partner.

> **Trust is essential for a woman to continue getting turned on to her partner.**

It is easy for a man to be turned on to a woman he is attracted to. It is not so automatic to keep that attraction. It is not enough for a man to love a woman. He needs to feel that she is attracted to him, that she is open to him. He needs to feel that he can make her happy.

> **A man needs to repeatedly experience that he can make a woman happy if he is to stay attracted and turned on to her.**

Why Passion Is Easy in the Beginning

In the beginning of a relationship, as she looks into his eyes and then casually looks away, he gets the clear message that he could be the one to make her happy. This look gives him the courage to risk rejection and initiate a relationship.

Later on, when he has disappointed her several times, she stops giving him that look, and he stops feeling that he can make her happy. Suddenly or gradually, the attraction stops. He may love her, but he is no longer attracted to her.

He may fantasize about having sex with other women, or he may eventually just suppress his sexual tendencies. He is still monogamous, but there is no passion. To remain a prisoner in a passionless relationship is not a choice that people today are willing to make. Using advanced relationship skills in bed and out can ensure that passion stays alive and sex continues to get better and better.

The Ebb and Flow of Passion

It is both healthy and natural that the wave of passion in a relationship rises and falls. Just as it is normal not to feel in love with your partner at times, it is also normal not to feel sexually attracted to your partner.

> **Just as it is normal not to feel in love with your partner at times, it is also normal not to feel sexually attracted to your partner.**

Times when you don't feel this sexual attraction are like cloudy days when the sun doesn't shine. A cloudy day does not mean the sun is not there. It just means that it is temporarily covered. Cloudy days are the times when temptation knocks on our doors. When attraction is blocked in a relationship, many times we feel attracted elsewhere.

To maintain the possibility for passion to come back to your relationship, ideally it is best not to indulge your passions or fantasies.

At times, I have found myself getting turned on to another woman. This doesn't mean I don't love my wife. It just means that my attraction is not fully locked in to my wife. It takes years of commitment before a man's passions flow only in the direction of his partner.

When a Man Is Tempted

When I am turned on to another woman, I look down at myself and think, "I'm glad everything down there is working." Then I point in the opposite direction and say, "Home, James."

This is called "dick discipline!"

I never tell myself I'm bad for feeling attracted to someone else, but I take that arousal and bring it back to my wife. If I get home and it is gone, I know I just have to begin using my advanced relationship skills to make her feel loved, happy, and special. Gradually, the attraction always comes back.

Just by containing my sexual feelings and repeatedly directing them to my wife, I increase my ability to be turned on to her. Also by controlling my feelings when I am away from her, I have more control in sex.

When a Man Can Control His Passion

When a man can both feel his passion and control it, a woman can begin to let go of control, release her inhibitions, and start to really feel her passions. As a man learns to control his passions, not only does he help his partner reach higher levels of fulfillment, but he also can experience greater levels of sexual pleasure and love.

> When a man can feel his passion and control it, a woman can begin to let go of control, release her inhibitions, and start to really feel her passions.

When a man is in control, it means that his passion is so great that he could easily have an orgasm, but instead he holds back and gradually builds up his partner's passion.

The Importance of Monogamy for Wild and Uninhibited Sex

This control is not exercised just in bed but extends into the world. When a man is in touch with his sexual feelings but directs his sexual energies only to his partner, this control has a definite effect on her.

Every time a man is tempted by the possibility of sex and maintains his monogamous commitment, he is creating the safety for his partner to enjoy sex more. By not indulging in his fantasies of other women, he learns to control his sexual energies so that he can slow down the process of release and last longer for her. Certainly, thoughts and images may cross his mind, but as long as he comes back to an awareness of his partner, his passion and control will continue to grow.

Some men can easily last long but have little passion. Other men have tremendous excitement and passion but little control. Once they get started, they are quickly finished. They ejaculate and have an orgasm, but it is not a full body orgasm. Using the skills of polarity sex can help a man last longer, but through years of passionate monogamy, he will automatically find more control.

How a Woman Can Help a Man Last Longer

Just as a man affects a woman's ability to relinquish control and go wild, a woman's trust and ability to open up and receive from his touch and love can help a man stay in control.

When a woman is able to surrender and fully receive a man, he can easily maintain control while feeling increasing passion. When she is able to relax, receive, and enjoy his loving touch, he can last longer. He can continue giving as long as she is fully receiving.

If, however, she tries to take control and start turning him on, she can unknowingly push him out of control or turn him off. When he is focused on giving to her and arousing her, but she is trying to turn him on rather than let him turn her on, she can actually block the flow of his energy into her and cause him to have an orgasm before he is ready.

When her sexual reactions are a response to him rather than an attempt to arouse him, he can grow in controlled passion. But when her responses are not genuine reactions to his skillful touch, he doesn't feel the growth of passion and may suddenly lose control. He either gets too excited and ejaculates or he gets turned off. In both cases, he doesn't know what happened, nor does she. By her being overly excited to his touch in this manner, she can actually turn him off.

Repeating the Fourth of July

One afternoon, Donald and Connie had great, fantastic, memorable sex. Afterward, Donald told her how much he loved it. He particularly loved the way she was moving on top of him. He felt that he had driven her wild, and after a while all he had to do was lie there as she freely expressed her passion.

Two days later when they were having sex, right away she began making the same moves from the time before. This time it was a turnoff for him, even though she was repeating what she had done before to please him.

He didn't understand at first what had gone wrong. Then he realized that the previous time when he had liked it so much, her movements were the spontaneous result of his turning her on. The next time, she was mechanically doing it to turn him on, and that is why it didn't work. Her passionate movements and feelings were not an automatic response to him but instead were her loving attempt to please him again.

Quite innocently, she was just doing what she knew

he had liked before. After discussing this, Connie learned that her honest and natural expression would turn Donald on the best, particularly when he was trying to turn her on. This awareness freed her to look even more deeply to her authentic sexual responses.

Balancing Her Pleasure with His

When a man finds himself about to have an orgasm before she is ready, he can easily regain control by reducing his excitement and increasing hers. By focusing his attention on her and not letting her focus on giving more pleasure to him, he can begin to increase her pleasure. As she begins to receive more pleasure than he does, his control comes back.

During intercourse, he can regain this control sometimes without having to come out of her by reaching down and directly stimulating her clitoris. At other times, he can move her on top and signal her to not move much by holding her hips for a moment and then, while she is on top, he can stimulate her clitoris. As she is more drawn into herself and he begins to relax, his control will come back.

Choosing to Slow Down

Sometimes a man feels that once he is moving in a woman, if he is a real man he should just keep thrusting and plunging deep inside her. Quite the opposite is true. A woman appreciates that she can turn a man on so that he begins to lose control. This is a turn-on for her. When he needs to pause and not continue to thrust, she feels successful in exciting him and she feels he is considerate of her. His slowing down to pace his energy and pleasure with hers is a sign of great skill and control and has the effect of increasing her pleasure.

Without an understanding of how she feels, he may feel inadequate and out of control because he can't continue pumping. She, however, will feel happy that he is in so much control that he can slow down for her.

If he is so aroused in his genitals that he can't continue intercourse without having an orgasm before she does, he should just slow down and either lie quietly inside her for a few minutes to calm down or gently pull out and continue stimulating her.

Whenever he is pumping and starting to lose control, it is generally a sign that she can't keep up. Sometimes to seem as if she is keeping up, she will intensify her passion, hoping to please him or catch up. At this point, he will tend to lose control and ejaculate too soon. Neither he nor she feels very good when this happens.

Mistakes do happen, and certainly we should never expect sex to be "perfect" each time. When a man does occasionally come before a woman, instead of feeling bad, he can just make a mental note to make sure that next time he gives her an orgasm before he has his.

He might playfully say:

"I owe you one, honey."
"You were just too irresistible tonight, next time I'll make sure you get yours."
"I love you sweetheart, next time will be all for you."

After this, it's best not to talk much about it but just behave as if everything is fine. If he seems disappointed and moody, the best thing she can do is to act as if everything is fine and leave him alone for a while. If, however, she is disappointed and feels a need to have an orgasm right away, she can simply begin touching herself and bring herself to climax while he holds her or helps by touching and stimulating her.

When a Man Doesn't Get an Erection

Just as a man may easily lose control, he may also not get an erection right away. As a rule of thumb, in both cases the solution is the same. He should focus more on her pleasure. As her pleasure increases and she lets go of control, he regains his control. Couples generally make the mistake of focusing on him as if he has a problem. The more the woman focuses on trying to make him hard, the more difficult it becomes.

When a man doesn't get an erection or has difficulty maintaining control, he should simply focus more on her pleasure.

Although sometimes it can be helpful to see a counselor for assistance, it is best to first ignore a man's lack of control when it occurs and focus on ways he can help her feel loved in the relationship. Then when it comes to sex, they can both focus on her fulfillment for a while without depending on his erection.

A tremendous amount of pleasure can be shared sexually without a man having to be erect. The best solution is generally to focus on what techniques he can use to skillfully turn her on. Automatically, his erections will then begin to come back.

Although it is important not to be mechanical in sex, it is also important to understand in very concrete terms the basic mechanics of sex. In the next chapter, we will explore our different sexual anatomies and different ways to successfully stimulate each other.

CHAPTER 12

*S*exual Anatomy *S*and Oral Sex

Because touching the clitoris is so important for a woman's fulfillment and because it is so small and easily overlooked, I would like to take a moment to review some basic terms about a woman's anatomy. The term "vulva" describes all the female external genital organs, including the labia majora, the labia minora, the clitoris, and the entrance to the vagina.

The labia majora is like another set of lips. The labia majora are outside the labia minora, which are the smaller folds of flesh inside the external lips. Both sets of lips contain thousands of delicate nerve fibers running up and down, which, when delicately stroked, provide much stimulation, pleasure, and fulfillment.

At the south end of the labia is the vagina, which is

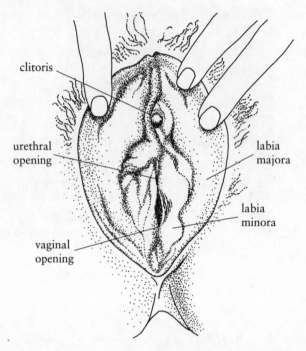

clitoris

urethral
opening

labia
majora

labia
minora

vaginal
opening

the canal where the man inserts his penis and enters her body. At the north end of the labia is the clitoris. Because it is so small and because he does not have one, a man doesn't realize how delicious it is for a woman when he touches her there. As a general rule, it is very important for a man to remember to go north before he goes south.

> **It is very important for a man to remember to go north before he goes south.**

Touching the Clitoris

The clitoris is partially covered by a little flap of skin, or hood. When a woman becomes aroused, the clitoris becomes erect or engorged. Like a penis, the more erect it becomes, the more it wants to be touched.

When a woman is very aroused, a man can stimulate her even more intensely by pressing a couple of fingers just north of the clitoris and then pulling back, fully exposing it. This, however, should be done cautiously. If the clitoris is touched with too much pressure or too soon, even if she is in the mood for an orgasm, she may not be able to have one. Too much pressure can temporarily numb her sensations.

Men should aim to have a feather touch down there. When the woman wants it harder, she can easily let him know by pushing her pelvis higher or placing her hand on his and pushing it in harder.

Camping Out "Down South"

While touching a woman's genitals, a man needs to remember to vary his approach from time to time. Instead of using the same finger, try another one. Then use two, then three. Occasionally use the whole palm as you gently but firmly sweep up from the south to the north.

Sometimes it is good to grab a pillow and plan to camp out down south for a full fifteen minutes. You should just resign yourself to the fact that you are not going anywhere else for quite a while. In this relaxed way, you can experiment with some of these suggestions.

Start with the inner thighs leading up to the labia. Stroke up and down the labia. Then take the fluids secreted from the vagina and with your fingers draw them up to the clitoris. Gently circle the clitoris, always making sure it is lubricated so the friction doesn't cause her pain. Gently and rhythmically move up and down.

After a while, move back and forth, and then move up and down again.

Try moving with the rhythm of her breathing. As she becomes more excited, increase the pace. Then slow down. Increase and decrease, no hurry, nowhere to go. If she is also stimulating your penis, you can copy her pace.

After moving in all directions, you can begin to circle the clitoris. Circle to the left and then circle to the right. Make big circles and then make little circles. Then shift to spirals. Spiral from a big circle around the whole vulva, around and around, circling smaller and smaller in toward the clitoris. After spending some time making very little and precise circles around the head of the clitoris, you can slowly begin to make bigger circles.

When you pull back the hood of the clitoris, instead of directly touching the clitoris, you can stroke up and down the nerves leading down to the clitoris from above. A variety of movements without rhyme or reason can be very stimulating for her.

While using different movements, you should listen to her responses to know what is working best that day and do more of it. Play with the movement. Do variations of it, and then come back to it. Even a winning movement can become boring if it is used too much. Yet once she is very excited, keeping a steady and consistent movement can assist her in reaching higher levels of pleasure.

> **Once she is very excited, keeping a steady and consistent movement can assist her in reaching higher levels of pleasure.**

While touching the clitoris, you might try tracing your fingers over her clitoris as if you are writing out the alphabet. See if certain letters get a bigger response.

When your fingers get a little tired, you can just relax your hands and use your tongue. She will love it. It will provide a whole different sensation. Especially when she is very aroused, flicking your tongue over her clitoris can be very exciting for her.

Oral Sex for Women

I remember clearly the first time I gave oral sex to a woman. After being a celibate monk for nine years, I was just about to have intercourse with a woman for the first time when she said, "Oh, before you enter me, I would love it if you would first *lick* my clitoris. It feels really good."

I was totally shocked. Those words reverberated in my head: "lick my clitoris." Before that moment, I hadn't even been aware of oral sex for women. The thought had never entered my mind.

I still remember that moment. As I moved down on her, it was like taking a deep breath and then going down into the deep end of a pool for the first time. I remembered her words, "It feels really good." Those words gave me the courage to keep going.

Once I was down, I discovered the great joys of fulfilling a woman with the tongue. She loved it, and every woman since has loved it. It is not that a woman wants to be licked every time, but she definitely appreciates it if he does it sometimes. A man might feel more comfortable performing oral sex on a woman when he realizes that as long as she keeps herself clean and is healthy, licking her vaginal secretions is quite sanitary. In fact, in the Far East the vaginal secretions were once considered the elixir of immortality.

If, however, a man is uncomfortable licking her fluids,

he can still use his tongue and his own saliva, and he doesn't have to take in her fluids.

While licking her with his tongue, he can simply lick in the same ways he would touch her. The added advantage of licking is that the sensation for her is super smooth and lubricated. To provide another sensation, he can delicately suck the clitoris into his mouth and then flick it with his tongue or sometimes just suck it into his mouth and gently massage it back and forth.

Sometimes while licking or sucking her clitoris, he can gently insert one or two fingers in her vagina and slowly move in and out. This can add more pleasure to her experience. Reaching in her in this way, he can stimulate another point that some sex researchers call the G-spot, located about two inches in and toward her front rather than her back. Rubbing the G-spot can add another dimension to her arousal.

The problem with getting too technical in these descriptions is that we run the risk of becoming too technical in sex. Sometimes when men go hunting around for the G-spot, a woman again begins to feel performance pressure. As a general guideline, it is enough to remember the clitoris.

Oral Sex for Men

Oral sex is one of the few ways a woman can directly give her love to a man. Oral sex can be a beautiful gift of her love for him, or it can leave her with an uncomfortable feeling. When a few basic issues about oral sex that concern women are handled, it becomes easy for women to enjoy giving this special gift.

The first issue is something that men all around the world seem to do. No matter where I've taught my semi-

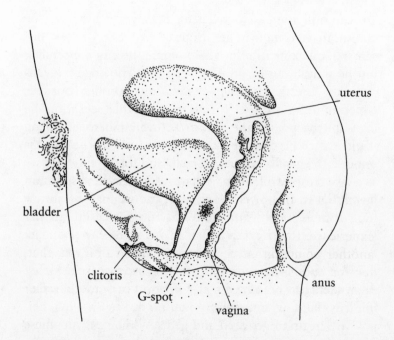

nars, I've heard women from many different cultures repeatedly complain about something they don't like about oral sex when a man starts to have an orgasm.

Quite commonly, a man will put his hands on either side of her head and ram her head in. This is not a comfortable feeling for her. Until that moment, she feels that she is giving the man she loves a special gift of pleasure. Then when he rams her head in, it begins to feel as if he is taking from her, and it is no longer her gift.

If a man wants her to continue giving this treasured gift, he simply needs to put his hands to the side of his body and not ram. A man does not know his own strength at the time of orgasm. It is as though a thunderbolt comes through him, and it can be very frightening to her.

Another complaint women have is that when he comes in her mouth, he expects her to swallow his semen. It is certainly fine if she does swallow the semen, but he should not be disappointed if she doesn't. It is her personal preference and choice. She should not be expected to.

With the possibility of contracting HIV from semen, some experts consider choosing to swallow a man's semen a high-risk activity. A man should be extra sensitive and respectful about whatever feelings his partner has about it. If, however, she does choose to swallow, as long as he is truly healthy and not a carrier of HIV, there is nothing unsanitary about it.

Another condition that occurs during oral sex that may make it uncomfortable for the woman is lockjaw! As a woman is holding a man's penis in her mouth, sucking it while moving up and down on it, after a while her jaw will begin to get tired and ache. While he is moaning in pleasure, she also is moaning—in pain!

Making Oral Sex Painless

Oral sex should be a positive experience each time for a woman. There is no need for her to suffer while pleasing him. It can be comfortable and easy. There is an automatic mechanism that men have that can make it much easier for a woman.

Just about the time her jaw begins to get tired or ache, it seems every man universally will cock his head back, close his eyes, and move his head blissfully from side to side. When a woman notices this happening, she can just take her mouth off his penis, rest her jaw, and use her hand on his penis. He won't know the difference.

After a while, he will notice something is different and

look to see what she is doing. At that point, she can just put his penis back in her mouth, and he will go back to his heavenly experience. After a while, he will begin to appreciate all that she can do with her hand as well.

Friction and Compression

Basically, there are two ways to stimulate the penis: friction and compression. Friction is generated by rubbing up and down, and compression is created by holding the penis and squeezing and releasing. Just as it is very exciting for him when she moves up and down, it is also exciting when she squeezes and releases in a pumping action.

A man is generally very happy with whatever a woman does when she is stimulating his penis, but there are movements that can drive him wild with pleasure. While a woman is relaxing her jaw, she can start out with the standard up and down hand job.

Up and Down, Over the Top, Squeeze and Release

After a while, she can begin adding variations in the movement, pressure, grip, and rhythm. She could then move from up and down to over the top. She moves her hand up, cupping his penis. Then instead of going back down, she goes over the top and then down the other side. Then she comes back up and over and repeats this for a while.

Then as his pleasure is increasing, she can just hold his penis and repeatedly squeeze and release, squeeze and release. Now she can start all over and put her mouth on the penis, protecting it from her teeth with her lips, and begin sucking while moving up and down.

Sometimes she can move slow and then speed up.

While moving up and down with her mouth, she can also use her hand and grip the penis around its base. As she pulls her head up, her hand can follow it up, then as her hand goes back down, her mouth can follow.

Again while relaxing her jaw, she can use the basic up and down movement quickly without a lot of pressure. This fast movement can actually help him to control ejaculation better because it is less intense than vaginal intercourse.

If she wants to increase the intensity, she can squeeze tighter as she moves up and down. Another secret is to keep his penis well-lubricated with saliva. Just as man should not stimulate a dry clitoris, a woman should be careful to keep his penis lubricated with her saliva so as not to create friction burn.

Another basic movement she can use occasionally with the up and down, over the top, and squeeze movements is the clutch movement. Holding his penis, using a back and forth wrist action, she can provide another sensation. She can then combine this twisting around clutching movement with an up and down movement. The effect is a twisting around as you go up and then twisting back as you come back down.

When holding his penis from above, she can provide another unique sensation. She can imagine that she is opening a jar. With that same twisting motion, she provides another different kind of stimulation. All these different varied movements and grips provide increasing stimulation for him but also fun for her.

Spreading Out the Pleasure

Once she has stimulated his penis for a while, the rest of his body becomes much more sensuous. To increase his pleasure, she can then begin to spread the pleasure out around his body.

As his penis is stimulated, the rest of his genitals and body also become more aroused and want to be touched. While holding and compressing his penis in her hand, she can then begin licking his testicles. This can drive him wild.

Then she may want to calm him down by slowly licking up and down the shaft of his entire erect penis. She can thereby cool his energy down and yet continue to pleasure him greatly.

Holding his penis firmly in her hand, she can occasionally move her head up his body, licking all around, gently biting his nipples, and eventually kissing him in a deeply passionate manner.

The rim of the head of his penis is also a specific area to stimulate for a while. She can lightly and quickly stimulate it much the same way she would want her own clitoris touched or licked. Then she may choose to change and intensify the pressure.

Just as a man needs feedback, so does a woman. When she is doing something that he really likes, it is OK for him to say, "I really like that movement." Various sounds of pleasure can also let her know what he likes most.

Another very sensitive area is the perineum, a point halfway between the base of the penis and the anus. This point is a nerve-ending point for the whole body. When it is licked gently, stroked, or pressed in firmly, it can send a man to a whole new level of pleasure.

When a man is very excited, she can intensify his pleasure *and* give him more control by pushing up firmly on the whole perineum area with her palm. Palming him in this way when he is close to orgasm can be incredibly satisfying for him.

By using a variety of pressures and alternating between intense movement and light movement, a woman can build his energy up and then let it settle down. Each time she builds his energy back up, his pleasure will be greater.

Simultaneous Oral Sex

Although women like receiving oral sex, men tend to like receiving it more. Simultaneous oral sex is also very exciting to most men. While it is certainly fun to do, a man needs to remember that particularly for a woman who gives a lot in her life, it is hard to give and receive at the same time. For her to really enjoy receiving, ideally she should focus on herself and not on his pleasure. Simultaneous oral sex is not always going to be as exciting for her as for him. A man giving oral sex to a woman is just too intense for her sometimes, while at other times she may really be into it. For her to enjoy him giving her oral sex, it must be on her timetable. He should not try to perform oral sex on her all the time. A man needs to remember that variety is very important to women.

Just as a woman giving a man oral sex is very exciting and important to him, romance is exciting to women. In oral sex, a man gets to relax and be loved at a time when he is most vulnerable. It is his time to receive, after all his efforts to give. Similarly, romance is a way a man can give to a woman and let her know that he loves her and appreciates her efforts.

In the next chapter, we will explore different rituals for lasting romance.

Keeping the Magic of Romance Alive

While men hunger for great sex, women long for romance. Even the tough-minded, goal-oriented, high-powered executive woman places great value on romance. Romance has a magical effect on women everywhere.

Women spend billions of dollars each year on romance novels. To fulfill a woman's need for romance, a man first needs to understand what romance is. Receiving cards, cut flowers and little presents; moonlit nights; spontaneous decisions; and eating out all spell romance.

It is not that men are unwilling to create romance. A man just doesn't get why it is so important. He is happy to be romantic in the beginning to show her how special she is, but once he has behaved romantically, he doesn't instinctively realize why he has to keep doing it. Probably if he had repeatedly witnessed his father being romantic to his mother, it wouldn't have to be a learned skill.

The Magic of Cut Flowers

I remember once asking my wife to pick up some flowers at the grocery store. I knew that women like cut flowers, but after a while I wondered why I should keep getting them. After all, I casually thought, she could easily pick them up while she was shopping.

To her, this kind of reasoning was definitely not romantic. Through eventually discovering the importance of buying her cut flowers, I was able to understand the importance of all romantic gestures.

To feel romanced, a woman doesn't want to buy her own flowers. She wants her lover to do it. She doesn't even want to ask for them. If she has to ask, it doesn't count as romance.

His self-motivated purchase of cut flowers for her is a symbol that he cares for her and understands her needs. These kinds of symbols are a very important part of romance.

> **His self-motivated purchase of cut flowers for her is a symbol that he cares for her and understands her needs.**

She does not want a potted plant but cut flowers that will die in five days. Why cut flowers? So that in five days he will again go out and prove his love for her by purchasing more flowers!

Buying a potted plant is just not romantic. It is one more thing she will have to take care of.

How a Woman Can Help Him Be Romantic

When I forget to buy flowers, Bonnie sometimes helps me to remember. Instead of buying them herself or asking me to buy them, she will put out empty vases. In this way, I get to notice and then take full credit for bringing them home.

Not only do I feel charming and dashing, but she gets to feel more fully that I care. If she puts out the vases and I still forget, instead of buying flowers herself, she will sometimes ask me.

Although it is not as romantic, she can then appreciate the flowers and I will feel closer to her because I did get them. Once again, after I experience how happy the flowers make her, I tend to remember to buy them.

Why Romance Works

When a man plans a date, handles the tickets, drives the car, and takes care of all the small details, that is romance. When a man takes responsibility to take care of things, it allows a woman to relax and enjoy feeling taken care of. It is like a mini vacation that assists her to come back to her female side.

> **Romance is like a mini vacation that assists her in coming back to her female side.**

Romantic moments are particularly helpful for women who don't feel comfortable sharing their feelings. On a romantic date, without having to talk about her feelings, a woman can feel acknowledged, adored, understood, and supported. She receives the benefits of talking without having to talk.

A man's romantic behavior says repeatedly that he acknowledges her, and by anticipating her needs, he signals that he understands and respects her. These kinds of actions give her the same support that talking does. In both cases, she feels heard.

Why Romance Is Important

Romance is so important today because it assists a woman to come back to her female side. For most of the day, she is doing a traditionally male job that requires her to move more to her male side. To find relief, she needs her partner's help to return to her female side.

Romance clearly places the woman in the feminine role of being special and cared for. When a man passionately focuses on fulfilling her needs, she is able to release her tendency to take care of others. For romance to stay alive, however, eventually there must be good communication.

Romance and Communication

For romance to thrive, a woman needs to feel heard and understood on a day-to-day basis. In the beginning of a relationship, the woman really doesn't know the man and can imagine that she is truly seen, understood, and validated. This positive feeling is the fertile ground of romance and passion. After several disappointments, however, this magic spell is broken.

When the man is untrained in the skills of listening to and understanding a woman, or when the woman resists sharing the feelings that naturally come up, she eventually feels unheard and is turned off. She generally doesn't even know what happened. He may even make romantic overtures, but they don't have the same magical feeling.

Even cut flowers lose their potency if a woman doesn't feel heard on a daily basis.

Talking is a major feminine need. I fully develop this advanced relationship skill in my other books on relationships and communication. Creating romantic rituals that say, "I love you and I care about you" can, however, go a long way to communicate love without words. With the support of romance, communication is much easier.

Creating Romantic Rituals

In my relationship with Bonnie, we have several rituals that nurture her female side while supporting my male side. Romantic rituals are simple actions that acknowledge he cares about her and she appreciates him. Here's an example.

> **Romantic rituals are simple actions that acknowledge he cares about her and she appreciates him.**

As a writer, I have an office in my home. When I hear her come home during the day, I immediately stop, get up, and find her. I greet her with a hug. Like bringing flowers, this little ritual creates a feeling that I care about her and she is loved. When she lights up after I greet her in this way, I also feel loved and appreciated.

If I forget to greet her, she will find me, not always right away, and greet me by asking me for a hug and then really appreciating it.

For many women, the thought of having to ask for a hug seems paradoxical. A hug makes her feel supported. To have to ask for a hug affirms that she is not supported. Certainly, it is more romantic if the man offers to give the hug, but if he forgets, it is better to ask than to miss out and be resentful.

> It is more romantic if the man offers to give the hug, but if he forgets, it is better to ask than to miss out and be resentful.

Asking for Love: The Big Step

I remember when Bonnie first asked for a hug. It made such a difference in our relationship. Instead of resenting me for not offering hugs, she would simply ask.

It was such a gift of love to me. She began to understand that the way to love me best was to help me be successful in loving her. This is a very important advanced relationship skill.

I still remember the first day she asked for a hug. I was standing in my closet, and she was making different sounds of exhaustion. She said, "Ooohhh, what a day."

Then she took a deep breath and made a long sigh on the exhale. In her language, she was asking for a hug. What I heard was a tired person and wrongly assumed that she probably wanted to be left alone.

Instead of resenting me for not noticing or responding to her request, she took the big step to ask for what she wanted, even though to her it seemed obvious.

She said, "John, would you give me a hug?"

My response was immediate. I said, "Of course." I went straight over to her and gave her a big hug.

She let out another big sigh in my arms and then thanked me for the hug. I said, "Any time."

She chuckled and smiled. I said, "What?"

She said, "You have no idea how hard it was to ask for a hug."

I said, "Really? Why should it be hard? I am always willing to give you a hug, if you want one."

She said, "I know, but it feels so humiliating to have to ask. I feel like I am begging for love. I want to feel like you want to give me a hug as much as I want one. I have this romantic picture that you will notice that I need a hug, then automatically offer one."

I said, "Oh . . . well, from now on I will definitely try to notice and offer to give you hugs. And I really thank you for asking. If I forget to notice in the future, I hope you will keep asking."

Acknowledge Her When She Seems Distant

Just this morning, I noticed a little distance from my wife. Instead of giving her a lot of space or ignoring her, I immediately asked her how she was feeling. This is another important ritual.

I said, "Are you feeling OK?"

Bonnie said, "I am feeling a little lonely, like the wife of an author."

Instead of taking this as an invitation for an argument regarding how much time I spend on writing versus on our relationship, I heard what she was really saying. She was just feeling lonely. She didn't mean anything more except that she would love a hug. So instead of defending myself, I said emphatically, "Ohhh, come here . . . let me give you a hug."

Eating Out

This same principle of asking for what you want applies to all romantic rituals. When Cindy is tired, her husband, Bob, offers either to make dinner or to take her out. If he doesn't notice or offer, she will ask, "Bob, would you take us out to eat tonight?" or "Bob, would you pick up something to go and bring it home for dinner?" or "Bob, would you make dinner tonight?"

The flip side of this ritual is that when they are finished eating out, Cindy always thanks Bob for a wonderful meal. Even though it is *their* money that pays for the meal, she thanks him. If he brings home food, she appreciates it in the same way as when he makes a meal.

Ordering the Meal

Another little ritual while eating out is for the man to ask the woman what she is going to order and then order it for her when the waiter arrives. Although a man need not always do this, when he does, it makes dinner special. It gives her the message that he is attentive to her, he remembers what she likes, and he cares.

When he orders for her, it does not imply that she can't order for herself. His ordering for her is just a romantic ritual that says, "You are always doing so much for me and others, so let me do this for you."

Another way to create a little romance in the restaurant is for him to suggest things that he knows she likes. This increases her feeling that she is seen, heard, and known. Ironically, if she suggests foods for him to eat, he may feel as if she is mothering him, which is not romantic. What may be romantic for her is not romantic for him.

How Men Take Credit

One way a woman can create some romance when they eat out is simply to have a good time and appreciate the food or the restaurant. When he takes her out, on an emotional level he will tend to take credit for the dinner. If she likes the dinner, he feels, "Yes, I cooked that dinner."

When a man takes a woman out, she has a golden opportunity to make him feel special as well. When she appreciates what he provides for her, he feels more intimate with her.

When a man and woman go to a movie and she likes the movie, then again, a part of him takes credit. He feels, "Yes, I wrote that movie, I directed it, and I starred in it." Of course, intellectually he knows he didn't create the movie, but emotionally it is as if he did.

To keep the romance, she can be sensitive to his feelings when she is not happy with a movie. She doesn't need to point out to him in great detail that she didn't like the movie. A man feels most romantic when he feels successful in providing for her happiness.

Focusing on the Good

Sometimes a man will sense that she didn't like the movie and for reassurance ask, "Did you like the movie?" He doesn't really want an accurate answer about the movie but some nice and friendly comment so that he doesn't feel he ruined the evening.

To support him at those vulnerable and embarrassing times, she needs to focus on the positive and look for something that was good or that she appreciated. She could pause for a while to let him know that she is working hard to find something good about the movie. The longer she takes, the more he knows she didn't like the movie, and the more he'll appreciate her for not complaining about it. After pausing to find something that she liked, she can still be honest but not critical. She could say, "I really liked that sunset scene. That was beautiful photography."

Even if there was absolutely nothing good about it, she could say, "I don't think I have ever seen a movie like that." He will get the message right away and change the subject.

Or she could say, "I just enjoyed being with you." He will definitely appreciate her.

She will find it easier to make the effort to give these kinds of supportive comments when she understands that he is really asking for her to help him save face.

Just as little gifts and caring attention from a man to a woman make her feel loved and romantic, when a woman appreciates a man's efforts and what he provides for her, he feels more loved and romantically inclined.

It is attention to the little things that creates lasting romance. When men and women take each other for granted, the romance disappears.

Some Things Are Better Left Unsaid

Once in my seminar, while sharing this example about reacting to a movie, a woman said, "It just doesn't feel honest to me to do that. Why can't I just tell him?"

I said, "I can understand your frustration, but to help you understand the situation better, let me ask you a question."

She smiled and nodded her head.

I said, "What should a man say when his wife is getting dressed and looking into the mirror and says, 'Do you think I am getting fat?'" She immediately began to laugh and said she got the message.

When it comes to romance, there are just some things better left unsaid, particularly at sensitive moments. The reason men and women tend to be insensitive is that they do not instinctively understand their different sensitivities. A man might think, "Why do I have to keep bringing her flowers or opening doors for her?" and a woman might think, "Why do I have to acknowledge the things he does?" As we understand each other better, these little rituals become fun and playful, and, most important, they are loving, kind, and considerate.

> As we understand each other better, these little rituals become fun and playful, and, most important, they are loving, kind, and considerate.

Survival Skills for Dating

If a woman doesn't understand this delicate point, while dating she can easily turn her partner off without even realizing it.

Here is another example. Bonnie and I were going to see a really great movie. We both loved it. But what I remember even more clearly than the movie was the comment a woman made on her way out to her date.

He had just asked her if she liked the movie. She responded that she hated it. I watched his posture droop as he then said, "What would you like to do now?"

She said, "I'd like to stand outside this theater and tell every person how awful this movie was." I still remember the defeated look in this fellow's eyes.

This woman didn't even have a clue that she was destroying whatever chance of romance they had that evening. This man was definitely going to hesitate before ever picking another movie with her again.

Telling the Truth

Telling the truth in a relationship is essential for intimacy and romance to thrive, but timing is equally important. Lasting romance requires talking at the right time and in a way that doesn't offend, hurt, or sour your partner.

> **Telling the truth in a relationship is essential for intimacy and romance to thrive, but timing is equally important.**

Having lots of successful romantic rituals gives both men and women the emotional support they need to be more honest, particularly about the important things. When a man feels appreciated, it is easier for him to hear and respond lovingly to her feelings and needs. When he doesn't feel appreciated and hears her talk about problems, he feels as if she is saying he is not doing enough.

> **Having lots of successful romantic rituals gives both men and women the emotional support they need to be more honest, particularly about the important things.**

Listening to a woman's feelings is a new skill for men. Traditionally, men have *not* been expected to empathetically listen to women's feelings. If a woman was upset, he would "do something" or "fix something" to make her feel better. When a woman needed empathy, to get emotional support, she didn't talk to a man, she went to other women. Until recently, women didn't even want to talk with men about their feelings.

Why Talking Helps Romance

Today women don't have time for each other. To various degrees, they are all feeling overwhelmed with too much to do. Lacking the support of other women *and* having to talk in a very goal-oriented way at work, many women today are not merely hungry to share their feelings at the end of the day, but starving. In a magical way, this new dilemma can actually be a terrific opportunity for romance.

As we have discussed before, men need to feel needed and appreciated. This is their primary emotional fuel. A big problem arises when women can provide for and protect themselves. In a very real way, men are out of work; they have been laid off from the job they have exclusively held for thousands of years.

Although women are no longer as dependent on men as providers and protectors, they suddenly have a new emerging need: a man to talk to; a partner who truly cares and listens. Women today need to communicate and feel heard at the end of the day.

The Importance of Communication

Sometimes even before she can appreciate romantic gestures, a woman needs to communicate and feel heard. Just as sex connects a man to his feelings, communication connects a woman to her need for and appreciation of romance.

> **Just as sex connects a man to his feelings, communication connects a woman to her need for and appreciation of romance.**

For the last twenty years, the lack of communication in intimate relationships has been the major complaint of women. The reason for this is simple: Overworked women need to talk more about their feelings to successfully cope with the stress of being overwhelmed.

> **Overworked women need to talk more about their feelings to successfully cope with the stress of being overwhelmed.**

By learning to fulfill this new emerging need to talk with his mate, a man is back in the saddle and able to provide for his partner in a new and equally important way. By gradually learning to listen, a man helps a woman be released from feeling overwhelmed and gives her a reason to greatly appreciate him.

Opening the Car Door

Romantic rituals or habits are ways the truth of your deepest feelings can be easily expressed. Opening the car is another of those rituals. Particularly for men, doing such things is a way of showing love. When a woman appreciates his efforts, not only does he feel closer to her, but her heart begins to open as well.

> **Romantic rituals or habits are ways the truth of your deepest feelings can be easily expressed.**

When couple goes out on a date, he should go to her side of the car and open the door—even if the car automatically unlocks with a little beeper. If he starts forgetting to do this, she can remind him the next time as they approach the car by simply wrapping her arm inside his so he naturally escorts her to the door.

Even if he is opening the door for her, the very feminine act of cuddling next to her man and wrapping her arm around him is very nurturing both for her and for him.

Write It Down

Another romantic ritual is to write down a request. When a woman asks for something and he can't give her an immediate response, the next best thing is for her to see him write it down. If he doesn't write it down, she feels that she will have to remember and remind him again and again. A woman feels romanced by a man who hears her and quickly addresses her requests or at least writes them down. This kind of immediate response gives her the feeling that he is really there for her. Just as men like women to respond in sex, women like men to respond to little requests.

> Just as men like women to respond in sex, women like men to respond to little requests.

Whenever possible, if her request can be met immediately in just a couple of minutes, the best way to ensure lasting romance is for him to "do it now." A quick response is so comforting for a woman. When she says, for example, "The light bulb upstairs went out," he can think, "That only takes two minutes, do it now," and then say, "I'll change it right now." Before I understood that it was the little things that make a big difference with women, I would have just put it on the bottom of my to-do list because other lights were working. I would not have gotten around to doing it until much later.

The truth is it only takes two minutes for a man to get a light bulb and screw it in. When a woman makes a little request like this, a smart man immediately responds, and she loves it.

I don't want to imply that men should just stand around waiting to do whatever she wants. Of course, men can be very busy or very tired, and they need to do things for themselves just as they do things for her. If she says the yard is a mess, he doesn't have to jump up and start working on it. That kind of request takes hours to fulfill. It can go on the "to be done later" list.

Just as a man needs to listen and respond to her needs and requests in whatever way he can, a woman's way of creating romance is to not take anything he does for her for granted. Certainly, there will be times that she doesn't respond with appreciation, just as there will be times when he doesn't respond immediately to her requests, but by being aware of these basic dynamics at work, they will always be moving in the right direction.

As couples practice keeping romance alive, it actually gets easier and easier. When a man anticipates he will be appreciated for doing something, he has more energy to do it. When a woman anticipates he will hear her and respond, she feels much more appreciative and can more easily acknowledge all he does and be more forgiving at those times when he makes mistakes or seems self-centered or lazy.

When a woman consistently lets a man know what a great guy he is for the little things he does, he will continue to do them. It brings out the best in him. Without her support, he will probably unconsciously go back to focusing on the big things like making money and being a good provider. When he does little things for her, it gives her the chance to feel her love for him again and again.

She may love him, but if he doesn't do things for her, it is also hard for her to feel her romantic feelings for him.

Rituals take time to develop, but each time a man gets into the habit of doing something a woman likes, and she continues to express her appreciation instead of taking it for granted, he will automatically be motivated to do a little more.

Going for a Walk Together

One of Robert and Cher's romantic rituals is to walk together. Cher loves to go for walks. In the beginning of the relationship, Robert was more of a workaholic. When Cher asked him if he wanted to go for a walk, he would say no because he needed to work.

One day, he realized that a walk only takes about fifteen minutes, and since Cher loved to walk, it would probably be very good for their relationship. He remembered that when she was upset, she would say things like, "We are so busy, we never have time for each other."

As an experiment, he started taking little walks with her. In the beginning, he didn't get much out of it, but now he loves it. At first, they would walk and she would talk. His mind was rather distracted by the pressures of work. She easily could have gotten upset that he was thinking about work the whole time, but instead she wisely enjoyed being with him, without expecting anything more from him. Cher was content to talk about how beautiful the trees were.

Gradually because it was something that made her happy, he began to like it more and more. Now he goes for walks even when she is not around. He likes it. It is a great break, and when he comes back he is more relaxed, clear, and efficient.

Our Night Out

Philip and Lori make sure that at least one night a week, they go out and have fun without feeling the pressures of their home and family. Sometimes, of course, they go out several times, but they always go out on Tuesday night.

Tuesday night is their movie night. They both love movies. Then every other week they will additionally do something more cultural like attending the theater or a concert.

These kinds of little rituals are particularly important for women because they give them an inner sense of security that they will get the special emotional support they need from a relationship to cope with the stress of daily life.

Going Out With the Guys

Each week, Craig has a ritual of going to the movies or doing something with his male friends. They generally go and see a "guy" movie, the kind of movie his wife, Sarah, doesn't like.

Although at first this kind of ritual may not seem to support their relationship, it really does. Spending time with the guys keeps him from expecting to get all his support from Sarah. Time away helps him to feel completely free to be himself. As a result, he begins to miss her and want to be with her even more.

Sarah understands this because she greatly appreciates the support he gives her to spend time with her women friends. He recognizes that it is vitally important for her to get many of her needs met by women friends so that she is not looking to him for everything.

When he goes out with the guys, her accepting attitude about it really makes him feel her support. It used to be that she would look at him in a hurt way whenever he went out with the guys. Now she even reminds him to go out when he forgets.

Building Fires

Charley and Carol have a ritual around building fires. In the wintertime, when Charley got cold he used to just go turn up the heater. Now instead he will find his wife first and ask her if she is cold. Just including her in that way makes her feel special.

When he wants to create more romance, he will offer to build a fire. There is something very special when a man builds a fire for a woman. Certain primal feelings are awakened. There is a good reason that so many resorts have fireplaces in the bedrooms.

When they first moved into their forest home, Carol was planning to make lots of changes. Charley thought they were all good ideas. As he continued to support her ideas, he kept thinking of what he would want.

He wanted one of those automatic fireplaces that burns gas. When a switch was turned, it would automatically light, and the fire was all ready. Carol, however, was not into high-tech fireplaces.

When he suggested it, in a positive way she said, "That sounds like a good idea. I can see why you would want that."

After a pause, he started thinking, "OK, she's going to go for it."

Then she said, "I don't know. Something very special happens inside me when you build me a fire. It is very primal." Because he understood the power of these romantic rituals, he gave up on the idea of the high-tech fireplace and is now glad he did.

All it takes sometimes to create a special romantic

mood at home is for him to build a fire. He will wait till she is home and then carry in the heavy logs. Then he will sit down and begin building the fire.

She appreciates every effort he makes. It is special for her to feel that he is taking care of her. Sometimes she will build a fire herself, and although it is nice, it doesn't automatically kindle the fires of their romantic feelings.

Who Carries the Wood

In her day-to-day existence, a modern woman no longer experiences as strongly the feeling that a man is taking care of her. Sure, he is still going out and working hard for her, but she also is going out and working hard. Romance is anything that helps her to feel that she is not alone and that someone is there for her. Any little thing he can directly do for her says he cares and creates romance.

At one point Charley began asking Jeff, who helps with the yard once a month, to stack the wood for fires inside the house and set up a fire. When he would start these fires that Jeff built, he noticed that it didn't have the same effect on his wife as when he exerted himself and took the time to build the fire.

Intellectually, he could say, "I pay Jeff, so I should get the credit." But from Carol's emotional perspective, it didn't matter if Charley paid Jeff to do it. For romance to be created, sometimes a woman needs to directly experience her partner toiling for her.

This is a very important aspect of romantic rituals. Women like to see their men toil or make sacrifices for them. On a deep emotional level, if her husband carries in the heavy logs and takes the time to build a fire, she feels that he is exerting himself for her well-being, and she feels loved.

It is very different from exerting himself for others who pay him and then bringing home the money. On an emotional level, when he is earning money, he is directing his attention and energy toward the people he works for and with and not toward her. For romance, a woman needs to feel a man's energy being spent and exerted directly for her.

> For romance, a woman needs to feel a man's
> energy being spent and exerted directly for her.

Taking Out the Trash

A woman particularly appreciates it when a man is happily willing to do something he really doesn't want to do. A great example of this is taking out the trash. Larry never used to take out the trash. But with Rose's persistence in asking him to empty it in a nondemanding manner and then appreciating him when he complied, his attitude changed.

Now whenever she seems a little distant or frustrated, he starts looking to see if the trash needs to be emptied. This response happens because he repeatedly experienced how much she appreciates it when he empties it. Not only does it help out, but it is also a symbol of much more.

It says he is willing to come down off his ladder of success and do what it takes to make their life together work. It says he is not above housework. It says she is not alone, and he appreciates her efforts and is willing to help lighten her heavy load. It says he cares. When he gets home, he is now happy to be the "maintenance man" for her.

Helping with the Dishes

When Bonnie and I first got married, I told her that I would be very involved in raising our children and doing some housework, but I didn't like doing dishes.

I said, "I don't like doing dishes, and I don't want someone trying to make me feel guilty when I don't do them. If you don't like doing dishes, we can hire someone to do them."

She said it was fine and that she was happy doing them. When she was pregnant with our daughter Lauren, I could see that she was getting really exhausted doing dishes at night. I told her that for the rest of the pregnancy, I would do dishes, but that afterward we would go back to the old system.

Every night when I did the dishes, she was so appreciative. She treated me as if I was such a wonderful guy for doing them. A few months after Lauren was born, I very happily handed the job back to her. Again she was very appreciative that I had done it for so many months and didn't at all mind taking it back.

Well, after a few weeks, I began to miss how wonderful it felt when she appreciated me for doing the dishes. I would wait for her to look tired and then I would come in and offer to help. Each time, she was so happy and relieved.

Now, many years later I do dishes much of the time. Doing dishes is a way I can instantly get her love. She never takes it for granted and always appreciates me.

One day, someone asked my kids who does the dishes the most. They unanimously said me. Bonnie said she did, and the kids argued. I explained to the kids that she did the dishes more but that there was a good reason they thought I did.

In a playful manner, I said, "I only do dishes when someone can see me." Like any other romantic ritual, doing dishes is a little way I can help her and she can appreciate me. I do the dishes as a way to fill up with Bonnie's appreciation as well as to help.

Doing Dishes Is Great Foreplay

Sometimes when my wife is really tired and goes to bed without cleaning the kitchen, I will stay and do the dishes. It rarely takes more than twenty or thirty minutes. When she gets up the next morning and finds a clean kitchen, she feels an incredible mixture of joy and relief. In an instant, her love for me dramatically goes up.

On many occasions, she has come back upstairs to awaken me in a most delightful manner. As she gently strokes my thigh, she whispers in my ear, "Was that you who cleaned the kitchen?" I smile and say, "Um-hum." She smiles back and continues providing me with a most enjoyable and pleasurable morning delight.

This does not mean that every time I do the dishes, she is supposed to have sex with me. That would not be romance. That would be a business deal.

Doing the dishes commonly turns into sex because it makes her feel loved. Naturally, she begins to feel turned on. Knowing how much she appreciates my help makes doing the dishes a fulfilling activity for me as well.

Going to Cultural Events

Grant and Theresa go to cultural events as a romantic ritual. Both Grant and Theresa enjoy going to the movies, but sometimes Theresa also likes to go to the theater or a concert. It took years before Grant realized how important it was for her to attend something besides just movies. He thought that since he was having such a good time at the movies, she was too.

She enjoyed going to the movies, but she also wanted to do other things. Now their romantic ritual is for her to mention certain events, and then he takes charge and schedules a date and buys the tickets.

All she has to say is that there is new play in town, and he will take the hint and plan a date. He might say, "That sounds like a good idea. Let's go next Thursday night." When he makes a date in this way, she feels loved, romanced, and taken care of.

Grant still remembers when he first recognized the importance of cultural events for creating romance. It was before he started taking charge of these matters. After hinting around for a while about going to the symphony, Theresa went ahead and bought the tickets for them to go.

It was a great concert, and afterward when they were driving home, she greatly surprised him. He knew she had liked it, but he didn't realize how much.

She said, "Thanks so much for taking me. It was so good." Then, after a pause, she said, "I'm feeling really wet."

He said, "Wet?!"

She nodded. "Yeah."

He go so excited that when they got home and into their own garage, they took off their clothes and did it in the car.

Needless to say, the next morning Grant got up early and called to get season tickets to the symphony.

Giving Compliments

Another little ritual is to compliment a woman whenever she gets dressed up, wears something different, or in any way seems to have put some effort into how she looks. Women can become very frustrated when men don't notice.

While Lucille was taking more time to get ready to go out, her husband, Steve, would wait downstairs. Then she would walk down the stairs and, instead of rushing, she would stop in the middle of the stairs for Steve to look at her and appreciate her beauty.

He didn't understand this female ritual and instead of complimenting her, he would say, "Come on, we're late." This did not go over well.

Eventually, she decided to help him out. The next time, when Lucille paused on the stairs, she said, "How do I look?"

Still not realizing the importance of this question, Steve said, "You look fine. Come on, we're late."

Again this didn't go over well. As Steve finally started learning about how men and women are different, he eventually realized his mistake.

Now when she comes down the stairs, he takes the time to notice how beautiful she is. Here is a list of expressive phrases men can use to most effectively compliment a woman:

"You look so beautiful."
"You look really great tonight."
"I love how you look in that dress."
"You look really wonderful."
"Fabulous, fabulous."
"You look great."
"I love the way you look tonight."
"You look really good."
"Your earrings are really great."
"I really love your colors."
"You look so spectacular."
"You are amazingly beautiful."
"You are so stunning."

"You are so hot."

"You really look sexy tonight."

"I love your legs."

"You are so radiant."

"You look really very lovely tonight."

"You are so gorgeous."

"You look so exquisite."

With each of these compliments, don't hesitate to add lots of embellishments, like "*really* beautiful," "*very* beautiful," or "*so* beautiful."

The Power of Touch

A man reaching out to touch or hold hands is a turn-on for women. While men generally hold hands in the courting stage, they stop after a while. This is a big loss. A woman loves to feel that a man wants to connect with her in this way. She doesn't feel loved if the only time he wants to touch her is when he wants sex.

> **A woman doesn't feel loved if the only time a man wants to touch her is when he wants sex.**

If a man wants his partner to feel receptive to sex, he needs to touch her in an affectionate way many times each day when he is not wanting sex. He can hold hands, put his arm around her, stroke her shoulders and arms, all without implying that he is wanting sex. If the only time he touches her is when he wants sex, she begins to feel used or taken for granted.

> **If the only time he touches her is when he wants sex, she begins to feel used or taken for granted.**

When he is holding her hand, he should remember to be attentive. Many times a man will forget he is holding her hand and she is left holding a limp, lifeless hand. When he needs to shift his attention, he should just release her hand. She doesn't want to hold hands *all* the time. It is just a way to connect for a few minutes.

When I started being more affectionate and touching Bonnie more of the time, it made a tremendous difference. I couldn't believe that one simple little shift could have such a big influence. I had heard that women need to be touched twenty times a day in a nonsexual way to build high self-esteem. When I heard this, I thought I would experiment. I started out with ten times a day, and it worked great. Immediately, she began to shine more. Now I am much more affectionate when I am around her.

In the beginning, I did it just because I knew she liked it. Each time I would touch her, I could clearly sense that she was drinking it up. She loved it. I thought, "What a great discovery." Then as time passed, I started to really enjoy it myself.

Not only is touching her a great way to connect and feel close at any time, but it also softens the rough edges at times and brings us back to feeling our love for each other.

Lasting Love, Romance, and Sex

All these romantic rituals are simple but powerful. They assist us in reconnecting with those very special feelings of attraction and passion that we can only feel when we are emotionally connected. These rituals ensure that the man can always do something to win his partner's love, and the woman can get the special attention and support she needs to stay passionately attracted to her partner.

> These rituals ensure that the man can always do something to win his partner's love, and the woman can get the special attention and support she needs to stay passionately attracted to her partner.

By keeping the romance alive and practicing advanced bedroom skills, you can and will continue to enjoy great sex. May you always grow in love and passion and enjoy God's special gift. You deserve it.